The Cambridge Companion to Mary Wollstonecraft

Once viewed solely in relation to the history of feminism, Mary Wollstonecraft is now recognised as a writer of formidable talent across a range of genres, including journalism, letters, and travel writing, and is increasingly understood as an heir to eighteenth-century literary and political traditions as well as a forebear of Romanticism. *The Cambridge Companion to Mary Wollstonecraft* is the first collected volume to address all aspects of Wollstonecraft's momentous and tragically brief career. The diverse and searching essays commissioned for this volume do justice to Wollstonecraft's pivotal importance in her own time and since, paying attention not only to *A Vindication of the Rights of Woman*, but also to the full range of her work across disciplinary boundaries separating philosophy, letters, education, advice, politics, history, religion, sexuality, and feminism itself. A chronology and bibliography offer further essential information for scholars and students of this remarkable writer.

CAMBRIDGE COMPANIONS TO LITERATURE

The Cambridge Companion to Greek Tragedy
edited by P. E. Easterling

The Cambridge Companion to Old English Literature
edited by Malcolm Godden and Michael Lapidge

The Cambridge Companion to Medieval Romance
edited by Roberta L. Kreuger

The Cambridge Companion to Medieval English Theatre
edited by Richard Beadle

The Cambridge Companion to English Renaissance Drama
edited by A. R. Braunmuller and Michael Hattaway

The Cambridge Companion to Renaissance Humanism
edited by Jill Kraye

The Cambridge Companion to English Poetry, Donne to Marvell
edited by Thomas N. Corns

The Cambridge Companion to English Literature, 1500–1600
edited by Arthur F. Kinney

The Cambridge Companion to English Literature, 1650–1740
edited by Steven N. Zwicker

The Cambridge Companion to Writing of the English Revolution
edited by N. H. Keeble

The Cambridge Companion to English Restoration Theatre
edited by Deborah C. Payne Fisk

The Cambridge Companion to British Romanticism
edited by Stuart Curran

The Cambridge Companion to Eighteenth-Century Poetry
edited by John Sitter

The Cambridge Companion to the Eighteenth-Century Novel
edited by John Richetti

The Cambridge Companion to Victorian Poetry
edited by Joseph Bristow

The Cambridge Companion to the Victorian Novel
edited by Deirdre David

The Cambridge Companion to American Realism and Naturalism
edited by Donald Pizer

The Cambridge Companion to Nineteenth-Century American Women's Writing
edited by Dale M. Bauer and Philip Gould

The Cambridge Companion to the Classic Russian Novel
edited by Malcolm V. Jones and Robin Feuer Miller

The Cambridge Companion to the French Novel: from 1800 to the present
edited by Timothy Unwin

The Cambridge Companion to Modernism
edited by Michael Levenson

The Cambridge Companion to Australian Literature
edited by Elizabeth Webby

The Cambridge Companion to American Women Playwrights
edited by Brenda Murphy

The Cambridge Companion to Modern British Women Playwrights
edited by Elaine Aston and Janelle Reinelt

The Cambridge Companion to Virgil
edited by Charles Martindale

The Cambridge Companion to Ovid
edited by Philip Hardie

The Cambridge Companion to Dante
edited by Rachel Jacoff

The Cambridge Companion to Goethe
edited by Lesley Sharpe

The Cambridge Companion to Proust
edited by Richard Bales

The Cambridge Companion to Thomas Mann
edited by Ritchie Robertson

The Cambridge Companion to Chekhov
edited by Vera Gottlieb and Paul Allain

The Cambridge Companion to Ibsen
edited by James McFarlane

The Cambridge Companion to Brecht
edited by Peter Thomson and Glendyr Sacks

The Cambridge Chaucer Companion
edited by Piero Boitani and Jill Mann

The Cambridge Companion to Shakespeare
edited by Margareta de Grazia and Stanley Wells

The Cambridge Companion to Shakespeare on Film
edited by Russell Jackson

The Cambridge Companion to Shakespeare Comedy
edited by Alexander Leggatt

The Cambridge Companion to Spenser
edited by Andrew Hadfield

The Cambridge Companion to Ben Jonson
edited by Richard Harp and Stanley Stewart

The Cambridge Companion to Milton
edited by Dennis Danielson

The Cambridge Companion to Samuel Johnson
edited by Greg Clingham

The Cambridge Companion to Mary Wollstonecraft
edited by Claudia L. Johnson

The Cambridge Companion to Keats
edited by Susan J. Wolfson

The Cambridge Companion to Jane Austen
edited by Edward Copeland and Juliet McMaster

The Cambridge Companion to Charles Dickens
edited by John O. Jordan

The Cambridge Companion to George Eliot
edited by George Levine

The Cambridge Companion to Thomas Hardy
edited by Dale Kramer

The Cambridge Companion to Oscar Wilde
edited by Peter Raby

The Cambridge Companion to George Bernard Shaw
edited by Christopher Innes

The Cambridge Companion to Joseph Conrad
edited by J. H. Stape

The Cambridge Companion to D. H. Lawrence
edited by Anne Fernihough

The Cambridge Companion to Virginia Woolf
edited by Sue Roe and Susan Sellers

The Cambridge Companion to James Joyce
edited by Derek Attridge

The Cambridge Companion to T. S. Eliot
edited by A. David Moody

The Cambridge Companion to Ezra Pound
edited by Ira B. Nadel

The Cambridge Companion to Beckett
edited by John Pilling

The Cambridge Companion to Harold Pinter
edited by Peter Raby

The Cambridge Companion to Tom Stoppard
edited by Katherine E. Kelly

The Cambridge Companion to Herman Melville
edited by Robert S. Levine

The Cambridge Companion to Edith Wharton
edited by Millicent Bell

The Cambridge Companion to Henry James
edited by Jonathan Freedman

The Cambridge Companion to Walt Whitman
edited by Ezra Greenspan

The Cambridge Companion to Henry David Thoreau
edited by Joel Myerson

The Cambridge Companion to Mark Twain
edited by Forrest G. Robinson

The Cambridge Companion to Edgar Allan Poe
edited by Kevin J. Hayes

The Cambridge Companion to William Faulkner
edited by Philip M. Weinstein

The Cambridge Companion to Ernest Hemingway
edited by Scott Donaldson

The Cambridge Companion to F. Scott Fitzgerald
edited by Ruth Prigozy

The Cambridge Companion to Robert Frost
edited by Robert Faggen

The Cambridge Companion to Eugene O'Neill
edited by Michael Manheim

The Cambridge Companion to Tennessee Williams
edited by Matthew C. Roudané

The Cambridge Companion to Arthur Miller
edited by Christopher Bigsby

CAMBRIDGE COMPANIONS TO CULTURE

The Cambridge Companion to Modern German Culture
edited by Eva Kolinsky and Wilfried van der Will

The Cambridge Companion to Modern Russian Culture
edited by Nicholas Rzhevsky

The Cambridge Companion to Modern Spanish Culture
edited by David T. Gies

The Cambridge Companion to Modern Italian Culture
edited by Zygmunt G. Baranski and Rebecca J. West

THE CAMBRIDGE
COMPANION TO

MARY
WOLLSTONECRAFT

EDITED BY

CLAUDIA L. JOHNSON

Department of English
Princeton University

CAMBRIDGE
UNIVERSITY PRESS

PUBLISHED BY THE PRESS SYNDICATE OF THE UNIVERSITY OF CAMBRIDGE
The Pitt Building, Trumpington Street, Cambridge, United Kingdom

CAMBRIDGE UNIVERSITY PRESS
The Edinburgh Building, Cambridge CB2 2RU, UK
40 West 20th Street, New York, NY 10011-4211, USA
477 Williamstown Road, Port Melbourne, VIC 3207, Australia
Ruiz de Alarcón 13, 28014 Madrid, Spain
Dock House, The Waterfront, Cape Town 8001, South Africa

http://www.cambridge.org

First published 2002

Printed in the United Kingdom at the University Press, Cambridge

Typeface Sabon 10/13 pt.   *System* LaTeX 2_ε [TB]

A catalogue record for this book is available from the British Library

ISBN 0 521 78343 7 hardback
ISBN 0 521 78952 4 paperback

CONTENTS

Notes on contributors   *page* ix
Acknowledgments   xiii
Chronology   xv
Texts and abbreviations   xxi

1 Introduction   1
    CLAUDIA L. JOHNSON

2 Mary Wollstonecraft's letters   7
    JANET TODD

3 Mary Wollstonecraft on education   24
    ALAN RICHARDSON

4 Mary Wollstonecraft's *Vindications* and their political tradition   42
    CHRIS JONES

5 Mary Wollstonecraft's French Revolution   59
    TOM FURNISS

6 Mary Wollstonecraft's literary reviews   82
    MITZI MYERS

7 The religious foundations of Mary Wollstonecraft's feminism   99
    BARBARA TAYLOR

8 Mary Wollstonecraft and the literature of advice
    and instruction   119
    VIVIEN JONES

CONTENTS

9 Mary Wollstonecraft's *A Vindication of the Rights of
   Woman* and the women writers of her day   141
   ANNE K. MELLOR

10 Mary Wollstonecraft and the poets   160
   SUSAN J. WOLFSON

11 Mary Wollstonecraft's novels   189
   CLAUDIA L. JOHNSON

12 *Letters Written During a Short Residence in Sweden, Norway,
   and Denmark*: traveling with Mary Wollstonecraft   209
   MARY A. FAVRET

13 Mary Wollstonecraft and the sexuality of genius   228
   ANDREW ELFENBEIN

14 Mary Wollstonecraft's reception and legacies   246
   CORA KAPLAN

   Select bibliography   271
   Index   277

NOTES ON CONTRIBUTORS

ANDREW ELFENBEIN is Professor of English at the University of Minnesota – Twin Cities. He is the author of *Byron and the Victorians* (1995) and *Romantic Genius: The Prehistory of a Homosexual Role* (1999). He is currently engaged on a project involving the history of socialism and sexuality.

MARY A. FAVRET is Associate Professor in the English department at the University of Indiana in Bloomington, where she teaches courses on British Romanticism, among other things. She is the author of *Romantic Correspondence: Women, Politics and the Fiction of Letters* (1993) and the coeditor of *At the Limits of Romanticism* (1994). The legacy of Jane Austen and the representation of war in the romantic era currently compete for her research time and attention.

TOM FURNISS is a Senior Lecturer in the Department of English Studies at the University of Strathclyde in Glasgow, Scotland. He is the author of several articles and essays on Wollstonecraft, while his *Edmund Burke's Aesthetic Ideology* (1993) includes an account of Wollstonecraft's engagement with Burke. He is currently working on two books about the discourse of radical nationalism.

CORA KAPLAN is Professor of English at Southampton University. The author of *Sea Changes: Essays on Culture and Feminism* (1986), her most recent book, coauthored with David Glover, is *Genders* (2000). A new collection of her essays *Victorians: Histories, Fictions, Criticisms* will be published in 2002. She is now completing a book on *Gender and Racial Thinking* in Victorian Britain.

CLAUDIA L. JOHNSON is Professor of English at Princeton University. She is the author of *Jane Austen: Women, Politics, and the Novel* (1988), *Equivocal Beings: Politics, Gender and Sentimentality in the 1790s* (1995). She is currently finishing *Jane Austen's Cults and Cultures*, which investigates the permutations of Austen's mythic status from the Victorian period to the present, and *Raising the Novel*, which ponders the history of novel studies.

CHRIS JONES is Senior Lecturer in English at the University of Wales, Bangor. His *Radical Sensibility: Literature and Ideas in the 1790s* (1993) explores radical developments in the ideas and techniques of sensibility across gender and genre. He has published articles on the prose writers of the period, including Godwin, Hazlitt, and Helen Maria Williams and is currently working on Jane Austen.

VIVIEN JONES is Senior Lecturer in English at the University of Leeds. She is editor of *Women in the Eighteenth Century: Constructions of Femininity* (1990), and of *Women and Literature in Britain, 1700–1800* (2000), and has published widely on Wollstonecraft and on gender and writing in the eighteenth century. She is currently completing a book on *Contexts for Jane Austen*, and is General Editor of the Oxford World's Classics Jane Austen.

ANNE K. MELLOR is Professor Above Scale at UCLA. She is the author or editor of numerous books and articles on women's writing and British Romantic literature, including *Blake's Human Form Divine* (1974), *English Romantic Irony* (1980), *Romanticism and Feminism*, ed. (1988), *Mary Shelley: Her Life, Her Fiction, Her Monsters* (1988), *Romanticism and Gender* (1993), *British Literature, 1780–1830*, ed. with Richard Matlak (1996), and *Mothers of the Nation – Women's Political Writing in England, 1780–1830* (2000). She is currently working on the intersection of race and gender in British Romantic-era writing.

MITZI MYERS teaches English and writing at UCLA. She has published many authoritative essays on Mary Wollstonecraft, Hannah More, Maria Edgeworth and children's literature. She is currently working on a literary life of Maria Edgeworth, the Norton Anthology of Children's and Young Adult's Literature, and the subject of war and violence from the Irish Rebellion of 1798 to modern times.

ALAN RICHARDSON is Professor of English at Boston College. His books include *British Romanticism and the Science of the Mind* (2001), *Literature, Education, and Romanticism: Reading as Social Practice, 1780–1832* (1994), and (as co-editor) *Romanticism, Race, and Imperial Culture 1780–1834* (1996). He has also published numerous essays on Romantic-era literature and culture, particularly in relation to gender, childhood and education, colonialism, and early neuroscience.

BARBARA TAYLOR teaches history at the University of East London, and is an editor of the History Workshop Journal and director of the international research project, "Feminism and Enlightenment, 1650–1850." Her book *Mary Wollstonecraft and the Radical Imagination* will be published in 2002.

JANET TODD is the Francis Hutcheson Professor of English Literature at the University of Glasgow. She has written many books on women writers and has recently completed two biographies, *The Secret Life of Aphra Behn* (1996) and *Mary Wollstonecraft: A Revolutionary Life* (2000). She has just edited the letters of Mary Wollstonecraft and is working on a study of Wollstonecraft's pupil Margaret King.

SUSAN J. WOLFSON, Professor of English at Princeton University, is the author of *Formal Charges: The Shaping of Poetry in British Romanticism* (1997), coeditor of *The Romantics and their Contemporaries* (1999), editor of *The Cambridge Companion to John Keats*, and a contributor to several other Romantic-era volumes in this series.

ACKNOWLEDGMENTS

In recent years, Mary Wollstonecraft has been exceedingly well served by scholars working in the fields of literature, history, feminist and gender studies, and political philosophy. It has been a privilege to collaborate with many of the leading figures in Wollstonecraft studies and in the history of her period. My deepest thanks go to the colleagues who joined me in this volume, for their splendid essays as well as for their patience with my editorial nagging; and to the anonymous readers for Cambridge University Press, whose advice and encouragement were decisive when this project was in its earliest stages. I am particularly grateful to Linda Bree's expert judgment not only as an editor but also as scholar of late eighteenth- and early nineteenth-century literature.

It is impossible to think about Mary Wollstonecraft without being haunted by the untimeliness of her death. This volume is perhaps doubly haunted, for in the course of its production, one of its contributors, Mitzi Myers, died suddenly. Myers's work on late eighteenth- and early nineteenth-century writers has been wide-ranging and illuminating, and her many publications on Wollstonecraft have been particularly influential. Critics and scholars of the period will feel her loss keenly. This volume is dedicated to her.

1759	MW born on 27 April in Spitalfields, London to Edward John Wollstonecraft, the son of a weaver, and Elizabeth Dickson Wollstonecraft, who was Irish. MW is the second of seven children. Her older brother, Edward (Ned) was born in 1757; Henry followed in 1761, Elizabeth (Eliza) in 1763, Everina in 1765, James in 1768, and Charles in 1770.
1763–68	Determined to set up as a gentleman farmer, MW's father moves his family successively from London to Epping, Barking (both outside London), and Beverley (in Yorkshire). Unsuccessful in these (and later) efforts, MW's father is violent at home. Disgusted with her father's brutality, contemptuous of her mother's acquiescence to it, and resentful of their shared preference for her older brother, MW is intensely unhappy at home and driven to seek affection and nurture elsewhere. While in Beverley, MW develops a close friendship with Jane Arden.
1774	The Wollstonecraft family moves to Hoxton, on the outskirts of London. MW is befriended by a neighboring clergyman, Mr Clare, and his wife, who assist in MW's education and become a second family for her.
1775	Through the Clares, MW first meets and develops an intense friendship with Fanny Blood, later the model for Ann in *Mary* and the namesake of her first daughter.
1776	The Wollstonecraft family moves to Laugharne, Wales
1777	The Wollstonecraft family returns to Walworth, a suburb of London.
1778	As her father's finances continue to deteriorate, MW resolves to live away from home and takes a job as a paid companion to Mrs Dawson, of Bath, one of the few kinds of employment conventionally open to women of Wollstonecraft's position.

While employed by her, MW visits Bath, Windsor, and Southampton.

1781 MW's mother becomes sick, and MW goes to London to nurse her.

1782 MW's mother dies. MW's father remarries and moves to Wales. Angry with the familial indifference of her older brother, now an attorney in London, MW feels responsible for the care of her siblings. MW moves in with Fanny Blood's family in Walham Green, west of London, and helps to support them as well. In October, MW's sister Eliza marries Meredith Bishop.

1783 MW's sister Eliza gives birth to a daughter in August, and thereafter suffers from acute postpartum depression. Fearing a repeat of her parents' marriage, MW attributes her sister's unhappiness to Bishop's cruelty.

1784 MW convinces Eliza to take the bold step of running away in secret from her husband and child, who dies later in the year. After an attempt to start a school in Islington fails, MW starts one at Newington Green, a dissenting community north of London, with Fanny Blood and Eliza. MW begins a friendship with the celebrated non-conforming preacher Richard Price, and she becomes a member of his circle. MW is introduced to Dr. Samuel Johnson. Everina Wollstonecraft joins her sisters at Newington Green.

1785 Fanny Blood leaves the school at Newington Green, and sails for Lisbon to marry Hugh Skeys. MW journeys to Lisbon to assist Fanny during her pregnancy. Fanny dies in childbirth in late November. MW returns to London in December.

1786 MW closes her school because of financial problems that had mounted during her absence. To raise money and improve her spirits, MW begins *Thoughts on the Education of Daughters.* Faced with debts, MW helps her sisters find positions as teachers, and agrees to become a governess for the Viscount Kingsborough family of Mitchelstown (County Cork) in Ireland. On her way to Ireland, MW visits Eton, confirming her disapproval of public school education and suggesting material she would later use in her education writings. MW passes the winter with the Kingsboroughs in Dublin.

1787 *Thoughts on the Education of Daughters* is published by Joseph Johnson, earning MW 10 guineas, which she gives to the Blood family. MW travels with the Kingsboroughs to Bristol, and composes *Mary* and "Cave of Fancy." In August Lady

Kingsborough dismisses MW, in part because she disapproves of her daughter's attachment to her. Returning to London and working as a reader and translator with Joseph Johnson, MW begins her career with a hard-earned sense of satisfaction. She joins Johnson's circle of progressive writers and artists, eventually meeting such figures as Thomas Holcroft, Henry Fuseli, Joel Barlow, Horne Tooke, and Anna Letitia Barbauld.

1788   *Mary: A Fiction, Original Stories from Real Life* and *Of the Importance of Religious Opinions* (trans. from Necker) published by Joseph Johnson. MW begins reviewing for the *Analytical Review*, a monthly progressive periodical recently started by Joseph Johnson and Thomas Christie.

1789   *The Female Reader* published, under pseudonym of Mr. Cresswick. On 14 July, the Bastille falls, and the French Revolution begins.

1790   MW publishes *Young Grandison*, a translation of Maria van de Werken de Cambon's adaptation of Richardson's novel, and a translation of Salzmann's *Elements of Morality*, illustrated by William Blake. On 29 November, MW publishes *A Vindication of the Rights of Men* anonymously, in response to Burke's *Reflections on the Revolution in France* (published 1 November). On 18 December, MW's second edition is published, bearing MW's name and establishing her reputation as a partisan of reform.

1791   MW publishes a second edition of *Original Stories*, illustrated by Blake, and starts writing *A Vindication of the Rights of Woman*. MW meets William Godwin for the first time through Joseph Johnson in November.

1792   MW's portrait is painted by an unknown artist. In January, MW publishes *A Vindication of the Rights of Woman*, which receives several favorable reviews. MW meets Talleyrand, whose proposals regarding women's education in France had disappointed her. A second edition of the *Rights of Woman*, somewhat revised, is published later that year. MW plans to write a "Second Part" but never does so, though Godwin published her "Hints [Chiefly designed to have been incorporated in the Second Part of the Vindication of the Rights of Woman]" in her *Posthumous Works* (1798). MW becomes passionately attached to the painter Henry Fuseli. After Fuseli and his wife refuse to let her join their household as she wishes, MW departs alone for France in December. In Paris, she meets leading Girondins and English friends of the Revolution, including Helen Maria Williams and Tom Paine.

1793   On 21 January, Louis XVI is executed. On 1 February, France declares War on England, and English nationals come under suspicion. MW meets American fellow radical Gilbert Imlay and begins her affair with him. MW's friends, the Girondists, fall from power in late May. The Reign of Terror begins, dampening MW's enthusiasm for the Revolution. In June, MW moves from Paris to Neuilly to escape increasing revolutionary violence. MW is pregnant and returns to Paris in September. Although they are not married, Imlay registers MW at the American Embassy as his wife so that she can claim the protection of American citizenship (America being an ally of France during this time). On 16 October, Marie-Antoinette is executed.

1794   In January MW moves to Le Havre and starts writing *An Historical and Moral View of the Origin and Progress of the French Revolution*. Fanny Imlay born in May at Le Havre. In late July, Robespierre falls and the Terror ends. Imlay returns to England, leaving MW and Fanny alone. In December, MW's *An Historical and Moral View of the French Revolution* is published in London.

1795   In April, MW returns to London to join Imlay, and learns of his infidelity. MW attempts suicide, but is prevented by Imlay. In June, MW agrees to travel to Scandinavia with her infant daughter Fanny and with Marguerite, their maid, in connection with Imlay's business concerns. MW returns to England in September. In October, increasingly depressed over her disintegrating relationship with Imlay, MW attempts suicide by jumping off Putney Bridge into the Thames. Anti-sedition legislation is passed in England.

1796   In January, MW publishes *Letters Written during a Short Residence in Sweden, Norway, and Denmark*. In March, she meets Imlay for the final time, and in April meets Godwin again. MW starts to write *Wrongs of Woman*. By mid-summer, MW begins her relationship with Godwin.

1797   John Opie paints MW's portrait. On 29 March, MW marries Godwin at Old St. Pancras Church, although the couple retain separate households. Their marriage is something of a scandal, in part because Godwin had denounced marriage as an monopolistic institution, and in part because its occurrence underscored the fact that MW had not in fact been previously married to Imlay. Some friends drop MW as a result. Their daughter, Mary, born on 30 August. MW dies on 10 September of complications resulting from childbirth, and is buried at St. Pancras Churchyard.

1798   Godwin publishes MW's *Posthumous Works*, including *The Wrongs of Woman, or Maria*, "The Cave of Fancy," her *Letters to Imlay* and other miscellaneous pieces. Also included is Godwin's own controversial *Memoirs of the Author of A Vindication of the Rights of Woman*, MW's first biography.

TEXTS AND ABBREVIATIONS

The following is a list of the short titles of Mary Wollstonecraft's works cited in this volume. Except where otherwise indicated, all citations from texts by Wollstonecraft are taken from *Works of Mary Wollstonecraft*, 7 vols., eds. Marilyn Butler and Janet Todd (London: Pickering & Chatto; New York: New York University Press, 1989). The abbreviation, volume, and page numbers will be provided parenthetically; errors have been silently emended. Citations from Wollstonecraft's letters are from *The Collected Letters of Mary Wollstonecraft*, ed. Ralph M. Wardle (Ithaca: Cornell University Press, 1979).

AR	Reviews for the *Analytical Review*
CF	"Cave of Fancy"
FR	*Female Reader*
Hints	"Hints"
HMV	*Historical and Moral View of the French Revolution*
IRO	*Thoughts on the Importance of Religious Opinions*
L	*Lessons*
Letters	*The Collected Letters of Mary Wollstonecraft*
LI	*Letters to Gilbert Imlay*
M	*Mary, A Fiction*
MI	*Letters on the Management of Infants*
OP	"On Poetry"
OS	*Original Stories*
PCFN	"Letter on the Present Character of the French Nation"
SR	*Letters Written During a Short Residence in Sweden, Norway, and Denmark*
TED	*Thoughts on the Education of Daughters*
VRM	*A Vindication of the Rights of Men*
VRW	*A Vindication of the Rights of Woman*
WWM	*Wrongs of Woman, or Maria*
YG	*Young Grandison*

I

CLAUDIA L. JOHNSON

Introduction

Even though Mary Wollstonecraft had little to no presence in history or literature curricula as recently as a generation ago, she has never exactly been a minor figure. Some, certainly, have wished her so. A dauntless advocate of political reform, Wollstonecraft was one of the first to vindicate the "rights of man," but in her own – brief – lifetime and ever since, she achieved notoriety principally for her championship of women's rights. And while some of this notoriety took the particular form of scandal of the sort that often attends women directly involved in public affairs, some of it she directly sought in her writing and in her conduct. Controversy always inspired Wollstonecraft, always sharpened her sense of purpose. Whether writing about education, history, fiction, or politics itself, she was always arguing – even her travelogue, written as a series of letters to her faithless lover, is an ongoing argument. And in turn, Wollstonecraft always inspired controversy. A revolutionary figure in a revolutionary time, she took up and lived out not only the liberal call for women's educational and moral equality, but also virtually all of the other related, violently contested questions of the 1790s – questions pertaining to the principles of political authority, tyranny, liberty, class, sex, marriage, childrearing, property, prejudice, reason, sentimentality, promises, suicide, to mention only a few. Clearly, she struck many a raw nerve. Although her *A Vindication of the Rights of Woman* (1792), for example, at first received fairly respectful reviews as a tract on female education,[1] after England and France declared war, it was increasingly (and correctly) read against the backdrop of its broader progressive agendas on behalf of liberty. Thereafter, efforts to vilify Wollstonecraft, though sometimes marked by an air of puerile jocularity, were hysterically intense. Horace Walpole famously called the champion of women's rights a *hyena in petticoats*; Richard Polwhele arraigned her as the foremost among modern-day *unsexed females*; and the *Anti-Jacobin Review* of 1798 went so far as to index her under "P" for *Prostitute*, presumably because no woman could conceivably wish to criticize standards and practices of female modesty unless she wanted to breach them with impunity.[2] No one could possibly arouse this sort of animus unless she is perceived to have posed an urgent, an important threat indeed. Vindications of this great vindicator are marked by a comparable intensity. When Blake invokes a "Mary" persecuted by "foul Fiends," or later in the nineteenth century when Elizabeth Robins Pennell likens her to Saint Vincent de Paul and to Joan of Arc, it is clear that Wollstonecraft was regarded as a formidable figure who challenged the sexual and moral norms of her society in radical ways and who was martyred as a result.[3]

But assailed, revered, or lamented – anything but actually forgotten, even when her memory seemed to go underground – Wollstonecraft's celebrity rested principally on the narrative that makes up her life, particularly as it was first related in Godwin's *Memoirs of* in 1798. As Cora Kaplan observes here in her compelling essay on Wollstonecraft's legacies, Ralph Wardle concludes his path-breaking 1951 biography by fully acceding to the assumption that it has not been her writing but rather her "personality" that "has kept her memory alive," opining that for every "one" person who plodded her or his way through *A Vindication of the Rights of Woman*, "dozens" thrilled to the story of her courage and idealism.[4] There is no denying that ever since her death in 1797, Wollstonecraft endured as a story whose outlines are both highly charged and highly conventional – a story about a passionate but difficult woman's idealism in love (her daring affair with Gilbert Imlay) as well as in politics (her hope for the French Revolution); about her struggles with crushing disappointment in both (Imlay abandoned her and their infant daughter; the French Revolution degenerated into the Terror); about her daring efforts to be independent and original in a world that demonized feminine independence and would not tolerate deviations from the commonplace; about her discovery of "true" love and happiness with William Godwin later in life, only to be cut short by her death in childbirth, of all deaths the one that confirms (as detractors observed) the "wrongs" to women she attempted to ameliorate. Only in the late 1960s and 1970s, when feminist studies began to make an impact on literary and historical studies in the academy, and when the *Rights of Woman* was issued in several paperbound editions – in the twentieth century, it had previously been available only in a 1929 Everyman Classic version alongside John Stuart Mill's *The Subjection of Women* – did attention begin to turn from Wollstonecraft's life to Wollstonecraft's works. Today, at the outset of the twenty-first century, as "feminism" is now acknowledged only to be part of Wollstonecraft's project, *The Rights of Woman* itself, though surely still her popular work, is read with *Mary, The Wrongs of Woman; or Maria*, and *Letters Written During a Short Residence in Sweden, Norway, and Denmark*, all readily available in paperbound editions. And with the complete *Works of Mary Wollstonecraft* issued for the first time, we can now say, contra Wardle, that "dozens" of readers are familiar with Wollstonecraft as a writer for every "one" who has ever read Godwin's first biography of her, *Memoirs of the Author of The Rights of Woman* (1798), or pondered her remarkable afterlife as a personal story.

While committed to investigating Wollstonecraft's crucial and distinctive stature as a figure, the present volume of essays is also inspired by this relatively newfound sense of Wollstonecraft's breadth as a writer. Wollstonecraft is well suited for a volume in the Cambridge Companion series because her career encompasses writing of so many different kinds. As the late Carol Kay has observed, in *A Vindication of the Rights of Woman*, Wollstonecraft writes as a "philosopher" and a "moralist," as an authority on the education of women, a book reviewer, a non-sexual voice of intuitive reason and ecstatic religious contemplation, and as political projector whose ideas should change the French Constitution and the entire course of the French Revolution. This multiplicity of rhetorical voices has at times been read as Wollstonecraft's personal failure of intellectual control or as her noble effort to sustain a female critique of male discursive forms, when in fact, in Kay's words, the "miscellaneous" forms Wollstonecraft employed are "symptoms of the diversity of literature and philosophy of [her] time." The novels, essays, sermons, or pamphlets of writers demonstrably important to Wollstonecraft – take, for example, Rousseau, Burke, Richard Price, or Samuel Johnson – display similar traits of miscellaneousness and a similar decision to eschew being methodical in favor of being accessible to wide ranges of topics and sudden fluctuations of tone and mood.[5] In Wollstonecraft's case, such diversity has proved quite confounding, for working across the tidy disciplinary boundaries we have since constructed to organize disciplines within the academy as well as within the literary marketplace itself, she has seemed to elude our efforts to categorize or even to name her. Do we call her a novelist? An educationist? A political theorist? A moral philosopher? An historian? A memoirist? A woman of letters? A feminist? Wollstonecraft was all of these things, of course, but to describe her as any single one of them would not only diminish the range as well as the wholeness of her achievement, but also impose decidedly anachronistic territorial distinctions on her literary endeavor.

Because thinking about the miscellaneous appearance of Wollstonecraft's career as a writer entails rethinking the way we map out fields of knowledge, putting together a volume of this nature is a compelling venture. But, considered more narrowly, it also poses something of a challenge. To be sure, Wollstonecraft's contributions to specific genres are important, and this collection does not neglect them. As Janet Todd's essay shows, for example, Wollstonecraft excels as a writer of familiar letters, and any student or scholar interested in understanding her profound originality could do no better than to start here. Moreover, the recent availability of the complete *Works of Mary Wollstonecraft* makes Wollstonecraft's wide-ranging work as a reviewer for the *Analytical Review* readily available to readers for the first time. Mitzi Myers's essay demonstrates how Wollstonecraft's literary reviews enabled her not only to educate herself but also to develop her own voice as novelist, a subject I in turn take up in my essay on Wollstonecraft's fiction and its efforts to disrupt customary assumptions about the relations of gender and genre. Nevertheless, the sorts of discrete thematic and generic demarcations that describe other writers' careers do not always offer us the most productive way of conceiving of Wollstonecraft's. She does not, in other words, treat religion in one work, education in another, politics and the French Revolution somewhere else, and fiction in a separate place altogether. On the contrary, her works are always re-visiting and re-thinking the same questions – pertaining to moral improvement, liberty, sensibility, reason, duty. Accordingly many of the essays here recur to these same sets of issues in Wollstonecraft's works, albeit from different angles. Thus, Tom Furniss's essay on Wollstonecraft and the French Revolution not only examines less well-known works like *Vindication of the Rights of Men* and *An Historical and Moral View of the French Revolution* but also traces surprising changes of her attitude towards monarchy in such later and very different works as *Letters Written During a Short Residence in Sweden, Norway, and Denmark*, a work which Mary Favret on the other hand elucidates by uncovering the tension between mobility and confinement as it marks Wollstonecraft's entire career. Similarly, Alan Richardson and Vivien Jones each agree that everything Wollstonecraft wrote was essentially and urgently about education, but Jones illuminates *A Vindication of the Rights of Woman* as a species of advice and conduct literature, and Richardson assesses it vis-à-vis the pedagogical theory of the time. For Barbara Taylor, *A Vindication of the Rights of Woman* is rooted in Wollstonecraft's deepest convictions about religion, while for Chris Jones it is rooted in related, but quite distinct, political traditions of the period. It is hoped that these overlapping discussions, differing in their objectives and emphases and sometimes in their conclusions, promote an expansive as well as an intensified appreciation of Wollstonecraft's work.

As these essays explore Wollstonecraft's affiliations with specific religious, political, and social traditions, others develop still other new ways of apprehending Wollstonecraft's achievement. For Susan Wolfson, Wollstonecraft works and thinks foremost as a close, critical, and often highly resistant reader of the high canonical texts of English poetry – Shakespeare, Milton, Pope, among others – and was in a sense the first practicing cultural critic, one who ironically, however, subsequently came herself to constitute a text for the Romantic poets of her own generation, who reinscribed her into the poetic traditions she attempted so incisively to intervene in and transform. Foregrounding the issue of sexuality, a vexed one since Wollstonecraft's own time, Andrew Elfenbein argues that Wollstonecraft saw herself in terms of an emerging discourse of *genius* which encouraged and licensed her to upset, among other things, conventional indices of sexuality. As many scholars have noted, the late eighteenth century witnessed an exponential rise of women's activity in the literary marketplace,[6] and Ann Mellor's essay suggests how Wollstonecraft directly or indirectly inspired traditions and counter-traditions among her female contemporaries. Finally, pondering the question of Wollstonecraft's presence not in her own time, but in ours, Cora Kaplan's essay finds that, much as Wollstonecraft herself recurs to the problem of female sensibility and the construction of feminine erotic imagination through literature, so too does Wollstonecraft's life and work exemplify for modern feminist theory and practice the vexed status of affect and its relation to gender.

If Wollstonecraft only recently had the peculiar status of being a major figure who was nevertheless typically unread, today students are likely to read Wollstonecraft's works in a wide variety of contexts – in eighteenth-century as well as Romantic studies, in courses on the history of feminism and the emergence of women writers, and in classes about the history of sensibility or of English radical thought. This collection of essays is designed to help students encounter this powerful, daring, and often difficult writer whose career and whose example and whose work continue to inspire and to haunt us.

NOTES

1. For a fine discussion of Wollstonecraft's early treatment at the hands of reviewers, see Regina M. Janes, "On the Reception of Mary Wollstonecraft's *A Vindication of the Rights of Woman*," *Journal of the History of Ideas* 39 (1978), 293–302.
2. See *Letters of Horace Walpole*, ed. Paget Toynbee (Oxford, 1905), 15:337–8; Richard Polwhele, *The Unsex'd Females* (London, 1798), pp. 13–15.
3. See William Blake's "Mary," lines 41ff; Elizabeth Robins Pennell, *Life of Mary Wollstonecraft* (Boston, 1884), 1, 32–3. Countering the still common assumption that Wollstonecraft had no discernible influence on women writers until the late twentieth century, Roxanne Eberle demonstrates Wollstonecraft's impact on nineteenth-century fictional representations of women in general and fallen women in particular throughout *Chastity and Transgression in Women's Writing, 1792–1897: Interrupting the Harlot's Progress* (Palgrave, 2001), and especially in "Concluding Coda: Writing the New Wollstonecraft." I am much indebted to Eberle's study.

4. Ralph M. Wardle, *Mary Wollstonecraft: a Critical Biography* (Lincoln: University of Nebraska Press, 1966), 341. This book was first published in 1951.
5. See "Canon, Ideology, and Gender: Mary Wollstonecraft's Critique of Adam Smith," *New Political Science* 15 (Summer 1986), 69.
6. For the most important recent studies on this score, see Harriet Guest's splendid, "The Dream of a Common Language: Hannah More and Mary Wollstonecraft," *Textual-Practice* 9:2 (Summer 1995), 303–23; and *Small Change: Women, Learning, Patriotism, 1750–1810* (Chicago: University of Chicago Press, 2000); and Gary Kelly, *Women, Writing, and Revolution, 1790–1827* (Oxford: Clarendon Press, 1993) and *Revolutionary Feminism: the Mind and Career of Mary Wollstonecraft* (Basingstoke: Macmillan; New York: St. Martin's, 1992).

2

JANET TODD

Mary Wollstonecraft's letters

Mary Wollstonecraft is one of the most distinctive letter writers of the eighteenth century. Her works from her juvenile productions as a young girl in the Yorkshire town of Beverley to her final notes to her husband and future biographer William Godwin are instantly recognizable. Indeed Wollstonecraft's value is as much in letter writing as in public authorship; often she seems almost to live through her correspondence, expressing within it her numerous roles: child, daughter, companion, friend, teacher, governess, sister, literary hack, woman of letters, lover, wife, rationalist, and romantic. She wrote incessantly throughout her life, priding herself on her frank expression and often berating her correspondents for not rising to her expansive standards. She might have said with Amelia Opie, a friend from her final years, "If writing were an effort to me I should not now be alive . . . and it might have been inserted in the bills of mortality – 'dead of letter writing A. Opie.'"[1]

Wollstonecraft's letters were self-aware certainly but they were also dashed off as the overflow sometimes of joy, more often of bitterness, ennui, and self pity. They are occasionally funny, often engaging, but most frequently moving in their self-centered vulnerability. In them Wollstonecraft grows from the awkward child of fourteen to the woman of thirty-eight facing her death in childbirth. One can see where she matured and where she remained entangled in childhood emotions, noting in the swift reading of a lifetime's writing the unity in temperament from beginning to end, the eerie consistency of tone. At different times the letters reveal her wanting to reconcile different irreconcilables – integrity and sexual longing, the needs and duties of a woman, motherhood and intellectual life, fame and domesticity, reason and passion – but all are marked by similar strenuousness, a wish to be true to the complexity she felt. As a result she never seems quite to have said the last word: there are numerous PSs in her letters, mentions of the paper or letter itself and her need to write to its end, to fill in, to dominate her pages. No space should be left empty, no mood untouched by expression: "I can hardly bid you adieu, till I come to the bottom of my paper," she wrote.

A letter will conclude by promising silence, only to be followed by another begun a few hours later.

Wollstonecraft's letters were not written with half a glance at the public in the manner of some of the Romantic poets like Lord Byron, who expected a place in literary history. At the same time no letter writer of the time assumed complete one-to-one privacy. Runs of letters were kept, handed around among coteries or colleague groups. When Wollstonecraft asked for her letters back from a correspondent, she was confident that she would receive them intact. Yet inevitably for the modern reader there is a sense of intrusion in reading private writing, even after so long. Those anxious about the tastelessness of the act might look at the words of another friend of her latter years, Mary Hays. Unlike Wollstonecraft, Hays lived long enough to collect her own correspondence, and she wrote, "Should this book fall into the hands of those who make the human heart their study, they may, it is possible, find some entertainment, should the papers continue legible, in tracing the train of circumstances which have contributed to form a character, in some respects it may be singular and whimsical, yet affording I trust something to imitate, though more to warn and pity."[2]

Wollstonecraft, like Hays, was aware that she was expressing an inner reality. Inevitably there were outside influences: some letters mentioned reading, usually of improving books, but mostly the modern reader grasps little of the world around – much more appears in her sister Eliza's letters. For Wollstonecraft's response to the great events of her time, the French Revolution and the English reaction, or the deaths of literary and political figures we must turn to the published writings, to her three polemical works: *A Vindication of the Rights of Men*, *A Vindication of the Rights of Woman*, and *An Historical and Moral View of the Origin and Progress of the French Revolution* or to her journalism with *The Analytical Review*. But she does not, by contrast in her letters, describe a domestic private world outside the public political one; unlike most eighteenth-century letter writers, especially women, she did not give immense detail of interiors, gardens, consumer objects, dresses, and materials. The letters of Jane Austen and Frances Burney are full of muslins, gauzes, and hats, as well as of shops and streets they have entered and walked down. Wollstonecraft's letters, often sent from the same fashionable locations, reveal mostly her thoughts, sensations and emotions. In many respects offending the canons of good letter writing, she was rarely concise, graphic, direct, realistically detailed, or detached.

Good letter writing of the time was described by the Scottish literary critic Hugh Blair, whose popular *Letters on Rhetoric* Wollstonecraft discovered when she was a governess in Ireland in 1786 and 1787. She valued the work but the remarks on letter writing had little influence on her practice. Blair had expressed the Augustan notion of correspondence as good conversation, sprightly, witty, and seemingly natural, above all entertaining, with a constant eye to the recipient. Although she tended to be more open about her feelings with some correspondents than others, these were not always especially appropriate for confidence or especially close in family or friendship. Indeed she seems to have had little concern for the particular effect of her writing on her correspondent; for example, she remarked to an old friend, George Blood, that he might dread hearing from her if she continued moaning; yet this fear did not inhibit further complaint. She simply did not accept the Augustan advice to calibrate tone and detail according to the recipient. Great letter writers in this tradition such as Horace Walpole took a single event and reported it in different ways for different correspondents. Wollstonecraft was not a leisured and literary letter writer like this; she did not have Walpole's temperament nor his time and space; she was writing on the hoof, in cramped lodgings, on swaying boats, in the wilds of Scandinavia or in freezing Paris before queuing for bread, or between reviewings in London, or indeed before plunging into the Thames in an attempt to end her life. In such circumstances she was concerned with expressing her emotions as she felt them, not entertaining or worrying about her effect. So she could reveal herself fully to men such as her future publisher Joseph Johnson when she hardly knew him or display her melancholy to a chance acquaintance like the clergyman Henry Gabell.

Perhaps her secret determination to become a writer gave all her communications value in her eyes, however self-obsessed and repetitive they might sound to her correspondent. Just occasionally she sought to entertain – when she replied to her sister Eliza, whom she knew to be gloomy, she tried "fabricat[ing] a lively epistle" – but this was a rare aim and, if her letters to her other sister are anything to judge by, she soon fell back on her preachy homiletic style or her habit of detailing her moods almost as if conversing with herself rather than another. She was concerned to get herself across to herself as well as to both private recipients and public readership, whatever the cost. As a result of this self-concern there was less distinction than one might have expected between her letters to her lover and those to her sisters or distant friends.

The main impression given by her letters, then, is of self-absorption but not lack of self-awareness; often, they seem more like a diary than correspondence, a communion with the self or perhaps a self-created other. Wollstonecraft talked and thought on paper. The strengths of the letters were that, while they were not witty entertainments, they were also not sentimental or exaggeratedly exclamatory in the contemporary feminine mode – letters from Mary Hays or Mary Robinson are examples – nor did they use prepackaged phrases. Instead they sought to dramatize feelings, tease out the meaning from sensations, enacting moods on paper rather than simply describing them. Indeed the letters themselves often formed a large part of the drama of her life. Wollstonecraft would begin to write in one state and end in another or write herself into dramatic misery. She portrayed herself awaiting the post, then hearing that nothing had arrived; her fiery brain burnt and she rushed from the room for air. All was captured on paper.

Wollstonecraft's letters create a distinctive world, a sense of inner vitality, revealing a consistent character. Unhappy in Scandinavia, she told her forsaking lover Gilbert Imlay,

> there is such a thing as a broken heart! There are characters whose very energy preys upon them; and who, ever inclined to cherish by reflection some passion, cannot rest satisfied with the common comforts of life. I have endeavoured to fly from myself, and launched into all the dissipation possible here, only to feel keener anguish, when alone with my child.[3]

Her huge sense of the "I" is always believable and fully present. It is quite unlike the self image of, for example, Lady Mary Wortley Montagu or the bluestocking writers such as Elizabeth Carter and Catherine Talbot. The bluestockings wrote to each other as friends, but their letters, which seem designed to be passed around among a coterie, have a public quality lacking in Wollstonecraft. Lady Mary Wortley Montagu had a very different temperament from Wollstonecraft, as she disclosed when she wrote her wonderfully sharp and witty letters earlier in the century. Although both struggled for self-mastery – Wollstonecraft through religion in the beginning, then through rationalism – unlike Lady Mary she was not concerned in her letters to discipline her sorrows or to distance her subject matter from herself. She did not try to express herself stoically.[4] Part of the difference lay in their different circumstances. Montagu had her aristocratic status to uphold where Wollstonecraft had little social status but a great deal of valued identity to express.

As her letters indicate, Wollstonecraft believed in getting to truth through investigating her own experience; so her mode of writing was in the main intensely personal. She argued the value of her expression with Godwin, who had been critical of her raw careless style,

> I am compelled to think that there is some thing in my writings more valuable, than in the productions of some people on whom you bestow warm elogiums – I mean more mind – denominate it as you will – more of the observations of my own senses, more of the combining of my own imagination – the effusions

of my own feelings and passions than the cold workings of the brain on the materials procured by the senses and imagination of other writers.

(Letters, no. 242)

Her points remain valid for her public writings or her personal letters.

Wollstonecraft's extant letters begin in 1773 when she was still a child and end on 30 August 1797, a few hours before the childbirth that would kill her. They are scattered in libraries in the US and England but the bulk of them exists in two collections, the larger among the Abinger manuscripts in the Bodleian Library, Oxford, and the smaller, including the juvenile letters, in the Pfortzheimer Library in New York. In addition, the letters to the Liverpool philanthropist William Roscoe are in the Walker Art Gallery in Liverpool. The edition by Ralph M. Wardle in 1979 lists 346 letters; my edition will have 354, including a recently discovered letter to Catharine Macaulay whom Wollstonecraft praised in A Vindication of the Rights of Woman and to whom she sent a copy of her The Vindication of the Rights of Men. Many of the letters are undated; consequently their placing depends on an interpretation of the life.[5]

Wollstonecraft's letters survive where someone else wished them to do so. For all his rebuffing, Gilbert Imlay chose to save and then return his lover's letters. His successor, Godwin, read them and found them wonderful and passionate, seductive of the later reader if not of their first recipient; they were in keeping with his image of Wollstonecraft as an author of genius. So, remarkably for the times, as proof of this genius he chose to print an intimate record of the intense obsessive love felt by his wife for a former lover. Perhaps we also owe to Godwin the unflagging intensity of the letters. He liked to see Wollstonecraft as an emotional writer and was less interested in her as a political and economic commentator. Consequently he cut out the sections of the letters from Scandinavia that concerned the business on which Wollstonecraft was traveling (his excisions might also be due to the nature of this business, which was the pursuit of a case arising out of French efforts to circumvent the British blockade during the war between the two countries). As a comparison of these letters with others to her family suggests, he also made them more coherent and corrected the punctuation.

Two other series of letters over which Godwin had control were those between himself and Wollstonecraft and those from Wollstonecraft to her publisher and friend Joseph Johnson. The former he did not publish but largely kept intact. Many of the interchanges simply consist of notes about quotidian matters, appointments, cold dinners, arrangements for Wollstonecraft's little daughter by Imlay. Others are longer or more serious, describing the new deep love for Godwin in fleeting voluptuous or tender moments, combined, as always in Wollstonecraft, with moods and displays of neediness and self-assertion. The others to Johnson Godwin published together with the Imlay letters in *Posthumous Works*.[6] These also sometimes discuss business – literary assignments and the debts which Wollstonecraft was constantly running up with Johnson – but they also reveal again her troubling mixture of independence and dependence, her conflicting desire to rely on and impress another. Like the Imlay letters, the originals of the Johnson letters were presumably destroyed by Godwin once he had prepared them for publication. There are thus no manuscripts from which to check his editing.

In Godwin's view, the great absence from the letters he was publishing were the extant letters Wollstonecraft wrote to the artist and cultural critic Henry Fuseli, for whom she had had what she described as a "rational passion" during the early 1790s. They would certainly have been of value since they must have been a record of her mind when she was writing her great polemical works, *A Vindication of the Rights of Men* and *A Vindication of the Rights of Woman*; in addition they would have thrown light on her tortuous efforts to reconcile reason and passion. When she had been at a low ebb after her suicide attempt in 1795, Wollstonecraft had asked Fuseli as well as Imlay to return her letters. Imlay complied but Fuseli did not. After her death when Godwin was writing his *Memoirs* in loving if undiplomatic remembrance of his wife, he asked Fuseli – whom he knew well but without intimacy – if he might see these letters. Although he had not even opened some of them, so importunate and repetitive had they become in his mind, he had retained them. He showed them in a drawer to Godwin but refused him access; they remained among his papers at his death in 1825. They then became the property of his executor and biographer, John Knowles. Since his subject was Fuseli not Wollstonecraft, Knowles quoted only briefly from them in his 1831 biography.[7] After his death they came into the hands of his son, E. H. Knowles, who announced his possession in 1870.[8] In 1884 E. H. Knowles sold them to Sir Percy Florence Shelley, Mary Shelley's son and Wollstonecraft's grandson. As the child of scandal, brought up to value restraint and propriety, Sir Percy is unlikely to have acquired them for their literary value but rather to stanch the poison of notoriety that seemed to afflict his family – they were after all intense personal letters written from an unmarried woman to a married man. Sir Percy refused Elizabeth Robins Pennell permission to use them for her biography in 1885. Since then they have disappeared and it has long been presumed by scholars that the Shelleys – Sir Percy's wife Jane survived him and was much concerned with the family's legacy – destroyed them.[9]

The letters to Godwin can be explicated through Godwin's own letters, which he also saved; the letters to Imlay have no replies except the fragments quoted within them; the letters to Fuseli exist only in a few quotations by Knowles; one other series of romantic letters surfaces even more shadowily in a newspaper account. Joshua Waterhouse, a clergyman don from St. Catherine's College, Cambridge, unmentioned in Wollstonecraft's extant letters, was visiting the fashionable spa of Bath where young Mary was working as a lady's companion. After his murder in 1827, a cache of love letters was discovered in his possessions:

> Amongst the many fair ones to whom the singular rector of Stukeley paid his addresses was the once-famous Mary Wollstonecraft, distinguished during the period of the French Revolution for her democratical writing.... How far the rev. gentleman sped in his wooing with this intellectual amazon we have not been able to ascertain....[10]

The letters have since disappeared.

The greatest gap for our understanding of Wollstonecraft's emotional development is neither the letters to Fuseli nor the supposed ones to Waterhouse but those to Fanny Blood, the main love of her youth. Wollstonecraft was clear about Fanny's significance in a letter she wrote to Jane Arden:

> I enjoyed the society of a friend, whom I love better than all the world beside, a friend to whom I am bound by every tie of gratitude and inclination: To live with this friend is the height of my ambition . . . her conversation is not more agreeable than improving. . . .

To Godwin Wollstonecraft later described it as "a friendship so fervent, as for years to have constituted the ruling passion of [my] mind."[11] Unhappily not a single letter between the pair survives from this period of Wollstonecraft's accelerated emotional and intellectual development.

What does survive is the series of letters to Fanny Blood's younger brother, the enthusiastic George, as well as those to her own youngest sister Everina, these latter perhaps the most revealing of all she wrote since they are rarely inhibited except about the objects of her affections and they cover the longest period of her life. Everina held on to these letters until her death in 1843. They were therefore not available to Godwin when he wrote his *Memoirs*, although he had requested them. Everina refused access because she felt she had already suffered enough from her sister's scandalous life – she believed her employment prospects damaged by the relationship. Also she neither liked Godwin nor wished to cooperate on what she regarded as an unwise display of her sister's failings – "stripping his dead wife naked" as the poet Southey termed it.[12] The counterpart to the Everina letters is the much smaller series to the third sister Elizabeth Bishop, the most troublesome of the family correspondents and the nearest in temperament and yearnings to Wollstonecraft herself; since Eliza Bishop became thoroughly alienated from her famous sister, even pretending that she was dead through several periods of her life, she probably destroyed some of this correspondence; only one letter survives from Wollstonecraft's later years and it was copied in outrage for her sister Everina to read.

The letters to Everina Wollstonecraft and George Blood have a similar tone; they are often complacent, dominating, dogmatic, frank, complaining and self-assertive: they are deeply interested in the welfare of their recipients but they also blame both for their failures as correspondents and occasionally they make it clear that Wollstonecraft regarded herself as their intellectual and temperamental superior. To George Blood she became remarkably close after Fanny Blood's death, before she awkwardly withdrew from what was perhaps more compromising than she had meant. At other times she felt comfortable berating George for his and his family's failings as if she had really been his older sister or mother. On his side he seems to have given unqualified admiration: Wollstonecraft became the "Princess," a nickname she relished since she referred to it in several of her letters. Without the crucial correspondence with Fanny Blood, this with her brother best charts Wollstonecraft's love affair with the Blood family and her alienation from them as she came to realize their severe limitations (selfishness and fecklessness) and intellectual shortcomings. Poor George, who had been her main comfort through periods of anguish at the loss of Fanny, was later told not to read books above his capacities. The letters to George, like those to her sisters, trail off as Wollstonecraft emotionally outgrew both family and surrogate family.

With her sister Everina, frequently called a "girl" despite her adult status, Wollstonecraft could be frank and bossy:

> your mind certainly requires great attention – you have seldom *resolution* to *think* or *exert* the talents nature, or to speak with more propriety, Providence has given you to be *improved* – our whole life is but an education for eternity – virtue is an *acquirement* – seek for the assistance of Heaven, to enable you *now* to be wise into Salvation, and regret not the time which is past, which, had others taken the greatest pains to form your mind could only have opened it to instruction – and made you capable of gaining experience – no creatures are so situated but they may obtain His favor from whom *only* TRUE comfort flows *if they seek it.* (Letters, no. 51)

While often being dogmatic and homiletic, the letters to her sisters, especially those to Everina, are revelatory and in many ways moving, revealing the transformation of all three of them from vital yearning young girls to sour melancholic women, a character which only Wollstonecraft escaped with her genius and dramatic action. Depression and self-dramatization marked all the siblings – except the youngest brother Charles – as well perhaps as a certain resilience of which, curiously, Wollstonecraft herself seems to have had the least amount. But the letters reveal more than shared temperament: they also display a family of obligations. Each must circulate the last pound when necessary though each is entitled to grumble about his or her generosity. If a brother turns up broke on any sister he will be fed and helped; in return he will leave his dreams with the women who cannot go to sea or speculate in land. When they earn money the younger brothers think of their sisters – as they do again when they lose it. And always there is the parental black hole beneath the tracery of the letters – the father who ruined their childhood and then soaked up whatever money any of them managed to save, the father who often with all his vices and faults was not quite repudiated – not even by Mary, who refused to see him. Johnson rightly emphasized how much Wollstonecraft gave to her siblings and parent – as she did herself. The placing of her letters among those of her family displays how intricate was the network of dependence. Eliza Bishop gave to her father when she herself was almost destitute. Everina sent money to Mary in France as Mary had sent money to her before. In marked contrast, Imlay, outside the blood family, never gave anything to the sisters as a proper husband should have done, nor did he honor the bond for his daughter.[13]

Finally, there are letters to miscellaneous friends and colleagues. The most interesting are a series to her girlhood friend in Beverley, Jane Arden. These letters are a remarkable record of a young girl's hopes and fears, her development and lack of development – for in many ways the bemused, emotional girl of fourteen, who begins the series, is not much different from the woman of twenty who ends it. At one point in the correspondence Wollstonecraft accused Jane Arden of not valuing her letters. In fact, while Jane Arden's letters have not survived, those from Wollstonecraft were carefully preserved. Later in Wollstonecraft's life other letters went to literary colleagues, a few to liberal men like the United Irishman, Archibald Hamilton Rowan, or the Liverpool abolitionist, William Roscoe, more to other literary women written in the last years of her life when she was a celebrity and regarded as such by her fellow writers. Her letters to these women were familiar, often bossy. She came over as both friend and professional, strenuous, formidable, frank, and sometimes downright rude. She could be both helpful and haughty towards a fellow writer like Mary Hays whose tone she found irritating, then slightly priggish but affectionate to the quirky, overfamiliar young Amelia Alderson, who she rightly feared held conventional attitudes beneath her modish radicalism.

The Arden letters begin in 1773 or early 1774 and address Jane when she is away staying with a friend in Hull; they continue on her return when Mary is hurt and jealous at Jane's attentions to other girls: "I am a little singular in my thoughts of love and friendship; I must have the first place or none," she wrote. Jane argued that a person could have many equal friends but Mary doubted it and the girls quarreled and refused to speak to each other. So Mary dashed off an aggrieved note:

> I once thought myself worthy of your friendship; – I thank you for bringing me to a right sense of myself. – When I have been at your house with Miss J – the greatest respect has been paid to her; every thing handed to her first; – in short, as if she were a superior being: – Your Mama too behaved with more politeness to her. (Letters, no. 5)

Such letters with their authentic tone of aggrieved adolescence deliver a prickly, needy but proud girl, eager to prove her value. She was keen to suggest her cultural awareness – her letters were at times a tissue of quotations from writers young people were supposed to read, mingled with doggerel from local poets – as well as her worth as a writer. She might not have the proper pens or have been taught as formally as Jane, but she knew she was expressing authentic "true" emotion. She also knew that writing was powerful and that she might control others with her words.

The youthful letters already indicate her sense of her dysfunctional family. The eldest girl in a family of seven, she had been caught in her parents' downward social spiral and in her own envy for her eldest brother Ned, who had been singled out by their mother's favor and by their grandfather's excluding will, which left a third of his estate to this one child. By the time the Arden letters commence her family had already moved from London, where her father had been an apprenticed weaver, to a farm in Essex, where he had played gentleman farmer, then to another farm in Beverley. With each move be became more drunken and violent and it was clear to onlookers that he was incapable of flourishing or managing what had once been an adequate inheritance. "Many people did not scruple to prognosticate the ruin of the whole family, and the way he went on, justified them for so doing" (Letters, no. 10).

The Beverley period ended abruptly in 1775 when Edward Wollstonecraft returned south with his family. The gloom of this move was lightened for his daughter only by her meeting with the engaging Fanny Blood, with whom she soon dreamt of making a life. Her family meanwhile continued its wandering and decline, and it was with relief that she left home at the age of nineteen to become a companion in Bath. There she reestablished contact with Jane Arden, now a governess in Norfolk. Her letters, expressing her love for Fanny, revealed continuities with the childhood letters but also a temperamental change. She had become strenuously pious and there was a new depressive strain that would dog her throughout her life:

Pain and disappointment have constantly attended me since I left Beverley. I do not however repine at the dispensations of Providence, for my philosophy, as well as my religion will ever teach me to look on misfortunes as blessings, which like a bitter potion is disagreeable to the palate tho' 'tis grateful to the Stomach. . . . Young people generally set out with romantic and sanguine hopes of happiness, and must receive a great many stings before they are convinced of their mistake, and that they are pursuing a mere phantom; an empty name.

(Letters, no. 10)

The sulky demanding girl of Beverley had become a scornful and depressive young lady, a "spectator" of pleasure, an alienated being marginalised in an uncaring society: "I wish to retire as much from [the world] as possible – I am particularly sick of genteel life, as it is called; – the unmeaning civilities that I see every day practiced don't agree with my temper; – I long for a little sincerity, and look forward with pleasure to the time when I shall lay aside all restraint" (Letters, no. 12). Yet, despite the moaning, she had kept intact a sense of "consequence," now expressed as a pride in puritanical austerity and in proper alienation among the trivial.

Wollstonecraft's time as companion was interrupted by family disasters. Her mother was ailing and she returned home to help with nursing. Shortly after Mrs Wollstonecraft's death, the second daughter Eliza married Meredith Bishop. Wollstonecraft regarded her as too young for marriage and was unsurprised when, after the birth of a child, Eliza fell into deep melancholy. Wollstonecraft's response was vigorous: she removed her sister from her new husband and baby. The event was delivered in a series of breathless notes to the third sister Everina, brilliantly capturing the shifting moods and fears provoked by the drama: "I knew I should be the . . . *shameful incendiary* in this shocking affair of a woman's leaving her bed-fellow," Wollstonecraft wrote at one moment; at another, "[Eliza] looks now very wild – Heaven protect us – I almost wish for an husband – for I want some body to support me."

To help keep Eliza, herself – and in due course her friend Fanny Blood and her sister Everina – she founded a small school in the progressive Dissenting community of Newington Green. The next years are sparsely covered by letters – which is a pity since it was a time of considerable intellectual growth. The period and the school came to an end when Wollstonecraft left for Portugal to be with Fanny Blood during her confinement – consumptive, Fanny had quit the school to be married the year before. After Fanny's death,

Wollstonecraft returned to England depressed and lonely; the school collapsed and she accepted a diminished future as governess to the daughters of Lord and Lady Kingsborough in Ireland. The letters during these months and those following, addressed to Fanny's brother George Blood and to Everina Wollstonecraft, primarily describe a prolonged and deep depression, unmitigated by the continuing piety. "I am here shut out from domestic society – my heart throbs when I see a hand written by any one to whom my affections are attracted," she lamented. The triviality of life in Mitchelstown Castle and the Dublin townhouse appalled her: "conversations which have nothing in them" and rituals of dress that consumed time. "I see Ladies put on rouge without any, mauvais honte – and make up their faces for the day – five hours, and who could do it less in – do many – I assure you, spend in dressing – without including preparations for bed washing with Milk of roses &c &c." Her letters, always much concerned with her sensations, now became more specific about her mental and physical ailments:

> Don't smile when I tell you that I am tormented with *spasms* – indeed it is impossible to enumerate the various complaints I am troubled with; and how much my mind is harrassed by them. I know they all arise from disordered nerves, that are injured beyond a *possibility* of receiving *any* aid from medicine – There is no cure for a broken heart! (Letters, no. 54)

During the time in Ireland Wollstonecraft added a new correspondent, Joseph Johnson, the London bookseller who had published her book on education, written on her return from Portugal. He had become a kind of confidant, but he may also have symbolized for her an independent future; so her letters tried to impress him with both her intellect and sensibility. Certainly they eased her forward to a new life which began in 1787, when Lady Kingsborough dismissed her. Declaring herself excitedly to Everina as "the first of a new genus," Wollstonecraft then went to work for Johnson as an author and reviewer on his new periodical the *Analytical Review*. The letters to Everina and George Blood became fewer, more aware of growing intellectual distance. They revealed her continuing care for her family and surrogate family, but now mingled with a growing irritation at their failure to flourish independently; her irritation made her franker and more astringent than she had been when she needed their comfort.

One discrete series gives an idea of her developing sense of herself: it was written to Everina during a short vacation in Warminster with the clergyman schoolteacher Henry Gabell, whom she had met on her way to Ireland. Now closeted with him and his new wife, she cast a jaundiced eye on the couple's married bliss, revealing in the process her own ambivalent attitude to coupledom and domesticity, as well as her awareness of her own intellectual gifts:

> Whenever [I] read Milton's description of paradise – the happiness, which he so poetically describes fills me with benevolent satisfaction – yet, I cannot help viewing them, I mean the first pair – as if they were my inferiors – inferiors because they could find happiness in a world like this – A feeling of the same kind frequently intrudes on me here – Tell me, does it arise from mistaken pride or conscious dignity which whispering me that my soul is immortal & should have a nobler ambition leads me to cherish it?   (Letters, no. 95)

Her detailed sense of her intellectual progress during this time was kept primarily for Fuseli, with whom she must have discussed her two polemical triumphs of the early London years, the *Vindications*, both written as sort of public letters in angry reaction to texts by men she considered both powerful and wrong-headed, especially Burke's *Reflections on the Revolution in France* and Rousseau's *Emile*.

Wollstonecraft must have been writing to Fuseli constantly to create the stack of letters Godwin later glimpsed and it was thus a considerable emotional wrench when, repulsed by him and his wife in her efforts to form a *ménage à trois*, she left for France. It was the fourth year of the Revolution and the Jacobin Terror was about to begin. Vulnerable and yearning for old friends, she soon replaced the middle aged *enfant terrible* Fuseli with a very different man, an American merchant, speculator and liberal author, the tall handsome Gilbert Imlay. Their love burgeoned. When the French grew antagonistic to English wellwishers after the declaration of war between the two countries, she had to move from Paris to a nearby village. There she began the long series of letters to Imlay which would chart her next few haunted years. They tell a dismal story: of the growth, short flowering and long decline of their relationship through Paris, Le Havre, where their child Fanny was born, through a sad reunion in London, through the first suicide attempt, the business trip to Scandinavia, the dreary return and further suicide attempt, to the slow recovery of health and peace.

"Everybody allows that the talent of writing agreeable letters is peculiarly female," remarked the ironic hero of Austen's *Northanger Abbey*. Letter writing certainly filled up a good deal of the literate woman's time but the great letter writers of society were perhaps more men than women, Walpole or Byron, rather than the bluestocking ladies. But, when it came to the emotional personal letter, the exemplary exponent was agreed to be the seventeenth-century French Madame de Sevigné, whose love object was her daughter. Only fiction matched this intensity in Wollstonecraft's period and it was the male hero, Werther, in Goethe's *The Sorrows of Young Werther* who had become the standard of passion. In the letters to Imlay Wollstonecraft bears comparison with Madame de Sevigné and Werther.

Indeed the latter parallel was made by Godwin. The Imlay letters contained "possibly...the finest examples of the language of sentiment and passion ever presented to the world." He went on, "in the judgement of those best qualified to decide upon the comparison, these Letters will be admitted to have the superiority over the fiction of Goethe. They are the offspring of a glowing imagination, and a heart penetrated with the passion it essays to describe" (LI 6:367). The letters were variously crafted, sometimes dashed off and sometimes carefully composed; sometimes they had a literary ring, as though Wollstonecraft were aware of her place among celebrated and passionate female letter writers such as Ovid's fictional Heroides or the medieval nun Heloise. She was often pleading and abject; at the same time she displayed a very real self-respect: Imlay was berated as lover and failed reader for misunderstanding her message and value. Frequently she broke off in passion, in frustration at her lover's obtuseness and her own desire. Her longings vacillated between neediness and dependence on the one hand and longing for freedom and autonomy on the other. Constantly they grappled with the problem of female sexual desire within society and addressed the value, power and seduction of the imagination within human relationships:

> Ah! my friend, you know not the ineffable delight, the exquisite pleasure, which arises from a unison of affection and desire, when the whole soul and senses are abandoned to a lively imagination, that renders every emotion delicate and rapturous. Yes; these are emotions, over which satiety has no power, and the recollection of which, even disappointment cannot disenchant; but they do not exist without self-denial. These emotions, more or less strong, appear to me to be the distinctive characteristic of genius, the foundation of taste, and of that exquisite relish for the beauties of nature, of which the common herd of eaters and drinkers and *child-begeters*, certainly have no idea. You will smile at an observation that has just occurred to me: – I consider those minds as the most strong and original, whose imagination acts as the stimulus to their senses.
>
> Well! you will ask, what is the result of all this reasoning? Why I cannot help thinking that it is possible for you, having great strength of mind, to return to nature, and regain a sanity of constitution, and purity of feeling – which would open your heart to me. – I would fain rest there!   (Letters, no. 180)

The correspondence with Imlay was returned by him when she requested it; although it must have increased her pain, perhaps when she reread it she realized that letter writing was her forte, her form. In her final years her works use the epistolary structure repeatedly: for example in her most successful unison of political commentary and personal experience, *Letters Written During a Short Residence in Sweden*, as well as in the fragment

"Letters on the Management of Infants." Letters also form the largest part of her unfinished novel, *The Wrongs of Woman*.

Wollstonecraft had met William Godwin when she had been in her robust vindicating phase; he had found her strident and unprepossessing. Now in 1796 they met again and he was impressed with her grief-induced mellowness. They rapidly became close friends and within a few months lovers. Occasionally over the period of courtship and commitment she wrote to him the kind of erotic notes she had earlier addressed to Imlay:

> Now by these presents let me assure you that you are not only in my heart, but my veins, this morning. I turn from you half abashed – yet you haunt me, and some look, word or touch thrills through my whole frame – yes, at the very moment when I am labouring to think of something, if not somebody, else. Get ye gone Intruder! though I am forced to add dear – which is a call back –
>
> When the heart and reason accord there is no flying from voluptuous sensations, I find, do what a woman can. (Letters, no. 247)

On other occasions they read too much into each other's words and ended in emotional tussles. Once Wollstonecraft sent Godwin a fable of a sycamore in which she tried to express her vulnerability and fears about another attachment after the disaster with Imlay; Godwin was obtuse and read the letter as a desire to end the relationship. Or they quarrelled and Godwin would try to remonstrate in a reasoned letter about her extreme irrational spoken words. Mostly, however, they wrote short notes making arrangements, sending over cold dinners, complaining about household duties, or organizing visitors. Both relished a secret life going on below the public meetings, for, until their marriage in March 1797, they kept up a fiction that they were friends but no couple. Always theirs was a literary relationship, whose intimacy was embodied in the communal bottle of ink. Ever impecunious and distracted by domestic details, Wollstonecraft asked Godwin to send her some ink because she had run out. Later he asked for his bottle back and one can imagine it traveling between the two unconventional households as, now married and about to be parents, they fiercely guarded their independence and signified both their togetherness and separation in their habit of writing rather than speaking – though they saw each other daily and were only a few doors apart.

During the last months of Wollstonecraft's life, two series of letters are revelatory of her newfound strength yet continuing insecurity and vulnerability to melancholy and suicidal moods. The first concerned her anxiety over Godwin's apparent flirtation with Miss Pinkerton. She remonstrated with him, bringing up the past and reliving her rejections; then she herself wrote the letter of dismissal, leaving Godwin to emend and send it. The

JANET TODD

other series arose out of Godwin's visit to the Wedgwoods in Etruria. He had always been self-conscious about his more elaborate letters, for example at the outset of their relationship trying out various forms of love letter, not always to Wollstonecraft's taste. This time he thought hard about an appropriate style and decided at first on a jocular man-to-man one, varied with more intimate tones, "Take care of yourself, my love...."¹⁴ As the visit progressed, however, he hid the social embarrassments he was suffering in Etruria and adopted a detached tone of travel narrative. It did not suit Wollstonecraft, who regarded his letters less as addressed to her and more of an *aide memoire* for himself. She might cajole her readers, but she rarely forgot them altogether, as she accused Godwin of doing. It was epistolary vanity and self-indulgence she thought.

The letters to Godwin tragically end with the short notes written by Wollstonecraft just hours before the birth which would kill her. Her last recorded writing provides a moving conclusion to her life in its echo of the dying words of her own mother. Mrs. Wollstonecraft had declared, "A little patience, and all will be over!" her daughter's final written words were, "Mrs Blenkinsop [the midwife] tells me that I am in the most natural state, and can promise me a safe delivery – But that I must have a little patience" (Letters, no. 354).

Wollstonecraft is now mainly delivered as an Enlightenment feminist – as indeed she was. In this role she echoes many of the sentiments of the thinking women of her day both liberal and conservative. The life and opinions delivered in the letters are more revolutionary and distinctive however. The desultory and experiential form suited her style, allowing for her devotion to candor. So in the letters she grapples with the complexities of woman's lot as she rarely does in the published work: their emotional neediness as well as their desire for independence, their anxiety over motherhood as well as their enthusiasm, and their attraction to the romance they might theoretically despise.

The letters sometimes appear melodramatic and self-indulgent but part of this is the fashion of the times, and they need to be judged beside the extreme self-dramatizing of her sister Eliza for example or indeed of her friend Mary Hays, similarly caught up in unrequited love. Taken together they form a remarkable autobiographical document. Unlike a diary or retrospective, they record not a finished ordered life but the dynamic process of living and experiencing, and inevitably they tell a tale no biography can truly match. They do not reveal the hindsight of commentary, nor do they show the steady progress towards a full articulateness of any vision; instead they reveal flashes of the genius that makes their writer worth recording and reading in the twenty-first century. The novelist Samuel Richardson believed the "converse of the pen" made distance presence and "even presence but body, while absence becomes the soul..." At their best, this is the effect of Mary Wollstonecraft's letters.

NOTES

1. J. Menzies-Wilson and Helen Lloyd, *Amelia: the Tale of a Plain Friend* (London: Oxford University Press, 1937), v.
2. *Love-Letters of Mary Hays*, ed. A. F. Wedd (London: Methuen, 1925), 13–14.
3. *The Letters of Mary Wollstonecraft*, ed. Janet Todd (Penguin: 2002), no. 193.
4. After Wollstonecraft there are other women writers whose private letters reveal a similar intimate self-dramatizing, self-revealing quality. For example, Charlotte Brontë and Virginia Woolf.
5. My proposed dates differ on many occasions from Ralph Wardle's in his 1979 edition; for example I have used the dates of Wollstonecraft's mother's death and of the births of her brother Edward's children to reassign several of the letters to Jane Arden.
6. *Posthumous Works*, 6: 349–446.
7. *Life and Writings of Henry Fuseli* (London, 1831), 3 vols.
8. *Notes and Queries* 1870 (November 19), 434.
9. See Richard Garnett, ed., *Letters about Shelley* (London: Hodder and Stoughton, 1917).
10. See T. Lovell, *Narrative of the Murder of the late Rev. J. Waterhouse* (1827).
11. Godwin, *Memoirs of the Author of the Vindication of the Rights of Woman* (London, 1798), 19.
12. Ford K. Brown, *The Life of William Godwin*, London: Dent, 1926, 134.
13. I have made this family network a major theme of my biography, *Mary Wollstonecraft: a Revolutionary Life* (London: Weidenfeld and Nicolson, 2000).
14. Note to letter 329.

3

ALAN RICHARDSON

Mary Wollstonecraft on education

A keen and vital concern with education, especially the education of girls and women, runs throughout Mary Wollstonecraft's writing and remains a dominant theme to the abrupt end of her career. The title of her first book, *Thoughts on the Education of Daughters*, speaks for itself; her single most important work, *A Vindication of the Rights of Woman*, begins as a plea for the equal education of women and includes an ambitious and farsighted proposal for a national schools system. Both of her novels, *Mary* and the unfinished *Maria*, centrally address the self-education of their heroines while seeking to fill a pedagogical role in relation to their female readers.[1] More directly, Wollstonecraft produced a book for children (*Original Stories*) in the innovative, progressive mode of the day, edited an innovative reader specifically designed for the use of girls, and frequently commented on children's books and educational treatises for the *Analytical Review*. Among the projects left unfinished at her death were a treatise on the "Management of Infants," barely begun, and a primer, provisionally entitled "Lessons," that, if completed, might have changed the early history of the British children's book.

Education was critically important to Wollstonecraft both as a liberal reformer and as a radical theorist and proponent of women's rights. A broad spectrum of reformist writers and activists – from conservatives wishing to shore up the status quo to "Jacobins" wishing to overturn it – saw education as a, if not the, key locus for promoting social stability or engineering social revolution.[2] According to associationist psychology, influentially applied to schooling and pedagogy in Locke's *Some Thoughts Concerning Education* (1693) and subscribed to by nearly every important writer on education in Wollstonecraft's time, childhood was the crucial period for the formation of individuals, and hence of social groups. As Wollstonecraft herself writes (in a chapter of the second *Vindication* on the "Effect which an Early Association of Ideas has upon the Character"), early education has a "determinate effect" upon later character, and the associations built up over the course of childhood can "seldom be disentangled by reason" in later life (VRW 5:185–6). Not simply the consciously held ideals but the unconscious habits, prejudices, and character traits of men and women are established during childhood.

The efforts of parents and teachers cannot do everything, following associationist logic, since dominant social manners and institutions have a large formative effect in themselves. Yet education could at least do something to form rational and virtuous moral subjects who could then, in turn, help set a better social tone and establish more progressive social institutions. In contrast to skeptics like Anna Barbauld, who noted the contingencies and uncontrollable aspects of the child's early environment, most liberal and radical intellectuals of the time viewed education as the cornerstone of any movement for social reform.[3] This was especially true for Dissenting intellectuals, "non-conformist" Protestants excluded from the educational institutions (including both English universities) under official Anglican control. Left to build their own network of schools and academies, with considerable success, Dissenters had a practical stake as well as a theoretical and political interest in education. Although Wollstonecraft came from an Anglican family, her intellectual career brought her into sustained contact with Dissenting culture, from Richard Price's circle at Newington Green to Joseph Johnson's celebrated group in London, and her thought on education and childhood shows a good deal of coherence with leading non-conformist ideas.[4]

If education was preeminent in forming individual subjects, it was equally powerful, Wollstonecraft eventually argued, to deform the subjective lives of women. Building on Catharine Macaulay's *Letters on Education*, Wollstonecraft came to see the history of female education as a virtual conspiracy of male educators and writers seeking to render women more weak and less rational than they would otherwise have become. For the amelioration of women's abject social condition, then, and for the rise of a revolutionary generation of rational, freethinking, independent women, educational reform was crucial. Moreover, women could argue from their traditional role as nurturers and early educators of children for a sounder and more rational education. If women were to be wholly or largely consigned to the domestic sphere, that is, they could make this domestic form of subjection the very ground for educational reform, since only a thoughtful, well-informed, strong mother could be expected to provide her children with a truly adequate rearing and education.[5] Such arguments, made by Wollstonecraft in company with a wide range of female reformers, running the ideological spectrum from conservatives like Hannah More to radicals like Macaulay and Mary Hays, were inevitably double-edged. They challenged a key aspect of patriarchal domination – the subordination of women through an invidious education meant to confine them to the domestic sphere – through urging a revised conception of that very domestic role.[6]

In addition, their traditional role as mothers, nurturers, and educators of the young gave women writers an experiential base from which to draw on in writing about – and to – children. Wollstonecraft herself worked as a domestic companion, a schoolmistress, and a governess, three of the few "respectable" (if "humiliating") careers then open to women (VRW 5:219). These experiences resonate throughout her completed books, as her experience as a mother (to Fanny Imlay) informs the tantalizing fragments published by William Godwin after her death. The two years Wollstonecraft spent managing and teaching in her own school on Newington Green left an indelible mark on *Thoughts on the Education of Daughters*, the book that first established her as an author.

Published by Johnson in 1787, *Thoughts* owes a good deal to Wollstonecraft's reading in earlier educational treatises (the title itself echoes Locke's *Some Thoughts on Education*) and in the conduct-book tradition. In fact, if Wollstonecraft had not gone on to write the two *Vindications*, it is doubtful that anyone now would find *Thoughts* a "radical" text.[7] For the most part, the book reads like the work of a young author wishing to appeal to mainstream taste by reiterating received ideas, more interested (as Harriet Jump writes) in "selling the book" than in developing original views.[8] Many of the leading ideas are familiar from the Lockean tradition: the ideal of a domestic education supervised by parents; the bourgeois distrust of servants, for the most part an "ignorant and cunning" lot; the banishment of "improbable tales" and "superstitious accounts" (like fairy tales) from the children's library; the importance of an "inflexible" adherence to rules, once set, on the part of parents, along with due affection and an avoidance of "needless" restraint (TED 4:8, 10, 22, 38). Sound habits and "fixed principles" do far more in educating children than empty precepts can, best inculcated by example rather than by rote (TED 4:42). In other words, "I wish them to be taught to think" (TED 4:11). As throughout the Lockean tradition, this mental independence must be tightly constrained by the habitual and principled adherence to things as they are: Wollstonecraft summarizes the "main articles" of early education as "a strict adherence to truth; a proper submission to superiors; and condescension to inferiors" (TED 4:11).

Insofar as girls specifically are concerned, Wollstonecraft argues for a reasoned assent to reigning social values, urging (like most contemporary writers on female education) the development of a sound moral understanding over the mindless cultivation of "exterior" accomplishments like drawing and music (TED 4:12). Unfortunately, rote accomplishments, empty "manners," and "vicious" examples are what can be expected from most girls' boarding schools, which should be avoided – unless the children would otherwise be left with servants, "where they are in danger of still greater corruptions" (TED 4:22). The primary object of early education is to "prepare a woman to fulfill the important duties of a wife and mother," best taught by the children's mother herself. The emphasis throughout on "domestic duties," however, does not mean that there are no glimmers in *Thoughts* of Wollstonecraft's later feminist views (TED 4:21–2). Early marriage, for example, is to be avoided because mothers cannot be expected to "improve a child's under-standing, when they are scarcely out of childhood themselves" (TED 4:31). Wollstonecraft will later argue that women, within patriarchal society, are kept in a "state of perpetual childhood" and that the entire "false system of education" must be dismantled as a result (VRW 5:73, 75). As several critics have noted, *Thoughts* is unprecedented in passionately decrying the paucity of careers for women, and in lamenting the "disagreeble" lot of the governess, the "humble companion," and the school teacher – "only a kind of upper servant, who has more work than the menial ones" (TED 4:25). Here, as in the trenchant remark that schools cannot be well managed given the "low" fees parents currently expect to pay, the voice of experience can be heard (TED 4:12). Although marriage and motherhood remain the default goals of female education, Wollstonecraft notes that the contracted compass of the wife's "province" tends to result an underdeveloped subjectivity, for "nothing calls for the faculties so much as the being obliged to struggle with the world" (TED 4:32). The security of the married state will not be available to all educated women, and it will come at a distinct cost at least to some.

Thoughts veers away from the Lockean mainstream in other ways as well. One is the strong note of piety that brings Wollstonecraft, perhaps surpris-ingly, closer to the devout Sarah Trimmer than to secularists like Richard and Maria Edgeworth, whose influential *Practical Education* (1798) has nothing like the stress on the "promises of the Gospel" and "presence of the Deity" that marks *Thoughts* (TED 4:24, 41). Despite her general adherence to associ-ationist principles, Wollstonecraft also departs from the Lockean consensus in giving a formative role as well to "innate" principles of truth and to "feelings which nature has implanted in us as instinctive guards to virtue." These inborn principles and feelings give children a certain "artless" and "beautiful" simplicity which vicious habits and harmful associations should not be allowed to override (TED 4:9). Artificial manners obscure natural "sincerity" and conceal the "genuine emotions of the heart"; fine clothes and "made-up" faces should not take the place of "unaffected manners" and natural play of thought and emotion revealed by a "'mind-illumined face'" (TED 4:14, 17). As will Joanna Baillie a decade later, Wollstonecraft criticizes the theater of the time for the "false display of the passions" characteristic of the period's acting, missing the "delicate touches" that convey real emotion (TED 4:46).[9] Wollstonecraft employs a standard of nature as well as a standard of reason in seeking to improve on the artful and ornamental female education retailed by boarding schools and fashionable governesses.

Even writing, instrumental for forming "rational and elegant" habits of conversation, should strive for a certain nakedness of expression. "Young people are very apt to substitute words for sentiments, and clothe mean thoughts in pompous diction" (TED 4:18–19). The ideal of artlessness recurs in *The Female Reader* (1789), a collection of short pieces and extracts edited by Wollstonecraft but published by Johnson under a popular writer's name ("Mr. Cresswick"). Taking William Enfield's *Speaker* – designed for use in the Dissenting academies – as her model, but aiming at the "improvement of females," Wollstonecraft again advocates "simplicity and sincerity" in style as well as behavior, with "natural and touching" extracts from "the Scriptures, Shakspeare, etc." as prime examples (FR 4:55). The anthology (along with the translations of European books for children Wollstonecraft produced for Johnson at about the same time) has been described as "hackwork," fairly enough, but the "Preface" is by no means without interest.[10] In addition to advocating a "pure and simple style," Wollstonecraft recommends "works addressed to the imagination" over "cold arguments and mere declamation," and characterizes children formed by "rote" learning as miseducated "monsters," as William Wordsworth more famously will in *The Prelude* (FR 4:56, 58).[11] Well before *Maria*, one can detect a Romantic strain in Wollstonecraft's writing.

Original Stories, however, is often seen as the antithesis to the nascent Romantic cult of childhood innocence and imagination, and has been typically described as a "series of harsh moral tales."[12] Published by Johnson in 1788, reissued in 1791 (with illustrations by William Blake) and in several further editions through 1835, Wollstonecraft's book for children was her first commercial success. Its full title gives a sense of the book's openly didactic purpose: *Original Stories from Real Life; With Conversations, Calculated to Regulate the Affections, and Form the Mind to Truth and Goodness.* Two recent experiences left a profound mark on *Original Stories*: Wollstonecraft's stint as governess to the daughters of Lord and Lady Kingsborough in Ireland, from late 1786 through the summer of 1787, and her enthusiastic reading of Rousseau's *Emile* during the same period.[13] At the Kingsborough estate, Wollstonecraft strove to reform her spoiled, aristocratic charges, through a program based on personal example, rational conversation, and affectionate bonding, much like that of her fictional Mrs. Mason in *Original Stories*. The form and many of the discursive strategies of that book, however, owe a great deal to the literary example of Rousseau, whose influence on the late eighteenth-century children's book is almost as great as that of Locke.

Like other British admirers of Rousseau – Thomas Day, David Williams, John Aikin, and the Edgeworths among them – Wollstonecraft found *Emile* extravagantly idealistic yet accepted a number of its arguments concerning education. The most important, as she states in a sympathetic review of Williams's *Lectures on Education*, is Rousseau's guiding principle of "instructing by circumstances, instead of wasting time ... in formal lessons and severe rebukes." Children learn by active experience guided by a wise and uncompromising parent or tutor. "Dry lessons" and "cold precepts" are at best useless, at worst liable to "form artificial characters"; one cannot truly "cultivate the mind without exercising it" (AR 7:142–3). The difficulties of translating Rousseau's pedagogical program in *Emile* into a children's book format should be immediately obvious, for what is didactic fiction if not a series of dry lessons culminating in cold precepts? As Day had before her in the first two volumes of *Sandford and Merton* (1783–6), Wollstonecraft attempts to overcome this paradox by building the text around a series of fictionalized but credible experiences – "stories from real life" – with the precepts gradually emerging from simulated "conversations" rather than bluntly spelled out as moral tags. Reviewing the third and final installment of *Sandford and Merton* in 1789, Wollstonecraft places it "conspicuously foremost" among the recent spate of "useful books" in the new, post-*Emile* mode, seeking to unfold the minds of their young readers through "questions, conversations, and lively representations of actions, leveled to their comprehensions" (AR 7:174). The characterization of Day no less aptly fits her own innovative children's book, published the year before.

Wollstonecraft acknowledges the inherently compromised nature of the fictionalized object lesson in the book's preface, noting the vast superiority of proper habits, "imperceptibly fixed" by daily experience, over the "precepts of reason" found in books. But given the "present state of society," parents, with their "own passions to combat" and "fastidious pleasures to pursue," can hardly be expected to correctly form the "ductile passions" of their children (OS 4:359). (The Kingsborough family had given Wollstonecraft ample evidence to the contrary.) The "cruel necessity" of teaching by precept rather than parental example recurs in the basic outline of the book's plot, with Mrs. Mason, a family friend rather than paid governess, seeking to reform the characters of two girls left to the care of servants, "or people equally ignorant" (OS 4:361). Having caught "every prejudice that the vulgar casually instill," the girls must be broken of their invidious habits and false associations before these grow too deeply rooted in their "infant minds" (OS 4:361, 383). (Caroline and Mary are aged twelve and fourteen.) Guided by the living example of Mrs. Mason through a series of dialogues and revelatory experiences and encounters, the girls will shed their vulgarities and, assisted by the reemergence of their innately good qualities, pursue a rationally independent future.

Readers' reactions to *Original Stories* tend to be shaped by their attitude toward Mrs. Mason, who has been alternately described as "icy and merciless" and "compassionate," a bloodless "monster" and a "woman of feeling."[14] One oft-quoted passage, concerning the first of the children's many object lessons, can be read either way. In the course of breaking the girls of their habitual cruelty to animals (which, from the power of association, will inexorably lead to cruelty towards people), Mrs. Mason takes charge of a pair of larks shot by an idle boy. The female is worth trying to save; the male is doomed and in "exquisite pain" besides (OS 4:368–9). Pointing out that it would be cruel to leave him to suffer, Mrs. Mason "put her foot on the bird's head, turning her own another way." Cool, certainly; but also an unforgettable lesson in overcoming empty sentiment and weak-minded fastidiousness with rational (if unavoidably fatal) kindness. More chilling is an exchange a bit earlier in the same episode, when the girls try to defend their behavior after running "eagerly after some insects to destroy them." "You are often troublesome," Mrs. Mason tells them, "I am stronger than you – yet I do not kill you" (OS 4:367–8). Even if this is supposed to be uttered half-jokingly, it is probably not a sort of humor that children enjoy.

In the course of their pursuit of instructive experiences and moral examples, Mrs. Mason's charges, like Day's Sandford and Merton before them, receive an incidental education in liberal and radical causes as well. They hear the story of a prisoner in the Bastille, meet a Welsh harper driven off his land by a tyrannical landlord, meet a shopkeeper ruined by wealthy customers too lofty to pay their bills. They also encounter a series of exemplary women, who (along with Mrs. Mason) provide them with models of female virtue, rationality, and autonomy. The village schoolmistress, Anna Lofty, maintains her valued "independence" through minimizing her desires and devoting her time to the improvement of others (OS 4:428). Mrs. Trueman, in contrast, embodies rational domesticity, providing her children with a model education while enjoying a companionate marriage. Mrs. Mason herself, having lost her spouse and "darling child," prefers to continue single and bestow her considerable energies upon the larger community (OS 4:432). Negative examples are provided as well. Mrs. Mason tells the story of a "gentle girl" who, terrified of poverty, marries a wealthy "old rake" only to be reduced to the mad-house by his vices and "ill-humour" (OS 4:405); this cautionary figure recurs as the "lovely maniac" in *Maria* (WWM 1:95).

The radical politics and proto-feminist portrayals found throughout *Original Stories* should not blind criticism, however, to its pronounced disciplinary character. In keeping with much literature written for the "new child" of the 1780s and 90s, *Original Stories* seeks to reengineer the child reader's subjectivity along lines of self-surveillance and openness to adult control, and constructs a rational autonomy carefully delimited by habits of "oeconomy and self-denial" and guided by religious "duty" (OS 4:445, 449).[15] In addition to the virtual object lesson and the scripted "conversation," Wollstonecraft helps develop two strategies for disciplining the juvenile reader that become widespread in British children's fiction: convincing the child of her own legibility and leading her to construct a moral narrative out of her daily life. Both strategies amplify the Lockean view of the infant mind as a sheet of "white Paper" into a full-scale textualization of the child's developing subjectivity.[16] Throughout the book Mrs. Mason urges the children (and, by implication, the book's young readers) to view themselves as objects of constant surveillance, accountable for all of their actions, however seemingly trivial. Mrs. Mason herself exemplifies the penetrating gaze of authority, inescapable even in the dark: "I declare I cannot go to sleep, said Mary, I am afraid of Mrs Mason's eyes" (OS 4:389). Even their inmost thoughts and desires are subject to the all-seeing eye of God. "You must recollect," Mrs. Mason enjoins the girls, "that the Searcher of hearts reads your very thoughts; that nothing is hid from him" (OS 4:383). Construed as texts open to authoritative reading, the girls strive to bring their actions and "very thoughts" into line with Mrs. Mason's teaching. This ongoing program of textualization becomes explicit at the book's conclusion, when Mrs. Mason presents the girls with the written record of their experiences and discussions, presumably a version of *Original Stories* itself. "Recur frequently to it, for the stories illustrating the instruction it contains, you will not feel in such a great degree the want of my personal advice" (OS 4:449). The book is offered as a means to facilitate the girls' internalization of Mrs. Mason's pedagogy, by reconstructing their lives as a series of moral "stories" calculated to illustrate her precepts. For the future, Mrs. Mason urges the children to "write often" to her, again seeking to hide nothing: "but let me have the genuine sentiments of your hearts" (OS 4:450). The girls no longer require the constant presence of a monitor only because they have learned to monitor themselves.

Readings of *Original Stories* as a work of ideological "subversion" tend to downplay or ignore altogether its starkly and pervasively disciplinary tenor.[17] Yet in its treatment of gender, its advocacy of female "fortitude" and rationality, its condemnation of the "frivolous views" – "littlenesses" in the first edition – that "degrade the female character," Wollstonecraft's book for children is strikingly progressive (OS 4:410, 437). A passage from her 1789 review of *Sandford and Merton* suggests how isolated Wollstonecraft felt in her pursuit of an equal, more substantial, and rational education for girls. "Mr Day, above prevailing prejudices, recommends a very different mode of education for females, from that which some late writers on the subject, have adopted;...he wishes to see women educated like rational creatures, and not made mere polished play things, to amuse the leisure hours of men" (AR 7:176). A review of another work of educational reform published only a year later, however, shows Wollstonecraft possessed of a major new ally and her thinking given a significant new impetus. Described as the "turning point" in her intellectual career, Wollstonecraft's reading of Catherine Macaulay's *Letters on Education* provided her with the germ of the arguments on female education and conduct that she would develop to such lasting effect in *A Vindication of the Rights of Woman* (1792).[18]

"Perfectly coinciding in opinion with this sagacious writer," Wollstonecraft reviewed Macaulay's *Letters* at unusual length, eliciting and endorsing its more iconoclastic views on gender and education (AR 7:309). As Rousseau had insisted in *Emile*, "hardy habits" should be developed from infancy, with the important addition that the "amusements and instructions of boys and girls should be the same." The judicious reading program recommended in *Letters* is "equally designed for girls and boys"; in place of the submissiveness and other "negative" virtues enjoined by nearly every conduct writer, girls like boys should develop "habits of independence" (AR 7:311–12). Women are miseducated rather than educated under the reigning system, debilitated and "depraved" physically from lack of exercise and excessive restraint, debased morally by being taught only to "abstain" from vice but not how to attain to virtue. Summarizing this aspect of Macaulay's views as "*no characteristic difference in sex*," Wollstonecraft comments that her "observations on this subject might have been carried much farther, if Mrs M.'s object had not been a general system of education" (AR 7:314). Within a few years, Wollstonecraft would herself draw out the implications of Macaulay's radical critique, in her book-length investigation of the "rights of woman and national education" (VRW 5:65).

Writing in the brief period between the fall of the Bastille and the full-blown British reaction against the French Revolution, Wollstonecraft attacks the inequitable system of female education for its subversion of the republican values of liberty and equality. Having developed a defense of the ideals of the Revolution – "the *rights of men* and the liberty of reason" – two years before in *A Vindication of the Rights of Men* (1790), Wollstonecraft now demands civil rights and equal educational provisions for women in the name of those same ideals (VRM 5:7). Adapting (as had Macaulay)

Rousseau's standard of education for active citizenship developed throughout *Emile*, Wollstonecraft nevertheless relentlessly attacks Rousseau for limiting such an education to boys, consigning girls to a subservient "education for the body" alone (VRW 5:150). Even in their traditional role as mothers and nurturers, however, women require a much more substantial education. "If children are to be educated to understand the true principle of patriotism, their mother must be a patriot; and the love of mankind, from which an orderly train of virtues spring, can only be produced by considering the moral and civil interest of mankind" (VRW 5:66). Virtue must be "nursed by liberty," both positive freedom of intellectual inquiry and negative freedom from undue restraint (VRW 5:264). The proper mother is not an amiable, fashionable house-slave but a reasonable, liberated intellectual.

Wollstonecraft's radical reconceptualization of the maternal role overlaps with the reformist agendas of most of the period's writers on education for women, but goes much further in demanding a complete overhaul of the "false system" recommended by "all" writers on "female education and manners" from Rousseau to Gregory (VRW 5:73, 91).[19] In place of incremental reforms, she calls for "civil" equality and economic independence, as well as an "independence of mind" scarcely to be expected from women "taught to depend entirely on their husbands" (VRW 5:216–17, 222–3). Such independence demands in turn that women be free to step out of their seemingly natural role as wives and mothers, in order to pursue traditionally male professions, such as medicine, politics, and business (VRW 5:218–19). Moreover, the entire slate of "negative" virtues recommended throughout the conduct-book tradition must be repudiated for their morally as well as physically debilitating effects, including the cardinal virtue of female modesty. In the *Female Reader* Wollstonecraft had recommended "diffidence and reserve" as the "most graceful ornament of the sex," praising the modest blush as "more eloquent than the best turned period" (FR 4:56, 59). There is no longer a place in Wollstonecraft's thought for such temporizing. "I here throw down my gauntlet, and deny the existence of sexual virtues, not excepting modesty" (VRW 5:120). Her uncompromising dismissal of uniquely "feminine" virtues – which would facilitate her demonization in the reactionary period soon to follow – allowed Wollstonecraft to revise the existing system of female socialization, from the cradle up.

An education for mental independence and "strength, both of mind and body," begins with a freer and more vigorous infancy and childhood (VRW 5:75). Swaddling, bodily constraint, and close supervision should be kept to a minimum while infancy passes in "harmless gambols" and "almost continual" playful exercise (VRW 5:110). In *Thoughts on the Education of Daughters*, Wollstonecraft had praised the "diffidence" of a "sweet young creature, shrinking as it were from observation," in contrast to the girl who, left too much with servants, "soon grows a romp" (TED 4:11). Now she hopes, in riposte to *Emile*, that a "girl, whose spirits have not been damped by activity, or innocence tainted by false shame, will always be a romp," lively and athletic, less interested in dolls than in running "wild" (VRW 5:112). Growing girls should take the "same exercise as boys," and once they do so the alleged "natural superiority of man" in point of strength will prove to have been culturally exaggerated, if not altogether socially produced (VRW 5:155). In place of the sedentary, repetitive, and confining occupation of needlework, older girls should practice "gardening, experimental philosophy, and literature," likely to improve their conversation along with their health (VRW 5:144). More "good sense" and active virtue can be found among "poor women," despite their "few advantages of education," than among those of the middle and higher ranks, simply because their desperate situation demands activity verging on "heroic" exertion (VRW 5:145).

Turning to education proper, Wollstonecraft breaks both with the bourgeois liberal consensus of her time and her own earlier position in advocating an ambitious scheme of national education. Educational reformers from Locke to the Edgeworths recommend a "domestic" education supervised directly by parents – or a trusted, qualified tutor – over the boarding schools and day schools then available. Boarding schools regularly come in for special attack, and Wollstonecraft echoes this criticism in the chapter of the *Vindication* devoted to "national schools," the first third of which concerns schooling for boys (VRW 5:229–35). Schools, "as they are now regulated," are the "hot-beds of vice and folly"; too crowded for careful instruction and adequate supervision, their tone too often set by the worst impulses of the boys themselves. "The relaxation of the junior boys is mischief; and of the senior, vice." But, acknowledging the significant shift in her views, Wollstonecraft can no longer support "private" (domestic) education either. Children best learn to "think for themselves" among other children, working in concert to solve problems rather than passively relying on adults. The "social affections" require an atmosphere of "equality" in order to develop, and the friendships, open discussions, and "confidences" shared by children provide the best foundation for a frank, benevolent, and ingenuous character. Seeking a middle ground between the inadequate pedagogy and supervision of boarding-schools and the confinement of an adult-dominated "private" education, Wollstonecraft calls for the provision of "proper day-schools," where children can learn together while enjoying the domestic comforts – and maintaining the domestic ties – of home. Sounding rather like her old adversary Edmund Burke – the target of the first *Vindication* – she insists that "public virtues" must be rooted in domestic bonds: "if you wish to make good citizens, you must first exercise the affections of a son and brother" (VRW 5:234).[20]

As Wollstonecraft's ambitious proposal for a national schools system develops, however, it becomes clear that the needs of daughters and sisters are foremost on her mind. Other radical writers, most notably Thomas Paine, had also concluded that day schools funded by the state would best promote the spread of literacy, knowledge, and ultimately social and political equality. But Paine, like Joseph Priestley, William Godwin, and other radicals from Dissenting families, worried about the potential of a system controlled by the (officially Anglican) state to shape ideological uniformity and religious orthodoxy.[21] The national government should help parents meet educational expenses, but should have no part in establishing or directing the schools themselves. For Wollstonecraft, however, only a national system of day schools has the capacity to fundamentally change social relations between the sexes. She notes early in the second *Vindication* that "private education" can have only a limited effect in comparison to the implicit, insensible, constant education provided by the "opinions and manners" of society as a whole (VRW 5:90). But should education become a "grand national concern," an entire generation could be produced under fundamentally altered social circumstances (VRW 5:234). Raising girls together with boys in "national" day schools established throughout the country and making female education not only equal, but indistinguishable from (a reformed) male education, could enable the "improvement and emancipation of the whole sex" (VRW 5:247).

By being educated together with boys in "public schools" (that is, state-managed day schools), girls will learn to become "free" and "independent," the best foundation for genuine companionship with men in later life. Both sexes will learn true modesty together – that is, "modesty without those sexual distinctions" that make for an unequal social compact and "taint" both the male and female mind, rendering the former more sensual and the latter more cunning. Thanks to the "enlargement of mind" promised by a sounder education, women will learn to better appreciate the fine arts and the beauties of nature, in place of the "ignorance and low desires" all but guaranteed by the current system (VRW 5:237-8, 245). Wollstonecraft anticipates the stock charge that too much education will masculinize women by returning to her revisionary conception of motherhood and domesticity. Schooling in "political and moral subjects" will make women more rather than less "attentive to domestic duties," by giving them the strength of an "active mind" and a compelling alternative to the "love of pleasure." "Indolence and vanity," not the higher pleasures of "literary pursuits" and the "steady investigation of scientific subjects," poison domestic life (VRW 5:241). The scientifically trained mother will moreover be in a better position to "nurse" her family's physical and moral health, and the schools should therefore cover not only the "elements of anatomy and medicine," but teach the "anatomy of the mind" by "allowing the sexes to associate together in every pursuit," studying the progress of civilization and the "political history of mankind" (VRW 5:249). Here the force (and iconoclasm) of Wollstonecraft's critique of "sexual" virtues again becomes evident. Having dismantled the notion of a uniquely feminine "modesty," Wollstonecraft can argue not only for coeducation, but for the pursuit of supposedly immodest subjects like human anatomy.

The specifics of her proposal for a national schools system show that Wollstonecraft wishes to promote social equality not only in relation to gender but in relation to class as well, though within certain parameters. In the "elementary" day schools (for children from five to nine years old), "boys and girls, the rich and poor" are educated together with a single curriculum. School uniforms and a single code of discipline function to minimize the appearance of class distinctions. A large playground allows for the physical exercise and "relaxations" that young children need, as well as providing a natural classroom for studying botany, mechanics, and the like. As in *Original Stories* and other didactic children's books written in the wake of *Emile*, hands-on learning, active problem-solving, and "socratic" dialogues are the preferred forms of instruction (VRW 5:240). Older children, still unsegregated by gender, will be divided into two tracks. Those "intended for domestic employments, or mechanical trades," will be given a predominately vocational education, whereas "young people of superior abilities, or fortune," will pursue a version of the sound "liberal" education available in the great Dissenting academies: classical and modern languages, natural science, history, politics, and literature (VRW 5:242). This tracking may seem a concession to the starkly hierarchical class system of the time, and it is. Yet the possibility that children's futures might be determined by "abilities" rather than "fortune" reflects the radically progressive character of Wollstonecraft's imagined school of the future.

Much as Wollstonecraft's vision of coeducational, state-supported, universally available schooling – at once utopian and prophetic – represents a significant shift in her educational thought, the second *Vindication* manifests a fundamentally new approach to considering the relation between children and adults generally. With its emphasis on "proper submission to superiors," *Thoughts* had kept children in their traditional place of inferiority to adults, at least adults of the same or higher socioeconomic status. In *Original Stories*, despite its casual equation of the "lower class of mankind" with "children," the girls are instructed to consider themselves "inferior" even to servants, at least those "whose understandings are arrived at some degree of maturity" (OS 4:390, 412). But by the time she publishes her translation of de Cambon's *Young Grandison* (1790), Wollstonecraft has grown impatient with doctrines that "cramp" the child's understanding in making it "submit to any other authority than that of reason" (YG 2:215). According to *A Vindication of the Rights of Woman*, the "Divine right" of parents to their children's obedience is just as spurious as the divine right of kings to rule a people (VRW 5:228). In fact, these alleged "rights" equally make part of an overarching system of patriarchal despotism, both political and domestic, promoting the interest of "tyrants," from the "weak king to the weak father of a family" (VRW 5:67). Rejecting the "arbitrary principle" of parental authority and the "blind obedience" that renders children "slavish" in character, Wollstonecraft urges that parent–child relations be predicated instead on a principle of "reciprocal duty." Parents should earn their children's respect through carefully attending to their education as well as basic needs, and children return the obligation through caring for parents in their old age (VRW 5:224–6). In her *Strictures on the Modern System of Female Education* (1799) Hannah More had attempted to reduce the "*rights of woman*" to absurdity by anticipating a new treatise on the "*rights of children.*"[22] But for Wollstonecraft, there is clearly nothing absurd about the connection between women's and children's rights to rational self-determination. Among the few "Hints" she left toward the planned second volume of *A Vindication of the Rights of Woman*, one finds the thesis that "children should be taught to feel deference, not to practise submission" (Hints 5:273).

Two other works left in fragmentary form further extend Wollstonecraft's thought on education and childhood: her "Letters on the Management of Infants" and her "Lessons" for small children, both published by Godwin with the *Posthumous Works* in 1798. In the second *Vindication*, Wollstonecraft had argued that rational, independent-minded women would be better able to see through the reigning "prejudices" concerning infant care that had "thinned the human race"; if this were the *only* benefit of reforms in female education, it would be worth setting up a national schools network simply to save infants from being sacrificed to the "moloch prejudice" (VRW 5:248). Following the birth of her daughter Fanny in 1794, Wollstonecraft refused to let her daughter be tightly swaddled, dressed her in loose clothing, exposed her to fresh air and a rich environment, and adopted a "natural manner of nursing," all to the consternation of the local matrons.[23] The letters on infancy, of which only part of the first survives, were meant to illustrate a program of infant care based on "simplicity" and the author's own successful "practice" for women ready to depart from the conventional errors that contributed to the high infant mortality rate of the time (MI 4:459). Her healthy, vigorous daughter was a living argument both for rational motherhood and for giving children, even as infants, as much freedom and stimulation as possible.

Fanny also figures prominently in the fragmentary "Lessons," which address a "little girl" her age and were designed for her use in learning to read (L 4:468–74). In the manner of Barbauld's *Lessons for Children* (1778–88), Eleanor Fenn's *Cobwebs to Catch Flies* (1783), or the Edgeworths' *Parent's Assistant* (1796), Wollstonecraft seeks to provide the beginning reader with age-appropriate, concrete, engaging material in a simple style and parental voice. The first lesson is simply a list of nouns, all naming concrete objects, in the best Lockean manner. Verbs, a few adjectives, more abstract nouns (day and night), numbers and colors are added in the second lesson. The third lesson introduces phrases of two to four words, and also begins to establish a warm, intimate relation between the child reader and the adult writer: "Shake hands. I love you. Kiss me now. Good girl." The fourth lesson introduces a baby brother, enabling a series of comparisons that give the girl reader–protagonist insight into her own motoric, cognitive, and emotional development. She is steadily encouraged to take pride in her growing strength and mastery of the object world around her, while a life narrative develops that emphasizes the child's affectionate bonds with her family in place of the moral self-scrutiny insisted upon in *Original Stories*.[24] "You could only open your mouth, when you were lying, like William, on my knee. So I put you to my breast, and you sucked, as the puppy sucks now, for there was milk enough for you."

In his brief preface to the extant lessons (ten in all), Godwin states that the author has "struck out on a path of her own," a claim amply justified as the "Lessons" continue (L 4:467). For Wollstonecraft establishes a unique variant on the maternal voice of the "new" literature for children, one that includes a rare admission of parental vulnerability that contrasts strikingly with her own Mrs. Mason's seeming omnipotence. "At ten months you had four pretty white teeth, and you used to bite me. Poor mamma! Still I did not cry, because I am not a child, but you hurt me very much." The roles of parent and child are shown to be not fixed identities, but positions that shift with succeeding generations: "My mamma took care of me, when I was a little girl, like you." The child's growing autonomy is a source of parental pleasure rather than anxiety, something to endorse and encourage rather than qualify and circumscribe. "What you think that you shall soon be able to dress yourself entirely? I am glad of it: I have something else to do." The tenth lesson shows first the mother, then the father, in moments of weakness, ill and needing rest and quiet, and demonstrates to the child that she indeed knows "how to think" because she has learned from one parent how to spare the other. "I did not bid you be quiet; but you thought of what papa said to you, when my head ached. This made you think you ought not to make a noise, when papa was resting himself. So you came to me, and said to me, very softly, Pray reach me my ball, and I will go and play in the garden, till papa wakes." This is altogether a new voice in juvenile fiction. Had Wollstonecraft lived to complete "Lessons," it would have made a pronounced contrast to the steely didacticism of *Original Stories*, and would have provided an innovative and compelling model for children's writers to come.

The lasting impact of Wollstonecraft's writing about education and childhood cannot, however, finally be separated from her feminism. It was as a revolutionary thinker on female education, and its intimate relation to women's social, political, and domestic subordination, that Wollstonecraft both inspired and provoked her contemporaries. Although Macaulay had provided her with a foundation, Wollstonecraft's *A Vindication of the Rights of Woman* is unprecedented in the systematic character of its analysis of female subjection and in the vigor and precision of its critique of earlier prescriptions for women's education. Her willingness to attack the cultural edifice of feminine modesty, to advocate coeducation throughout the years of schooling, to demand political rights and economic independence for women, all made Wollstonecraft a ready target not just for criticism, but for demonization within the increasingly reactionary climate of the Romantic era. Yet even at a time when to name Wollstonecraft usually meant to mock or attack her, versions of her ideas on women's education tacitly informed later works in an entire range of genres, from domestic fiction to tracts on educational reform.[25] Wollstonecraft's powerful analysis of the role of educational methods, institutions, and disparities in maintaining social inequalities still resonates today.

NOTES

1. See Lisa Shawn Maurer, "The Female (As) Reader: Sex, Sensibility, and the Maternal in Wollstonecraft's Fictions," *Essays in Literature* 19 (1992), 36–54 and Mitzi Myers, "Pedagogy as Self-Expression in Mary Wollstonecraft: Exorcising the Past, Finding a Voice," *The Private Self: Theory and Practice of Women's Autobiographical Writings*, ed. Shari Benstock (Chapel Hill: University of North Carolina Press, 1988), 192–210.
2. For an overview, see Alan Richardson, *Literature, Education, and Romanticism: Reading as Social Practice, 1780–1832* (Cambridge: Cambridge University Press, 1994).
3. Anna Laetitia Barbauld, "On Education," *Works of Anna Laetitia Barbauld*, ed. Lucy Aikin, 2 vols. (London: Longman, Hurst, Rees, Orme, Brown, and Green, 1825) 2: 305–20.

4. Virginia Sapiro, *A Vindication of Political Virtue: the Political Theory of Mary Wollstonecraft* (Chicago: University of Chicago Press, 1992), 239–40.

5. Mitzi Myers first called attention to this strategy in "Impeccable Governesses, Rational Dames, and Moral Mothers: Mary Wollstonecraft and the Female Tradition in Georgian Children's Books," *Children's Literature* 14 (1986), 31–59.

6. For a ground-breaking study of this dilemma, see Elizabeth Kowaleski-Wallace, *Their Fathers' Daughters: Hannah More, Maria Edgeworth, and Patriarchal Complicity* (Oxford: Oxford University Press, 1991).

7. Jane Moore, *Mary Wollstonecraft* (Plymouth: Northcote House, 1999), 10.

8. Harriet Jump, *Mary Wollstonecraft: Writer* (New York: Harvester Wheatsheaf, 1994), 9.

9. Compare Baillie's Introduction to the third volume of *Plays on the Passions*, in *The Dramatic and Poetical Works of Joanna Baillie*, 2nd edn. (London: Longman, Brown, Green, and Longmans, 1853), 232–3.

10. Gary Kelly, *Revolutionary Feminism: the Mind and Career of Mary Wollstonecraft* (New York: St. Martin's Press, 1992), 74.

11. Compare *The Prelude* (1805 version), 5: 290–340, in *The Prelude, 1799, 1805, 1850*, eds. Jonathan Wordsworth, M. H. Abrams, and Stephen Gill (New York: Norton, 1979).

12. Janet Todd, *The Sign of Angellica: Women, Writing, and Fiction, 1660–1800* (New York: Columbia University Press, 1989), 222.

13. Emily W. Sunstein, *A Different Face: the Life of Mary Wollstonecraft* (New York: Harper and Row, 1975), 139.

14. Mary V. Jackson, *Engines of Instruction, Mischief, and Magic: Children's Literature in England from its Beginnings to 1839* (Lincoln: University of Nebraska Press, 1989), 148; Moore, *Mary Wollstonecraft*, 29; Geoffrey Summerfield, *Fantasy and Reason: Children's Literature in the Eighteenth Century* (Athens: University of Georgia Press, 1984), 229; Myers, "Pedagogy," 206.

15. For children's literature and the "new child" in late eighteenth-century Britain, see Jackson, *Engines*, 129–48.

16. Richardson, *Literature, Education, and Romanticism*, 127–42.

17. Moore, *Mary Wollstonecraft*, 28. Kelly, however, provides a refreshingly balanced view of the book's disciplinary and radical tendencies in *Revolutionary Feminism*, 58–67.

18. Kelly, *Revolutionary Feminism*, 83.

19. See Claudia L. Johnson, "Mary Wollstonecraft: Styles of Radical Maternity," *Inventing Maternity: Politics, Science, and Literature, 1650–1865*, eds. Susan C. Greenfield and Carol Barash (Lexington: University Press of Kentucky, 1999), 160–72.

20. Compare Burke – "In this choice of inheritance we have given to our frame of polity the image of a relation in blood, binding up the constitution of our country with our dearest domestic ties, adopting our fundamental laws into the bosom of our family affections" – in *Reflections on the Revolution in France*, ed. J. G. A. Pocock (Indianapolis: Hackett, 1987), 30.

21. Richardson, *Literature, Education, and Romanticism*, 87–88.

22. Hannah More, *Strictures on the Modern System of Female Education*, 6th edn., 2 vols. in one (London: Cadell and Davies, 1799), 1: 146–7.

23. Sunstein, *Different Face*, 257–63.

24. My reading of the "Lessons" concurs with that of Jump in *Mary Wollstonecraft*, 23–5.
25. For a subtle delineation of the indirect expression of feminist ideas in early nineteenth-century domestic fiction, see Claudia L. Johnson, *Jane Austen: Women, Politics, and the Novel* (Chicago: University of Chicago Press, 1988). For an example of a contemporary writer on education making extensive, though unacknowledged, use of Wollstonecraft's arguments, see Sydney Smith, "Female Education" (initially published in 1810 in the *Edinburgh Review*), *The Works of the Reverend Sydney Smith* (London: Longmans, Green, 1865), 175–86.

4

CHRIS JONES

Mary Wollstonecraft's *Vindications* and their political tradition

The republican milieu

When she set up her school in Newington Green in 1784, Wollstonecraft joined a circle rich in adversarial political experience. As religious Dissenters, they were opposed to the established Church of England. Dissenters could not take the oaths necessary to secure offices under the Crown or even to take degrees at English Universities. Politically they debated the terms of the Whig triumph of 1688 when parliament had seemingly affirmed its paramount power by dismissing James II and calling a Protestant monarch, William of Orange, to the throne. "Real," or "true," Whigs complained that Parliament, instead of extending its power and becoming more representative of the people, had used the influence of the throne to establish a monopoly of power in the hands of great landowners. James Burgh, whose widow was Wollstonecraft's personal friend, had compiled a damning dossier on the oligarchy of "borough-mongers," its manipulation of elections, its system of patronage and nepotism. Republican ideas, from a tradition including Greece, Rome, and Renaissance Italy as well as the seventeenth-century English Commonwealth, were frequently used to attack courtly corruption and democratic arguments were voiced, especially after the American Revolution. Many saw a remedy for corruption in extending parliamentary representation to newly populous towns and widening the franchise to make bribery and intimidation less common. However radical their ideas, few ventured to actually propose dismantling rather than reforming a constitution that purported to balance monarchical, republican, and democratic principles and had brought peace and prosperity to Britain. Richard Price, another close friend and Wollstonecraft's mentor in moral philosophy, was a member of the Real Whig club and a correspondent of Tom Paine, Benjamin Franklin, and Thomas Jefferson. He had opposed the American War and joined with Catharine Macaulay in the battles for "Wilkes and Liberty" against the power of the Crown, keeping alive the republican traditions of the Commonwealth. He attempted to pilot bills through Parliament to free Dissenters from the Tests which barred them from civic offices and worked with members of the renowned Warrington Dissenting Academy, Joseph Priestley, William Enfield, John Aikin, and Aikin's sister Anna Barbauld. Wollstonecraft maintained these connections when she moved to London to write for Joseph Johnson, the Liverpool-bred publisher. The overlapping circles of Price and Johnson included liberal Churchmen, Dissenters of many sectarian persuasions, educators, scientists, entrepreneurs, provincial and metropolitan radicals, some of whom, like John Horne Tooke and Thomas Brand Hollis, were continuators of mid-century groupings. Later in France Wollstonecraft met American radicals and entrepreneurs, representatives of the revolutionary United Irishmen, and the circle of Madame Roland, Brissot, Condorcet, and Helen Maria Williams, a group concerned initially with developing ideas drawn from English and American republican traditions and then with surviving the reign of Robespierre.

In politics Mary Wollstonecraft must be accounted a republican.[1] She hoped for the disappearance of monarchy and inherited distinctions, but she went further than Price and Macaulay in supporting "democratists" like Paine, looking towards the extension of the franchise to working men and women. She did not produce a specifically political program, however, and her political criticism is couched predominantly in terms of morality. Like most republicans she was concerned about virtue as the quality most needed to uphold the state, but her definitions of virtue are more moralistic and individualistic than the public virtues of traditional republicanism. While sharing the republican preference for a citizen militia, her criticism of a standing army concentrates less on its use as an instrument of despotism than on the way in which a soldier is fashioned into a stunted, ceremonious automaton and becomes a victim, like woman, of the inequalities of present society. She does not adopt the principle associated with the Commonwealth writer James Harrington and his eighteenth-century followers that political power should follow property and thus be attainable by the gentry and rising commercial classes. Possession of an economic "independency" did not guarantee political independence in these corrupt times. The goal of Wollstonecraft's political morality is the happinesss and self-determined advancement of each individual, not the good of the propertied, the majority, or the imaginary whole of society, a position that distinguishes her also from the utilitarianism of Priestley.

What Wollstonecraft gained from her radical friends was not just a set of doctrines but a way of life in which feeling and intellect gained social expression. Individuals such as Price, Johnson, Thomas Christie, her editor on Johnson's *Analytical Review*, and William Godwin gave her much-needed personal support and the close-knit groups of Dissenters and radicals provided a sort of extended family. Often collaborating in literary projects, they maintained a fiercely guarded intellectual independence. In defending Price against Burke's attacks in his *Reflections on the French Revolution* (1790) Wollstonecraft was praising the man who had done most to form her views, but though her portrait of Price in *A Vindication of the Rights of Men* (1790) is of a reverend patriarch she does not adopt a stance of uncritical reverence. His utopian speculations are admitted to be provocatively extreme, and the picture of the Dissenters as sharing "feminine" weaknesses in the conclusion of *A Vindication of the Rights of Woman* (1792) might be seen as critical of his political efforts to unify Dissenting opinion and by multiplied compromises bring some slight alleviation of their civic disabilities. Her milieu gave her the liveliest evidence of the progressiveness of what the eighteenth century called the "social passions," feelings that Blake celebrated in *Songs of Innocence* (1789) as the basis of social harmony in mercy, pity, peace, and love. Rousseau, the Prometheus of the passions, was a strong and early influence on Wollstonecraft's thinking. She was particularly drawn to his pictures of the republican Swiss canton with its patriarchal families, evoking a "Golden Age" in human society. In her travels in Scandinavia she was persuaded that it might exist, but always further north in inaccessible valleys. In her writings the term "patriarchal" has none of the pejorative implications of later feminist criticism; it is associated with a Rousseauistic vision of "independence and virtue; affluence without vice; cultivation of mind, without depravity of heart; with 'ever-smiling liberty;' the nymph of the mountain" (SR 6:308).

Sensibility in social thought

Wollstonecraft was scathing about some versions of Sensibility, but in that deeply rifted tradition of thought she definitely belonged to the radical wing. A common general term that united discourses dealing with feeling in medicine, religion, and the arts, Sensibility also came to signify the school of philosophy that saw human society as deriving from and sustained by bonds of feeling and sympathy. Shaftesbury, Hutcheson, Hume, and Adam Smith originated many of the leading ideas of the tradition, which were developed by philosophical historians, critics, and general essayists. In its more radical aspect Sensibility cut across distinctions of rank and wealth to elevate the subjectivity of the virtuous and cultured individual, broadening the idea of politeness and establishing an emulative culture of sociability. It purported to put the individual in touch with a more authentic "natural" self that also connected with authentic national traditions rather than classical models.

Its humanitarianism and benevolism were considered distinctive of modern society. Wollstonecraft educated herself in authors of this tradition and was convinced of its progressive tendency. Classical societies had denigrated woman, found entertainment in slaughter, glorified war, and justified slavery; they had not cultivated the humanizing warmth of fellow-feeling, the essentially democratic acknowledgment of a common nature. Slavery, the topic and the analogy she returns to in all her works, was the prime example of an evil which flourished by precedent and authority, the laws of property and trade, but which the enlightened heart of the age condemned. Many radicals in the republican tradition saw political progress as the key feature of the age and Price, Macaulay, Barbauld, Coleridge, and the Godwin circle welcomed the French Revolution with millenarian enthusiasm. Wollstonecraft, while not denying that it promised the greatest advance yet made on this globe, was more concerned with a broader concept of civilization, one which included the development of imagination and the feelings as well as intellectual and political improvement. Her work is not so much an extension of republican principles to domestic life as an effort to bring republican thought into line with the best aspects of domestic relations. Much as she reveres Catharine Macaulay, she finds her work deficient in "sagacity" and "fancy" and praises its "sympathy and benevolence" more than its argumentative closeness (VRW 5:175). Her own entry into political controversy emphasizes qualities of feeling rather than arguments of political theory.

In her *Vindication of the Rights of Men* Wollstonecraft maintains that "if the heart beat true to nature" vast estates would be divided into small farms, cottagers would be allowed to make enclosures from the commons and, instead of alms being given to the poor, they would be given the means to independence and self-advancement (VRM 5:56–7). Her condemnation of charity, like that of Godwin, sees it as sustaining an unequal society while giving the appearance of virtue to the rich. Wollstonecraft's emphasis on independence for the lower classes is moral as much as political. She praises the "civilizing relations of husband, father, and brother" just as Wordsworth was to elevate the domestic feelings characteristic of the independent farmers of the Lake District. For Wollstonecraft as well as Burke the political virtue of patriotism is an extension of domestic feelings, but interpreted very differently. Burke's version of domestic feelings is the product of history and association, cementing the bonds of a society of dependence by the family values of loyalty and heredity.[2] For him they act like instincts, having no need of reason. Wollstonecraft's version owes much to the egalitarian, experimental, but no less emotional relationships of progressive groups. Though it is from the heart that all that is great and good comes, it must be an educated heart. Wollstonecraft rejected the automatism of Burke's view of the passions. The gut-reactions he appealed to were not a mysterious wisdom of nature or of the body but habits of a superseded stage of society that could be analyzed and criticized: "Affection for parents, reverence for superiors or antiquity, notions of honour, or that worldly self-interest that shrewdly shews them that honesty is the best policy? all proceed from the reason for which they serve as substitutes; – but it is reason at second hand" (VRM 5:31).

Civilization was marked for Wollstonecraft by the "cultivation of the understanding, and refinement of the affections" (VRM 5:39). The passions may be involuntary but they can be subjected to analysis; in fact the strong reactions of passion are for her the stimulus of thought. There is no contradiction for her in holding the domestic affections sacred while applying to the relations of husband and wife or parents and children the Lockean doctrine of a contract with reciprocal duties. Family affections are civilizing because they impel reflection on the basis of the affections developed (or thwarted) in such relationships and so "refine" the affections. Her husband and wife must be equal and independent because true, refined affection can only subsist among equals. "Natural" (or should it be "refined"?) love of children makes no distinction among them but that of virtue (VRM 5:22) and does not favor sons above daughters or the first son above all. Burke's model of the family embodied the ideology – or "reason at second hand" – of the barbarous, aristocratic stage of society, and primogeniture, with its object of maintaining an illustrious name by passing an entire estate to the first son, was, she thought, mere "brutal" selfishness. Even the restriction of benevolence and patronage within the family circle was a defect, a lack of civilized refinement. Friendship ought to have the weight of relationship – and she defines friendship in terms of sympathy with virtue (VRM 5:24). Wollstonecraft may be distinguished from a republican line of moralists, including Hutcheson and Godwin, whose idea of benevolence is directed primarily towards the state and mankind in general, and who tend to denigrate the "partial" affections of family. Wollstonecraft's idea of family affections, however, makes the family the breeding ground of a republican or universal benevolence, a position shared by Coleridge and later by Godwin himself.

Natural feelings, natural rights

In the theory of Burke and Paine, the social contract is entered into for motives of fear, to protect oneself from the encroachment of others, and to add their strength to your own. For Wollstonecraft it is natural fellow-feeling, the imagination, and the social passions that initiate and sustain the social enterprise. In the age of the French Revolution, when human nature seemed to be born again, she looked to origins and Nature as well as to the progress of the Enlightenment for confirmation of the capacities of human nature. The myths of a golden age, of a state of nature, and an original contract of society were part of an eighteenth-century movement which often seems to see progress as recovering the past, a "natural" life that had taken a wrong turning. Dissenters like Priestley hoped to clear away the corruptions of Christianity; Major Cartwright and radical Whigs like Catharine Macaulay appealed to an original Anglo-Saxon constitution of liberty before the imposition of the "Norman Yoke." Coleridge investigated institutions to recover not their historical forms but an idea of their ultimate aim. Images of the past are often more or less consciously mythologized in obvious efforts to make them meet the urgent demands of the present. In the *Rights of Man* (Part One, 1791) Paine cites the Bible as his precedent for the equality of man, yet in his *Age of Reason* (1794) he can discard revelation and rely on the wondrous organization of nature for his belief in a God who talks the language of Newton and Locke. Burke extolled the pomp of monarchy and the grandeur of chivalry, outmoded fictions both, but in acknowledging that they were to a large extent the creation of his own rhetoric he insisted on the present need for such a moral "drapery" of the imagination. In response to the American and French Revolutions, events that were widely hailed as unprecedented, many, like Macaulay and Wollstonecraft, took their stand on inalienable natural rights, of which constitutional precedents such as Magna Carta or the Bill of Rights were only a compromised expression, rights granted rather than declared.

Price popularized the idea of natural rights when criticizing British policy towards America in his *Observations on the Nature of Civil Liberty*, published in the same year as Paine's *Common Sense* (1776). Applied to America, his theory was democratic in expression. He outlined a system of representative government and the term "civil liberty," liberty *under* the law, gave way in subsequent editions to "political liberty," the ability to make the laws that guaranteed freedom. In the established state of Britain his practical demands were usually limited to establishing the predominance of the "people" as represented in the House of Commons, eradicating corruption, and moderately extending representation. His sermon to the Revolution society in 1789 which roused Burke's ire asserted the right of the "people" to elect their governors and to "cashier" them for misconduct, rights that Price had maintained in most of his writings as the achievements of the Revolution of 1688. For him this showed an evolving understanding of the natural rights of man that should be extended to religious freedom and more equal representation. Price, though not as popular in his style as Paine, enunciated principles in a similarly pithy, often tabular, form that emphasized their simplicity, a mode also favored by Wollstonecraft. Complication, sophistication, and obfuscation in political and legal matters inhibited wide discussion and gave opportunites for corruption. Her own statements of principle, versions of the golden rule of doing as you would be done by, assertions of equality and of freedom limited only by prohibiting encroachment upon others' freedom, echoed the language of political pronouncements such as the American *Declaration of Independence* and the French *Declaration of the Rights of Men and of Citizens*. Though such principles were the product of historical experience and progressive political science – she traces them particularly to Locke – they appear the spontaneous products of "natural" morality or common sense. She regarded them as "eternal," requiring "only to be made known, to be generally acknowledged ... " (HMV 6:221).

Wollstonecraft could be accused of not confronting Burke on his own ground, the ground of political precedent and historical fact, but her attack on his emotional sincerity in *A Vindication of the Rights of Men* is a valid approach for one who values precedents only as they enlighten present responses. She finds his rhetoric cold and artificial, its professed basis in domestic feeling absurdly confined to primogeniture, and its aggressive masculinity outmoded bombast. Even her digs at his pension and motives for ingratiating himself with established power are legitimate in exposing the emotional malpractice he seemed to be perpetrating. In exhibiting her own emotional reactions with Rousseau-like openness, she is claiming a true contemporary sensibility, emotion confirmed by reflection, to contrast with Burke's hackneyed theatrical gestures and parade of prejudice. "Nature" and "natural" are words that she distrusts but cannot do without. They indicate the spontaneous reactions of a cultivated mind that is not afraid to re-examine its own possible prejudices and is prepared to root out those in others' thought.

Active citizens

For Price the affections and passions, although basically healthy and God-given, do not become morally admirable until transformed by the reason into a universal benevolence that strives to imitate that of God, and only such progress in virtue is a true preparation for the afterlife.[3] These rational passions seek to improve the world, not to justify its present state. Price's theory enabled Wollstonecraft to interpret Rousseau more positively. Rousseau's sensibility had seemed an isolating grandeur, all too easy to identify with in rejecting a society whose goals had become detached from real satisfactions. Much of her early work echoes Rousseau's sermons to himself to limit his desires to ends achievable within the given sphere of existence. When she gained the support of communities that embodied the mind and heart of a progressive culture Wollstonecraft recognized that Rousseau's sensibility had its heroic aspect as a rational passion urging him to progressive social ideals. In *A Vindication of the Rights of Woman* he becomes a "respectable visionary" whose passionate struggles with adversity prepare him better for the hereafter than for a comfortable life (VRW 5:143, 161). The sensibility with which he endowed his "noble savage" was improbable for that stage of human progress, but it embodied the basic feelings of sociability that underpinned human society, feelings that would be both developed by the progress of society and contribute to it.

Civilization in the individual and the collective is the result of strenuous effort. Self-development entails not merely absorbing doctrines but often painfully struggling toward new formulations. It is knowledge proved on the pulses and reacting with experience in order to work on society in activities such as Wollstonecraft's own journalistic activity and proposals for educational institutions. The emphasis on work, on earned distinctions rather than those of inherited wealth and rank, and the stress on duty and morality, links Wollstonecraft with the long middle-class cultural revolution against aristocratic values. The virtues of diligence, economic probity, foresight, and self-discipline, are not, however, ends in themselves. If her books for children encourage an "investment mentality" of self-denial, it is not directed toward the delayed gratification of accumulated wealth but toward amassing the means to personal independence and benevolence. Such virtues fit a man or woman to play a full part in the state, the wider sphere of benevolence. In her letter to Talleyrand prefacing *A Vindication of the Rights of Woman* she complains against the French exclusion of women from the ranks of "active citizens," empowered to take part in the political decisions of the nation. This complaint underlines the importance of political rights to Wollstonecraft since the new French constitution gave women far more independence in other ways, including the power to inherit an equal share of property, a provision to which even the republican Thomas Christie objected.[4] Wollstonecraft deviates from middle-class reformers not only in her feminism but also in her more general democratic sympathies.

A Vindication of the Rights of Men breathes fiery indignation at Burke's contempt for what he calls "the dregs of the people" (VRM 5:21) and adulation of the dissolute French queen. It defends the "respectable" market-women whom he reviled as monstrous when they marched on Versailles to demand bread. Attacking Burke's idea of property as the inherited wealth of the aristocracy, Wollstonecraft defends a Lockean notion of property as the product of personal labor and extends this idea to labor itself. The property of the rich is secure in England but not that of the mechanic, whose "property is in his nervous arms" (VRM 5:15). The press-gang is her key example of how the liberty and property of the poor are sacrificed to protect that of the rich. She comments on the idleness and vices of beggars and the urban poor but these moral failings are the result of their conditions, not their cause. They are the victims of the city's boasted commerce, thrown out of work by a "flux of trade or fashion," and also victims of false emulation as they copy the vices of the rich. A particularly concentrated passage yields a pregnant analysis of the relationship of the classes: "Envy built a wall of separation, that made the poor hate, whilst they bent to their superiors; who, on their part, stepped aside to avoid the loathsome sight of human misery." The mixed envy and hatred of *ressentiment* stifles the social passions of the poor, while the passions of the rich are not refined by the reflection that their wealth involves the poverty of others, turning them into loathsome creatures from which a fastidious taste revolts. They are rendered deaf to the appeal to fellow-feeling evoked by the allusion to the parable of the Good Samaritan. The remedy is a "more enlarged plan of society" in which man "did not seek to bury the sympathies of humanity in the servile appellation of master" (VRM 5:57–8). The poor, she asserts, "have a right to more comfort than they at present enjoy . . . " (VRM 5:55). With Price, she criticizes approaches to poverty like that of Burke, who held out hopes of heavenly compensation and preached Stoic resignation.

Heavenly justice promises a recompense, but only to those who improve their own natures. Both Price and Wollstonecraft expound a duty to ourselves that consists in training up virtue to perfection in this life of trial and adversity, and virtue demands benevolence directed towards the similar improvement of every individual. Beside breaking up large estates by abolishing primogeniture, Price wished to see property, happiness, and independence even more equally dispersed. He speculated that ideas of holding goods in common could be extended, but he favored schemes of self-help. His importance in the history of insurance stems from his efforts to introduce schemes whereby laborers might insure against old age and unemployment. A similar emphasis on self-help led Wollstonecraft to support the Evangelical Sarah Trimmer's involvement with the Charity School movement and the enterprises of the unitarian George Dyer in the 1790s, who proposed models of charitable institutions like miniature states run by simple, agreed, and well-publicized rules. Dyer and Wollstonecraft shared a dilemma in the 1790s, whether to emphasize the separate identity and interests of a group or to urge a communal response. Dyer stated bluntly that the poor were slaves, since they had no part in the social contract of society, yet he looked for a sharing of responsibility between rich and poor.[5] He described it as a kind of patronage, yet without the stigma attached to the term, just as Godwin and Coleridge urged similar ideas of stewardship of property. Wollstonecraft identified women as a group, and urged self-advancement, but she recognized the necessity for society as a whole to change. She criticized French society particularly for the barriers that it set up between classes. Paine's plans in the second part of his *Rights of Man* (1792) for redistributing wealth from the landed class in grants to the needy exacerbated the sense of a conflict of classes as aid was seen to be demanded, possibly to be extorted. Wollstonecraft's faith in the social passions could still, in the early 1790s, envisage social amelioration as a joint enterprise.

Progress

Wollstonecraft's vision of social progress owed much to the school of Scottish philosophical historians who chronicled social advancement through distinct cultural stages from savagery to the present "commercial" age, characterized by a weakening of the distinction of ranks, growing equality and sociability, and the cultivation of the arts and sciences. One of the later exponents of this view was John Millar who contributed to the *Analytical Review*. Though predominantly optimistic, his reservations about the blessings of progress and commercial society were similar to traditional republican fears that luxury, selfishness, and impatience of subordination would lead to its dissolution.[6] Burke too, seeing the English Constitution as the historical outcome of Providential wisdom, warned of the danger of "feminine" relaxation in the articles of subordination, property, and masculine military virtues. Wollstonecraft uses the idea of stages of growth, though she denies any "hidden hand" or historical determinism directing the process. While taking sociability and the cultivation of arts and sciences as the main motors of civilization, she is also aware of the possibilities of degeneration.

Her method of social criticism is very similar to that of Rousseau, and directed against aspects of "commercial society" that had engaged the ambivalence of historians such as Adam Ferguson and John Millar. Scattered throughout the two *Vindications* are jaundiced references to the commercial nature of present civilization, a civilization far from that she celebrated as the progressive unfolding of man's social and benevolent nature. In *A Vindication of the Rights of Men* they culminate in a Rousseauistic diatribe against "the polished vices of the rich, their insincerity, want of natural affections, with all the specious train that luxury introduces" (VRM 5:58). The "specious" social and sexual virtues upheld by this society are, again in Rousseauistic fashion, regarded as "substitutes" for the virtues themselves: regulations instead of principles, reputation in place of integrity, commercial treaties instead of friendship, legal prostitution instead of marriage.

Luxury, a term particularly rich in connotations of sexual and material-
istic indulgence, exploitation of labor and of colonial possessions, carries
for her also the intimations of nemesis. The great empires of the past fell because of such faults, and Wollstonecraft prophesies the fall of London and of
Paris.

When she undertakes to write on the French Revolution she has the ambition to contribute to the "history of man" in the same way as social historians, estimating the stage of civilization of the French and confronting
the questions which the violence of 1793 posed to her own idea of progress
(PCFN 6:444). Was the development of sociability and equality, the progress
of arts and sciences, really an aspect of "feminine" luxury, responsible for
the anarchy into which France had descended? In *A Historical and Moral
View of the French Revolution* (1794) she concedes that the "effeminacy"
of the French was responsible for anarchy, but maintains that this subverted
a Revolution that had been motivated by nobler motives. The influence
of the courtly, feudal system of society had vitiated the national character and temporarily overpowered emergent forces which would eventually
triumph. She uses the idea of stages of society to see old institutions as
necessary and in part beneficial stepping-stones to more advanced values.
Like Godwin and Coleridge, she views past constitutional battles of property and power between king, lords, and people as beneficial in establishing
a certain level of personal freedom, but, as the passion for empire dimin-
ishes, more refined feelings for justice, intellectual progress, and sociability
require new institutions. Similarly courtly society and the culture of politeness were a necessary stage in developing more comprehensive social
virtues.

The *Historical and Moral View* directly contradicts criticism of "the luxury
introduced with the arts and sciences; when it is obviously the cultivation of
these alone, emphatically termed the arts of peace, that can turn the sword
into a ploughshare" (HMV 6:23). In the gradual advance of civilization
in ancient and modern cultures the arts, including the arts of politeness
and sociability, are seen as deriving from courtly life. Under this "partial
civilization" a certain amount of civil liberty is possible but not political
liberty. True civilization, as in *A Vindication of the Rights of Men*, consists
of the widest diffusion of happiness and power among all citizens. Ancient
societies, like the Greek and Roman, and modern cultures, like those of
Florence and Holland, may have advanced in the arts, yet remained regressive
in their treatment of colonies and of those without the rights of citizenship:
they "trampled with a ferocious affectation of patriotism on the most sacred
rights of humanity." Her scheme of progress, however, "makes the perfection
of the arts the dawn of science ... " (HMV 6:15). In a similar stage of progress

the French court, frivolous, vain, and sensual as it was, cultivated a sociability that gave rise to intellectual curiosity and a patronage of ideas that were eventually to destroy it. The improvement of manners is "the harbinger of reason" (HMV 6:225). Paris, which had been the disseminator of courtly culture, gained a tone distinct from that of the court and spread the new ideas through enterprises such as the *Encyclopedia*. The capital itself, the creation of the courtly system and its luxury, became a "bulwark to oppose the despotism of the court," and the author of the revolution. Yet Paris also nurtured the Terror, and Wollstonecraft's attitude towards the metropolis is mixed: "the focus of information, the reservoir of genius, the school of arts, the seat of voluptuous gratification, and the hot-bed of vice and immorality" (HMV 6:223).

Just as Wollstonecraft's view of the capital is ambivalent as it displays aspects of old courtly corruption and new enlightenment so her view of commerce is divided. She can be quoted as the inveterate foe of commerce in its fraudulent, antisocial pursuit of profit and again as one of its great champions. Commerce was seen as the characteristic element of modern society and linked with the "*douce commerce*" of sociability. Wollstonecraft values commerce and industry for the same reasons as Adam Smith: they encourage independence and equality, broadening the basis of "polite" society. The command of a wage for his labor or a market for his goods emancipates man from slavish dependence on a feudal lord or the servile receipt of alms from the rich. The benevolent heroine of her novel *Mary* (1789) establishes "manufactories" as well as small farms, but they are not the industrial workhouses that Wollstonecraft condemned in the *Analytical Review* as the products of a "mistaken" theory of commerce (AR 7: 442). In the *Historical and Moral View* she voices the same criticism as Godwin of a system that turns men into unthinking, unprogressive automatons to make fortunes for individuals. From her early *Original Stories for Children*, where Mrs. Mason resists bargains and pays the right price for goods, to her insistence on fair mercantile profits in the *Historical and Moral View* (HMV 6:233) and her idea of a just proportion between profit and wages in the *Letters Written During a Short Residence* (SR 6:287), Wollstonecraft upholds a commerce regulated by ideas of justice and fairness and directed toward the ideals of independence and benevolence. This evolution too must come with an improvement of culture. In Scandinavia the smoke-filled rooms of profiteering merchants gave scant indication of sociability, and she felt that acquaintance with the arts and sciences would enlarge their minds to more benevolent prospects. Brissot, in his *Travels to America*, had similarly commented optimistically on the rage for commerce as a phase that the growth of civilization would moderate.[7] Price had warned the Americans of the dangers of commercialism, and Paine himself seemed to show an undiscriminating reliance on its power. For Paine, kings make war, republics make trade, and the most effectual way of improving the condition of man is by means of his interest.[8] Wollstonecraft's faith was that man would improve beyond the pursuit of narrow self-interest. In hoping that her lover, Gilbert Imlay, might be cured of his commercial greed by the refinement of cultured domestic life on an American farm, Wollstonecraft was applying the analogy of the progress of civilization to the growth of the individual that she uses throughout the *Historical and Moral View*.

Wollstonecraft used the "body politic" image to deal with corruption and luxury as sicknesses subject to cure. The work is full of medical terminology drawing analogies between the mental and physical state of France. Frustrated by artificial restrictions the imagination becomes a "wen" of "romantic," sensual fancies just as the capital is the seat of sensual, courtly corruption. Her optimistic viewpoint produces metaphors of antidotes and purgings, beside the more commonly used images of tempests, fermenting liquors or muddy water that will ultimately produce calm, clear progress. The work actually ends on an image of defecation.

French failings

Like many radical commentators Wollstonecraft blamed the excesses of the French Revolution on the corruptions of the old regime. She describes the brutalizing effect of feudal slavery and lessons of tyranny received by the lower classes, but her main focus is on the corruption of the aristocracy and, through them, of the national character. Most of the violence, she maintains, was due to the provocative intransigence of the nobility. The corruptions of the French are characteristic of their state of civilization, a polished, courtly society, in which morals have been sacrificed to manners. After her analysis of the influence of established inequalities on woman in *A Vindication of the Rights of Woman*, she could readily ascribe the notorious "effeminacy" of the French character to the same political causes. She reviews the components of the French public sphere with distaste. Their pleasure-gardens and grand galas minister to frivolity and the desire to cut a figure, while their theater is a place of declamation and rhetoric, a school of vanity. Accustomed to codes of politeness, the French, like women, think only of how to please and be pleased. In such a society the progressive ideas of modern philosophy become mere counters of fashionable intercourse, the weapons of self-glorifying wits and rhetoricians. The sincerity, the deeply pondered conviction necessary to make opinion a passion, is as foreign to their feminized natures as to Burke's. Imagination, nourished only by the senses, gives rise to sensual reveries or ambitions of personal glory, and even bursts of exalted sympathy are not sustained by the rational passion of humanity. Her account of the session of the Assembly in which the nobles and clergy renounced their privileges is of an orgy of competitive bids for the nation's praise. The same spirit, she maintains, led them to ignore the lessons of history and assert their unique leadership of the world. It is, she implies, a small step from the pre-Revolutionary situation in which each man considered himself the center of the world to the Terror when, having executed their king, every petty functionary considers himself a monarch.

Wollstonecraft shared the view of Helen Maria Williams that the French were advancing not too far but too fast.[9] They lacked the self-knowledge that might have brought success to more temperate reform. The abolition of the monarchy and of titles did not suit the state of public feeling, even though the progress of knowledge was tending toward such a goal. Their refusal of a second deliberative chamber spurned the wise American example of a senate and left the country open to the manipulation of the ruling faction of the day. Wollstonecraft, perhaps with the benefit of hindsight, is here departing from the more sanguine welcome given by Macaulay and Christie to the French experiment and from the simplicity of Paine's scheme.

The motives of the French Revolutionary legislature, their wish for popularity and prominence, their liablity to faction and demagoguery, leads to the deformation of the basis of the Revolution itself, the *Declaration of the Rights of Men and of Citizens*. She viewed this as a blueprint for a constitution that should have been promulgated with the same speed as the American. In its absence the rhetoric of the rights of man, always sure to gain popularity, gained precedence over the rights of security of person and property. The historical limits of her survey do not allow Wollstonecraft to use one of the most common explanations of the failure of Revolutionary ideals, the threat of invasion from hostile powers. She has to ascribe it to strictly internal moral and social causes. Wollstonecraft ends her volume by making the march on Versailles an example of the descent into factionalism and anarchy, a foretaste of the Terror to come. Instead of insisting on the respectability of the market-women, as in *A Vindication of the Rights of Men*, she emphasizes their monstrosity. Adopting a rumor current at the time, Wollstonecraft maintains that the market-women were corrupted by the vicious Duke of Orleans and made tools in his schemes. While seeming to capitulate to Burke's widely accepted version of this event as a demonstration of monstrous revolutionary violence, she is actually using it to isolate the insurgents from the "people." Her main criticism is that the Assembly did not investigate the violence effectively.

Surviving hopes

In absolving the people as a whole from the guilt of the Versailles marauders Wollstonecraft demonstrates her faith in the diffusion of knowledge and the ultimate progress of true civilization. Political causes have vitiated manners but politics will change when the French change their amusements and manners (HMV 6:213). The world of metropolitan society is far from representing French society as a whole and she often looks to the provinces for a civilization benefiting more solidly from the centrifugal rays of intellect radiating from the capital. Such a gradualistic hope sustained many reformers like Godwin and Helen Maria Williams and was in tune with the doctrine of stages of progress. Nevertheless, Wollstonecraft's sense of possibilities inherent in every point of history where "natural" relationships obtain and her refusal to see precedent as dictating the present often conflict with a linear model. She concedes that long ages might be necessary for the development of political and moral science and that it is "morally impossible" for the French people suddenly to throw off the influence of the old regime, but such a possibility is perpetually held out. The brutalized serf, enlightened by self-evident truths, experiences a "noble regeneration" of dignity and humanity (HMV 6:51). Even as she dismisses the superficial culture of the playhouse, pleasure-garden, and gala, she finds examples of the cultured domestic virtues making part of the public sphere in the capital. She praises couples living with the affection of the "civilest friends," attentive to the education of their children, and entertaining relations and acquaintances with cultural activities in the evening, perhaps a reference to the salons of Mme. Roland and Helen Maria Williams. Returning to their manors in the summer, they mingle with the peasants in their amusements and benevolences. In this "virtuous and useful life" French women are freer, and therefore less subject to unrealistic "romantic" obsessions than the more confined English (HMV 6:147–8). The public acts of the "people" and the National Guard are seen as exemplary in the early days of 1789. It is the court which shows the disunity and covert guile of faction as they oppose a movement of the nation itself. Yet the imposing spectacle of a nation united in improvement gives way to apparently congenital vice. The Palais Royale is described as a school of patriotism in the days of the Bastille, a spacious square where crowds flock to proclaim the sense of the nation (HMV 6:76), but within three months it has become a "den of iniquity … " (HMV 6:207).

The unlikely swiftness of this transformation questions both the prospect of speedy reform and the necessity of a tardy gradualism. Improvements in printing, the quick global communication of knowledge, the very fact of the Revolution itself, make reform a more immediate prospect to her in her

Scandinavian journeys. Though she proclaims her philosophical orthodoxy in considering particular national historical conditions when estimating stages of progress, anomalies still intrude. In Norway, a country subject to Denmark, she finds, instead of an enslaved province, the freest community in her experience. It seems to answer to her own criteria with its small farms, independent yeomen, mild laws, and local government responsive to democratic pressure: one district had "cashiered" a man who abused his power (SR 6:273). In Sweden the middle class, obsessed with etiquette and rank, are not in the improving, "natural" state she describes in *A Vindication of the Rights of Woman*; here it is the benevolence of the lower ranks that raises thoughts of a Golden Age.

Influence

Wollstonecraft played a part in making the independent agriculturalist a subject of ideological debate, a topic taken up particularly by Wordsworth and Cobbett. Her high valuation of economic independence was echoed in efforts to open more occupations to women later in the century but her concern for the independence and welfare of town workers as a whole and her criticism of large factories tended to be absorbed into a general Romantic antagonism to modern industrial systems which encouraged communitarian experiments, usually under the reforming banner of Robert Owen's efforts to ensure a fair proportion between profit and labor.

Wollstonecraft's influence on the political thought of Romantic writers is still being explored and this chapter has indicated some of the areas where it may be found. Her exceptional vitality of thought impressed all who knew her and Coleridge regarded her as a genius. Wordsworth might have followed her in looking for progress in recovering ways of thought and feeling deformed by modern, commercial society yet preserved in rural communities. Her development of republican and democratic principles in domestic and affective terms provided a powerful critique of Burke's use of domestic feelings to support the conservative model of community. In asserting the relative autonomy of the domestic sphere she indicated an alternative to totalitarian theories that subordinated all aspects of an age to its political or economic base. By maintaining the priority of lived social experience in transforming thought she influenced the Shelleyan attitude to political institutions as attempts, always outrun, to embody the spirit of progressive society. In seeing political institutions as responsive to the progressive civilization of social relationships she anticipated the "Cockney" culture of the later Romantics, whose "coterie" politics and utopian, pastoral art forms correspond to the

CHRIS JONES

domestic and imaginative values that Wollstonecraft hoped would reform the public sphere.[10]

NOTES

1. G. J. Barker-Benfield, 'Mary Wollstonecraft: Eighteenth-Century Common-wealthwoman', *Journal of the History of Ideas* 50 (1989), 95–115.
2. Edmund Burke, *Reflections on the Revolution in France*, ed. L. G. Mitchell (Oxford: Oxford University Press, 1993), 33–5.
3. Richard Price, *A Review of the Principal Questions in Morals*, ed. D. D. Raphael (Oxford: Clarendon Press, 1974), 74, 191, 260. See also *Sermons on the Christian Doctrine* (London: Cadell, 1787), 249.
4. Thomas Christie, *Letters on the Revolution in France* (London: Johnson, 1791), 268.
5. George Dyer, *The Complaints of the Poor People of England*, 2nd edn. (London: Johnson, 1793), 7, and *A Dissertation on the Theory and Practice of Benevolence* (London: Johnson, 1795), 31.
6. John Millar, *The Origin of the Distinction of Ranks*, 4th edn. (Edinburgh and London: John Murray, 1806), 101, 138.
7. J. P. Brissot de Warville, *New Travels to the United States of America Performed in 1788*, trans. Joel Barlow (London: J. S. Jordan, 1792), 110.
8. Thomas Paine, *The Rights of Man*, ed. H. Collins (Harmondsworth: Penguin, 1969), 234.
9. Helen Maria Williams, *Letters from France* (New York: Garland, 1975), First Series, 3:223.
10. Jeffrey Cox, *Poetry and Politics in the Cockney School* (Cambridge: Cambridge University Press, 1998), 11–12.

58

5

TOM FURNISS

Mary Wollstonecraft's French Revolution

When the fall of the Bastille on 14 July 1789 signaled to the world that some-thing extraordinary was taking place in France, Mary Wollstonecraft was already in a position, intellectually and socially, to respond with enthusiasm. From 1784 to 1785 she had lived in Newington Green, where she came under the influence of the Dissenting preacher Dr. Richard Price, then in his sixties, who was one of the leading radical intellectuals of the day. In 1787 she began working as a writer and translator for Joseph Johnson, a Dissenter and radical publisher whose home and bookshop at St. Paul's Churchyard was a focal point for London Dissenters and radicals. As a kind of surrogate daughter to Johnson, Wollstonecraft became part of one of the most forward-looking intellectual circles in Britain. Members of Johnson's circle hurried to Paris in the summer of 1789 and returned with enthusiastic accounts, hoping that a similar revolution might take place in Britain. The joy occasioned by the French Revolution's early phase bound this circle together, as Claire Tomalin puts it, "in the certainty that they knew the truth and that it was bound to prevail."[1]

The French Revolution was a drawn-out process rather than a single event. But the dramatic events of the Revolution's early phase provoked one of the most important political debates in British history. The "Revolution Controversy" of 1789–95 was as much about the implications of the Revolution for Britain as it was about the Revolution itself. This argument was sparked off by a sermon Richard Price delivered on 4 November 1789, which was published shortly afterwards, along with a letter of congratula-tion to the National Assembly in Paris, as *A Discourse on the Love of Our Country* (1789). Despite England's revolution in 1688–9, Price argued, lib-erty in Britain was neither secure nor complete (especially for those who, like Price himself, were Dissenters from the Church of England). In his con-clusion, Price enthusiastically hailed the French Revolution and implied that Britain ought to follow its example and thereby complete the political process that had begun in England's so-called "Glorious Revolution."[2]

Edmund Burke, a Whig politician and political theorist, was relatively untroubled by the French Revolution until he read Price's suggestion that it be imitated in Britain. He responded with a ferocious attack on Price and on the Revolution in his *Reflections on the Revolution in France* (published on 1 November 1790) – a text that has provoked readers ever since. Focusing on an event that took place on 5–6 October 1789 in which a crowd of Parisians marched to Versailles and forced the king and queen of France to return to Paris,[3] Burke represents the Revolution as the action of a mob bent on destroying all the social and cultural values of France that had been the model for the whole of Europe. This was the inevitable outcome of a concerted campaign by radical French philosophers to undermine traditional respect for the monarchy, aristocracy, and church. The result, he predicts, will be tyranny and the destruction of France. This was not a prospect to be celebrated, nor an example to be imitated. On the contrary, French revolutionary principles ought to be treated like a disease fatal to the ancient principles of the British constitution. Burke's attack on Price's sermon and character was thus an attempt to repress the symptoms of revolutionary enthusiasm at work in Britain.

Burke's *Reflections* stimulated a flurry of responses.[4] The first of these was Wollstonecraft's *A Vindication of the Rights of Men, in a Letter to the Right Honourable Edmund Burke; Occasioned by his Reflections on the Revolution in France* (Johnson, 1790). The first edition was published anonymously on 29 November 1790, barely a month after Burke's *Reflections* had appeared; a second, published on 18 December with her name on the title page, made Wollstonecraft instantly famous. As the full title indicates, Wollstonecraft's *Vindication* is principally interested in replying to Burke, its aim being "to shew you to yourself, stripped of the gorgeous drapery in which you have enwrapped your tyrannic principles" (VRM 5:37).[5] The text itself reveals that, at this stage, Wollstonecraft knew more about Burke's writings and political conduct than about the French Revolution.

Wollstonecraft begins by associating herself with a tradition of radical British writing, echoing John Locke's *Second Treatise of Government* (1690): "The birthright of man, to give you, Sir, a short definition of this disputed right, is such a degree of liberty, civil and religious, as is compatible with the liberty of every other individual with whom he is united in a social compact, and the continued existence of that compact" (VRM 5:9).[6] Whereas Burke argued that the people of Britain already enjoy liberty as a kind of property inherited from their ancestors, Wollstonecraft refers to a different kind of birthright – those "rights which men inherit at their birth, as rational creatures" (VRM 5:14). But no government on earth has yet instituted such rights: "Liberty, in this simple, unsophisticated sense, I acknowledge, is a fair idea that has never yet received a form in the various governments that have been established on our beauteous globe" (VRM 5:9). People have been denied their birthright because existing legal systems protect the property of the few rather than promote justice for all. Wollstonecraft thus reads Burke's celebration of English liberty as a defence of the property rights of the privileged minority: "Security of property! Behold, in a few words, the definition of English liberty" (VRM 5:14–15).

Burke's belief in the antiquity of the British constitution and the impossibility of improving upon a system that has been tried and tested through time is dismissed as nonsense. The past, for Wollstonecraft, is a scene of superstition, oppression, and ignorance. While Burke's politics are backward looking, Wollstonecraft's are orientated towards the future, looking forward to the possibility that the French Revolution might establish the rights of men for the first time in history by putting radical theory into practice. Like Price, Wollstonecraft assumes that the imperfections of the system of political representation in Britain are a major defect of the British constitution. She thus looks with interest to the alternative system being introduced in France which, in theory, "appears more promising" (VRM 5:59). Rejecting Burke's contemptuous dismissal of the National Assembly because it included in its ranks men from the middle and lower orders, she proposes that "Time may shew, that this obscure throng knew more of the human heart and of legislation than the profligates of rank, emasculated by hereditary effeminacy" (VRM 5:40). For Wollstonecraft, in short, the Revolution is a "glorious *chance*" to obtain "more virtue and happiness than has hitherto blessed our globe" (VRM 5:48).

Wollstonecraft's *Vindication* is particularly attentive to the way that Burke manipulates conventional ideas of gender and class in the *Reflections*. Burke presents the events of 5–6 October 1789, for example, as revealing a stark contrast between the refined beauty of the *ancien régime*, embodied by Marie Antoinette, and the uncivilized barbarity of the revolutionary mob, exemplified by the way the royal family was escorted from Versailles back to Paris "amidst the horrid yells, and shrilling screams, and frantic dances, and infamous contumelies, and all the unutterable abominations of the furies of hell, in the abused shape of the vilest of women" (*Reflections*, 165). Wollstonecraft deflates Burke's display of outraged sensibility with a precise socioeconomic description of the kind of women who participated in the Versailles march: "Probably you mean women who gained a livelihood by selling vegetables or fish, who never had had any advantages of education" (VRM 5:30). Civilized life in the monarchies of Europe consists of a mutually destructive conflict between the rich, corrupted by vice and luxury, and the poor, broken and brutalized by tyranny and poverty, and the outrages at Versailles or the

confiscation of the revenues of the Catholic Church are small prices to pay
for the opportunity to establish a more equitable society: "What were the
outrages of a day to these continual miseries?... Man preys on man; and
you mourn for the idle tapestry that decorated a gothic pile, and the dro-
nish bell that summoned the fat priest to prayer" (VRM 5:58). Countering
Burke's lament that the treatment of Marie Antoinette at Versailles shows
that "the age of chivalry" is dead (Reflections, 170), Wollstonecraft ridicules
Burke as a "romantic" writer (in the sense associated with the "romances" of
the Middle Ages in which the "age of chivalry" had been celebrated and/or
invented, and which involved notions of courtly love and female delicacy
that Wollstonecraft found damaging to women and men alike). By contrast,
Wollstonecraft celebrates reason, virtue, and consistency of sound principles.
This does not mean that she outlaws feeling. Attempting instead to distinguish between genuine feelings appropriate to the objects or events that cause
them and false feelings incommensurate with their objects, she holds that to
be touched with sympathy for the Revolution is a sign of humanity, while to
lament, as Burke does, for the fate of the French clergy is a sign of false sensibility: "The declaration of the National Assembly, when they recognized
the rights of men, was calculated to touch the humane heart – the downfall
of the clergy, to agitate the pupil of impulse" (VRM 5:53).

In 1790, then, Wollstonecraft was a fully paid-up enthusiast for the
Revolution. In December of that year she published a positive review in
Johnson's Analytical Review of Helen Maria Williams's Letters Written in
France, in the Summer, 1790, to a Friend in England; containing various
Anecdotes relative to the French Revolution (1790). As this and other re-
views suggest, Wollstonecraft used her work as a reviewer as a means of
filling in her education about the French Revolution and its prehistory.[7]

In September 1791 Wollstonecraft began working on what was to become
her most influential book, A Vindication of the Rights of Woman (1792).
The philosophical idealism of the early phase of the French Revolution had
culminated in the National Assembly's Declaration of the Rights of Man and
Citizen in August 1789. Despite its groundbreaking nature, the Declaration
grants the political rights of citizenship only to men. Yet revolutionary enthusiasm on both sides of the English Channel led some radicals to ask why
women should not have the same rights. In France, the idea of women's rights
was championed by the Marquis de Condorcet, in his Sur l'Admission des
femmes au droit de Cité (1790), and by Olympe de Gouges in her Déclaration
des droits de la femme et de la citoyenne (1791). But although the Girondins
in the National Assembly were sympathetic to women's rights, the new constitution of 1791 "excluded women from all areas of political life, conferring
citizenship only on men over 25" (VRW 5:66, note). This exclusion appeared

as if it were being consolidated by the Assembly's plans for national education. Charles Maurice de Talleyrand-Périgord's *Rapport sur l'instruction publique, fait au nom du Comité de constitution* (1791) recommended that the Constituent Assembly introduce free national education for all the children of France of both sexes. Though this was a revolutionary proposal in its own right,[8] it fell "short of Wollstonecraft's ideal in its concurrence with Rousseau's *Emile, ou de l'Education* (1762) that the education of women should be directed towards a subservient role."[9]

Wollstonecraft dedicated *A Vindication of the Rights of Woman* to Talleyrand, seeking to influence him to institute a system of education in France in which both sexes would be educated equally to become full citizens. Between the two editions of *Rights of Woman* in 1792 Talleyrand, visiting London to win support for the new order in France, called on Wollstonecraft. There is no record of their meeting, but the revision Wollstonecraft made to the opening paragraph of the dedication in the second edition indicates that she did not change his mind: "Sir . . . I dedicate this volume to you; to induce you to reconsider the subject, and maturely weigh what I have advanced respecting the rights of woman and national education" (VRW 5:65). She goes on to argue that the "glorious principles" that inspired the French Revolution necessarily included the rights of women (5:65–6), reminding Talleyrand that he had almost conceded this:

> Consider, Sir, dispassionately, these observations – for a glimpse of this truth seemed to open before you when you observed, "that to see one half of the human race excluded by the other from all participation of government, was a political phaenomenon that, according to abstract principles, it was impossible to explain." (67)

Yet Talleyrand went on to withdraw what he had seemed to concede: "If the debarring of women from public positions is a means for the two sexes of increasing their mutual wellbeing, it follows that it is a law which all societies should recognise and sanction."[10] It is this assumption, derived from Rousseau, which Wollstonecraft takes on in *Rights of Woman*. Thus if *Rights of Woman* is not actually *about* the French Revolution it can be seen as an attempt to steer it in a more radical feminist direction.

Wollstonecraft's Second *Vindication* became a best-seller and its author one of the most famous, and infamous, women in Europe. But *Rights of Woman* did not have the effect in France (or in Britain) she hoped for. As we will see, the rise of the Jacobins put an end to feminist debate. And while the revolution Wollstonecraft envisages in *Rights of Woman* was far more radical than that achieved in either the American or the French revolutions, she imagines that it would arise peacefully out of universal education and what she twice calls a "revolution in female manners" (pp.114, 265). Her assumption, then, was that patriarchal oppression would melt away when children of all classes and both sexes were educated together. This ignored what was perhaps the most difficult lesson that the French Revolution offered for progressives like Wollstonecraft – that the oppressive regimes of Europe would not peacefully abandon their power and had to be overthrown through violent struggle.

In the summer of 1792 Wollstonecraft and Johnson, along with the artist Henry Fuseli and his wife, planned an excursion to Paris. Wollstonecraft anticipated that the French translation of the *Rights of Woman* – as *Défense des droits des femmes* (1792) – would give her access to some of the leading spirits of the Revolution.[11] The trip was canceled because of the news that "Paris was in confusion and probably dangerous" (Tomalin, *Life and Death*, 151). In early September "the people" of Paris butchered about fourteen hundred prisoners – priests, political prisoners, common criminals, beggars, convicts, prostitutes, royalists, ex-courtiers – on the pretext that they were "enemies to the Revolution."[12] The September Massacres made it seem as if Burke had been right about the Revolution, and many English enthusiasts began to have doubts. Others, however, attempted to rationalize the massacres as a necessary purge or as the inevitable result of repression under the *ancien régime*. Wollstonecraft remained optimistic and decided to visit Paris alone. In a letter of 12 November 1792 she informs William Roscoe that she has "determined to set out for Paris" and urges him not "to mix with the shallow herd who throw an odium on immutable principles, because some of the mere instrument of the revolution were too sharp. – Children of any growth will do mischief when they meddle with edged tools" (Letters, 218).

Though Britain and France were on the brink of war, Wollstonecraft left for Paris on the 8 December 1792, intending to stay for about six weeks to write an account of the Revolution for English readers. The Paris she discovered was different from what she may have expected. The open hearted euphoria reported by Williams had disappeared in the aftermath of the Massacres. Spending Christmas alone in the town house of a French family, Wollstonecraft wrote a letter to Johnson on 26 December full of mixed and disturbed impressions raised by a glimpse of Louis XVI being escorted through the streets to be tried for treason:

> About nine o'clock this morning, the king passed by my window, moving silently along (excepting now and then a few strokes on the drum, which rendered the stillness more awful) through empty streets, surrounded by the national guards, who, clustering round the carriage, seemed to deserve their name. The inhabitants flocked to their windows, but the casements were all

shut, not a voice was heard, nor did I see any thing like an insulting gesture. – For the first time since I entered France, I bowed to the majesty of the people, and respected the propriety of behaviour so perfectly in unison with my own feelings. I can scarcely tell you why, but an association of ideas made the tears flow insensibly from my eyes, when I saw Louis sitting, with more dignity than I expected from his character, in a hackney coach going to meet death, where so many of his race have triumphed. My fancy instantly brought Louis XIV before me, entering the capital with all his pomp, after one of the victories most flattering to his pride, only to see the sunshine of prosperity overshadowed by the sublime gloom of misery. I have been alone ever since; and, though my mind is calm, I cannot dismiss the lively images that have filled my imagination all the day. – Nay, do not smile, but pity me; for, once or twice, lifting my eyes from the paper, I have seen eyes glare through a glass-door opposite my chair, and bloody hands shook at me. Not the distant sound of a footstep can I hear. My apartments are remote from those of the servants, the only persons who sleep with me in an immense hotel, one folding door opening after another. – I wish I had even kept the cat with me! – I want to see something alive; death in so many frightful shapes has taken hold of my fancy. – I am going to bed – and, for the first time in my life, I cannot put out the candle.   (Letters, 227)

Overcoming the gothic horror of this early experience, Wollstonecraft's contacts with Williams, Paine, Thomas Christie, and Madame Roland enabled her to meet and become friends with a number of the Girondin leaders. British radicals found the Girondins more congenial than the Jacobins: they were mostly middle-class lawyers and writers, "believers in religious toleration, sympathetic towards women's advancement, deeply concerned with social questions" (Tomalin, *Life and Death*, 172). Their philosophical heritage – Voltaire, d'Alembert, Rousseau – had imbued them with an admiration for English political institutions; indeed, they were sometimes referred to as the "English" party. Moving in such circles gave Wollstonecraft direct access to the current of ideas released by the Revolution. Tomalin suggests that during the Revolution's early phase (from 1789 to early 1793) Paris was the scene of a short-lived sexual and social revolution. Unmarried mothers, as Tomalin explains, "were to be assisted and not shamed, and divorce [was to be] easily and sensibly arranged" (168). Women such as Olympe de Gouges were given the opportunity to address the National Assembly. Diderot's *Supplément au voyage de Bougainville*, which attacked traditional Christian attitudes to sexual behavior, was circulated in manuscript. In the community of expatriate radicals, Wollstonecraft was surrounded by couples whose relationships broke with traditional mores. Wollstonecraft's own attitudes towards sexuality underwent a revolution as she witnessed the political revolution around her. She would shortly live out the theory.

Louis XVI was found guilty of treason and sentenced to death. This shocked the expatriate radicals in Paris, some of whom had attempted to persuade the French to vote for mercy. The king's execution on 21 January 1793 cast a gloom over the expatriates. On 1 February 1793 war was declared between Britain and France, adding to the sense of pessimism and danger. Correspondence between the two nations was cut off and many of Wollstonecraft's letters home during this period were not posted. As Robespierre and the Jacobins gained control the Revolution began to deviate from the liberal dreams of the Girondins and the British radicals. By the end of February, as Tomalin puts it, Wollstonecraft "was to see not only shops plundered but the presses of unpopular journalists destroyed: it was scarcely the freedom she or Godwin had in mind when they praised the Revolution" (Tomalin, *Life and Death*, 182).

During these unstable times, Wollstonecraft began what she intended to be a series of letters, in the manner of Helen Maria Williams, "on the present character of the French nation" (15 February 1793).[13] It seems as if the reality of the Revolution has already displaced her radical dreams:

> I would I could first inform you that, out of the chaos of vices and follies, prejudices and virtues, rudely jumbled together, I saw the fair form of Liberty slowly rising, and Virtue expanding her wings to shelter all her children! I should then hear the account of the barbarities that have rent the bosom of France patiently, and bless the firm hand that lopt off the rotten limbs. But, if the aristocracy of birth is levelled with the ground, only to make room for that of riches, I am afraid that the morals of the people will not be much improved by the change, or the government rendered less venal.   (PCFN 6:444)

These melancholy reflections on the French Revolution challenge Wollstonecraft's earlier optimism: "I cannot yet give up the hope, that a fairer day is dawning on Europe, though I must hesitatingly observe, that little is to be expected from the narrow principle of commerce which seems every where to be shoving aside *the point of honour* of the *noblesse*" (445). As things stand, the taints of the *ancien régime* seem to have been carried over into the new order:

> For the same pride of office, the same desire of power are still visible; with this aggravation, that, fearing to return to obscurity after having but just acquired a relish for distinction, each hero, or philosopher, for all are dubbed with these new titles, endeavours to make hay while the sun shines.   (PCFN 6:446)

Life in Paris under siege became difficult. Moves towards totalitarian terror included the establishment in March 1793 of the Revolutionary Tribunal, the Committee of Surveillance, and the Committee of Public Safety. Foreigners were put under surveillance and had to produce six witnesses in support of their respectability before they could be issued with a certificate of residence. Wollstonecraft considered leaving for Switzerland but could not obtain the appropriate passport. Then, "[o]n 12 April all foreigners were prohibited formally from leaving the country. The expatriates who remained, trapped in this uncomfortable situation, drew together anxiously" (Tomalin, *Life and Death*, 184). Under these circumstances, Wollstonecraft met and began a sexual relationship with Gilbert Imlay, an American businessman and writer, disdaining the necessity for the traditional institution of marriage. Wollstonecraft moved to a house in Neuilly, then a tiny country village northwest of Paris, where Imlay's visits allowed them to enjoy a kind of honeymoon (they never married). Wollstonecraft began work on a "a great book", as she described it to her sister, which was to become *An Historical and Moral View of the French Revolution* (Letters, 231). Meanwhile, life in Jacobin Paris had become nightmarish: festive revolutionary parades in the daytime were followed by nights of police raids in search of the republic's "enemies," including the English. Robespierre joined the Committee of Public Safety in July and the Terror got under way.[14] Marie Antoinette and the leaders of the Girondins were executed in October, followed by Madame Roland and others in November. In the same month, all the English still in Paris were arrested, including Helen Maria Williams.

When Wollstonecraft realized she was pregnant she moved back to Paris, Imlay having registered her at the American embassy as his wife, to give her the protection of US citizenship. With the Terror going on around her, and amidst "a round of prison visits and all too frequent news of the execution of her friends," Wollstonecraft continued working on *An Historical and Moral View* (Tomalin, *Life and Death*, 210). Wollstonecraft then followed Imlay to Le Havre, where she finished her book and gave birth to her baby. In a letter written in March 1794 to her sister Everina (which was not posted), Wollstonecraft reflects upon her situation:

> It is impossible for you to have any idea of the impression the sad scenes I have been a witness to have left on my mind. . . . death and misery, in every shape of terrour, haunts this devoted country – I certainly am glad that I came to France, because I never could have had else a just opinion of the most extraordinary event that has ever been recorded. (Letters, 250–1)

The Terror ended in July 1794 with the fall and execution of Robespierre. Imlay returned to Paris in August and, clearly tiring of his companion, proceeded to London on business. Wollstonecraft returned to Paris, predicting in a letter to Imlay that the restoration of the freedom of the press "will overthrow the Jacobins" (Letters, 264). But that winter was the coldest of the century. Most of Wollstonecraft's energy between September 1794 and the Spring of 1795, after she had delivered the manuscript of *An Historical and Moral View* to Johnson, was taken up with sheer survival, caring for her child and grappling with her feelings of abandonment (see Letters, 262–81). In a letter to Imlay written from Paris on 19 February 1795 Wollstonecraft resists the idea of returning to England: "Why is it so necessary that I should return? – brought up here, my girl would be freer" (Letters, 280). Despite the horrors of the Revolution, Wollstonecraft seems to have felt more optimistic about post-Terror France than about a British state at war against France and against British radicals (as witnessed by the Treason Trials of the Autumn of 1794, in which Thomas Hardy, John Thelwall and John Horne Tooke were tried for high treason; although they were acquitted, this did not stop the British government's "reign of terror" against radicalism). Wollstonecraft's letter reads like a farewell to Imlay, but Imlay's emotional power over her is revealed by the fact that her next letter to him is written from Le Havre on 7 April en route to England. Thus ended Wollstonecraft's direct experience of the French Revolution.

An Historical and Moral View of the Origin and Progress of the French Revolution; and the Effect it has Produced in Europe (1794) was presented as "Volume the First," but no further volumes appeared and only one edition was produced in Wollstonecraft's lifetime. As far as I am aware, there was not a second edition until the Pickering edition of *The Works of Mary Wollstonecraft* in 1989.[15] Perhaps the main reason for this neglect is that the revival of interest in Wollstonecraft has been primarily in her feminist writings.[16] What's more, if a reader wished to find out what happened in the French Revolution, modern histories would be more helpful.[17] Narrative was not her strong point, and her history is loaded with day-to-day detail and moral reflections. Yet there is a case for suggesting that *An Historical and Moral View* was Wollstonecraft's best work. It was important in 1794 to present an accurate history of the Revolution to counteract the increasing counter-revolutionary repression and hysteria in Britain. Wollstonecraft did this through drawing on journals, records, and documents then available in Paris and London. Equally important, *An Historical and Moral View* records Wollstonecraft's own struggle to hold on to radical principles despite the Terror. While many radicals abandoned the faith, Wollstonecraft minutely analyzed the Revolution in order to discover how it went wrong and what lessons could be learned from it. In doing this, she was a pioneer for the many radicals faced with similar crises. Like Wordsworth after her, Wollstonecraft abandoned the idea that social progress could be brought about through changing the political system. But unlike him and others, Wollstonecraft retained – but only just, and only at times – her belief that a just society would emerge from the Revolution in which the rights of men, and of women, would be the origin and end of government. In so arguing, Wollstonecraft offers one of the most profound discussions of revolutionary politics to emerge out of the Revolution Controversy.

In her Preface, Wollstonecraft foregrounds how the Revolution poses a problem of interpretation. An adequate understanding of the Revolution "requires a mind, not only unsophisticated by old prejudices, and the inveterate habits of degeneracy; but an amelioration of temper, produced by the exercise of the most enlarged principles of humanity." In addition, given the vicissitudes of the Revolution, "it becomes necessary to guard against the erroneous inferences of sensibility" because "reason beaming on the grand theatre of political changes, can prove the only sure guide to direct us to a favourable or just conclusion." The Revolution is represented as a dramatic spectacle containing so many terrible scenes that it requires a special kind of mind to interpret it correctly. It is crucial to reach a just conclusion about the Revolution because it involves the most important question about humanity – whether human nature and society are irrevocably fallen and corrupt or have the potential to become as elevated as the dreams of "the most enlightened statesmen and philosophers" (HMV 6:6). Wollstonecraft is clear about her own position, stressing that the notion of "original sin" is a superstitious fabrication upon "which priests have erected their tremendous structures of imposition, to persuade us, that we are naturally inclined to evil" (HMV 6:21-2). The fact that the civilizations of the past have repeatedly fallen back into barbarism does not mean that this is inevitable, but rather that rule by hereditary riches and rank is intrinsically unstable.

The task Wollstonecraft sets herself in *An Historical and Moral View* is to trace the origin and progress of the French Revolution in order to find causes for optimism and signs of progress amongst the folly and carnage. One way she does this is to differentiate the theoretical principles that originally animated the Revolution from the disastrous way they were put into practice. She also attempts to convince herself and her readers that, from a long-term perspective, the Revolution can be seen as merely one episode, apparently chaotic but actually progressive, within a larger history of humanity's gradual but inexorable development towards reason and liberty.[18] Yet the main text of *An Historical and Moral View* follows the Revolution's historical progress so minutely that it only reaches the end of 1789, never fully confronting the most violent phases of the Revolution. Only by restricting herself to 1789 can Wollstonecraft produce an analysis that supports her progressive optimism.

To convince her readers that the Revolution is indeed ushering in "the approaching reign of reason and peace" (HMV 6:17) Wollstonecraft needs to account for why the Revolution went wrong, salvage its principles from the wreckage, and somehow show that it is a necessary moment in the evolution of human freedom. Strikingly, Wollstonecraft hardly even hints that the Revolution may have gone astray because of its failure to set up a proper system of education for women or because it has not enabled women to take up full civil rights. The argument of *The Rights of Woman* makes no appearance here. Instead, *An Historical and Moral View* argues that the origin of most of the Revolution's ills can be traced to the degeneracy of the French national character. Given that Wollstonecraft rejects the possibility that human nature is intrinsically degenerate, she suggests that "the frivolity of the french character" has arisen from the particular conditions prevailing in France, and especially from their habits, education, and manner of living (HMV 6:230). But the primary corrupting influence derives from the political and cultural system of the *ancien régime*. The central paradox of the Revolution, in fact, is that while the Revolution was made necessary by the degeneration of the national character under the *ancien régime*, the degenerate nature of the national character made it unlikely that the French would be able successfully to carry out a Revolution.

For Wollstonecraft, the feudal system of the *ancien régime* meant that the majority of the people were little better than the slaves of the aristocracy. This material slavery was reinforced by the spiritual and intellectual slavery produced by the superstitions of Roman Catholicism. The aristocracy in turn was reduced to moral slavery by the corrupt absolutism of the royal court at Versailles. Influenced by Rousseau's critique of modern European civilization, Wollstonecraft argues that the common feature of all aspects of life under the *ancien régime* was an all-pervasive theatricality that eroded common sense and sound principles:[19]

> Their national character is, perhaps, more formed by their theatrical amusements, than is generally imagined: they are in reality the schools of vanity. And, after this kind of education, is it surprising, that almost every thing is said and done for stage effect? or that cold declamatory extasies blaze forth, only to mock the expectation with a show of warmth? (HMV 6:25)

The *ancien régime* was theatrical through and through. Under Louis XIV, even wars "were . . . theatrical exhibitions" (HMV 6:26). The theatricality of Versailles had a corrupting influence on Marie Antoinette: "A court is the best school in the world for actors; it was very natural then for her to become a complete actress, and an adept in all the arts of coquetry that debauch the mind, whilst they render the person alluring" (HMV 6:74). Brought up at Versailles, the king's character exhibited weakness and a "criminal insincerity" (HMV 6:171) fatal for him and for the Revolution (HMV 6:74). The general theatricality of the old order in France contaminated the whole nation. Animated by appearance rather than substance, by feelings rather than reason, by ceremony and dress rather than strength of character, the French have no character in the moral sense of the word: "Thus a frenchman, like most women, may be said to have no character distinguishable from that of the nation" (HMV 6:230).

It was a commonplace in eighteenth-century Britain to claim that the old order of France exhibited a fatal combination of political tyranny and luxury. But Wollstonecraft uses this analysis to explain both why the Revolution was necessary and inevitable, and why it went wrong. Yet this analysis does not explain how the French were able to overthrow the old order and attempt to build a new political system based on the ideals of the rights of man. Wollstonecraft accounts for this in part by suggesting that the ordinary people of France somehow escaped the corruption that tainted the higher orders. While admitting that "[s]everal acts of ferocious folly have justly brought much obloquy on the grand revolution, which has taken place in France," she yet claims that she feels "confident of being able to prove, that the people are essentially good" (HMV 6:46).

The advance of reason allowed the common people of France to understand their own dignity and the most advanced political principles. Having been slaves for centuries, the people began to ask "the most important of all questions – namely, in whose hands ought the sovereignty to rest?" The realization that political sovereignty ought to derive from the people led to "the universal demand of a fair representation, to meet at stated periods, without depending on the caprice of the executive power" (HMV 6:39). Thus the most important human agency of the Revolution was the people – by which, at times, she means the "twenty-five millions of centinels" that comprised the whole population (HMV 6:39). With the states-general in session, "the whole nation called [with one voice] for a constitution, to establish equal rights, as the foundation of freedom" (HMV 6:53). Thus the Revolution can be seen as the collective action of a whole nation awakening to political consciousness as the largest electorate in history (HMV 6:68).

The virtue of the French nation was most impressively demonstrated in the destruction of the Bastille on 14 July 1789 and in the defense of Paris against the king's forces.[20] In these events, political theory became a living reality:

> there was, in fact, an inconceivable solemnity in the quick step of a torrent of men, all directing their exertions to one point, which distinguished this rising of the citizens from what is commonly termed a riot. – Equality, indeed, was then first established by an universal sympathy; and men of all ranks joining in the throng. (HMV 6:88)

The way the whole population prepared for the attack of the armed forces assembled outside Paris exhibited a new consciousness in a nation rising to its own defense:

> Thus was the nation saved by the almost incredible exertion of an indignant people; who felt, for the first time, that they were sovereign, and that their power was commensurate to their will. This was certainly a splendid example, to prove, that nothing can resist a people determined to live free; and then it appeared clear, that the freedom of France did not depend on a few men, whatever might be their virtues or abilities, but alone on the will of the nation.
> (HMV 6:100)

These were the glorious days of the Revolution, unproblematic for most radicals. Wollstonecraft's challenge is to wring optimism out of subsequent events in which the people could no longer be figured as a virtuous nation shaking off its chains. The second chapter of Book v is devoted to the events of 5–6 October 1789, beginning with the entertainment at Versailles of the king's bodyguards, rumors about which aroused fears in Paris that the old order was about to begin a new attack on Paris and the Revolution. Such rumors, and the lack of bread, set the people of Paris in motion:

> The concourse, at first, consisted mostly of market women, and the lowest refuse of the streets, women who had thrown off the virtues of one sex without having power to assume more than the vices of the other. A number of men also followed them, armed with pikes, bludgeons, and hatchets; but they were strictly speaking a mob, affixing all the odium to the appellation it can possibly import; and not to be confounded with the honest multitude, who took the Bastille. – In fact, such a rabble has seldom been gathered together; and they quickly showed, that their movement was not the effect of public spirit.
> (HMV 6:196–7)

These events prompted Burke to condemn the whole Revolution as the barbarous work of "a band of cruel ruffians and assassins" (*Reflections*, 164). In *Rights of Men* Wollstonecraft retorted that Burke's "furies from hell" were ordinary fishwives. Here, however, she accepts Burke's account of the event while nonetheless trying to maintain that it was perpetrated by "a set of monsters, distinct from the people" (HMV 6:206). But the worst aspect of this episode was the response of the National Assembly, which failed to reassert its authority by properly investigating it and punishing the offenders:

> At this moment the assembly ought to have known, that the future respectability of their laws must greatly depend on the conduct they pursued on the present occasion; and it was time to show the parisians, that, giving freedom to the nation, they meant to guard it by a strict adherence to the laws, that naturally issue from the simple principles of equal justice they were adopting; punishing

with just severity all such as should offer to violate, or treat them with contempt.... Yet, so contrary was their conduct to the dictates of common sense, and the common firmness of rectitude of intention, that they not only permitted that gang of assassins to regain their dens; but instantly submitted to the demand of the soldiery, and the peremptory wish of the parisians – that the king should reside within the walls of Paris. (HMV 6:209)

By giving in to the Parisians' demands, the members of the Assembly "surrendered their power to the multitude of Paris." This enabled the Jacobins, with their base in the popular clubs, to take over the Revolution: "It is in reality from this epocha ... that the commencement of the reign of anarchy may be fairly dated" (HMV 6:212).

Wollstonecraft attempts to cope with the fact that the "dawn" of July quickly merged into the dark days of early October by differentiating the heroic citizens who stormed the Bastille from the ferocious mob, controlled from behind the scenes by high-ranked conspirators, who broke into Versailles. Her problem is that the heroic nation of the early days seemed to disappear or degenerate into the mob. In order to account for this she overrides her earlier suggestion that the nation (the people) somehow avoided the taint of the national character:

The character of the french, indeed, had been so depraved by the inveterate despotism of ages, that even amidst the heroism which distinguished the taking of the Bastille, we are forced to see that suspicious temper, and that vain ambition of dazzling, which have generated all the succeeding follies and crimes.... The morals of the whole nation were destroyed by the manners formed by the [previous] government. (HMV 6:123)

Wollstonecraft thus admits that the French susceptibility to theatricality had contaminated the people in general – especially the people of Paris (HMV 6:228). By training the people to be moved by theatre the *ancien régime* prepared them to be swayed by the demagogues that the Revolution unleashed (HMV 6:133). Indeed, the Revolution itself has now degenerated into a paltry theatricality:

If a relish for the broad mirth of *fun* characterize the lower class of english, the french of every denomination are equally delighted with a phosphorical, sentimental gilding. This is constantly observable at the theatres. The passions are deprived of all their radical strength, to give smoothness to the ranting sentiments, which, with mock dignity, like the party-coloured rags on the shrivelled branches of the tree of liberty, stuck up in every village, are displayed as something very grand and significant. (HMV 6:25–6)

Related to their love of the theatre and theatrical effect is the French susceptibility to enthusiasm, which "hurries them from one extreme to another"

(HMV 6:27). As a consequence, the people of France, especially Parisians, were liable to sway, or be swayed, in any direction, pushed and pulled by stage managers on all sides – the popular orators, the National Assembly, the court party, and so on (HMV 6:105). Far from being the virtuous heroes depicted earlier, the people now exhibit the worst qualities of the national character:

> These sudden transitions from one extreme to another, without leaving any settled conviction behind, to confirm or eradicate the corroding distrust, could not be seen in such a strong light any where as at Paris, because there a variety of causes have so effeminated reason, that the french may be considered as a nation of women ... so passive appears to be their imagination, it requires to be roused by novelty; and then, more lively than strong, the evanescent emotions scarcely leave any traces behind them.   (HMV 6:121)

The disastrous symptoms of the national character can also be detected in the leaders of the National Assembly. Echoing Burke's criticism in the *Reflections*, Wollstonecraft suggests that the National Assembly itself became a profane theatre in which the delegates played to the gallery:

> three parts out of four of the time, which ought to have been employed in serious investigation, was consumed in idle vehemence. Whilst the applauses and hisses of the galleries increased the tumult; making the vain still more eager to mount the stage. Thus every thing contributing to excite the emotions, which lead men only to court admiration, the good of the people was too often sacrificed to the desire of pleasing them.   (HMV 6:156)

One of the ways the Assembly sacrificed the people's good to the desire of pleasing them was by introducing a political constitution that was too advanced for the stage of political and moral development that the French had reached. The French were not yet politically mature enough to continue with a single chamber without the checks and balances needed in any society that falls short of moral perfection (HMV 6:161–2). The Assembly ought instead to have arranged for all future legislatures to be divided into a house of representatives and a senate, "for certainly no people stand in such great need of a check" as the French (HMV 6:165). In proceeding so precipitately, the Assembly revealed their ignorance of the national character and of the stage of political progress that had been reached in France. As a result, the Assembly introduced a political constitution "most improper for the degenerate society of France" and thereby gave the enemies of the Revolution the chance of mocking this ideal system as impossibly utopian (HMV 6:162).

But although the Revolution went astray when the National Assembly made itself subject to the people, this does not mean that the people are not sovereign or that government ought not to be responsive to its will;

instead, it means that the relationship between representative government and sovereign people ought to assume its proper form only when the people have developed political maturity and reason:

> The will of the people being supreme, it is not only the duty of their representatives to respect it, but their political existence ought to depend on their acting conformably to the will of their constituents. Their voice, in enlightened countries, is always the voice of reason. But in the infancy of society, and during the advancement of the science of political liberty, it is highly necessary for the governing authority to be guided by the progress of that science; and to prevent, by judicious measures, any check being given to it's advancement, whilst equal care is taken not to produce the miseries of anarchy by encouraging licentious freedom. (HMV 6:210)

Political reform, then, must be adjusted to the level of political development in the whole nation. The National Assembly, driven by a nation that thought itself more enlightened that it actually was, introduced too much liberty too soon (HMV 6:96).

Wollstonecraft's sustained examination of the impact of the French national character on the progress of the Revolution leads her to conclude, in the final chapter, that the people of France were "NOT PROPERLY QUALIFIED FOR THE REVOLUTION" (HMV 6:223). Although the *ancien régime* made the revolution necessary, even inevitable, it also made the people of France unfit to carry it out (HMV 6:230). But while the Revolution could not change the national character overnight, its achievements will bring about a gradual and beneficial change in that character:

> A change of character cannot be so sudden as some sanguine calculators expect; yet by the destruction of the rights of primogeniture, a greater degree of equality of property is sure to follow . . . As a change also of the system of education and domestic manners will be a natural consequence of the revolution, the french will insensibly rise to a dignity of character far above that of the present race; and then the fruit of their liberty, ripening gradually, will have a relish not to be expected during it's crude and forced state. (HMV 6:231)

And despite the National Assembly's blunders, Wollstonecraft still believes that "[t]he foundation of liberty was laid in the declaration of rights" (HMV 6:162). In this act, at least, the Assembly made an epochal contribution to the march of human progress:

> it was an honour worthy to be reserved for the representatives of twenty-five millions of men, rising to the sense and feeling of rational beings, to be the first to dare to ratify such sacred and beneficial truths – truths, the existence of which had been eternal; and which required only to be made known, to be generally acknowledged. (HMV 6:221)

Furthermore, the "many constitutional principles of liberty" that have been established in France will "greatly accelerate the improvement of the public mind, and ultimately produce the perfect government, that they vainly endeavoured to construct immediately with such fatal precipitation" (HMV 6:172).

In *An Historical and Moral View*, then, Wollstonecraft assumes that the theoretical principles of the rights of man are eternally true, unwaveringly asserting that humanity is on a teleological journey towards moral, intellectual, and political perfection. Yet her analysis of the origins and progress of the French Revolution yields incompatible conclusions. On one hand, the French introduced reforms too quickly and consequently lost control of the Revolution; on the other, it may be that violence is necessary to overthrow corrupt political systems in order to be able to introduce just ones. The Revolution thus raises two sets of questions and two sets of answers:

> 1st. If, from the progress of reason, we be authorized to infer, that all governments will be meliorated, and the happiness of man placed on the solid basis, gradually prepared by the improvement of political science[,] ... if every day extending freedom be more firmly established in consequence of the general dissemination of truth and knowledge: it then seems injudicious for statesmen to force the adoption of any opinion, by aiming at the speedy destruction of obstinate prejudices; because these premature reforms, instead of promoting, destroy the comfort of those unfortunate beings, who are under their dominion, affording at the same time to despotism the strongest arguments to urge in opposition to the theory of reason. Besides, the objects intended to be forwarded are probably retarded, whilst the tumult of internal commotion and civil discord leads to the most dreadful consequence – the immolating of human victims. (HMV 6:45–6)

But the history of the Revolution also leads Wollstonecraft to contemplate that which, in her two *Vindications*, was unthinkable – the possibility that the revolutionary violence may have been a necessary means of overthrowing a political order that could have been removed in no other way:

> But, 2dly, it is necessary to observe, that, if the degeneracy of the higher orders of society be such, that no remedy less fraught with horror can effect a radical cure; and if enjoying the fruits of usurpation, they domineer over the weak, and check by all the means in their power every humane effort, to draw man out of the state of degradation, into which the inequality of fortune has sunk him; the people are justified in having recourse to coercion, to repel coercion. And, further, if it can be ascertained, that the silent sufferings of the citizens of the world under the iron feet of oppression are greater, though less obvious, than the calamities produced by such violent convulsions as have happened in

France... it may be politically just, to pursue such measures as were taken by
that regenerating country...   (HMV 6:46)

This would appear to justify, in certain circumstances, the violent overthrow
of tyranny. Wollstonecraft also seems willing, at times, to excuse the ongoing violence in France (ibid.). Indeed, she concludes *An Historical and Moral
View* by exonerating the revolutionary violence she had criticized throughout, invoking the long standing metaphor of the body politic:

> Thus had France grown up, and sickened on the corruption of a state diseased.
> But, as in medicine there is a species of complaint in the bowels which works
> it's own cure, and, leaving the body healthy, gives an invigorated tone to the
> system, so there is in politics: and whilst the agitation of it's regeneration
> continues, the excrementitious humours exuding from the contaminated body
> will excite a general dislike and contempt for the nation; and it is only the
> philosophical eye, which looks into the nature and weighs the consequences
> of human actions, that will be able to discern the cause, which has produced
> so many dreadful effects.   (HMV 6:235)

Wollstonecraft finally figures herself, then, as one of those few observers with
a philosophical eye, a physician of the state capable of seeing the dreadful
effects of such purges as a reason to be optimistic for the body politic's future
well being.

The domestic happiness Wollstonecraft hoped for by joining Imlay in
England failed to materialize. By June of 1795 she was traveling with her
one-year-old daughter and their maid to Scandinavia on a business trip for
Imlay that would result in her most popular book, *Letters Written during a
Short Residence in Sweden, Norway and Denmark* (1796). This journey to
three countries at various stages of pre-revolutionary development allowed
her to reassess the Revolution, her characterization of the French, and the
efficacy of revolution itself as a means of promoting progress. Her attention
to political and social progress in Sweden, Norway, and Denmark reveals
that she is still pursuing what she refers to as her "favourite subject of contemplation, the future improvement of the world" (SR 6:338).

Although Wollstonecraft admits, in the opening letter, that she is still suffering from "the horrors I had witnessed in France, which had cast a gloom
over all nature" (SR 6:247), her observations of the people of Scandinavia
in Letter III suggest to her that the French Revolution is beginning to have
potentially beneficial effects in other countries. Thus she believes that she
can detect positive stirrings in Sweden:

> the french revolution has not only rendered all the crowned heads more cau-
> tious, but has so decreased every where (excepting amongst themselves) a re-
> spect for nobility, that the peasantry have not only lost their blind reverence

for their seigniors, but complain, in a manly style, of oppressions which before they did not think of denominating such, because they were taught to consider themselves as a different order of beings. (SR 6:255)

While admitting that the Revolution has caused her deep trauma, then, Wollstonecraft seems able to look forward with some optimism to further revolution on a European-wide scale.

Wollstonecraft's encounter towards the end of her journey with the indolence and ignorance of the Danes under an absolute monarch prompts her into making some intriguing adjustments to her assessment of the French national character. In Letter XIX, she confesses, "I believe I should have been less severe in the remarks I have made on the vanity and depravity of the french, had I travelled towards the north before I visited France." To "balance the account of horrors" in France, she now suggests that the common people of France have displayed "more virtuous enthusiasm ... during the two last years" than those of any other nation (326). In the following letter, she even wonders whether the French love of theater is not far preferable to the immoderate love of alcohol that characterises the "common people ... both in England and the northern states of Europe" and that impedes their "moral improvement" (SR 6:327).

Further complicating the account of the Revolution that emerges in the *Short Residence* is Wollstonecraft's encounter with French émigrés in Hamburg and Altona. She admires the way "[m]any emigrants have met, with fortitude, such a total change of circumstances as scarcely can be paralleled, retiring from a palace, to an obscure lodging, with dignity." She contrasts this fortitude with the "insolent vulgarity" of the men of commerce: "Still good-breeding points out the gentleman; and sentiments of honour and delicacy appear the offspring of greatness of soul, when compared with the grovelling views of the sordid accumulators of *cent. per cent*" (SR 6:340). While this may be part of Wollstonecraft's attack on Imlay's involvement with commerce, it also indicates that Wollstonecraft is beginning to think that the men of birth of the *ancien régime* were morally better than the men of commerce who have replaced them.

In an Appendix, Wollstonecraft offers general reflections on revolution and human progress:

> An ardent affection for the human race makes enthusiastic characters eager to produce alteration in laws and governments prematurely. To render them useful and permanent, they must be the growth of each particular soil, and the gradual fruit of the ripening understanding of the nation, matured by time, not forced by an unnatural fermentation. And, to convince me that such a change is gaining ground, with accelerating pace, the view I have had of society,

during my northern journey, would have been sufficient, had I not previously considered the grand causes which combine to carry mankind forward, and diminish the sum of human misery.

(SR 6:346)

The conclusion Wollstonecraft draws from her northern journey, then, confirms her sense that revolution, even hurried reform, results from a mistaken attempt to accelerate progress beyond its natural pace. While the ardent affection of enthusiastic characters leads them to make premature alterations in laws and government, it would be better simply to allow the general progress of Europe to stimulate home grown reforms that are suited to the particular soil of each nation. The example of the French Revolution has not dampened Wollstonecraft's optimism about the inevitability of gradual human improvement, but it has convinced her that revolution is not the best means of encouraging such improvement.

NOTES

1. Claire Tomalin, *The Life and Death of Mary Wollstonecraft* (Harmondsworth: Penguin, 1977), 130. For accounts of Wollstonecraft's experience in the Dissenting circles of Newington Green and St. Paul's Churchyard, see 44–63 and 89–109. The most recent and extensive biography of Wollstonecraft is Janet Todd, *Mary Wollstonecraft: a Revolutionary Life* (London: Weidenfeld and Nicholson, 2000).

2. Richard Price, *A Discourse on the Love of Our Country* (1789), in *Richard Price: Political Writings*, ed. D. O. Thomas (Cambridge and New York: Cambridge University Press, 1991), 176–96. For Wollstonecraft's review of Price's sermon in the *Analytical Review* of December 1789, see AR 7:185–7.

3. For an account of the events at Versailles on 5–6 October 1789, see Simon Schama, *Citizens: a Chronicle of the French Revolution* (London and New York: Penguin, 1989), 456–70.

4. See Edmund Burke, *Reflections on the Revolution in France* (1790), ed. Conor Cruise O'Brien (London and New York: Penguin, 1968). For extracts from some of the most important of the texts in this pamphlet war, see Marilyn Butler, ed., *Burke, Paine, Godwin, and the Revolution Controversy* (Cambridge: Cambridge University Press, 1984).

5. For discussions of *Rights of Men* as a reply to Burke, see Tom Furniss, "Gender in Revolution: Edmund Burke and Mary Wollstonecraft," *Revolution in Writing: British Literary Responses to the French Revolution* ed. Kelvin Everest (Milton Keynes and Philadelphia: Open University Press, 1991), 65–100, and Tom Furniss, *Edmund Burke's Aesthetic Ideology: Language, Gender and Political Economy in Revolution* (Cambridge: Cambridge University Press, 1993), 164–96.

6. See John Locke, *The Second Treatise of Government* (1690), 95–7, *John Locke: Two Treatises of Government*, ed. Peter Laslett (Cambridge and New York: Cambridge University Press, 1960, 1988), 330–2.

7. See AR 7:322–4, 375–8, 383–5, 390–3, 415–16.

8. See Carol H. Poston, ed., Mary Wollstonecraft, *A Vindication of the Rights of Woman*, 2nd ed. (New York and London: Norton, 1988), 3n2.

9. See VRW 5:65 nb.

10. Talleyrand, *Rapport*, translated in VRW 5:67n.

11. See Wollstonecraft to Everina Wollstonecraft (London, 20 June 1792), Letters, 213.

12. See the unflinching account in Schama, *Citizens*, 631–9.

13. William Godwin published this introductory letter, which Wollstonecraft never added to, in his edition of the *Posthumous Works of the Author of A Vindication of the Rights of Woman* (1798). See PCFN 6:443–6.

14. For a detailed account of the Terror, see Schama, *Citizens*, 726–847.

15. A facsimile of the first edition was published in 1975. See Mary Wollstonecraft, *An Historical and Moral View of the Origin and Progress of the French Revolution; and the Effect it has Produced in Europe*, introduction, Janet Todd (New York: Scholars' Facsimiles & Reprints, 1975).

16. Exceptions include: Vivien Jones, "Women Writing Revolution: Narratives of History and Sexuality in Wollstonecraft and Williams," *Beyond Romanticism: New Approaches to Texts and Contexts, 1780–1832*, eds. Stephen Copley and John Whale (London and New York: Routledge, 1992), 178–99; Harriet Devine Jump, "'The Cool Eye of Observation': Mary Wollstonecraft and the French Revolution," *Revolution in Writing: British Literary Responses to the French Revolution*, ed. Kelvin Everest (a revised version of this essay appears in Harriet Devine Jump, *Mary Wollstonecraft: Writer* [New York and London: Harvester Wheatsheaf, 1994], 90–110); Gary Kelly, *Revolutionary Feminism: the Mind and Career of Mary Wollstonecraft* (London: Macmillan, 1992), 149–70; Jane Moore, *Mary Wollstonecraft* (Plymouth: Northcote House and the British Council, 1999), 48–60. In her introduction to the special number of *Women's Writing* devoted to Mary Wollstonecraft Janet Todd claims that the contributors were self-consciously attempting to shift attention to Wollstonecraft's relatively neglected late writings, including *An Historical and Moral View*. See Janet Todd and Marie Mulvey Roberts, eds., *Women's Writing, Special Number: Mary Wollstonecraft: A Bicentennial* 4/2 (1997), 139–41. Speculating about the relative neglect of *An Historical and Moral View*, Ashley Tauchert's contribution develops a feminist psychoanalytical reading designed to "rescue it from oblivion"; see "Maternity, Castration and Mary Wollstonecraft's *Historical and Moral View of the French Revolution*," *Women's Writing*, 4/2, eds. Todd and Mulvey Roberts 173–99 (189).

17. The most impressive and detailed recent account of the French Revolution, which concentrates on the period Wollstonecraft wrote about and the period during which she lived in France, is Schama's *Citizens*. A more succinct account of the events of the whole Revolution can be found in Christopher Hibbert, *The French Revolution* (London and New York: Penguin, 1980).

18. See Jane Rendall, "'The grand causes which combine to carry mankind forward': Wollstonecraft, History and Revolution," in *Women's Writing*, 4/2, eds. Todd and Mulvey Roberts, 155–72.

19. For a brief discussion of Rousseau's critique of the theatre in *Lettre à d'Alembert sur les spectacles* (1758), see Gregory Dart, *Rousseau, Robespierre and English*

Romanticism (Cambridge: Cambridge University Press, 1999), 110. Dart's whole chapter – "Rousseau, Wollstonecraft and aesthetic education" (99–138) – is extremely interesting in terms of Wollstonecraft's response to the French Revolution.

20. For an account of these events, see Schama, *Citizens*, 369–425.

6

MITZI MYERS

Mary Wollstonecraft's literary reviews

Although they constitute a substantial portion of her writing, the reviews Mary Wollstonecraft wrote for Joseph Johnson's progressive journal, the *Analytical Review* (launched in 1788), rarely receive sustained critical attention. This omission is unfortunate, for these reviews collectively testify to the breadth of Wollstonecraft's reading and to the extent of her activity within the literary marketplace of her time. As such they are a valuable resource for and index to her opinions during perhaps the most decisive and yet also the most neglected period of her career. But just as importantly, the reviews deserve close attention because they show us how Wollstonecraft developed her own distinctive voice as a feminist cultural critic by engaging with the texts under review. The reviewing experience thus simultaneously educated the private, anonymous writer and her reading audience. As Wollstonecraft learns and teaches, she also moves from tentative confessional author to the authoritative public figure who altered the social, political, and literary sphere during the transitional period of the 1790s.

Wollstonecraft served her literary apprenticeship as a reviewer for the *Analytical Review* and worked again as a journalist in her latter years when she was on the verge of artistic maturity. Interestingly, then, her reviews of poetry and popular romance cluster around the periods when she was herself most intensely involved in creative activity.[1] Her early contributions laid the groundwork for her later achievements – showing affinities with the themes and language of the *Rights of Woman*, to take only one example. Clearly, her immersion in contemporary literature helped her to formulate her own special feminist stance, that peculiarly Wollstonecraftian blend of rational radicalism and precocious romanticism.

Before I turn to the place Wollstonecraft's reviews occupy in her career as a whole, it is important to address the problem of attribution. Consisting predominantly of quotations, most of Wollstonecraft's hundreds of reviews for the *Analytical Review* are short – in keeping with the common practice of the time, probably sent to the publisher on a single sheet – and they are signed at the end only with an initial or initials. Ascribing them to the various authors working for Johnson can thus be a risky venture. Mixing external evidence with stylistic and content analysis, Ralph Wardle argues in a pioneering article that Wollstonecraft contributed reviews under the signatures of M, W, and T and also the unsigned reviews in a run of short notices ending with such a signature. (He thought T might stand for "teacher" because he first noticed it in an essay on education.) Key evidence is that the M, W, and T signatures disappear while Wollstonecraft was abroad; after returning from France she picks up only the M. Subsequent scholars have queried parts of his hypothesis, but this essay substantially validates it.[2]

Although Wollstonecraft reviewed books about children, education, women, travel, and even boxing, fiction – sentimental fiction in particular – seems to have been her niche. Accordingly, Wollstonecraft's literary reviews are documents in the history of sensibility, offering a case study of how a female journalist, assigned seemingly unpromising "ladies' subjects" like sentimental novels, managed to create a resonant voice as cultural and literary critic. As such a critic, Wollstonecraft is a woman of sense who resists the model of femininity typically inscribed in these texts, which represent women according to a linguistic and structural etiquette of powerlessness and marginalization, often showing them being emotionally and physically carried away. Such is the stock-in-trade of even a first-rate popular novelist like Charlotte Smith. For the female writer and critic, sentimental fiction's overwrought language and behavioral code of extreme emotional responsiveness – a submission to forces outside the self that romanticizes passivity – poses a threat Wollstonecraft and others resist by recommending the power and the dignity of reason. If the latter eighteenth century witnessed the transformation of the *Man of Reason* (as Genevieve Lloyd's study labels patriarchal discourse) into the *Man of Feeling*, a comparable redefinition of womanly discourse empowered the female pen to include the rational along with the affective.[3] This appropriation of reason most notably informed educational writing by women – Wollstonecraft's *A Vindication of the Rights of Woman* (1792) is above all a pedagogical text critiquing female socialization in sensibility and advocating rational instruction in its place. Late in the century, this appropriation of reason also modified the feminine narrative tradition as well, the fiction of Maria Edgeworth and Jane Austen being only the most obvious examples. It especially directs the critical commentary of women of sense who worried about sensibility's effects on the readers of their sex, especially what they liked to call the "rising generation."[4]

But while Wollstonecraft demystifies the contemporary feminine specialty, the novel of sensibility so often "told in letters" and written by "A Lady" that was so instrumental in enabling her to evolve her own distinctive voice, she was certainly not ready to jettison the positive attributes associated with feminine sensibility. No reader could get beyond the early chapters of *Mary, A Fiction* (1788) or of *The Wrongs of Woman; or Maria* (1798), the novel she struggled to complete in the last months of her life, without recognizing their kinship with the contemporary sentimental narrative she so often reviewed. Indeed, her letters, the epigraph from Rousseau that supplies the theme of *Mary,* as well as the several *Analytical Review* essays on his writings, all testify to the fact that she, like numerous sister writers, was "half in love" with the seductive philosopher of feeling (Letters, 263). Wollstonecraft's whole career might be read, then, in terms of a dialectic of *sense* and *sensibility*, to recollect the title of Austen's later novel. But whereas Austen writes a text in which sisters for the most part grow up dichotomously and learn from one another's experience, Wollstonecraft assumes a maternal stance toward the imagined girl readers of the fictions she considers, and through her own voice offers an educative example of the integration she desires. The rationally responsible yet feelingly protective attitude she exhibits toward her pupils is encoded in her critical commentary as well as in her persona. While in real life, educating and socializing one's charges (and oneself) is problematic, the reviewer's authority can banish fears, remedy disorders, and textualize a strong self-image in the process of instructing others.[5] Along with the "Hints" set down for the unwritten second part of the *Rights of Woman* and with Wollstonecraft's most mature statement of her aesthetics, published in 1797 as "On Artificial Taste" and retitled "On Poetry, and Our Relish for the Beauties of Nature" by her widower William Godwin, Wollstonecraft's reviews both discuss and stylistically enact a poetics of change, an attempt to unite an aesthetic of spontaneity and affect with a morality of reason that is the hallmark of her career.

Sometimes sportive, sometimes serious, Wollstonecraft as feminist reader displays a lively critical intelligence and, in accordance with her revisionist ideology, a determination to exercise her own independent judgment. Her letters to Johnson sketch the reviewer's routine – returning the batch of books finished, asking whether "you wish me to look over any more trash this month." Her boredom sometimes surfaces in public laments about the lot of "poor Reviewers, who have lately perused so many bad novels," sometimes in digs at the run-of-the-press witlings who try her patience: "The writer of this Poem, we are informed, is between 15 and 18 years of age. We believe it." Most often and most instructively, however, her irritation focuses on women writers and readers, on the stereotypically feminine tales that these unthinking mothers and lovelorn daughters produce and consume. She takes for granted a growing and predominantly *female* readership hungry for narrative, describing the audience of the very popular Charlotte Smith as "her

fair countrywomen," for example.[6] She comments about the growing supply of authoresses eagerly catering to that appetite for fantasies. "The best
method, I believe, that can be adopted to correct a fondness for novels is
to ridicule them," she later observes in the *Rights of Woman*. The model of
reading based on therapeutic mockery she then details recapitulates much
of her own critical practice: "if a judicious person, with some turn for hu-
mour, would read several to a young girl, and point out . . . how foolishly
and ridiculously they caricatured human nature, just opinions" might replace "romantic sentiments" (VRW 5:258). Reading self-consciously as an
enlightened woman, shaping what she reads to serve her own controversial-
ist's purpose, Wollstonecraft criticizes her subjects for writing like Woman,
for serving as passive channels through which linguistic and cultural codes
flow without resistance. She finds oppression and repression inscribed in the
feminine texts she reads, never the self-expression her aesthetic demands.

Wollstonecraft's objections to her period's "scribbling women" are at once
aesthetic and ideological, for questions of literary artistry and questions of
human values are always intimately interrelated for her. Literarily, the scrib-
bles are vapid: "sweetly sentimental," "milk and water periods," "insipid
trifling incidents," "much ado about nothing," "matter so soft that the indulgent critic can scarcely characterize it" go her kinder descriptions.[7] A "great
number of pernicious and frivolous novels"– "those misshapen monsters,
daily brought forth to poison the minds of our young females" – waste the
time of readers, plunging them "into that continual dissipation of thought
which renders all serious employment irksome" as well as the time of writers,
especially schoolgirl romancers, who should work to improve their minds.
Instead, young consumers turn into young producers: "From reading to writing novels the transition is very easy."[8] When she finds a novel written by a
very young lady, Wollstonecraft repeatedly advises her to "throw aside her
pen" or even to "throw her bantling into the fire"; perhaps such an "author
will employ her time better when she is married." *Seymour Castle; or, the
History of Julia and Cecilia: An Entertaining and Interesting Novel* (1789) –
its title, like those of its sister works, weary with cliché – provokes her to
even stronger strictures: "This frivolous history of misses and lords, ball
dresses and violent emotions . . . is one of the most stupid novels we have
ever impatiently read. Pray Miss, write no more!"[9]

Often tart with women writers, Wollstonecraft counters the indulgent gallantry male reviewers usually reserve for a fair belletrist. Just as she later does
in the *Rights of Woman*, in her reviews she takes the position of the firm,
wise mother brooking no nonsense from the deficient mothers and daughters she instructs. Most female novels, she claims, adapting Pope, have no
character at all. Content to copy their predecessors in this "flimsy" kind of

writing– Richardson, who modernized romance; Burney, who feminized it; and Sterne, who whipped literary affect into syllabubs of sentimentality – "like timid sheep, the lady authors jump over the hedge one after the other, and do not dream of deviating either to the right or left." Wollstonecraft finds the typical woman's novel both stylistically and morally derivative. She recommends *Clarentine: A Novel* (1796) to "young female readers," who perhaps have more patience than "poor reviewers, condemned to read though dulness, perched on their eye-lids, invites to sleep or forgetfulness"; and though Sarah Harriet Burney's fiction was published anonymously, Wollstonecraft accurately locates the model for the normative lady's heroine "exactly proper, according to established rules.... an imitation of Evelina in water-colours."[10]

A work like Mrs. Elizabeth Norman's *The Child of Woe* (1789), having no "marked features to characterize it," Wollstonecraft pronounces "a truly feminine novel.... the same review would serve for almost all" of these "ever varying still the same productions." She registers her pleasure "when *written by a lady*, is not inserted in the title page" and insists that she can "guess the sex of the writer" by her "tissue of pretty nothings."[11] She even offers a "receipt for a novel" composed of favorite female narrative ingredients: "unnatural characters, improbable incidents, and sad tales of woe rehearsed in an affected, half-prose, half-poetical style, exquisite double-refined sensibility, dazzling beauty, and *elegant* drapery, to adorn the celestial body, (these descriptions cannot be too minute) should never be forgotten in a book intended to amuse the fair." Add to this framework the usual "decorations, the drapery of woe, grief personified, hair freed from confinement to shade feverish cheeks, tottering steps, inarticulate words, and tears ever ready to flow, white gowns, black veils, and graceful attitudes . . . when the scene is to be pathetic." "Sensibility," she finds, "is the never failing theme, and sorrow torn to tatters, is exhibited in . . . moping madness – tears that flow forever, and slow consuming death." Of course these staples serve woman's one plot: "The ladies are very fond of a dismal catastrophe, and dying for love is the favorite theme." They exalt weaknesses into excellences, and "the passion that should exercise the understanding" becomes "the grand spring of action, the main business of life."[12]

The women's heroines all come from the same mold: "these ladies, for such artificial beings must not be familiarly called women, are something like the cherubim under the organ-loft, soft, simple, and good." Like Austen in her juvenilia, Wollstonecraft satirizes authors' "pulling the wires to make the puppets . . . faint, run mad, &c., &c." And she is equally bored with infallible characters who "love and weep by rule," with "insipid goodness, so imperfect are we!"[13] The "faultless monster" is, like Helen Maria Williams's

Julia (1790), "viewed with [readerly] respect, and left very tranquilly to quiet her feelings, because," without real passion, too perfect for internal conflict, "it cannot be called a contest." The "most exemplary degree of rectitude in the conduct" of a heroine is not enough for satisfying fiction, which depends on "knowledge of the human heart, and comprehensive views of life." Wollstonecraft then turns her critique, as she often does, into a discussion of the fiction she values and would try to write in *The Wrongs of Woman; or Maria* – "A good tragedy or novel, if the criterion be the effect which it has on the reader, is not always the most moral work, for it is not the reveries of sentiment, but the struggles of passion – of those *human passions*, that too frequently cloud the reason, and lead *mortals* into dangerous errors . . . which raise the most lively emotions, and leave the most lasting impression on the memory; an impression rather made by the heart than the understanding: for our affections are not quite voluntary as the suffrages of reason." Although claiming passion and growth through error for her own heroine, Wollstonecraft can praise the pastel charms of first-rate women writers like Williams and Smith, despite their omitting the "workings of passion" from their tales. To the author of *Almeria Belmore: A Novel, in A Series of Letters,* "Written by A Lady" (1789), she is less generous: "no discrimination of character, no acquaintance with life, nor – do not start, fair lady! – any passion." And with the writer of *The Fair Hibernian* (1789), she is downright irascible: "Without a knowledge of life, or the human heart, why will young misses presume to write?" Such authors fuel Wollstonecraft's outburst in the *Rights of Woman* at "the reveries of the stupid novelists, who, knowing little of human nature, work up stale tales, and describe meretricious scenes, all retailed in a sentimental jargon, which equally tend to corrupt the taste, and draw the heart aside from its daily duties."[14]

Feminine fiction, Wollstonecraft argues, is "sentimental, pumped up nonsense," falsity masking negation. Affectation – phony feelings and incidents cobbled together from books – covers up a void, but strong writing cannot come "merely from reading . . . mocking us with the 'shadow of a shade.'" Because women writers prefer "unnatural sentimental flights" to "catching realities warm with life in the sun-beam that shoots athwart their own path," eschewing the individual and the original to "tread in a beaten track" (a favorite phrase), they warp their own experience, refining and perpetuating damaging stereotypes. She wanted a more serious and thoughtful examination of authentic human emotion and experience, not "artificial feelings, cold nonsensical bombast, and ever varying still the same improbable adventures and unnatural characters." Wollstonecraft was neither the first nor the last critic to lament how popular novels foster escapism and misleading expectations of life: "consequently *adventures* are sought for and created, when duties are neglected and content despised." Paradoxically, she demonstrates, flaccid fiction commands staying power through its very insubstantiality, its capacity to meld into the reader's daydreams and let her play at "becoming a heroine," as a modern study labels the process. However inaccurate as transcripts of life and emotion, the romance's artificial constructs possess a mysterious power to seep back out of literature and shape the life of which they are distortions in the first place, "to infuse insinuating poison into the minds of the inconsiderate."[15]

"No one was harder on women," one biographer justly remarks of Wollstonecraft's reviews, and no one was harder on cultural conditioning agents masquerading as fiction, precisely because she hoped to improve her sex and held the novel in high regard. If, as Derek Roper suggests in his survey of eighteenth-century reviewing, Wollstonecraft was more exacting than most of her fellow journalists, the reason surely lies in her ideological commitment, her antennae ever alert to "the circumstances that imperceptibly model the manners of a nation." Eighteenth-century conservatives and radicals alike fretted over women and novels; this period's model of the reading experience stresses the exemplary force, for good or ill, of the fiction one imbibes: you are what you read.[16]

Wollstonecraft's stories of reading, of the interaction between reader and text, factor gender into this inherited scenario. Her originality is neatly enlisting standard objections to serve the larger purposes of her revisionist social ideology; she makes routine moral cavils shoulder reformist, even radical, values. Wollstonecraft is very much an engaged critic, a contextual critic, a literary *and* cultural critic whose feminist literary critique, like that of her more recent sisters, is undergirded by cultural analysis, a reexamination of the interweave between art and society, a reassessment of prevailing values and female mythology. Literary commentary, she recognizes, is never purely aesthetic but always socially implicated. Her reviews show her forever exercised over how female life gets inscribed in literature and how literature molds life's rules and roles, simultaneously pandering to lovelorn "romantic notions" and prescribing narrow limits. "Why," Wollstonecraft complains of Elizabeth Inchbald's *A Simple Story* (1791), "do all female writers, even when they display their abilities, always give a sanction to the libertine reveries of men? Why do they poison the minds of their own sex, by strengthening a male prejudice that makes women systematically weak?"[17] Systematic weakness, systematic gaps in the texts where real women should be – so goes Wollstonecraft's typical indictment of the feminine novel, which acquires in her work an emblematic value, both a source and symbol of woman's artificiality, of her status as cultural fabrication.

Sweet, soft, and hollow, decorous and passionless mannequins, eighteenth-century images of women in literature yield neither the full-bodied female characters nor the liberating feminist values that Wollstonecraft values, that she desires to represent in her fiction to come, and that she already in fact epitomizes in her persona as a reader. Unlike the imitative feminine novelists she censures, Wollstonecraft self-consciously exemplifies the mature woman writer with "sufficient courage to think for herself, and not view life through the medium of books." Her critical presence is most obvious as the antithesis of that feminine negation she finds in the texts before her. Her self-confident assertion and decided views, her subjective candor (which again recalls early feminist literary criticism), her down-to-earth common sense, even her rough humor and ready wit function to differentiate her critical voice from the languishing maiden airs she derides and mark her as a strong-minded, rational educator, attuned to all the ways women have *not* been represented in literature. Indicatively, when Wollstonecraft does offer rare praise for a female character, it is the wise and resilient matron like Charlotte Smith's autobiographical Mrs. Stafford in *Emmeline* (1788) whom she singles out, not the passive romantic lead, the daughter, but the knowledgeable mother figure who has felt and thought deeply, who demonstrates women's "power . . . over themselves" rather than over their lovers called for in the *Rights of Woman*. No copybook tracery of a proper lady, Wollstonecraft reveals herself a real, complex woman with strong feelings and human foibles as well as rational understanding. Irascible, opinionated, enthusiastic, her varied emotional responses contribute to an ongoing dialogue that grants critical detachment and empathic involvement, sense and sensibility, each its due weight. As educative persona and exemplary reader, Wollstonecraft offers her female audience a resistant model of reading that counters their cultural predisposition toward submersion in the events of the text. She asks them to close the gap between their lives and their fantasies, to critique rather than internalize the shopworn images of women in literature, and her strictures on submissive female reading postures slide easily into a broader cultural analysis of female submission.[18]

Take her very first review – of *Edward and Harriet; or, The Happy Recovery: A Sentimental Novel*, "By A Lady" (1788) – with its anticipation of the *Rights of Woman*'s "judicious" reader. Arguing that "ridicule should direct its shafts against this fair game," the "*cant* of sensibility," she pronounces:

> Young women may be termed romantic, when they are under the direction of artificial feelings, when they boast of being tremblingly alive all o'er, and faint and sigh as the novelist informs them they should. Hunting after shadows, the moderate enjoyments of life are despised, and its duties neglected; and the

imagination, suffered to stray beyond the utmost verge of probability ... soon
shuts out reason, and the dormant faculties languish for want of cultivation;
as rational books are neglected, because they do not throw the mind into an
exquisite tumult ... false sentiment leads to sensuality, and vague fabricated
feelings supply the place of principles.[19]

Sentimental fiction is not a negligible literary vogue, Wollstonecraft emphasizes. Novels of sensibility matter because they shape behavior and serve as
an index to broader cultural ills. Such reviews point forward to the *Rights'*
fully developed analysis of contemporary female socialization in "over exercised sensibility." Woman is "made by her education the slave of sensibility,"
Wollstonecraft observes. Citing Samuel Johnson's definition – "quickness
of sensation; quickness of perception; delicacy" – she points out that the
"pretty feminine phrases" of sensibility stereotypically denoting the "sexual
characteristics of the weaker vessel" are "almost synonymous with epithets
of weakness." Novels, music, poetry, and gallantry "all tend to make women
the creatures of sensation":

> their understanding neglected, consequently they become the prey of their
> senses, delicately termed sensibility, and are blown about by every momen-
> tary gust of feeling ... All their thoughts turn on things calculated to excite
> emotion; and feeling, when they should reason, their conduct is unstable, and
> their opinions wavering ... Miserable, indeed, must be that being whose culti-
> vation of mind has only tended to inflame its passions! A distinction should be
> made between inflaming and strengthening them.[20]

The final distinction is characteristic and important. Although Wollstonecraft
as a reviewer of commonplace sentimental fiction may stress sense and strategically exemplify how a "judicious" woman must rate "love-lorn tales of
novelists," she is not immune to the legitimate charms of sensibility, and she
accords it a privileged role in her evolving feminist aesthetic (VRW 5:194).
The weak, false sensibility of cultural stereotype symbolizes imprisonment;
the strong, genuine sensibility of romantic genius signifies empowerment.

Wollstonecraft's reviews, then, imply not just alternative models of reading
and female selfhood, but also an alternative aesthetics. Most significantly,
her favorite critical counters range themselves firmly against the ways of
knowing and valuing that she attributes to popular literature. The derivative, prescriptive, imitative, and affected – false because copied rather than
freshly seen: these are her foils for originality, individuality, independence,
spontaneity; for the natural, innovative, imaginative, and real, true feeling – good because uniquely felt at firsthand. These are the characteristics of
"genius" – always a standard of value for Wollstonecraft and the heart of the
revisionist aesthetics she refines throughout her literary progression: direct

observation, independent thought, the primacy of the individual imagination as the source of aesthetic truth. To think and to feel for oneself: such phrases inform her reviews and her whole career, from the preface to her first novel, a neat little piece of expressionist aesthetics which unmistakably enrolls Wollstonecraft among the first English Romantics, to her "Hints" for the *Rights of Woman*, part two, probably written during her reviewing years and packed with maxims about originality, spontaneity, creativity, and imagination; from her personal letters to her final aesthetic manifesto, "On Poetry," initially and more appropriately entitled "On Artificial Taste." Like many of her reviews, the "Hints" connect strong passions and strong minds, "enthusiastic flights of fancy" and individuality: "a writer of genius makes us feel – an inferior author reason"; the "flights of the imagination" grant access to truths beyond the "laboured deductions of reason," necessary though these are (Hints 5:275, 276, 294).

And much as her reviews critique hackneyed sentimental fiction as a symptom of cultural malaise, of that overrefined "state of civil society . . . in which sentiment takes place of passion, and taste polishes away the native energy of character," "On Poetry" contrasts two styles of feeling and stages of society, the natural and the artificial, into a definitive exposition of Wollstonecraft's aesthetic values. (It is justly described by one biographer as a virtual call for a romantic revival in poetry.) Here she talks again about the natural as the "transcript of immediate sensations, in all their native wildness and simplicity," about "real perceptions" versus bookish declamation, revealing once more how much she values strong feelings, exquisite sensibility, and original genius. The last two are equivalent, she suggests, but she also insists that the "effusions of a vigorous mind" reveal an "understanding . . . enlarged by thought" as well as "finely fashioned nerves" that "vibrate acutely with rapture." Indeed, the understanding, she argues, "must bring back the feelings to nature."[21]

Here she also shows, as she does almost obsessively in so many reviews, a preoccupation with style, a conviction that style, substance, and consciousness indivisibly interconnect. Thus I can argue that Wollstonecraft's critical form and phrasing, to apply her own words, "forcibly illustrate what the author evidently wishes to inculcate." No one was more keenly aware of how ideological substance spills over into style – witness the often-quoted introduction to the *Rights of Woman* with its stress on sincerity, its hatred of "that flowery diction which has started from essays into novels, and from novels into familiar letters and conversation," and its allegiance to "things, not words!" and Wollstonecraft's way of scanning artistic expression for its ideological content illuminates her critical practice. In what she says – in the qualities she praises and the recurrent critical counters she deploys – and in the way she says it – in such associated juxtapositions as cold and warm, head and heart, reason and imagination, the "indolent weakness" of "copyists" and the "bold flights of genius," and in her distinctive style, much commented on and seldom analyzed – Wollstonecraft acts out the aesthetics of change she worked at and returned to throughout her career. Very different from the Latinate and often periodic constructions of her colleagues, her loose, informal sentences embody the associative movement of a thinking and feeling woman's mind as she strives to integrate the claims and languages of sense and sensibility, giving us, as does her ideal poet, "an image of [her] mind."[22] (Her final assessment of *Julia*, quoted above, is a good example.) Now spontaneously reactive, now reflective; now curt, now sprawling, her sentences enact her critical premises, according feminist issues a formal significance. Like her mix of Yorkshire colloquialisms and abstract philosophy and her attempts to unite imaginative excursus and rational inquiry, her "running" style – with its propulsive movement and its openness to experience – both mirrors her own mind and typifies the free play of the feminist mind as she defines it. Wollstonecraft has been – and still is – criticized for the supposed disorganization and awkwardness of her style and the seeming structural disorder of her work in general. Certainly her discursive, conjunctive style differs from the subordinated linear style typical of the period. The latter lays out ideas *already* classified and arranged; Wollstonecraft's syntactic structure mirrors the shifting perspective of the writer's mind, piling up clauses and phrases as they occur. It is the formal analogue of her ideological position, its roughness testifying to the sincerity and artlessness she values.[23]

Wollstonecraft's style affirms the emotive and imaginative complex that Romantic and feminist critics have accused Wollstonecraft of devaluing.[24] Her habitual contrasts of "warmth of imagination" and "truth of passion" with "romantic rants of false refinement" or "cold romantic flights" and "false enervating refinement" must be read as the thoughtful cultural critique that they are, as legitimate concern over the impact (especially on women and the young) of sensibility as literary and behavioral cliché. Like Jane Austen, Maria Edgeworth, and other female contemporaries who expose the literary dependence of feminine feelings, Wollstonecraft deplores a congealing of literary language into jargon, a hardening of the emotional arteries so that women feel and act by rote, casting themselves as derivative sentimental heroines and losing touch with cultural realities and their own thoughts and feelings. Wollstonecraft's real quarrel with women writers centers around affectation, falsity, and imitation; it is never with sensibility, passion, imagination, or fiction per se, and certainly not with narrative that feelingly renders female experience. That was her own aspiration in *The Wrongs of Woman; or Maria*: "it is the delineation of finer sensations which, in my opinion, constitutes the merit of our best novels. This is what I have in view," she states in the preface, and the novel values (perhaps even over-values) the heroine's "true sensibility, the sensibility which is the auxiliary of virtue, and the soul of genius." If Wollstonecraft as reviewer worries about the spurious sensibility of works that "engender false notions in the minds of young persons, who read with avidity such flimsy productions, and imagine themselves *sentimental*, when they are only devoid of restraining principles, the sure and solid support of virtue," Wollstonecraft the novelist tries to depict the real thing interacting with rational morality in a woman's mind.[25]

Throughout her career she defined sensibility in glowing terms, repeatedly equating it with genius and forever waxing ardent over Rousseau's ardors; her reviews talk of "that glow of imagination, which constitutes the grand charm of fiction"; and she voices genuine respect for the rare good novel, freshly and imaginatively realized. Praising Robert Bage's *Man As He Is* (1792), she observes that the increasing crop of novels, "the spawn of idleness," might lead "the inconsiderate . . . to conclude, that a novel is one of the lowest order of literary productions; though a very different estimation seems to be suggested by the small number of good ones which appear." She even offers a friendly welcome to romance as a genre (witness her review of the historical *Earl Strongbow* [1789] or Ann Radcliffe's Gothic *Italian* [1797]). She insisted early in her reviewing career that "to write a good novel requires uncommon abilities," something very different from "exhibiting life through a false medium" or a "sickly veil of artificial sentiment," and the final sentence of her last notice for the *Analytical Review*, published in May 1797, a few months before her death, makes an appropriate envoi. The story is *Hubert de Sevrac: A Romance of the Eighteenth Century* (1796) by Mary Robinson, a sister feminist who struggled, just as Wollstonecraft was then struggling with *Maria,* to mesh original cultural insights with the exaggerated effusions of feminine romance. All ornamental sentiment, the book has "no centre," Wollstonecraft observes, although "irradiations of fancy flash through the surrounding perplexity, sufficient to persuade us, that she could write better, were she once convinced, that the writing of a good book is no easy task," perhaps especially for a woman.[26]

But although Wollstonecraft's creative work cannot wholly escape from literary conventions, her critical practice demonstrates a surer mastery of these codes, a defter updating of textual femininity, not in the guise of a heroine but of a critical persona, who engenders an alternative selfhood while educating her audience. Embodying the ideal she would teach, this lively voice works against stale, parasitic, adulterated ways of living and feeling. Wollstonecraft explicitly urges women readers to think and feel for themselves; implicitly, she shows them how in a critical discourse that is also a mode of self-definition. Eager to encompass experience, following her consciousness even at the risk of apparent self-contradiction, Wollstonecraft as critic dances nimbly between the flaccid, love-fixated romance she deplores and the romantic genius she valorizes, between a narrative mode that formalizes passive subjection and one that facilitates passionate subjectivity, between fictive conventions and romantic freedoms. Although she emphasizes understanding and gibes at "double-refined sentiments," romantic impulse fuels Wollstonecraft's cultural ideology as much as it does that ideology's aesthetic analogue: individual protest, passion, and perception, as well as an insistence on personal growth, self-definition, and self-realization, undergird everything she wrote. Her social thought, literary criticism, and artistic experiments interplay and explicate one another, and they are all energized by her emergent feminist ideology's catalyzing force. Pursuing reason with emotional intensity, privileging passion while reining in sensibility, subtending a brisk no-nonsense critical posture with self-referentiality, Wollstonecraft the feminist reader shapes the critic's task to her own purposes and converts the bland fodder she reviews to nourish her own political aesthetics.

As a well-rounded woman exemplifying how reviews do indeed offer "points of access to the intellect and sensibility of the reviewer," Wollstonecraft demonstrates that a cool head need not preclude a warm heart, that "flights of feelings" are not incompatible with "the slow, orderly walk of reason," that women's heads can "become, a balance for our hearts." As woman critic and model to her readers, Wollstonecraft borrows the best of two discourses; appropriating reason, distinguishing true from false sensibility, she manages a stance and style that blend the languages of reason and feeling to her own humanist purposes.[27]

NOTES

1. The "forward-looking" *Analytical Review*, as Walter Graham points out, "encouraged...the romantic reaction in English literature," reflecting "the romantic or sentimental drift of literature during the 1790s better than any other periodical," *English Literary Periodicals* (New York: Thomas Nelson, 1930), 221, 195, 220.
2. See Ralph M. Wardle, "Mary Wollstonecraft, *Analytical Reviewer*," PMLA 62 4 (December 1947), 1000–9, and his 1951 biography *Mary Wollstonecraft: a Critical Biography*, (Lincoln: University of Nebraska Press [Bison Books], 1966). Working independently from unpublished papers, Elbridge Colby also identifies T, M, and unsigned reviews followed by M as Wollstonecraft's work; see his *The Life of Thomas Holcroft*, 1925, 2 vols. (New York: Benjamin Blom, 1968). In his "Mary Wollstonecraft's Reviews," *Notes and Queries* n.s. 5 (January 1958), 37–8, and in *Reviewing before the "Edinburgh," 1788–1802* (London: Methuen, 1978), Derek Roper criticizes Wardle's hypothesis, citing a

1796 review of *The Monk,* which he argues is not as moral as expected from Wollstonecraft. In 1961, however, this review (with three others, all signed only at the end) was identified by Eleanor L. Nicholes from manuscript as Wollstonecraft's work, "SC 15," *Shelley and His Circle, 1773–1822,* ed. Kenneth Neill Cameron (Cambridge: Harvard University Press, 1961), 1:152–57. Roper also questions attributions that would give Wollstonecraft an occasional brief notice on topics like boxing, but the kinds of reviews and the initials of different reviewers are remarkably consistent, as noted in Gerald P. Tyson's study of the journal's publisher, *Joseph Johnson: a Liberal Publisher* (Iowa City: University of Iowa Press, 1979). Finally Roper insists that truly anonymous material was part of the *Analytical Review,* as evidenced by unsigned final notices, but these are normally the abstracts from foreign periodicals, a special feature of the *Analytical Review.* Roper's 1978 book runs to the opposite extreme, attributing to Wollstonecraft (165) a review even Wardle's generous hypothesis did not countenance, one signed DM, Review of *Henry,* by the Author of *Arundel* [Richard Cumberland], *Analytical Review* 21 (May 1795), 511–16, when Wollstonecraft was romantically entangled with Gilbert Imlay and not reviewing. DM (and MD, its variant) are clearly the insignia of another reviewer.

The most thorough published study of attribution is Sally Stewart, "Mary Wollstonecraft's Contributions to the *Analytical Review,*"*Essays in Literature* 11/2 (Fall 1984), 187–99. Stewart points out some of the parallels between the M, W, and T reviews, suggesting these are by the same person. In addition to close stylistic echoes and content parallels, these reviews contain frequent internal cross references, indicating that one person was writing under the three signatures, and they dovetail with the style and concerns of Wollstonecraft's known works.

A hitherto unnoticed way to explain the T signature is that Wollstonecraft sometimes signs her name M Wt (e.g., Letters, 210); she may have dropped the W and T after her return because her usual signature then was Mary Imlay. Interestingly, two previously unnoticed brief reviews signed MI appear in March 1796: Review of *Maria; or, The Vicarage, Analytical Review* 23 (March 1796), 294; and Review of *Angelina: A Novel, in A Series of Letters,* by Mrs. Mary Robinson, *Analytical Review* 23 (March 1796), 293–4. (Letters, 385, verifies that Wollstonecraft had indeed read *Angelina.*) Shortly thereafter Wollstonecraft had her final break with Imlay; MI henceforth disappears and only M reviews continue until her death. These two reviews, however, are not stylistically distinctive enough to be conclusive. The editors of the *Works of Mary Wollstonecraft,* however, revert to a more conservative stance than Wardle or I take.

Because most of Wollstonecraft's reviews are brief, my references refer to the entire review. Most of Wollstonecraft's reviews are reprinted in *Works,* 7. For a more elaborated discussion, see my "Sensibility and the 'Walk of Reason': Mary Wollstonecraft's Literary Reviews as Cultural Critique," *Sensibility in Transformation: Creative Resistance to Sentiment from the Augustans to the Romantics,* ed. Syndy Conger McMillen (Rutherford: Fairleigh Dickinson University Press, 1990), 120–44, from which this essay draws.

3. See Genevieve Lloyd, *The Man of Reason: "Male" and "Female" in Western Philosophy* (Minneapolis: University of Minnesota Press, 1984).

4. For a discussion that places Wollstonecraft's views on novels and education alongside the views of other female educational reformers as well, such as Madame de Genlis, Clara Reeve, Catharine Macaulay, Anna Letitia Barbauld, Priscilla Wakefield, Hannah More, and Maria Edgeworth, see my "Impeccable Governesses, Rational Dames, and Moral Mothers: Mary Wollstonecraft and the Female Tradition in Georgian Children's Books," *Children's Literature*, 14, eds. Margaret Higonnet and Barbara Rosen (New Haven and London: Yale University Press, 1986), 31–59; and "'A Taste for Truth and Realities': Early Advice to Mothers on Books for Girls," *Children's Literature Association Quarterly* 12/3 (Fall 1987, 118–24).

5. I have argued further that Wollstonecraft's educative persona is at once maternal and self-reflexive in "Pedagogy as Self-Expression in Mary Wollstonecraft: Exorcising the Past, Finding a Voice," *The Private Self: Theory and Practice of Women's Autobiographical Writings*, ed. Shari Benstock (Chapel Hill: University of North Carolina Press, 1988), 192–210.

6. Letters, 178–9; Review of *The Young Lady of Fortune; or, Her Lover Gained by a Stratagem*, by A Lady, *Analytical Review* 4 (August 1789), 480 (T review); Review of *King Asa: a Poem in Six Books*, by T. May, *Analytical Review* 8 (December 1790) 464–5 (T is next signature); Review of *Ethelinde; or, The Recluse of the Lake*, by Charlotte Smith, *Analytical Review* 5 (December 1789), 484–6 (M is next signature).

7. Review of *Delia: a Pathetic and Interesting Tale*, *Analytical Review* 5 (Appendix 1789), 580 (M review); Review of *The Test of Honour: a Novel*, by A Young Lady, *Analytical Review* 4 (June 1789): 223 (M is next signature); Review of *The Parson's Wife: a Novel*, by A Lady *Analytical Review* 5 (October 1789), 216 (M is next signature); Review of *Mount Pelham: a Novel*, by the Author of Rosa de Montmorien, *Analytical Review* 3 (February 1789), 221–2 (W review); Review of *A Day in Turkey; or, The Russian Slaves: a Comedy*, by Mrs. Cowley, *Analytical Review* 13 (June 1792), 147–8 (W review).

8. Review of *Euphemia*, by Mrs. Charlotte Lennox, *Analytical Review* 8 (October 1790), 222–4 (T review); Review of *Henrietta of Gerstenfeld: a German Story*, *Analytical Review* I (June 1788), 209; Review of *Agitation; or, The Memoirs of George Woodford arid Lady Emma Melville*, by the Author of *The Ring* and *The False Friends*, *Analytical Review* 1 (June 1788), 208 (first issues unsigned).

9. Review of *The Vicar of Landsdowne; or Country Quarters: a Tale*, by Maria Regina Dalton, *Analytical Review* 4 (May 1789), 77 (W is next signature); Review of *The Cottage of Friendship: A Legendary Pastoral*, by Silviana Pastorella, *Analytical Review* 5 (October 1789), 216 (M review); Review of *Almeria Belmore: a Novel, in A Series of Letters*, by A Lady, *Analytical Review* 5 (December 1789), 488–9 (M review); Review of *The Fair Hibernian*, *Analytical Review* 5 (December 1789), 488 (M is next signature); Review of *Seymour Castle; or, The History of Julia and Cecilia: an Entertaining and Interesting Novel*, *Analytical Review* 5 (November 1789), 361 (M review).

10. Review of *The Fair Hibernian*; Review of *Juliet; or, The Cottager: a Novel, in A Series of Letters*, by A Lady, *Analytical Review* 3 (March 1789), 345 (M is next signature); Review of *Clarentine: a Novel*, [by Sarah Harriet Burney, Frances Burney's half-sister], *Analytical Review* 24 (October 1796), 404

(M review). Rereading *Clarentine* in 1807, Jane Austen was "surprised to find how foolish it is...It is full of unnatural conduct & forced difficulties, without striking merit of any kind," *Jane Austen's Letters to Her Sister Cassandra and Others*, ed. R. W Chapman, 2nd edn. (London: Oxford University Press, 1959), 180.

11. Review of *The Child of Woe*; Review of *Agitation*; Review of *The Bastile; or, History of Charles Townly: a Man of the World, Analytical Review* 4 (June 1789), 223 (M is next signature); Review of *Delia.*

12. Review of *The Child of Woe*; Review of *Emmeline, The Orphan of the Castle*, by Charlotte Smith, *Analytical Review* 1 (July 1788), 327–33 (M review); Review of *The Widow of Kent; or, The History of Mrs. Rowley, Analytical Review* 1 (July 1788), 208–9 (first issues unsigned); Review of *The Exiles; or, Memoirs of The Count of Cronstadt*, by Clara Reeve, *Analytical Review* 4 (June 1789), 221 (M is next signature).

13. Review of *Euphemia*; Review of *Calista: a Novel*, by Mrs. Johnson, *Analytical Review* 5 (September 1789), 98 (M is next signature); Review of *Adriano: or, The First of June, A Poem*, by the Author of *The Village Curate, Analytical Review* 7 (May 1790): 39–42 (M review).

14. Review of *Edward: Various Views of Human Nature, Taken from Life and Manners, Chiefly in England*, by [John Moore], *Analytical Review* 24 (January 1797), 23–5 (M review); Review of *Julia, a Novel: Interspersed with Some Poetical Pieces*, by Helen Maria Williams, *Analytical Review* 7 (May 1790), 97–100 (M is next signature); Review of *Ethelinde*; Review of *Almeria Belmore*; Review of *The Fair Hibernian*; VRW 5:256.

15. Review of *Heerfort and Clara: From the German, Analytical Review* 5 (December 1789), 487 (M is next signature); Review of *The Revolution: An Historical Play*, by Lieutenant Christian, *Analytical Review* 12 (April 1792), 431–4 (T review); Review of *The Negro Equalled by Few Europeans: Translated from the French, Analytical Review* 7 (August 1790), 462–3 (T is next signature); Review of *The Revolution*; Review of *Doncaster Races; or, The History of Miss Maitland: a Tale of Truth, in A Series of Letters*, by Alexander Bicknell, *Analytical Review* 4 (July 1789), 351 (W is next signature); Review of *Emmeline*; Review of *Doncaster Races.*

16. Emily W. Sunstein, *A Different Face: the Life of Mary Wollstonecraft* (New York: Harper and Row, 1975), 172; Roper, *Reviewing before the "Edinburgh,"* 168; Review of *Sketches of Society and Manners in Portugal, in A Series of Letters*, by Arthur William Costigan, *Analytical Review* 1 (August 1788), 451–7 (W review).

17. Review of *A Simple Story*, by Mrs. (Elizabeth) Inchbald, *Analytical Review* 10 (May 1791), 101–3 (M is next signature).

18. Review of *Celestina: A Novel*, by Charlotte Smith, *Analytical Review* 10 (July 1791), 409–15 (M review); Review of *Emmeline;* VRW 5:131.

19. Review of *Edward and Harriet; or, The Happy Recovery: a Sentimental Novel*, by A Lady, *Analytical Review* 1 (June 1788), 207–8 (first issues unsigned).

20. VRW 5:130, 195, 130, 132, 75, 130, 129.

21. Review of *Amusement: a Poetical Essay*, by Henry James Pye, *Analytical Review* 6 (March 1790), 326–7 (M is next signature); Wardle, *Mary Wollstonecraft*, 285; OP 7:7, 11.

22. Review of *Anna St. Ives: a Novel*, by Thomas Holcroft, *Analytical Review* 13 (May 1792), 72–6 (M review); VRW 5:76; Review of *Earl Goodwin: An Historical Play*, by Ann Yearsley, *Analytical Review* 11 (December 1791), 427–8 (M review); OP 7:8.

23. For other views of Wollstonecraft's style, see Gary Kelly, "Expressive Style and 'The Female Mind': Mary Wollstonecraft's *Vindication of the Rights of Woman*," *Studies on Voltaire and the Eighteenth Century: Transactions of the Fifth International Congress on the Enlightenment* 4 (1980), 1942–9; and Syndy Conger, "The Sentimental Logic of Wollstonecraft's Prose," *Prose Studies* 10/2 (September 1987), 143–58.

24. See, for example, Michael G. Cooke, *Acts of Inclusion: Studies Bearing on an Elementary Theory of Romanticism* (New York and London: Yale University Press, 1975), 159–63, and Jane Roland Martin, *Reclaiming a Conversation: the Ideal of the Educated Woman* (New Haven and London: Yale University Press, 1985), 70–102. Wollstonecraft herself observed that "reason and fancy are nearer akin than cold dulness is willing to allow," in Review of *Remarks on Forest Scenery, and Other Woodland Views, Relative Chiefly to Picturesque Beauty*, by William Gilpin, *Analytical Review* 10 (July 1791), 396–405 (M review).

25. Review of *Albert de Nordenshild; or, The Modern Alcibiades: a Novel Translated from the German* [by Carl Gottlob Cramer?], *Analytical Review* 24 (October 1796), 404 (M is next signature); Review of *Euphemia*; WWM 1:85; Review of *Original Letters of the Late Mr. Laurence Sterne, Never Before Published*, *Analytical Review* 1 (July 1788), 335 (W review).

26. Review of *New Travels into the Interior Parts of Africa, by the Way of the Cape of Good Hope, in the Years 1783, 84, and 85: Translated from the French of Le Vaillant*, *Analytical Review* 25 (May 1797), 464–75 (M review); Review of *Man As He Is: a Novel in Four Volumes* [by Robert Bage], *Analytical Review* 24 (October 1796), 398–403 (M is next signature); Review of *Earl Strongbow; or, The History of Richard de Clare and the Beautiful Geralda* [by James White], *Analytical Review* 3 (February 1789), 343–4 (M is next signature); Review of *The Italian; or, The Confessional of the Black Penitents: a Romance*, by Ann Radcliffe, *Analytical Review* 25 (May 1797), 516–20 (M review); Review of *Arundel*, by the Author of *The Observer* [Richard Cumberland], *Analytical Review* 3 (January 1789): 67–69 (W review); Review of *The Confidential Letters of Albert; from His First Attachment to Charlotte to Her Death: from "The Sorrows of Werter,"* *Analytical Review* 6 (April 1790), 466–7 (M is next signature); Review of *Hubert de Sevrac: a Romance of the Eighteenth Century*, by Mary Robinson, *Analytical Review* 25 (May 1797), 523 (M review).

27. Review of *Zelia in the Desart, from the French*, by the Lady who Translated *Adelaide and Theodore* [by Madame de Genlis], *Analytical Review* 4 (June 1789), 221 (M is next signature); Gerald P. Tyson, Review of *Reviewing before the "Edinburgh," 1788–1802* by Derek Roper, *Eighteenth-Century Studies* 14/1 (Fall 1980), 71; VRW 5:199, 161.

7

BARBARA TAYLOR

The religious foundations of Mary Wollstonecraft's feminism

> Gracious Creator of the whole human race! hast thou created such a being as
> woman, who can trace Thy wisdom in Thy works, and feel that Thou alone
> art by Thy nature exalted above her, for no better purpose . . . [than] to submit
> to man, her equal – a being who, like her, was sent into the world to acquire
> virtue? Can she consent to be occupied merely to please him – merely to adorn
> the earth – when her soul is capable of rising to Thee?   (VRW 5:136)

Admirers of Mary Wollstonecraft are often reluctant to see her as a religious
thinker. This should not surprise us. The reiterated "appeals to God and
virtue," in *A Vindication of the Rights of Woman* are "a dead letter to
feminists now," a leading feminist critic tells us, and if by dead letter is
meant a failed communication, then it is certainly true that of all aspects of
Wollstonecraft's thought it is her religious faith that has failed to speak to
modern interpreters.[1] Most studies do no more than gesture toward it, and
then usually dismiss it as ideological baggage foisted on her by her times,
with no positive implications for her views on women. *A Vindication of
the Rights of Woman* is generally located in a tradition of Enlightenment
humanism that is assumed to have been at least indifferent to religion, if not
actively hostile to it.

So it is startling, on looking closely at the *Rights of Woman,* to find that
it contains at least fifty discussions of religious themes, ranging from brief
statements on one or other doctrinal point to extended analyses of women's
place within a divinely-ordered moral universe. Nor are these discussions in
any sense peripheral to the main message of the text. If Wollstonecraft's faith
becomes a dead letter to us, then so does much of her feminism, so closely
are they harnessed together. The famous call for a "revolution of female
manners" in the *Rights of Woman* on close inspection proves to be first and
foremost a summons to women to a right relationship with their Maker. "In
treating . . . of the manners of women, let us, disregarding sensual arguments,
trace what we should endeavor to make them in order to cooperate . . . with
the Supreme Being" (VRW 5:90):

99

...for...if they be really capable of acting like rational creatures, let them not be treated like slaves; or, like the brutes who are dependent on the reason of man, when they associate with him; but cultivate their minds, give them the salutary sublime curb of principle, and let them attain conscious dignity by feeling themselves only dependent on God. (VRW 5:105)

It is through the exercise of "a rational will that only bows to God" that women may achieve that self-respect on which inner freedom is founded. "These may be Utopian dreams," Wollstonecraft writes, but "thanks to that Being who impressed them on my soul, and gave me sufficient strength of mind to dare to exert my own reason, till, becoming dependent only on Him for the support of my virtue, I view, with indignation, the mistaken notions that enslave my sex" (VRW 5:105). It was thanks to God, in other words, that Mary Wollstonecraft became a feminist.

Wollstonecraft's family were inactive members of the Church of England, and according to her husband and biographer, William Godwin, she "received few lessons of religion in her youth."[2] Nonetheless, for the first twenty-eight years of her life she was a regular churchgoer and her first published work, *Thoughts on the Education of Daughters* (1787), was steeped in orthodox attitudes, advocating "fixed principles of religion" and warning of the dangers of rationalist speculation and deism. For women in particular, the young Wollstonecraft argued, clear-cut religious views were essential: "for a little refinement only leads a woman into the wilds of romance, if she is not religious; nay more, there is no true sentiment without it, nor perhaps any other effectual check to the passions" (TED 4:33). In the same year that *Thoughts* was published, however, Wollstonecraft stopped attending church, and by the time she produced her last published book, *A Short Residence in Sweden,* she had performed an apparent volte face, writing approvingly of freethinkers who "deny the divinity of Jesus Christ, and...question the necessity or utility of the christian system" (SR 6:276). The abandonment of christian orthodoxy, however, only served to underline her commitment to what had become a highly personal faith. "Her religion," as Godwin wrote in his *Memoirs* of her shortly after her death, "was almost entirely of her own creation. But she was not on that account less attached to it, or the less scrupulous in discharging what she considered as its duties" (Memoirs, 215).[3]

At the time Godwin met Wollstonecraft she had not been a churchgoer for over four years. Nonetheless, on that occasion they managed to have a row about religion in which, as Godwin recalled, "her opinions approached much nearer to the received one, than mine" (Memoirs, 236). When they met again, in 1796, Godwin was an atheist. This meeting was much more successful than the first: they became friends, then lovers, then husband and wife – and meanwhile went on disagreeing about religion. "How can you blame me for taking refuge in the idea of a God, when I despair of finding sincerity here on earth?" Wollstonecraft demanded at one low point two months before her death.[4] At any rate, little as he would have wanted it, it was Godwin who had the last word, since after his wife's premature death it was left to him to produce an account of her religious beliefs in his *Memoirs*.

Wollstonecraft's religion, Godwin wrote, was "in reality, little allied to any system of forms" and "was founded rather in taste, than in the niceties of polemical discussion":

> Her mind constitutionally attached itself to the sublime and the amiable. She found an inexpressible delight in the beauties of nature, and in the splendid reveries of the imagination. But nature itself, she thought, would be no better than a vast blank, if the mind of the observer did not supply it with an animating soul. When she walked amidst the wonders of nature, she was accustomed to converse with her God. To her mind he was pictured as not less amiable, generous and kind, than great, wise and exalted. (Memoirs, 215)

This representation of Wollstonecraft's deity as a wishful mental projection owes too much to Godwin's own religious skepticism to be wholly reliable.[5] Her friend Mary Hays's alternative depiction of Wollstonecraft's God as "a being higher, more perfect, than visible nature" whom she "adored . . . amidst the beauties of Nature, or . . . in the still hour of recollection," better captures Wollstonecraft's *credo*.[6] Both Godwin and Hays rightly stress the central role of passion and imagination in Wollstonecraft's theology. Both also – much less plausibly – represent her as indifferent to theological controversy. Her "faith relied not upon critical evidence or laborious investigation," Hays claimed,[7] which in Godwin's version became a depressingly condescending portrait of his wife's mind in action. "She adopted one opinion," Godwin wrote, "and rejected another, spontaneously, by a sort of tact, and the force of a cultivated imagination; and yet, though perhaps, in the strict sense of the term, she reasoned little, it is surprising what a degree of soundness is to be found in her determinations" (Memoirs, 272–3).

"She reasoned little . . . ": and this of the woman who translated and reviewed theological works in three languages, was conversant with major theological debates of her period, and who consistently argued that true religion was not a mere matter of enthusiastic sentiment but rather "a governing principle of conduct, drawn from self-knowledge, and rational opinion respecting the attributes of God" (VRW 5:184). This refusal to take

Wollstonecraft seriously as a religious thinker was symptomatic of the anxieties aroused in Godwin by his wife's intellectual status. But it was also indicative of an important shift of opinion in the eighteenth century, as religious belief became increasingly aligned with the feminine and both came under the rule of sentiment, what Godwin described as the "empire of feeling." In the second edition of his *Memoirs* Godwin revised his account of Wollstonecraft's "intellectual character" so as to make some of these connections more explicit. The difference between the sexes, he argued there, corresponds to the psychological opposition between reason and emotion – and he and Wollstonecraft exemplified this divide, he being dominated by "habits of deduction" while she enjoyed an "intuitive sense of the pleasures of the imagination" which eventually aroused his own emotions as well: "Her taste awakened mine; her sensibility determined me to a careful development of my feelings" (Memoirs, 276–7). So while the Philosopher could not follow his wife into her religious beliefs, he nonetheless became a convert to the deep sense of personal truth reflected in them, the "fearless and unstudied veracity" of Wollstonecraft's womanly heart.

This portrait of the woman of sensibility (at one point Godwin called Wollstonecraft a "female Werther") tells us less about Wollstonecraft than it does about prevailing sexual mores – and Godwin's haphazard attempts to keep his wife's stormy history within the boundaries of them. This is not to deny that Wollstonecraft enjoyed donning the cloak of female Wertherism at times. But the idea of a uniquely feminine emotionality was anathema to her, a central target of her feminism. Religious sentimentality of the kind typically associated with women she particularly disdained. Drawing a line between this sort of "irrational enthusiasm" and the deep emotions of the true believer was not easy, however, and Wollstonecraft worked hard at clarifying the distinction. Her ambiguous attitude toward sensibility (which has so received much attention from recent commentators) is best understood in this context, as part of her wider endeavor to define an authentic religious subjectivity. What shape does a woman's inner life take when it is lived in a right relationship with her Maker?

For a feminist, this question inevitably raised issues of power and entitlement. The centrality of religion to Wollstonecraft's worldview is evident in virtually every aspect of her thought, from her uncompromising egalitarianism to her hostility toward British commercialism – modern mammon, as she saw it – to her ardent faith in an imminent age of universal freedom and happiness. The utopian optimism coloring her politics was basically Christian in origin, although marked by other influences too, most notably Rousseauism. Elsewhere I have traced in detail the religious roots of her radical *credo*, in its many diverse manifestations.[8] In this essay I concentrate specifically on her feminist ideals, as enunciated in *A Vindication of the Rights of Woman* (1792) and prefigured in her first novel, *Mary, A Fiction* (1788). Historians seeking to identify the origins of modern Western feminism have generally located them in secular developments: the rise of liberal political ideals, the reformist intellectual programme inaugurated by Enlightenment, the expressive opportunities opened to women by the eighteenth-century expansion of print culture. These, *inter alia*, are important factors. But for proto-feminist lines of argument with the longest pedigree and greatest ideological clout, we must look first to religion, or rather to that body of Christian doctrine which, at its most consistent, had strongly positive implications for women's private and public status. Pushed to the limit of their revisionary potential, teachings pertaining to the equality of souls and human likeness to God offered female believers a vision of sacralized selfhood sharply at odds with worldly subordination. Gender distinctions and their social consequences were both thrown into question. "Human nature itself, which is complete in both sexes, has been made in the image of God," Saint Augustine had written, and thus in the spirit "there is no sex,"[9] or as Simone de Beauvoir put it with characteristic trenchancy centuries later, "religion.... cancels the advantage of the penis".[10] Attacking misogynist representations of women as weakly infantile, Wollstonecraft repeatedly accused their inventors of purveying the Muslim viewpoint that women "have not souls" (VRM 5:45; VRW 5:73,88) (a popular misreading of Islamic doctrine at the time). As children of God, we are all equal in His sight, Wollstonecraft reminded readers of the *Rights of Woman*; thus "[i]t be not philosophical to speak of sex when the soul is mentioned" (VRW 5:103).

The appeal of this stance to pro-woman thinkers long antedated Wollstonecraft, and has long survived her. Feminism, it is worth recalling, has for most of its history been deeply embedded in religious belief. Eighteenth- and nineteenth-century western feminists were nearly all active Christians, and even the more secularized varieties of feminism that emerged in western societies in the 1970s still carried powerful undercurrents of religious belief. Obviously, the religions which have engaged feminists internationally over the centuries have been so varied that any attempt to offer a general account of them would be foolhardy. But given the centrality of Wollstonecraft to the self-image of western feminism, understanding her theology may give us more than local insights into the religious impulse as it has operated across the feminist tradition.

In Wollstonecraft's Protestant England, the spiritual equality of women had long been an important minority theme. Puritan sects in particular, with their fierce emphasis on the democracy of God's grace, had provided generations of female believers with a language of spiritual self-assertion; and even the Church of England had harbored godly feminists. "Whatever... Reasons Men may have for despising Women, and keeping them in Ignorance and Slavery, it can't be from their having learnt to do so in Holy Scripture," the High Anglican Mary Astell claimed in 1700, adding stoutly that "the Bible is for, and not against us..."[11] Calls to a higher life – whether it meant an intensification of female piety in the home or even, as in the case of seventeenth- and eighteenth-century women preachers, leaving their households to spread God's Word – was a route to enhanced self-esteem and moral status, and sometimes to the potential subversion of Female Duty. "I chose to obey God rather than man," one female preacher wrote on abandoning her husband in order to serve her Maker,[12] and the appeal of such forms of religious obedience to many insubordinate female spirits is easily imagined.

The religious revival which swept Britain from the 1730s on carried such aspirations in its wake, although with mixed results. The decline of the militant spirit which had fostered the revival, combined with stricter policing of sexual divisions within its ranks, led to women's claims often being pushed to the margins of the movement or outside evangelicalism entirely. By the 1780s, at the point when Wollstonecraft began pronouncing on such matters, St. Paul's strictures against the ministry of women had become a staple of popular sermonizing. The eruption of female voices that occurred during the early stages of the French Revolution intensified repressive criticism. "The influence of religion is to be exercised with discretion [by women]," the leading Evangelical tractarian Hannah More (one of Wollstonecraft's fiercest detractors) warned in 1799, since "a female Polemic wanders almost as far from the limits prescribed to her sex, as a female Machiavel."[13]

These fluctuations in the fortunes of female believers were accompanied by changing perceptions of the significance of gender in the Christian self. The soul may be sexless, but its earthly vehicles patently are not: a fact assigned increasing significance over the course of the eighteenth century. From the mid-century on preachers of all stripes could be heard arguing that female religious feeling was intrinsically more powerful than that of men, a view reinforced by the idealization of pity as the primary Christian sentiment. The cult of feminine sensibility, evident in both fiction and moral literature, derived largely from this source. Womankind, the Newcastle vicar John Brown explained in a sermon delivered in 1765, has a greater "sensibility of pain" than men, and thus a greater capacity to emphathize with the sufferings of others, while at the same time taking its "highest Delight... in a grateful Subordination to its Protector."[14] These emotional predispositions, combined with the "calmer" lives women lead, mean that while "in man, Religion is generally the Effect of Reason" in women "it may almost be called the Effect of Nature" (13). Such innate piety, Brown concluded (on a note heard with increasing frequency over succeeding decades) gave women a uniquely authoritative role in moral life, since

> a Mind thus gentle and thus adorned exalts subordination itself into the Power of Superiority and Command... the Influence and irresistible Force of Virtue.
>
> (15)

Women may be men's inferiors in social and political life, but in matters of the spirit they are preeminent. This line of argument clearly had attractions as a defense against women's secular claims. But it could also pose serious hazards for sexual conservatives, particularly in its more militant formulations. Wollstonecraft's first novel, *Mary, A Fiction* exemplified these dangers. *Mary*, published in 1788, features a heroine of such radiant piety that she outshines the feebler moral lights of all around her. Even as a child, Mary's emotional life is dominated by "devotional sentiments" (M 1:11); as a young adult, which is where the novel finds her, she is, if anything, even more saintly, with a mind focused always on God and a heart so attuned to the needs and sufferings of her fellow man that for her no "sensual gratification" can compare to the joy of feeling her "eyes moistened after having comforted the unfortunate" (M 1:59). This compassionate sensibility benefits everyone around her (although they remain disappointingly ungrateful) while at the same time bestowing an "enthusiastic greatness" on Mary's soul. She "glanced from earth to heaven," Wollstonecraft tells us, and "caught the light of truth" which, like her author, she was then ever eager to shed on others – "her tongue was ever the faithful interpreter of her heart" (M 1:59). And why should Mary keep silent, when heart and soul have so much to say? Christian militancy irresistibly posed the question, and even women ostensibly opposed to all that Wollstonecraft stood for, often found themselves responding to the call in unconventional ways. Hannah More may have held female polemicists to be ungodly, but this didn't prevent her from publishing tens of thousands of pious works exhorting women to use their superior moral influence against Satan, the slave trade, and French "democratical" politics. Soon (although not in Wollstonecraft's lifetime) many women Evangelicals began explicitly linking doctrines of female moral leadership to demands for practical improvements in women's own political and legal status.

Being a proper Christian woman, then, was a paradoxical affair, bestowing important ethical prerogatives to be exercised only under conditions of psychological and practical submission. In Book v of *Emile*, his famous statement on women's nature and entitlements, Rousseau had argued that a woman should always defer to the religious views of her father or husband,[15] and most women probably agreed – "conforming", as Wollstonecraft put it, "as a dependent creature should, to the ceremonies of the Church which she was brought up in, piously believing that wiser heads than her own have settled that business..."(VRW 5:118). Certainly mainstream moralists were as likely to denounce women with independent religious views as they were to condemn the godless. The immensely influential handbook of advice to young women written by Dr. John Gregory (and criticized by Wollstonecraft in the *Rights of Woman*) specifically counseled them against all religious study while at the same time emphasizing that "even those men who are themselves unbelievers dislike infidelity in *you.*" Lack of piety in women, Gregory noted, was taken as "proof of that hard and masculine spirit, which of all your faults, *we* [men] dislike the most" while its presence was men's best security for "that female virtue in which *they* are most interested," i.e., chastity.[16] James Fordyce similarly condemned any sign of intellectual independence in women while at the same time recommending public devotions as a way of displaying female face and form to most pleasing effect.[17] "Why are women to be thus bred up with a desire of conquest?" was Wollstonecraft's irritable response to all this: "Do religion and virtue offer no stronger motives, no brighter reward?" (VRW 5:164).

Women conduct-book writers by contrast tended to emphasize women's intellectual relationship to God, urging close study of the Bible and familiarity with major theological works. Women writers published biblical commentary, entered into public debate with male theologians, and wrote essays in which Female Duty was spelled out with fierce moral stringency. The brand of female devotion promoted by these women was based on mind as well as heart, and in this they were clearly spiritual sisters to the heroine of Wollstonecraft's *Mary, A Fiction*, and also to the redoubtable Mrs. Mason of Wollstonecraft's *Original Stories From Real Life*, written for children. Mrs. Mason, a Christian propagandist with a formidable sense of her own self-worth, tells her little pupils that they must learn not only to love God but also to mimic Him. "[T]o attain any thing great," she informs them, "a model must be held up to our understanding, and engage our affections" in such a way that we learn "to copy his attributes" and "imitate Him." "We are his children when we try to resemble Him...convinced that truth and goodness must constitute the very essence of the soul..." (OS 4:423, 431). The tone is conventionally didactic, but to urge a little girl to find "dignity and happiness" from mimicking God when the most to which she was generally meant to aspire was (in the words of the *Rights of Woman*) "to model her soul to suit the frailities of her [husband]" (VRW 5:101) was not just pious conventionalism. This affirmation of women's capacity to apprehend and identify with the divine, expressed in nearly all female writings of the period, was so fundamental to women's sense of ethical worth, and so far-reaching in its egalitarian implications, that it can properly be described as one of the founding impulses of feminism.

The young Mary of Wollstonecraft's first novel is clearly indebted to these protofeminist elements of English Protestantism while at the same time rejecting evangelical extremism and Establishment reaction. "The cant of weak enthusiasts have made the consolations of Religion ... appear ... ridiculous," Wollstonecraft wrote to her sister in 1784,[18] and by the time she wrote *Mary, A Fiction* this view was hardening into a wholesale condemnation of all varieties of Christian "fanaticism." The fictional Mary begins her career as a professing Anglican with an evangelical tinge. But as the novel progresses she becomes increasingly unorthodox. Like her author, she feels closest to God not in church but in the contemplation of His works, particularly "the grand or solemn features of Nature" in which her sensitive heart delights. She does not scorn Scripture, but nor does she unthinkingly accept it, for "her mind was not like a mirror" merely reflecting what was before it, but an instrument of rational criticism. Traveling in Portugal, she enters a Catholic church in the company of some "deistical" Englishmen, and then:

> Mary thought of both the subjects, the Romish tenets, and the deistical doubts; and though not a sceptic, thought it right to examine the evidence on which her faith was built. She read Butler's Analogy, and some other authors: and these researches made her a christian from conviction, and she learned charity, particularly with respect to sectaries; saw that apparently good and solid arguments might take their rise from different points of view; and she rejoiced to find that those she should not concur with had some reason on their side.
>
> (M 1:29)

Mary, in other words, is well on her way to becoming a typical Enlightenment intellectual, eschewing blind faith and evangelical purism in favor of "rational religious impulses" and liberal toleration. The trajectory roughly followed Wollstonecraft's own. Four years before the publication of *Mary* she had moved with her sisters to Newington Green, north of London, to run a girls' school there. Newington Green had long been a hotbed of religious and political radicalism; its presiding spirit at the time of Wollstonecraft's arrival was Richard Price, minister to the local community of Rational Dissenters (or Unitarians, as they became known). Price and his fellow Unitarian, the Birmingham scientist and preacher Joseph Priestley, were leading figures in the English radical intelligentsia, and while Wollstonecraft never became a Unitarian she attended Price's chapel, studied his sermons, and came to deeply admire his personal and political integrity. Price was "one of the best of men," she wrote shortly after his death, in the *Rights of Woman* (VRW 5:85).

Rational Dissent was a variety of Protestant Nonconformity forged by and for the *avant-garde* educated middle class. The most cerebral of the Nonconformist sects, Rational Dissent offered its adherents a bracing brew of Lockean psychology, Newtonian cosmology, rationalist morality and reform politics. Its creed was anti-trinitarian (the divinity of Christ was denied) and its deity was a benign Supreme Being with a judicious regard for all His creatures and no taste for hellfire. Calvinism, with its savagely anti-humanist ethos, was repudiated in favor of a vision of mankind as essentially good and inherently perfectible. "We must get entirely clear of all the notions...of original sin...to leave room for the expansion of the human heart," as Wollstonecraft wrote in 1794 (HMV 6:21–2).

In common with all Nonconformists, Rational Dissenters were subject to the Test Acts – discriminatory laws barring them from holding office under the Crown or in municipal corporations, and from taking degrees at Oxford and Cambridge. The struggle to repeal the Acts, which lasted many decades, was at its height when Wollstonecraft was attending Price's chapel, and the political stridency with which it infused the Unitarians' rhetoric clearly struck a chord in their young fellow-traveler. The analogy between the oppression of women and the penalties suffered by Dissenters was readily drawn, and Wollstonecraft herself drew it in the *Rights of Woman* (where she also claimed however that both Dissenters and women were psychologically deformed by their secondary status). But more important for her feminism was Unitarianism's emphasis on private reasoned judgment as the foundation of true religion: a principle to which the circumstances of both Dissenters and women gave real political bite. The fictive Mary's cool weighing of doctrinal choices, and her insistence that all religious beliefs (including those of "sectaries," i.e. Dissenters) be respected, reflected this viewpoint – its radicalism much heightened in this instance by the sex of its proponent. By 1790, in her *A Vindication of the Rights of Men*, Wollstonecraft was prepared to be more explicit. "I look into my own mind," she wrote,

> my heart is human, beats quick with human sympathies – and I FEAR God. . . . I fear that sublime power, whose motive for creating me must have been wise and good; and I submit to the moral laws which my reason deduces from this view of my dependence on him. It is not his power that I fear – it is not to an arbitrary will, but to unerring *reason* I submit.　　　　(VRM 5:34)

"[T]o act according to the dictates of reason," she wrote further on, "is to conform to the law of God" (VRM 5:51).

This appeal to the inner authority of the individual believer was at the heart of all varieties of Enlightened theism. "*Intra te quaere Deum,*" as Basil Willey has noted, was the motto of the age:

look for God within thyself. And what exactly would you find when you looked within? Not the questionable shapes revealed by psycho-analysis, but something much more reassuring: the laws of God and Nature inscribed upon the heart...[19]

The will of God, as Rousseau put it in his immensely influential credo of the Vicar of Savoyard, is "written by nature with ineffaceable characters in the depths of my heart. I have only to consult myself..."[20] Wollstonecraft's fictive Mary, contemplating scenes of public devotion, observes that true religion "does not consist in ceremonies" but in doing good and loving God. She, like her author, experiences her deepest religious emotions during moments of solitary contemplation, when the absence of all loved ones makes her particularly "sensible of the presence of her Almighty Friend" (M 1:27).

Rational Dissent did not go so far as this in rejecting religious observance, but its political case for toleration was founded on the same reverence for personal conviction. "Every man ought to be left to follow his conscience because then only he acts virtuously," Price argued. [21] No earthly power has any rights over our private judgments, and no restriction on conscience is ever legitimate. "Liberty," Price wrote in his 1758 *Review of the Principal Questions and Difficulties in Morals* (with which Wollstonecraft was clearly familiar) "is the power of acting and determining: And it is self-evident, that where such a power is wanting, there can be no moral capacities."[22] Liberty and reason, Price went on, "constitute the capacity of virtue"; or as Wollstonecraft put it: "the conduct of an accountable being must be regulated by the operations of its own reason; or on what foundation rests the throne of God?...Liberty is the mother of virtue" (VRW 5:105). Only those free to think and act for themselves will take their place by God's throne. Rousseau's ideal woman may have expected men to legislate for her in religious matters, or Milton's Eve may have willingly deferred to male spiritual authority – "God is thy law, thou mine: to know no more / Is women's happiest knowledge and her praise" Eve warbles away to Adam in *Paradise Lost* – but against these models of feminine self-abnegation Wollstonecraft invoked the protestant imperative for direct dealing with one's Maker. If no priest may stand between creature and Creator, why should a mere man stand between a woman and her God?

> For if it be allowed that women were destined by Providence to acquire human virtues, and, by the exercise of their understandings, that stability of character which is the firmest ground to rest our future hopes upon, they must be permitted to turn to the foundation of light, and not forced to shape their course by the twinkling of a mere satellite. (VRW 5:89)

Only a soul "perfected by the exercise of its own reason" is "stamped with the heavenly image," but "man ever placed between [woman] and reason, she is always represented as only created to see through a gross medium" and so is estranged from her own moral potential. This alienation from grace is the nadir of female oppression, since it denies to women that inner mirroring of God's virtues which leads to ethical fulfilment. Universal reason is God's gift to all, the manifestation of His presence within, but men's jealous claims to reason's prerogatives would damn women to spiritual ignorance, and thus flout God's purpose. For if the Father of All Creation smiles equally on all His offspring, who are men to raise themselves to a higher position in His sight? "Let us then, as children of the same parent . . . reason together, and learn to submit to the authority of Reason . . ." Wollstonecraft urges her readers. For "they alone are subject to blind authority who have no reliance on their own strength. They are free – who will be free!" (VRW 5:170–1).

Seen in this light, women's emancipation is not only a *desideratum* for this life, but the chief prerequisite for women's eternal salvation. This emphasis in the *Rights of Woman* on secular gains as a means to spiritual goals is possibly one of the most difficult to appreciate today, yet Wollstonecraft's text is suffused with it. The line of argument is clear. If the human soul were not immortal – if our brief existence invariably terminated at death – then female oppression, however censurable in itself, would be only one more of those infinite woes which make up our lot in this vale of tears. Social revolution throws into relief the injustice of women's subordinate status and offers opportunities for change; but it is the prospect of life beyond all such mortal contrivances which makes women's sufferings as a sex wholly reprehensible – for in enslaving women on earth men have also been denying them heaven. Rational Dissent held mortal existence to be a probationary state, a trial period, from which the souls of the virtuous alone would emerge into eternal bliss. Wollstonecraft consistently endorsed this view, and then pointed out its implications. For if women are disallowed the conditions necessary for the acquisition of virtue, then "how [they] are to exist in that state where there is neither to be marrying nor giving in marriage, we are not told":

> For though moralists have agreed that the tenor of life seems to prove that *man* is prepared . . . for a future state, they constantly concur in advising *woman* only to provide for the present. Gentleness, docility, and a spaniel-like affection are, on this ground, consistently recommended as the cardinal virtues of the sex; and disregarding the arbitrary economy of nature, one writer has declared that it is masculine for a woman to be melancholy. She was created to be the toy of man, his rattle, and it must jingle in his ears whenever, dismissing reason, he chooses to be amused. (VRW 5:102).

But "if morality has an eternal foundation" then "whoever sacrifices virtue, strictly so called, to present convenience . . . lives only for the passing day" at the expense of futurity. To propitiate men, women neglect absolute morality in favor of the relative merits – chastity, humility, diffidence – assigned to their sex, and the result is their spiritual nullification. "I wish to sum up what I have said in a few words," Wollstonecraft wrote in conclusion to the third chapter of the *Rights of Woman*, in what could well serve as a *coda* to the entire text: "for I here throw down my gauntlet, and deny the existence of sexual virtues. . . . For man and woman, truth must be the same" (VRW 5:120).

Here indeed is the puritan voice, stiff with ethical rigor. Moral absolutism of this kind has always had strong appeal for feminists, wary of the laid-back pragmatism of elite sophisticates, and hostile to the traditionalist morality of Burkean conservatives. It is all very well, as Wollstonecraft told Burke, for those in power to pretend to moral instincts which are somehow, mysteriously, always in accord with the *status quo*; for the disenfranchised, however, the assertion of ethical imperatives that transcend and potentially subvert the moral commonsense of an age is a powerful weapon against established authority. "It is time to separate unchangeable morals from local manners" she insisted in the *Rights of Woman* (5:114), to bring all humanity under God's law. But as far as women are concerned,

> the fanciful female character, so prettily drawn by poets and novelists, demanding the sacrifice of truth and sincerity; virtue [to them] becomes a relative idea, having no other foundation than utility; and of that utility men pretend arbitrarily to judge, shaping it to their own convenience. (VRW 5:120)

Where there is no absolute standard of right, power maintains its own codes of expedience. Men, like all despots, seek grounds for their rule in precept and custom, so that the ruled appear duty-bound to obey. Wollstonecraft's refutation of this authoritarianism further revealed her debt to Rational Dissent, and in particular to its anti-voluntarist view of the respective obligations of God and mankind. Anti-voluntarist theology, at its simplest, holds that the power of God is constrained by His goodness; or as Price put it, in his *Review of Morals*, God's "sovereign authority" derives "not merely from his almighty power" but from the "infinite excellencies of his nature as the foundation of reason and wisdom".[23] Worship, in other words, is not blind submission to an omnipotent force, for (in Wollstonecraft's words) "what good effect can the latter mode of worship have on the moral conduct of a rational being?" (VRW 5:115). Conservatives like Edmund Burke might hold that unthinking deference was authority's due, but for Wollstonecraft, as she told Burke in the *Rights of Men*, true worship was never servile but a rational reverence for those divine perfections that human virtues mimic. It is not to arbitrary might but to Virtue itself to which she submits:

> Submit – yes; I disregard the charge of arrogance, to the law that regulates his just resolves; and the happiness I pant after must be the same in kind, and produced by the same exertions as his – though unfeigned humility overwhelms every idea that would presume to compare the goodness which the most exalted being could acquire, with the grand source of life and bliss.   (VRM 5:34)

We love God because He deserves our love, not because He commands it; and the fruit of this worship is that "enlightened self-love" which is every believer's entitlement.

This emphasis on *esteem* as the key element in religious devotion had important consequences beyond the theological. For if it is not power but virtue that elicits respect in the divine sphere, why should this not be true of intimate human relationships as well? "It were to be wished," Wollstonecraft writes, "that women would cherish an affection for their husbands, founded on the same principle that devotion [to God] ought to rest upon" – which sounds shockingly retrograde until one realizes her precise meaning: that husbands, like deities, should be loved inasmuch – and only inasmuch – as they possess virtues entitling them to wifely respect. "No other firm base is there under heaven – for let [women] beware of the fallacious light of sentiment; too often used as a softer phrase for sensuality" (VRW 5:115). It is not power, romance, or – most emphatically – sexual desire which should tie women to their menfolk, but only shared love of the Good.

Wollstonecraft's astringent attitude to heterosexual love has attracted criticism from some modern feminists, repelled by what they regard as her chilly prudishness. Perusing the *Rights of Woman*, the grounds for this criticism would seem incontestable. "The depravity of the appetite which brings the sexes together," Wollstonecraft writes, is deplorable – inside marriage as well as out. "Nature must ever be the standard of taste – the gauge of appetite-yet how grossly is nature insulted by the voluptuary" (VRW 5:208) which is redeemable only, and barely, by the natural requirements of reproduction. "The feelings of a parent mingling with an instinct merely animal, give it dignity" by mixing "a little mind and affection with a sensual gust" (VRW 5:208); but once children have arrived the duties of parenthood are incompatible with further erotic indulgence.

> In order to fulfil the duties of life, and to be able to pursue with vigour the various employments which form the moral character, a master and mistress of a family ought not to continue to love each other with passion. I mean to say that they ought not to indulge those emotions which disturb the order of

society, and engross the thoughts that should otherwise be employed....I will go still further, and advance, without dreaming of a paradox, that an unhappy marriage is often advantageous to a family, and that the neglected wife is, in general, the best mother.... (VRW 5:99)

Even for an age of intensifying sexual restrictions, this was pretty repressive stuff. And it is views like these, unsurprisingly, that have led scholars like Mary Poovey and Cora Kaplan to brand Wollstonecraft a sexual puritan. The *Rights of Woman*, Kaplan has eloquently and influentially argued, "expresses a violent antagonism to the sexual, it exaggerates the importance of the sensual in the everyday life of women and betrays the most profound anxiety about the rupturing force of female sexuality."[24] Mary Poovey, in her major study of Wollstonecraft's relationship to eighteenth-century sexual ideology, develops a similar argument, pointing out that Wollstonecraft's sexual outlook was heavily inflected by the repressive codes of propriety characteristic of the new middle class.[25] In one sense this is clearly right. Both in spirit and content, much of Wollstonecraft's anti-erotic rhetoric can easily be recognized as part of that bourgeois project – so characteristic of the eighteenth-century middle class – to enhance middle-rank standing by contrasting its sober-minded decency to the moral laxity of the idle rich. The image of the eroticized woman to be found throughout Wollstonecraft's writings is thus both polemical and class specific: a caricature of aristocratic womanhood common to virtually all middle-class morality literature. "Love, in their bosoms, taking place of every nobler passion," Wollstonecraft writes of "women of fashion," "their sole ambition is to be fair, to raise emotion instead of inspiring respect; and this ignoble desire, like the servility in absolute monarchies, destroys all strength of character" (VRW 5:105).

There is far more to be said on this question of class bias in Wollstonecraft's sexual thinking than I have space for here. But the emphasis given to it by Kaplan, Poovey, and likeminded commentators has been at the expense of a larger historical point. Evaluating Wollstonecraft's erotic ideals in isolation from her wider philosophic commitments, particularly her religious convictions, obscures their psycho-ethical content and reduces their revisionary force. Like all eighteenth-century moralists, Wollstonecraft's ideas about sexual love were not freestanding but embedded in a universalist ethical creed, which in her case meant in her idiosyncratic brand of enlightened Christianity. Erotic attachments were not (or at least not only) the stuff of private passion and politicking, as they are for modern feminists, but modes of psycho-ethical relating – to oneself as well as to others – with transcendent significance. For Wollstonecraft, in other words, love was a sacred affair.

Reflecting on what has been said thus far about the pivotal part played by religion in Wollstonecraft's feminism, it is not difficult to see why this was so. Striving to free women not just from male power but from the inner corruption induced by oppression, the aspect of female love that concerned Wollstonecraft the most was its impact on women's moral destiny and ethical self-image: matters for which, in the 1790s, religion still provided the most compelling paradigm. For Wollstonecraft, what was at stake in heterosexual love was not just what a woman was permitted to *feel*, but who she was able to *be*: what kind of feminine self is inscribed in the erotic bond, and how does this love bear on the infinitely higher attachments of which every soul is capable? The answer the *Rights of Woman gives* is unequivocal: "[I]f [women] be moral beings, let them have a chance to become intelligent; and let love to man be only a part of that glowing flame of universal love, which, after encircling humanity, mounts in graceful incense to God" (VRW 5:136).

For Wollstonecraft, loving God is the basis of a rightly ordered moral personality. Unlike the Rational Dissenters of her circle who, anxious to avoid "enthusiasm," generally confined their devotional sentiments to the judiciously appreciative, for Wollstonecraft to know God is to adore Him – and this not only because His perfections inspire adoration but because the epistemic impulse toward Him is essentially erotic in character. The love Wollstonecraft had for her Maker, according to Mary Hays, was a "delicious sentiment," a "sublime enthusiasm" fueled by a "fervent imagination, shaping itself to ideal excellence, and panting after good unalloyed."[26] It was this passionate idealizing attachment that, for Wollstonecraft, was the emotional basis of ethical self-identity. "The mind of man is formed to admire perfection," she wrote to her sister Everina in 1784, "and perhaps our longing after it and the pleasure we take in observing a shadow of it is a *faint line* of that Image that was first stamped on the soul."[27] This amatory yearning after the Good is love's fullest expression, since "He who formed the human soul, only can fill it, and the chief happiness of an immortal being must arise from the same source as its existence" (CF 1:206). Yet this pious ardor, while infinitely superior to human love, should not – as in so many brands of Christian theology – be treated as the antithesis of earthly love, but rather as its product and proper fulfillment. Love of others, including physical love, is the emotional ground from which transcendent love arises.

> Earthly love leads to heavenly, and prepares us for a more exalted state; if it does not change its nature, and destroy itself, by trampling on the virtue, that constitutes its essence, and allies us to the Deity.   (CF 1:206)

This theme – human love as the progenitor of divine love – first appeared in Wollstonecraft's writings in the late 1780s, and persisted, with some modifications, until her death.[28] An unpublished allegory drafted in 1787, *The Cave of Fancy*, rehearsed the argument which was then more fully dramatized a year later in *Mary, A Fiction*. Caught up in an adulterous passion for a dying romantic genius, the fictive Mary defends her feelings by insisting (quoting Milton) that "earthly love is the scale by which to heavenly we may ascend"; on the death of her lover she turns her heart wholly toward her Maker with the consoling reflection that true happiness is to be had only in His presence (M 1:46, chapters. 25–31). Eros may begin its upward flight with the human affections, but its ultimate route must be heavenward.

Scattered references throughout her writings signal Wollstonecraft's awareness of the platonic roots of this ideal. If women are merely to be loved for their "animal perfection," she rebuked Burke in 1790, then "Plato and Milton were grossly mistaken in asserting that human love led to heavenly"; but if one accepts the platonic view that love of the divine is "only an exaltation of [earthly] affection" then women too must be loved for their rational virtues rather than their physical attributes (VRM 5:46). The feminist twist was new, but the general argument had its source in what James Turner has described as the "Christianisation of the Platonic Eros" to be found in Augustine and many varieties of post-Augustinian theology, leading up to Milton.[29] "Thy affections are the steps; thy will the way;" Augustine had written, "by loving thou mountest, by neglect thou descendest."[30] Desires that ascend toward God are to be radically distinguished from those that descend toward earthly things, yet both are designated as eros – the love which links humanity to the divine. Those moralists who would disdain earthly affections, Christian platonists therefore argued, are in fact apostates, denying their connection to God. "They ... who complain of the delusions of passion," Wollstonecraft wrote, "do not recollect that they are exclaiming against a strong proof of the immortality of the soul" (VRW 5:143).

The most immediate sources for this platonic element in Wollstonecraft's thought were obviously Milton, whom she quoted endlessly and whose ambiguous views on women she worried at throughout the *Rights of Woman*, but also, and even more equivocally, Rousseau, for whom Plato's had been the "true philosophy of lovers"[31] and whose platonic-romantic heroine, the saintly Julie of his 1761 novel *La Nouvelle Héloïse*, set a fashion for ideal love across late 18th century Europe. Wollstonecraft's quarrel with Rousseau's depiction of women in *Emile* – an argument framing much of the *Rights of Woman* – is sometimes assumed to imply her wholesale repudiation of his ideas. In fact the sharpness of her critique is not the anger of an entrenched opponent but that of a disappointed disciple, lambasting her favourite mentor for substituting prejudice for truth. Rousseau's views on women, as

Wollstonecraft pointed out, were in fact notoriously contradictory. While the female protagonist of *Emile*, Sophie, is a patriarch's dream of feminine decorum and submission, Julie of *La Nouvelle Héloïse* is very much the Wollstonecraftian woman: strong-willed, morally authoritative, and engaged in a "perfect union of souls" with her lover, St. Preux, that ultimately draws them both closer to God.[32] Julie's shadow falls long over Wollstonecraft's divinized love philosophy. "An imagination of this vigorous cast," Wollstonecraft writes of Rousseau's novel, "...can depict love with celestial charms, and dote on the grand ideal object – it can imagine a degree of mutual affection that shall refine the soul, and not expire when it has served as a 'scale to heavenly', and, like devotion, make it absorb every meaner affection and desire..." (VRW 5:143).

In the *Rights of Woman*, Wollstonecraft holds up Julie as an example of a "modest" woman, meaning one who, while in this case not technically chaste (Julie and St. Preux make love twice) is pure in heart and mind (VRW 5:196). Modesty in women – a topic to which Wollstonecraft devotes an entire chapter – is not, contrary to conventional opinion, a narrowly feminine virtue but rather the moral condition proper to all of God's human creation (VRW 5:196). The modest woman, like the modest man, is dignified, reserved, self-respecting, and sexually continent – the last, however, not for reasons of "worldly prudence" or public reputation but because she knows her body is a "Temple of the living God" (VRW 5:199). In addition to this, the modest woman is also – as Wollstonecraft carefully demonstrates over the course of the *Rights of Woman* – a natural feminist: resolute of mind, fiercely independent (even in relation to male relatives), and possessed of "the dignity of a rational will that only bows to God" (VRW 5:104). As an ideal of emancipated womanhood, this may seem a long way from recent feminist ambitions. But if we bypass it in favor of a more familiar, secularized version of Wollstonecraft's project, we lose both the historic woman and her principal mission: to liberate women from masculine tyranny not in order that they should become free-floating agents, stripped of all obligatory ties, but in order to bind them more closely to their God.

NOTES

1. Ann Snitow, "A Gender Diary", *Feminism and History*, ed. Joan Wallach Scott, (Oxford University Press, 1996), 529.
2. William Godwin, *Memoirs of the Author of a Vindication of the Rights of Woman*; first published 1798 (Harmondsworth: Penguin, 1987), 215.
3. This emphasis on Wollstonecraft's piety in *Memoirs* does not seem to have registered with many readers, including one who claimed that Godwin's book gave "a striking view of a Woman of fine talents...sinking a victim to the strength of

her Passions & feelings because destitute of the support of Religious principles"
(James Woodrow, quoted in Gary Kelly, *Women, Writing and Revolution, 1790–
1827* [Oxford: Clarendon Press, 1993], 27.)

4. Letter to William Godwin, 4 July 1797. Letters, 404.

5. A note found in Godwin's papers after his death, written sometime in 1787,
   contained the following: "Religion is among the most beautiful and most natural
   of all things; that religion which 'sees God in clouds and hears Him in the wind',
   which endows every object of sense with a living soul, which finds in the system
   of nature whatever is holy, mysterious, and venerable, and inspires the bosom
   with sentiments of awe and veneration" (quoted in Charles Kegan Paul, *William
   Godwin: His Friends and Contemporaries* [1876], 1:28). The similarity to the
   views he attributed to Wollstonecraft is obvious.

6. Mary Hays, "Memoirs of Mary Wollstonecraft," *Annual Necrology*, 1797/8
   (1800), 416.

7. *Ibid.*, 416.

8. Barbara Taylor, *Mary Wollstonecraft and the Feminist Imagination* (Cambridge
   University Press, 2002).

9. Quoted in Genevieve Lloyd, *The Man of Reason: Male and Female in Western
   Philosophy* (London: Methuen, 1984), 30–1.

10. Simone de Beauvoir, *The Second Sex*, 1949 (English ed., Harmondsworth:
    Penguin, 1972), 633. De Beauvoir's discussion of the egalitarian implications of
    Christianity for women is in many respects very reminiscent of Wollstonecraft's,
    although her perspective is that of an analytical unbeliever: "A sincere faith is a
    great help to the little girl in avoiding an inferiority complex: she is neither male
    nor female, but God's creature" (633).

11. Mary Astell, "Some Reflections Upon Marriage," first published in 1700; 1706
    edn. reprinted in Bridget Hill, *The First English Feminist* (Aldershot: Gower
    Publishing, 1986), 84.

12. A Methodist woman preacher quoted in L. F. Church, *More About the Early
    Methodist People* (London, 1949), 168.

13. Hannah More, *Strictures on the Modern System of Female Education* (London,
    1799), 1:7.

14. John Brown, DD, *On the Female Character and Education* (London, 1765), 12,
    10.

15. Jean-Jacques Rousseau, *Emile, or On Education*, 1765 (English edn. London:
    Penguin, 1991), 377–8.

16. Dr. John Gregory, *A Father's Legacy to His Daughters* (London, 1823), 159–60.

17. James Fordyce, *Sermons to Young Women*, 1765 (London, 1766), 2:163.

18. Letter to Everina Wollstonecraft, January 1784, Letters, 87.

19. Basil Willey, *The Eighteenth Century Background* (London: Chatto and Windus,
    1946), 7.

20. Rousseau, *Emile*, 286.

21. Richard Price, *Review of The Principal Questions and Difficulties in Morals*,
    1756 (Oxford: Clarendon Press, 1974), 180.

22. Ibid., 181.

23. Ibid., 113.

24. Cora Kaplan, "Wild Nights: Pleasure/Sexuality/Feminism," *Sea Changes:
    Culture and Feminism* (London: Verso, 1986), 41.

25. Mary Poovey, *The Proper Lady and the Woman Writer: Ideology as Style in the Works of Mary Wollstonecraft, Mary Shelley, and Jane Austen* (University of Chicago Press, 1984).

26. Hays, "Wollstonecraft," 416.

27. Letter to Everina Wollstonecraft, January 1784, Letters, 87.

28. For a fuller account of the evolution of this idea over the course of Wollstonecraft's intellectual career, see my *Wollstonecraft and the Feminist Imagination*.

29. James G. Turner, *One Flesh: Paradisial Marriage and Sexual Relations in the Age of Milton* (Oxford: Clarendon Press, 1987), 32.

30. Quoted in Turner, *One Flesh,* 32. For an influential discussion of the relationship between divine and earthly love in Christian theology, see Anders Nygren, *Agape and Eros* (London, SPCK, 1982), and for the significance of Christian Platonism in the formation of eighteenth-century British moral philosophy see John K. Sheriff, *The Good-Natured Man: the Evolution of a Moral Ideal, 1660–1880* (Tuuscaloosa: University of Alabama Press, 1982).

31. Jean-Jacques Rousseau, *La Nouvelle Héloïse,* 1761; translated as *Eloisa, or a Series of Original Letters* (London, 1767), 2:14.

32. Ibid., 34.

8

VIVIEN JONES

Mary Wollstonecraft and the literature of advice and instruction

In 1789, Wollstonecraft included extracts from John Gregory's *A Father's Legacy to his Daughters*, one of the most popular of eighteenth-century conduct books, in her anthology *The Female Reader*; in 1792, in *A Vindication of the Rights of Woman*, she claimed to "entirely disapprove of his celebrated Legacy," and Gregory was among those singled out as "writers who have rendered women objects of pity."[1] On the face of it, this looks like a radical change of opinion: a clear symptom of a newly politicized Wollstonecraft explicitly rejecting the kind of advice literature which she had been prepared to reproduce, and even to emulate, as a struggling freelance writer in the late 1780s but which, in the revolutionary atmosphere of the early 1790s, she recognized as one of those repressive cultural mechanisms responsible for turning women into mere "creatures of sensation" (VRW:130). But to read this as a straightforward volt face on Wollstonecraft's part would be far too simple an account of her view of Gregory, or of the wider tradition of female conduct literature which his text represents. Furthermore, it would be a serious misunderstanding of Wollstonecraft's relationship with the multifarious genre of advice writing more generally. As an autodidact, and then as an independent woman trying to make a living from her writing, Wollstonecraft relied throughout her life on those instructional genres through which moral principles and enlightenment knowledges were offered up to a popular audience. Her first publication, *Thoughts on the Education of Daughters* (1787), was a kind of conduct book, and *Rights of Woman* itself still bears a more than passing resemblance to the genre. In each case, advice on "improvement" is a primary characteristic, and the moral agenda which underpins this urge to (self-)improvement means that distinctions between attaining proper standards of personal "conduct," defining oneself as a virtuous domestic woman, aspiring to an appropriate education, and simply expanding one's knowledge, can become blurred: for modern readers, often uncomfortably so. What, we might ask, can the moralized literature of advice and conduct – based, as it so often is, in a belief in "natural" sexual difference and an asexual feminine ideal – have to do with Wollstonecraft's feminism? In this essay I want to suggest that the connections are sometimes surprisingly close. I shall try to justify this answer by defining the various strands of advice literature which most significantly inform Wollstonecraft's ideas and writings, and by plotting her discriminating, and shifting, relationship with them. A *Vindication of the Rights of Woman* is obviously a key text here, precisely because it is in *Rights of Woman* that Wollstonecraft, though writing from within the genre, most clearly modifies the conventions of advice literature, and subjects particular examples to her most explicit critique. But Wollstonecraft's intimate relationship with advice writing can be properly understood only by first examining the two quite orthodox examples of conduct literature which she produced at the beginning of her career: *Thoughts on the Education of Daughters* and *The Female Reader*.

Thoughts on the Education of Daughters

Thoughts on the Education of Daughters was the first product of Wollstonecraft's determination to escape, as she called them in *Thoughts*, the more "humiliating" and "disagreeable" "modes of earning a subsistence" – as a paid companion, schoolteacher, or governess – and to earn an independent living through writing.[2] The "humiliating" and "disagreeable" alternatives were all too real. *Thoughts* was written as the school in Newington Green which Wollstonecraft ran with her sisters began seriously to fail and just before she became governess to the Kingsboroughs in Ireland. Like many other women writers in comparable circumstances, Wollstonecraft turned in *Mary* (1788) to fiction; but – also like many other women – she turned in the first instance, and more substantially, to various kinds of instructional text, reliably popular and therefore potentially lucrative genres. *Thoughts* was followed in 1788 by *Original Stories from Real Life ... Calculated to Regulate the Affections and Form the Mind to Truth and Goodness* and in 1789 by *The Female Reader ... for the Improvement of Young Women*. Like these slightly later texts, with their disciplinary emphasis on "regulation" and "improvement," the full title of Wollstonecraft's first publication – *Thoughts on the Education of Daughters: with Reflections on Female Conduct, In the more important Duties of Life* – combines education with conduct and duty. To Wollstonecraft's contemporary audience, this title would have suggested an entirely orthodox addition to the literature of female instruction in which any improvement in girls' education was intended to prepare them for the "important Duties" of marriage and motherhood. For modern readers, however, the title at once appears to embody a contradiction – between "education," with its potentially liberating promise of individual intellectual development, and the restrictive and repressive implications of "conduct" and "duty." Since the publication of Mary Poovey's *The Proper Lady and the Woman Writer* in 1984, in which Poovey analyzes women's writing as bearing the repressive scars of the cultural imperative that women become a version of the "proper lady," conduct books have been seen as symptomatic of, indeed have been held responsible for, most of the ills of eighteenth-century bourgeois femininity. Poovey's reading of the power of the conduct book's domestic ideal was reinforced and sophisticated by Nancy Armstrong in her *Desire and Domestic Fiction* (1987), where she argues that it was "[o]n the domestic front" that "the middle-class struggle for dominance was fought and won"; that "this body of writing [conduct literature]... helped to generate the belief that there was such a thing as a middle class" and that the modest, submissive but morally and domestically competent woman it described was the first "modern individual".[3] Both Poovey and Armstrong homogenize conduct literature and, in doing so, play down not only the differences between individual texts of instruction and advice but also the constant and sometimes disruptive interaction of "conduct literature" with a growing commitment in the course of the eighteenth century to the improvement of female education. They reflect, in other words, our modern feeling that the project of conduct literature is incompatible with an ideal of self-improvement through education – and that it is even more inimical to anything that might be described as a "feminist" position.

But though modern readers might want to drive an ideological, and thus a generic, wedge between writings on female education on the one hand, and "conduct literature" on the other, the actual textual evidence makes the distinction very difficult to maintain – as more recent commentators have begun to suggest. Kathryn Sutherland, for example, explores the symptomatically mixed inheritance of Hester Chapone's *Letters on the Improvement of the Mind* (1773). Chapone's modest but rigorous educational program can be seen as part of an unbroken tradition of educated women's writing stretching back to the beginning of the century; at the same time, however, it is directly indebted to the conduct writer Wetenhall Wilkes, who endorses a rational education for women, but only on the grounds that it should enhance their strictly domestic function to "refine the joys, and soften the cares of humanity."[4] And writers like Mary Anne Radcliffe, Priscilla Wakefield, Hannah More – and Wollstonecraft herself – were able to use "the generic scope of the conduct manual" (Sutherland, "Writings on Education and Conduct," 40) to mount public campaigns for female education, employment and, in the case of More, patriotism. Indeed, Gary Kelly goes so far as to claim that by "defining woman as domestic yet insisting on her human

dignity and her importance to both private life and the life of the nation,"
female-authored conduct literature at least is "the context for Revolutionary
feminism."[5]

The best strategy, it would seem, is to see "conduct books," educational
writings, and in some cases proto-feminist tracts, as part of a wider tradition of advice literature dedicated to personal and social improvement, but
within which the particular textual and ideological allegiances of individual
examples must be carefully teased out. It is conduct books, rather than writings on education or women's rights, which are least likely to get the benefit
of this kind of reading. Alan Richardson, for example, in his excellent study
of educational writing in the period, establishes careful political distinctions
between examples of women's instructional writing, but is less concerned
to distinguish between two rather different conduct books: James Fordyce's
Sermons to Young Women (1766), and the text with which I began, John
Gregory's *A Father's Legacy to his Daughters* (1774).[6] Yet it is only through
careful definition and discrimination of particular conduct texts that we can
hope to understand their precise meaning for a contemporary audience. (As
we shall see, though Wollstonecraft was disapproving of both Fordyce and
Gregory in *A Vindication of the Rights of Woman*, she nevertheless distinguished sharply between them.) Equally importantly, by reading in this way,
we can begin to break the spell of the "proper lady" by exposing the inconsistencies and contradictions which make the ideological effects of conduct
books rather less predictable.[7]

How, then, should we read and categorize *Thoughts on the Education of
Daughters*: written by the woman who at the turn of the second millenium is
an icon of modern feminism; but described by one critic as "a conventional
conduct book, in which the arguments and topics of a hundred-year tradition
of such manuals by men and women weigh heavy" (Sutherland, "Writings on
Education and Conduct," 41)? One temptation is to read *Thoughts* teleo-
logically: to tell Wollstonecraft's story as one of ideological consistency, and
look for moments of radicalism which appear to anticipate the two *Vindications*. An alternative strategy would be to dismiss *Thoughts* as a politically
naive potboiler, written before Wollstonecraft's outraged response to Edmund Burke's *Reflections on the Revolution in France* "converted" her, as
this particular life-narrative would see it, to radicalism. But to disentan-
gle the "conventional" from the potentially radical in *Thoughts* is not so
straightforward. A "hundred-year tradition" of advice literature undoubtedly informs this text (as it does *A Vindication of the Rights of Woman*)
but, as inherited by Wollstonecraft, it is a tradition in which it's possible
to trace various contributory strands. I want to draw out three of these
here: writings "on the subject of female education and manners" (VRW:91);

the radical Dissenting tradition of moral and spiritual discipline; and moral satire, in which representations of women are closely associated with attacks on luxury and commercial excess. Sometimes working harmoniously, sometimes producing interesting points of tension, these are the traditions which shape Wollstonecraft's discussion of love and marriage, of women's opportunities and their intellectual and moral capacities, and of acceptable and unacceptable forms of feminine identity and behavior.

On several occasions throughout *Thoughts*, Wollstonecraft endorses the domestic priorities of current writings on girls' education and conduct. "No employment of the mind is a sufficient excuse for neglecting domestic duties," she asserts in her chapter on "Reading"; and discussing "Boarding-Schools" (of which she disapproves, preferring home education), she affirms: "To prepare a woman to fulfil the important duties of a wife and mother" should be the main object of her education (TED:21, 22). More problematically for modern readers, she seems in her chapter on "Matrimony" to endorse a particularly asexual version of adult womanhood: "There are a thousand nameless decencies which good sense gives rise to . . . It has ever occurred to me, that it was sufficient for a woman to receive caresses, and not bestow them" (32). At first glance, Wollstonecraft here seems to endorse a version of John Gregory's notorious advice to his daughters "never to discover to [a man] the full extent of your love, no not although you marry him,"[8] advice which she later briskly dismisses in *Rights of Woman*: "Voluptuous precaution, and as ineffectual as absurd" (VRW:98). And her phrasing echoes Adam's praise of Eve in *Paradise Lost*: "Those thousand decencies that daily flow/From all her words and actions."[9] Writers of female advice literature often approvingly invoked Milton's image of the submissive prelapsarian Eve. These very lines from *Paradise Lost* were to be quoted, for example, by the conservative Hannah More in her anti-Wollstonecraftian *Strictures on the Modern System of Female Education* of 1799, where More describes them as "that beautiful picture of correct and elegant propriety" – as an image, in other words, of the proper lady.[10]

More congenial to modern readers are those passages in which Wollstonecraft is more evidently uneasy with the current commonplaces of gender difference. At one point, for example, she lashes out against women's lack of opportunity in terms which very obviously anticipate *Rights of Woman*:

> Women are said to be the weaker vessel, and many are the miseries which this weakness brings on them. Men have in some respects very much the advantage. If they have a tolerable understanding, it has a chance to be cultivated. They are forced to see human nature as it is, and are not left to dwell on the pictures of their own imaginations. (TED:32)

And the dominant tone is one of barely suppressed disappointment, of resignation to the reality of life as an inevitable but often unsuccessful struggle:
against the effects of an uncultivated understanding; against the likely treach-
ery of men towards fashionably educated, but socially inferior, women;
against the limitations ("Her sphere of action is not large") even of a comfortable marriage (26, 32). Indeed, one of the chapters is entitled "The Benefits
which arise from Disappointments," a title which sits oddly among the more
standard headings of practical and moral advice on "Dress" or "Card-
playing," "Love" or "Benevolence."

At such moments, however, Wollstonecraft deviates less than we might
assume from the orthodoxies of female advice literature, whether by men or
women. Indeed, this particular chapter title simply makes explicit a preoccupation which is already very much part of that tradition. In female advice
texts, the suggestion that women might very often need to resign themselves
to, indeed might benefit from, less than perfect circumstances goes right
back to George Savile, Marquis of Halifax's *The Lady's New Years Gift: Or,
Advice to a Daughter*, first published in 1688 and reprinted at least twenty
times during the eighteenth century. Savile regretfully but unquestioningly
accepts the socioeconomic conventions of his class which will more than
likely condemn his bright, beloved daughter to marriage though her "*in-
ward Consent* might not entirely go along with it": "You are . . . to make the
best of what is *settled* by *Law* and *Custom*, and not vainly imagine, that
it will be *changed* for your sake."[11] Sarah Pennington, in *An Unfortunate
Mother's Advice to her Absent Daughters* (1761), writes from the assumption
that women might have slightly more say in their choice of marriage partner,
but she is nevertheless similarly dubious about the possibility of finding a
husband who is also a friend: "so great is the hazard, so disproportioned the
chances, that I could almost wish the dangerous die was never to be thrown
for any of you." And Pennington spends some considerable time itemizing
the kinds of "chearful compliance" needed to cope with the many unacceptable forms of masculinity.[12] With varying degrees of conviction, such
texts chillingly advise women to exercise a self-discipline of uncomplaining
submission to the inequalities of marriage. In doing so, however, they give
voice to dissatisfactions which only a slight shift of emphasis would turn into
much more explicit criticism of the gender system which condemns so many
women to a life either of disappointment or, at best, to what Wollstonecraft
in *Rights of Woman* would call "a lawless kind of power resembling the
authority exercised by the favourites of absolute monarchs" (VRW:226).

In *Thoughts*, this potential for critique remains largely latent. Instead,
Wollstonecraft emphasizes the pleasures of resignation, in terms which invoke the consolations of a private religious sensibility rather than those of

worldly power or political resistance. She writes, for example, of "that calm satisfaction which resignation produces, which . . . shall sanctify the sorrows, and dignify the character of virtue" (TED:30). And her chapter on "The Benefits which Arise from Disappointments" ends with a moment of explicit sublimation:

> [W]hen we look for happiness, we meet with vexations . . . And yet we were made to be happy! But our passions will not contribute much to our bliss, till they are under the dominion of reason, and till that reason is enlightened and improved. Then sighing will cease, and all tears will be wiped away by that Being, in whose presence there is fulness of joy. (37)

Although, as I have suggested, advice to women often manifests latent anxieties about the actualities of their role as wives and mothers, its concern is nevertheless to persuade them of their overwhelming usefulness in that role. *Thoughts* follows the forms rather than the spirit of that project. The language in this passage is not that of female domestic virtue; rather, it recalls the essentially ungendered program of rational and spiritual improvement (reason "enlightened and improved") associated with religious Dissent. This other advice tradition – of Dissenting sermons, moral treatises, and educational tracts – weighs as heavily in *Thoughts* as does that of specifically female advice literature. And when it erupts, in passages like this, we see clearly the connections between *Thoughts* and Wollstonecraft's almost exactly contemporary novel, *Mary: A Fiction*. As in the novel, dissatisfactions are registered not as yet through any clearly formulated goal or articulate protest, but at moments in which the language of longing and aspiration hints uncertainly at the possibility of an alternative to the conduct-book world of simply "*marrying*, [and] giving in marriage."[13]

During 1786, when Wollstonecraft was writing *Thoughts*, she was living and working in Newington Green, north of London, home of the prominent group of radical Unitarian Dissenters associated with Dr. Richard Price. Wollstonecraft's title pays tribute not simply to John Locke's *Some Thoughts Concerning Education* (1693), but also to *Thoughts on Education* (1747) by the Dissenter James Burgh, whose widow Hannah was particularly supportive of Wollstonecraft's project. Though its detailed curriculum is designed primarily for boys, the basis of Burgh's educative program is an explicitly non-gendered rational ideal: "it is of great consequence to the youth of both sexes, that they be early led into a just and rational way of thinking of things, and taught to be extremely cautious of judging according to outward appearances, or the superficial opinion of the multitude."[14] The only way to prepare "a young person" for this rational independence of mind is by early discipline, on broadly Lockean principles:

Previous to every other step . . . is the forming and breaking his temper; by cherishing and encouraging the good qualities of it, as Emulation, or a laudable desire of excelling, Curiosity, or thirst after knowledge, Humility, Tractableness, Meekness, Fearfulness of offending, and the rest; and by crushing and nipping in the bud the luxuriant or pernicious ones, as Anger, Pride, Resentment, Obstinacy, Sloth, Falshood, and so forth.

(Burgh, *Thoughts on Education*, 6–7)

Burgh's goal is the development not just of social and moral, but also of political, awareness: "a rational set of *political principles*, . . . the love of *liberty* and their *country*, and consequently the hatred of Popery, Tyranny, Persecution, Venality, and whatever else is against the interest of a free people" (12).

Burgh's Dissenting discourse typically combines spiritual meekness with rational independence of mind and a commitment to liberty. Wollstonecraft, too, advocates a "meek spirit" in her chapter on "The Temper." The juxtaposition with Burgh reveals its more radical possibilities:

A constant attention to the management of the temper produces gentleness and humility, and is practised on all occasions, as it is not done "to be seen of men". This meek spirit arises from good sense and resolution, and should not be confounded with indolence and timidity; weaknesses of mind, which often pass for good nature. She who submits, without conviction, to a parent or husband, will as unreasonably tyrannise over her servants; for slavish fear and tyranny go together. (TED:23)[15]

Like Sarah Pennington's worries about the difficulties her daughters might encounter in finding a decent husband, the implications of Wollstonecraft's observations here are more radical than the advice given. The aim, after all, appears still to be submission: just submission with rather than without "conviction." But the language of tyranny and slavery implicitly invites critique both of the husband who demands "slavish fear," and of the abuse of class power in the tyrannic woman's treatment of her servants.

Wollstonecraft's allusion to Eve might also be re-read in terms of Dissenting ideals, which would emphasize the "union of mind" and soul, and not just the "sweet compliance," in Miltonic marriage: " . . . love / And sweet compliance, which declare unfeigned / Union of mind, or in us both one soul; / Harmony to behold in wedded pair."[16] And elsewhere in *Thoughts*, Wollstonecraft advises women that: "Goodwill to all the human race should dwell in our bosoms, nor should love to individuals induce us to violate this first of duties" (TED:44). In all these instances, the domestic principles most closely associated with the conduct tradition are qualified by the language of spiritual aspiration, self-discipline, and equality associated with Dissent.

The two are clearly far from being incompatible: domestic advice literature draws constantly on religious traditions as a way of establishing the providential nature of the gender roles it advocates. But the Dissenting tradition, clearly identifiable in *Thoughts*, also pulls in a more disruptive direction: both in its stress on independence of mind over "the superficial opinion of the multitude" (Burgh, *Thoughts on Education*, 53), and in the way in which its human, rather than gendered, regime of spiritual self-discipline works in the service of a wider, communitarian, political ideal.

Within the Dissenting tradition, the good man (and not just the good woman) "avoids all parade and ostentation; ... He shuns all the excesses of pleasure and voluptuousness."[17] And in eighteenth-century moral discourse more generally, the opposition between superficiality and substance, ostentation and retirement, is all-pervasive. *Thoughts*, however, offers a conventionally gendered version of that retiring ideal. It moves from "The Nursery" in the first chapter, to "Public Places" in the last, and from the ideal mother to her dangerous alter ego, the "fine Lady": the female embodiments of substance and superficiality who inhabit those spaces. It begins with the rational duty of mothers: to ensure, by breastfeeding and by consistent, affectionate government, that their offspring achieve the Lockean (and classical) ideal of sound minds and bodies (TED:7–8).[18] It ends with warnings against the frivolous woman of fashion, sound in neither mind nor body, "still a child in understanding, and of so little use to society, that her death would scarcely be observed" (48).

Wollstonecraft's portraits are indistinguishable from the classic conduct-book opposition between acceptable and unacceptable modes of middle-class femininity: inner virtue and "use" compared with superficial display; the "empty airy thing" who, in Savile's formulation, "sail[s] up and down the House to no kind of purpose" compared with the woman whose "propriety of behaviour [is] the fruit of instruction, of observation, and reasoning."[19] But, like Savile's grotesque image, Wollstonecraft's caustic suggestion that the fine lady's death would go unnoticed suggests another generic connection: with the dismissive, and often cruel, portraits which are a commonplace in satire. In Pope's "Epistle to a Lady," pleasure-seeking women are: "Fair to no purpose, artful to no end, / ... / Alive, ridiculous, and dead, forgot!"; and Edward Moore's popular versified conduct-book *Fables for the Female Sex*, describes a

> Fair, flutt'ring, fickle, busy thing,
> To pleasure ever on the wing,
> Gayly coquetting for an hour,
> To die, and ne'er be thought of more.[20]

Throughout the eighteenth century, there were close connections between female advice writing and satire, most importantly through the pervasive influence of Joseph Addison and Richard Steele's moral satirical essays in *The Spectator* (1711–14). *The Spectator* encourages its readers, who importantly include women, to identify with the new bourgeois culture, in which commercial values are refined and mitigated by domestic pleasures and "polite" taste. Indeed, it makes female improvement both a sign of, and, in its stress on "well regulated Families," a means to, social progress. The effect is mixed. Women are addressed as "reasonable [i.e. rational] creatures," and invited to participate as readers in the virtual public sphere of "Knowledge and Virtue"; but their actual sphere of influence is implicitly limited to the domestic, the role to which "those Virtues which are the Embellishments, of the Sex" are most suited.[21] *The Spectator*, and the periodical tradition which it initiated, urge women to greater seriousness by repeating for a new consumer society the age-old accusation that they are "smitten with every thing that is showy and superficial."[22]

Wollstonecraft's thorough familiarity with periodical satire becomes most apparent in *The Female Reader*, where her extracts include *Spectator* 15, under the title "Female Passion for Dress and Show."[23] In *Thoughts*, the satirical voice surfaces only occasionally: when Wollstonecraft meaningfully misquotes Pope, for example: "Most women, and men too, have no characters at all" (TED:36);[24] or, as we have seen, in her pitiless dismissal of the fine lady's uselessness. This moment of virulence anticipates what one critic has described as Wollstonecraft's "feminist misogyny": her fierce critique in *Rights of Woman* of the "false refinement" which "not only renders [women] uncomfortable themselves, but troublesome . . . to others" (VRW:130).[25] And in *A Vindication of the Rights of Men*, she would put gendered satirical commonplaces to powerful political effect. *Spectator* 15 rejects those women "who consider only the Drapery of the Species" rather than "those Ornaments of the Mind, that make Persons Illustrious in themselves, and Useful to others."[26] In *Rights of Men*, Wollstonecraft scorns the "gorgeous drapery" in which Edmund Burke "enwrapped [his] tyrannic principles," turning the familiar vocabularies of superficiality and substance against Burke's defence of tradition which, she claims, undermines "religion and virtue to set up a spurious, sensual beauty."[27]

Such radicalism was in the future, however. *Thoughts on the Education of Daughters* fits more or less seamlessly into the continuum of advice writing which connects periodicals with the literature of conduct, education, and spiritual improvement. The text's manifest tensions – between resigned compliance and the possibility of alternative consolations; between spiritual meekness and rational independence; between domestic duty and the desire for participation in a wider sphere – are themselves typical of these genres. Wollstonecraft is as yet reproducing, rather than self-consciously exploiting, the central contradiction of advice traditions in which instruction on how to conform to established patterns of behavior is based in an appeal to readers' individualistic desires for self-improvement.

The Female Reader

Almost immediately after its publication, substantial extracts from *Thoughts* appeared in three consecutive issues of *The Lady's Magazine*. The following year, a pirated edition was published in Dublin in a volume which included *Instructions to a Governess* by the influential enlightenment educationist and theologian François Fénelon, and the anonymous *Address to Mothers*. Two chapters, on "Obstinacy" and "Needle-work," have been silently added to Wollstonecraft's original text, and it comes with an authoritative recommendation quoted from *The English Review*:

> These thoughts are employed on various important situations and incidents in the ordinary life of females, and are, in general, dictated with great judgment. Mrs. Wollstonecraft appears to have reflected maturely on her subject; . . . while her manner gives authority, her good sense adds irresistible weight to almost all her precepts and remarks. We would therefore recommend these Thoughts as worthy the attention of those who are more immediately concerned in the education of young ladies.[28]

Even without this reviewer's approval, the acceptability of *Thoughts* is amply evident from the way in which it was so readily absorbed and reproduced by a publishing industry ever eager to cash in on the lucrative market for such texts. One of the most significant characteristics of advice writing as a phenomenon within print culture is the endless recycling which went on, both of selected extracts and of whole texts: as reprints, legitimate or otherwise; in compendium editions; or, most typically perhaps, in miscellanies of all kinds, whether periodicals, anthologies, or improving "readers." In *The Lady's Magazine*, for example, Wollstonecraft's chapters on "Exterior Accomplishments," "Dress," "Boarding-Schools," "Matrimony," "The Treatment of Servants," and "Public Places" appear as part of the usual women's magazine farrago of serialized fiction, news digests, sentimental poetry, puzzles, historical narratives, and handy hints (in the first issue in which Wollstonecraft appeared, these are on the "Description and Culture of Bulbous Rooted Flowers"): in short, as the editors point out in introducing their unattributed selections from Wollstonecraft, of "whatever has a particular tendency to improve the female character in wisdom, virtue, and knowledge, and to assist in forming a proper estimate of exterior accomplishments" (*Lady's Magazine*, 18:227). Wollstonecraft's "proper estimate" of "Dress" is expressed in by now familiar terms: "By far too much of a girl's time is taken up in dress...The body hides the mind, and it is, in its turn, obscured by the drapery" (TED:16). *The Lady's Magazine's* interpretation of "a proper estimate" is a good deal more flexible (after all, the magazine regularly includes fashion plates and the latest fabric designs), but Wollstonecraft's singleminded preference for "a cultivated mind" over such frivolous "drapery" can nevertheless be happily accommodated within eighteenth-century women's magazine culture's professed commitment to "improving" the female character.[29]

Wollstonecraft's own moneyspinner anthology, *The Female Reader*, though much less heterogeneous in content than periodicals like *The Lady's Magazine*, is directed at a similar market. Such anthologies were a popular spin-off from the growing concern with female education. Consisting, as Wollstonecraft put it in her preface, of "the most useful passages of many volumes," they offered digestible gobbets of improving literature, designed to "imprint some useful lessons on the mind" and "cultivate the taste" of a still comparatively new, and supposedly vulnerable, female audience.[30] Like *Thoughts*, *The Female Reader* slotted neatly into its niche market: very soon after publication it was included in the revised list of recommended reading in a new edition of Pennington's *Advice to her Daughters*, alongside Vicesimus Knox's *Elegant Extracts* and several of the periodicals on which *The Female Reader* draws.[31]

But "hack-work" though it might have been, it is not necessarily contradictory also to see *The Female Reader* as a text which, in the words of one critic, "exposes Mary Wollstonecraft's ideas and personal characteristics more sharply than any other early work."[32] It certainly gives a good indication of her early reading – or, at least, of the books she had to hand, either in her own library, or available to her, in some cases as texts for review in the *Analytical Review*, in the office of her publisher Joseph Johnson. It also, importantly, indicates the generic variety which advice writing, broadly defined, might include; and it establishes a canon of texts – from Shakespeare to Sarah Pennington; Milton to Mrs. Chapone – which Wollstonecraft categorizes as by "our best authors" (FR:55) because of their usefulness within a wider instructional project.

"[P]rincipally intended for the improvement of females," *The Female Reader* makes the ability to "read well" (FR:55) the basis of a gradualist program of proper refinement: in taste, feeling, reason, morality, and, ultimately, piety. "[T]he taste should very gradually be formed," Wollstonecraft asserts; and her ordered series of readings will, she claims, "awaken the affections and fix good habits" (FR:56). The major advice traditions evident in *Thoughts* also shape *The Female Reader*. In her insistence on the cultivation of taste as a moral undertaking, Wollstonecraft works within the orthodoxies of eighteenth-century politeness, maintaining *The Spectator*'s programme of "constant and assiduous Culture";[33] in her concern to inculcate "good habits," she follows enlightened Lockean educational theory, which works with feeling and curiosity to bring the passions under the discipline of reason; whilst the inclusion of devotional pieces which can "still the murmurs of discontent" (FR:56), reproduces the quietist advice of the female conduct tradition. In its mode of organization and choice of texts, as well as its belief in the "external accomplishment" of reading aloud as both the means to, and the sign of, inner virtue, *The Female Reader* again demonstrates an immediate allegiance to Dissenting educational literature.

Wollstonecraft's model, as she herself makes clear, was William Enfield's *The Speaker: or, Miscellaneous Pieces, selected from the Best English Writers, and disposed under proper heads, with a view to facilitate the improvement of youth in Reading and Speaking* (1774), a new edition of which was published by Joseph Johnson in 1786. *The Speaker* was originally produced for pupils at the Warrington Dissenting Academy, where Enfield (who was later to write a favorable review of *Rights of Woman*) was tutor, secretary, and Rector.[34] Johnson acted as London publisher for the Warrington group, whose members included Joseph Priestley and Anna Letitia Barbauld, and the idea of producing a parallel collection for women readers very probably came from him. *The Female Reader* offers a more general program of "improvement" than Enfield's *Speaker*. His collection was a contribution to the elocution movement, which encouraged "standard" English as the spoken dialect of the professional classes. Wollstonecraft's title identifies reading rather than speaking out, modesty rather than performance, as the more suitable occupation for women: her collection has no equivalent of the "Orations and Harangues" or, indeed, of the "Argumentative Pieces" which Enfield includes. *The Speaker* has no equivalent to Wollstonecraft's "Book VI: Devotional Pieces, and Reflections on Religious Objects," nor does it draw on the Bible, as Wollstonecraft does throughout. Her textual choices emphasize humanitarian feeling, piety, and the familiar moral discipline of depth over surface: a recurrent preoccupation, particularly in "Book II: Didactic and Moral Pieces," is "Dress subservient to useful Purposes" (FR:121).[35]

So, although it shares some sources with *The Speaker* (most notably Shakespeare and a wide range of periodicals), Wollstonecraft's instructional

VIVIEN JONES

reader encourages a distinctly feminized and moralized taste. That taste also has a particular political identity, however. In terms of literary texts, Wollstonecraft's preference for Cowper's poetry of feeling, community, and the natural world over Pope's acerbic Tory satire is typical. Certainly, it reflects popular opinion at the end of the century, shaped by the "feminine" cult of sensibility; but Wollstonecraft's selections also make clear the attraction of Cowper for a Dissenting, and incipiently radical, readership. Joseph Johnson had sent Wollstonecraft a copy of the two-volume edition of Cowper's *Poems* which he published in 1787.[36] Alongside reflections from *The Task* on domestic happiness, or a short poem comparing a "silent and chaste" stream to a "virtuous maid," Wollstonecraft includes substantial extracts in which Cowper celebrates the common bonds between human beings or between humans and animals, as well as passages attacking the offences to liberty represented by slavery or the Bastille, where those common bonds are given specific political application. *The Female Reader* contains a wider generic range than does *The Speaker*, and Joseph Johnson publications are also well represented in Wollstonecraft's choice of non-literary texts. She includes a generous selection from Lavater's *Aphorisms on Man*, for example, published by Johnson in 1788 in a translation by Henry Fuseli, with a frontispiece by William Blake. These moral reflections are alien to a modern taste, but were admired by the Johnson circle as a voice of European enlightenment humanism. Anna Laetitia Barbauld, the only woman writer in *The Speaker* (because of her membership of the Warrington group), appears in Wollstonecraft's anthology as poet, but also as essayist; and, among other women writers, Wollstonecraft includes the educationists Sarah Trimmer (also published by Johnson) and Mme. de Genlis (whose *Tales of the Castle* had been translated in 1785 by the Jacobin novelist Thomas Holcroft).[37] "Hack-work" for Joseph Johnson, then, is hack-work that nevertheless reflects the rigorous moral tastes of the English middle-class Enlightenment and invites women to participate in the program of intellectual and social inquiry which Dissenting writers shared with other radicals of Johnson's circle.

Wollstonecraft's as yet comparatively orthodox approach to gender difference must be understood in this intellectual context. *The Female Reader* begins with a quotation from John Gregory's *Comparative View of the State and Faculties of Mankind* (1765): "As the two sexes have very different parts to act in life nature has marked their characters very differently, in a way that best qualifies them to fulfil their respective duties in society." It is followed by Hester Chapone, who contrasts men's pride in their "power, . . . wealth, dignity, learning, or abilities" with women's desire simply that men "be in love

132

with their persons, careless how despicable their minds appear," and insists that "[t]he principal virtues or vices of a woman must be of a private and domestic kind" (FR:67). Wollstonecraft begins her course of improving reading with questions of difference and sameness: implicit approval of a gendered division of social responsibility is followed by a concern that women have allowed difference to render their minds "despicable." She draws yet again on the female educationists' familiar program of female mental improvement as a means of escape from fashionable uselessness. But she draws, too, on rationalist inquiries into categorisation and definition, and the responsibilities incurred by difference: in Gregory's case, an inquiry influenced by his position within Scottish Enlightenment circles. Later in *The Female Reader*, for example, Wollstonecraft quotes Gregory's comparison between animals and humans – the latter "distinguished by the moral sense" – and follows it immediately with Cowper's mobilization of that moral sense through the sympathetic aesthetic of sensibility: "The heart is hard in nature, and unfit / For human fellowship . . . / . . . that is not pleas'd / With sight of animals enjoying life" (FR:288). Wollstonecraft prided herself on organizing the texts in *The Female Reader* into thematic groups, "carefully disposed in a series that tends to make them illustrate each other" (55). The anthology's juxtapositions invite her readers to reflect on the relationship between rational improvement and moral responsibility – and on what it means to be a human, as well as a gendered, subject.

Central to the traditions of advice and instruction within which Wollstonecraft works, these are the questions which are to shape *A Vindication of the Rights of Woman*. The less disruptive liberal sensibility of *The Female Reader*, however, stresses responsibilities rather than rights, difference rather than sameness. It can therefore easily accommodate a conduct writer like Gregory who, like other Scottish Enlightenment writers – and, of course, the periodical tradition going back to *The Spectator* – associates femininity with civilization and makes complementarity the basis of gender equality. Priding himself on his "honourable point of view," Gregory sees women, "not as domestic drudges, or the slaves of our pleasures, but as our companions and equals; as designed to soften our hearts and polish our manners."[38] *The Female Reader* draws extensively both on Gregory's *Comparative View* and on *A Father's Legacy to his Daughters*. In *Rights of Woman*, however, Gregory's well-meaning version of "equal" gender relations is subjected to extensive critique. Trained in advice traditions which value "a just and rational way of thinking of things" (Burgh, *Thoughts on Education*, 53), Wollstonecraft turns the Enlightenment scrutiny of categories back on itself, exposing the inequalities produced by definitions of difference and making careful distinctions within the category of advice writing itself.

A Vindication of the Rights of Woman

In Wollstonecraft's "Introduction" to *A Vindication of the Rights of Woman*, both the continuities and the breaks with the various advice traditions I have been discussing are immediately evident:

> The conduct and manners of women... prove that their minds are not in a healthy state;... One cause... I attribute to a false system of education, gathered from the books written on this subject by men who, considering females rather as women than human creatures, have been more anxious to make them alluring mistresses than affectionate wives and rational mothers;... the understanding of the sex has been so bubbled by this specious homage, that the civilized women of the present century... are only anxious to inspire love, when they ought to cherish a nobler ambition, and by their abilities and virtues exact respect.
>
> In a treatise, therefore, on female rights and manners, the works which have been particularly written for their improvement must not be overlooked;... the books of instruction, written by men of genius, have had the same tendency as more frivolous productions...   (VRW:73)

The moralists' familiar opposition between superficiality and depth, irresponsibility and duty, structures Wollstonecraft's introduction as it does the rest of *Rights of Woman*: in the sexualized juxtaposition of "alluring mistresses" with "affectionate wives and rational mothers"; and in Wollstonecraft's concern that women should "exact respect" through the quality of their minds, "abilities and virtues," rather than remaining content simply to "inspire love", a concern that clearly echoes the extract from Hester Chapone which opens *The Female Reader*. Like most writers on conduct and education, Wollstonecraft continues to emphasize the duties of marriage and motherhood as women's primary goal. "Do passive indolent women make the best wives?" she asks later in the text (103). And satirical attacks on feminine luxury and commercial excess continue to resonate in her scorn of those other women who "supinely dream life away in the lap of pleasure" and "have nothing to do but to plume themselves, and stalk with mock majesty from perch to perch" (VRW:98, 125).

What is new here, however, is the polemical confidence with which Wollstonecraft attributes the unhealthy state of women's minds to "books of instruction," and to "men of genius" in particular, and makes "female rights" central to any discussion of women's "conduct and manners." As I have suggested, Wollstonecraft inherited a language of rational equality and liberty from the Dissenting educational project: a critique of "slavish fear and tyranny" (TED:23) which at times threatened to disrupt the more pragmatic and biddable advice offered in *Thoughts on the Education of Daughters*. That language is again evident here: "rather as women than as human creatures"; "bubbled by this specious homage." But it is now used self-consciously to expose the contradictions within discourses of female improvement, contradictions crystalized by Wollstonecraft's involvement in French Revolutionary debates, and particularly by her devastating analysis, in *A Vindication of the Rights of Men*, of Edmund Burke's "libertine imagination," the "Gothic gallantry" which underpinned both sexual and national systems of inequality (VRM:46, 37). In *Rights of Woman*, empowered by the daring and success of her earlier attack on so public a figure, she is ready to assert her political and intellectual independence further and to "effect a revolution in female manners" (VRW:114) by turning her critical gaze on other influential men: specifically, on those whose "books of instruction" had been formative in establishing a dominant cultural idea of femininity – but who had therefore also been central to her own intellectual development.

Milton, Rousseau, and John Gregory are the three writers singled out for treatment: Milton, the republican poet whose image of Edenic domesticity shaped eighteenth-century conceptions of sexual relations; Rousseau, Revolutionary political and educational theorist; and Gregory, author of a popular conduct book based in his Scottish Enlightenment humanism. Their prominence in *Rights of Woman* is indicative of the personal significance each held for Wollstonecraft. In each case, it is their symptomatic inconsistencies that she is concerned to analyze: inconsistencies which have a common end result, "to render women pleasing at the expence of every solid virtue"; and a common source, "into similar inconsistencies are great men often led by their senses" (VRW:91, 89). It is sexuality, in other words, seeping into the instructional relationship, which distorts women's equal progress in intellectual, political, and domestic virtue.

Wollstonecraft freely acknowledges the centrality of Rousseau (with whom she confessed in a letter to being "half in love"[39]) to her vision of intellectual independence. Warning against the limitations of "mere instruction," she cites Rousseau in support of her assertion that, though the "sagacious parent or tutor may strengthen the body and sharpen the instruments by which the child is to gather knowledge... the honey must be the reward of the individual's own industry" (VRW:177, 183 and n.16). Elsewhere in the same chapter, however, he is vehemently attacked for the "eager fondness" (160) which leads him in *Emile* to exclude Sophie (and thus all women) from precisely that opportunity to exercise her own industry. Earlier in *Rights of Woman*, the political inconsistency arising from Milton's fond representation of Eve comes under similar scrutiny. Milton "seems to coincide with me," Wollstonecraft allows, quoting Adam's plea for a mate: "Among unequals what society / Can sort, what harmony or true delight."[40] Yet in his description of "our first frail mother," the political principle of equality "bends to the indefeasible right of beauty" (VRW:88–9). And John Gregory's *Legacy to his Daughters*, so extensively quoted in the early sections of *The Female Reader* and approached in *Rights of Woman* with "affectionate respect," is ultimately judged to have had "the most baneful effect on the morals and manners of the female world" because it has "two objects in view":

> ... wishing to make his daughters amiable, and fearing lest unhappiness should only be the consequence, of instilling sentiments that might draw them out of the track of common life without enabling them to act with consonant independence and dignity, he checks the natural flow of his thoughts, and neither advises one thing nor the other. (VRW:166)

It is Gregory's protective timidity which Wollstonecraft particularly objects to: fearful that his daughters will be hurt, he encourages a "system of dissimulation," a "desire of being always women" which is "the very consciousness that degrades the sex" (168, 169). The anxiety of the father is allowed to compromise an enlightened faith in ungendered transparency: "a cultivated understanding, and an affectionate heart [which] will never want starched rules of decorum" (167).

The approval, however qualified, allowed to these men of the Enlightenment sharply differentiates them from the only other text analyzed in any detail in Wollstonecraft's chapter on "Writers Who Have Rendered Women Objects of Pity." James Fordyce's *Sermons to Young Women* were, as Wollstonecraft points out, "frequently put into the hands of young people" (VRW:166). First published in 1766, their popularity was similar to that of Gregory's *Legacy* and Wollstonecraft makes clear that this is why she has "taken more notice of them than, strictly speaking, they deserve" (166).[41] Fordyce is neither cited nor quoted in either *Thoughts* or *The Female Reader*: a clear measure of his unacceptability when Wollstonecraft was prepared to draw on George Savile's *Advice to a Daughter* for conventional warnings against vanity or even on Lord Chesterfield's *Letters to his Son* on the dangers of indolence (FR:138–41, 128). Just why Fordyce was so unacceptable becomes clear when Wollstonecraft quotes one of his most absurd, but also most dangerous, passages: "They [women] are timid, and want to be defended. They are frail; o do not take advantage of their weakness. Let their fears and blushes endear them."[42] Such "lover-like phrases of pumped up passion," she objects, sin against both "sense and taste": "I have heard rational men use the word indecent, when they mentioned them with disgust" (VRW:163–4). As Wollstonecraft's analysis reveals, Fordyce shares other male advice writers' sexually compromised attitude to women, but what she calls his "sentimental rant" signals a significantly different quality of infantilizing sexual prurience, unmitigated even by "the language of the heart" (163), much less by any wider belief in liberty or equality.

Wollstonecraft's careful discriminations between Gregory and Fordyce are based in stylistic analysis. In *The Female Reader*, Wollstonecraft's program of carefully chosen texts was intended to "imprint some useful lessons on the mind, and cultivate the taste at the same time" (FR:55). As in the periodical tradition, a refined taste is seen as inseparable from moral and intellectual improvement. The method of *The Female Reader*, the exercise of rational taste through close reading, is central to Wollstonecraft's political analysis of advice writings in *Rights of Woman*. Gregory's ideological inconsistency is signaled by the conjunction of an "easy familiar style," which invites confidence and respect, with "a degree of concise elegance ... that disturbs this sympathy" (VRW:166). Fordyce's stylistic sins against taste, the "cold artificial feelings" on display in his "affected style," are continuous with his tyrannic reduction of women to "house slave[s]" and "domestic drudge[s]" (163, 162, 165). But because of this, Wollstonecraft believes, both his sexual politics and his mode of instruction are doomed to failure: "esteem, the only lasting affection, can alone be obtained by virtue supported by reason. It is respect for the understanding that keeps alive tenderness for the person" (166).

Wollstonecraft's discriminating analysis here makes manifest the complex effects of advice writing for women. Her own ambivalent response to Gregory, particularly, is at one level symptomatic of precisely those gendered power relations which the intimate form of address in many conduct books insidiously perpetuates: Wollstonecraft herself registers daughterly affection for the "familiar" authority of the father's voice, one effect of which, as she clearly sees, can be to lull women into "a system of slavery" exactly comparable to "the servility in absolute monarchies" (101, 105). Far worse, however, she suggests, is the complete lack of either rational or affective esteem for women revealed by Fordyce's cold linguistic excess: his *Sermons* "have contributed to vitiate the taste, and enervate the understanding of many of my fellow-creatures" (166). The tendency of both Gregory's and Fordyce's texts is to encourage women to focus on their gendered, rather than their shared human, identity. But Wollstonecraft is alert (as she was in the case of Burke) to the sexual threat in Fordyce's predatory "voluptuousness," by which "all women are to be levelled, by meekness and docility, into one character of

yielding softness and gentle compliance" (165). Gregory's sympathetic esteem, by contrast, like that of other advice writers for whom conduct and
manners are inseparable from a wider horizon of education and "improvement," at least implicitly acknowledges a potentially productive "respect for
the understanding."

Rational independence for women is the goal of Wollstonecraft's own,
transformed, advice book: a human ideal which she contrasts constantly
with the gendered "art of pleasing," through which, a certain kind of advice literature persuades its female readers, they will achieve power (97). "I
do not wish them to have power over men; but over themselves" is Wollstonecraft's forceful response; "[t]he conduct of an accountable being must
be regulated by the operations of its own reason; or on what foundation
rests the throne of God?" (131, 105). Control over the self; right conduct;
accountability; regulation; religious aspiration; an emphasis on intellectual
substance over superficial pleasure: the vocabularies of duty and discipline
through which Wollstonecraft envisages her "revolution in female manners"
are still recognizably derived from the program of improvement offered in
eighteenth-century moral traditions. But for Wollstonecraft, the virtue which
is the object of that self-discipline is an absolute: "I here throw down my
gauntlet, and deny the existence of sexual virtues." Too often in advice writing, Wollstonecraft suggests, the effect of gender is that "virtue becomes
a relative idea, having no other foundation than utility, and of that utility men pretend arbitrarily to judge, shaping it to their own convenience"
(120). In *A Vindication of the Rights of Woman*, Wollstonecraft makes her
feminist declaration of independence by exposing that inconsistency from
within.

NOTES

1. VRW 5:97.
2. TED 4:25.
3. Mary Poovey, *The Proper Lady and the Woman Writer: Ideology as Style in the Works of Mary Wollstonecraft, Mary Shelley, and Jane Austen* (Chicago and London: University of Chicago Press, 1984); Nancy Armstrong, *Desire and Domestic Fiction: a Political History of the Novel* (New York and Oxford: Oxford University Press, 1987), 24, 66.
4. Wetenhall Wilkes, *A Letter of Genteel and Moral Advice to a Young Lady* (1740), quoted in Kathryn Sutherland, "Writings on Education and Conduct: Arguments for Female Improvement," *Women and Literature in Britain 1700–1800*, ed. Vivien Jones (Cambridge: Cambridge University Press, 2000), 31. Wollstonecraft approved of Chapone's *Letters*; see VRW 5:174.
5. Gary Kelly, *Revolutionary Feminism: the Mind and Career of Mary Wollstonecraft* (Basingstoke and London: Macmillan, 1992), 29.

6. Alan Richardson, *Literature, Education, and Romanticism: Reading as Social Practice 1780–1832* (Cambridge: Cambridge University Press, 1994), 172.
7. See Vivien Jones, "The Seductions of Conduct: Pleasure and Conduct Literature", *Pleasure in the Eighteenth Century*, eds. Roy Porter and Marie Mulvey Roberts (London and Basingstoke: Macmillan, 1996), 108–32.
8. John Gregory, *A Father's Legacy to his Daughters* (1774), *Women in the Eighteenth Century: Constructions of Femininity*, ed. Vivien Jones (London and New York: Routledge, 1990), 51.
9. John Milton, *Paradise Lost*, Book 8, lines 601–2.
10. Hannah More, *Strictures on the Modern System of Female Education* (1799), *Women*, ed. Jones, 132.
11. George Savile, Marquis of Halifax, *The Lady's New Years Gift: or, Advice to a Daughter* (1688), *Women*, ed. Jones, 18, 19.
12. Sarah Pennington, *An Unfortunate Mother's Advice to her Absent Daughters* (1761), *The Young Lady's Pocket Library, or Parental Monitor* (1790), ed. Vivien Jones (Bristol: Thoemmes Press, 1995), 96, 102.
13. M 1:73.
14. [James Burgh], *Thoughts on Education* (London: G. Freer; M. Cooper, 1747), 52–3.
15. Wollstonecraft includes the first two sentences of this quotation in FR 4:68.
16. *Paradise Lost*, Book 8, lines 602–5
17. Richard Price, *A Sermon delivered to a Congregation of Protestant Dissenters at Hackney...* (1779), quoted in D. O. Thomas, *The Honest Mind: the Thought and Work of Richard Price* (Oxford: Clarendon Press, 1977), 69.
18. "A Sound Mind in a sound Body, is a short, but full Description of a Happy State in this World," John Locke, *Some Thoughts Concerning Education*, eds. John W. and Jean S. Yolton (Oxford: Clarendon Press, 1989), 83.
19. Savile in *Women*, ed. Jones, 21; Hester Chapone, *Letters on the Improvement of the Mind, Addressed to a Young Lady*, 2nd edn., 2 vols. (London: H. Hughs for J. Walter, 1773), 2:97.
20. Alexander Pope, "An Epistle to a Lady. Of the Characters of Women" (1735), lines 245, 248; Edward Moore, *Fables for the Female Sex* (1744), "Fable II: The Panther, the Horse and Other Beasts," *Young Lady's Pocket Library*, ed. Jones, 193. Wollstonecraft includes "Fable III: The Nightingale, and Glow-worm" in FR 4:269–70.
21. *The Spectator*, 10 (12 March 1711).
22. *The Spectator*, 15 (17 March 1711).
23. Wollstonecraft includes extracts not just from *The Spectator*, but also from *The Guardian*, *The World*, *The Lounger*, *The Mirror*, and *The Connoisseur*, and from Samuel Johnson's *Rambler* and *Adventurer*.
24. See Pope, "Epistle to a Lady," lines 1–2: "Nothing so true as what you once let fall, / 'Most Women have no Characters at all.' "
25. Susan Gubar, "Feminist Misogyny: Mary Wollstonecraft and the Paradox of 'It Takes One to Know One,'" *Feminist Studies* 20:3 (1994), 453–73.
26. Quoted in FR 4:114.
27. VRM 5:37, 48.

28. *The Lady's Magazine* 18 (1787), 227–30, 287, 369–70; *Mrs. Wollstonecraft's Thoughts on the Education of Daughters. With Reflections on Female Conduct, in the more important Duties of Life. To which is added Fenolon* [sic]*Archbishop of Cambray's Instructions to a Governess, and an Address to Mothers* (Dublin: W. Sleator, 1788), sig. [4]r. Since one of the added chapters refers approvingly to James Fordyce, we can safely assume they are not by Wollstonecraft.

29. Wollstonecraft's preference for "a cultivated mind" appears in TED 32, in a passage reproduced in *The Lady's Magazine* 18:288.

30. FR 4:55.

31. Pennington, *Unfortunate Mother's Advice*, 86–7.

32. Moira Ferguson, Introduction, *The Female Reader* (Delmar, NY: Scholars' Facsimilies and Reprints, 1980), xxviii. And this in spite of its being published (perhaps to give it a spurious kind of authority) under the name of "Mr. Cresswick, Teacher of Elocution" rather than Wollstonecraft's own. Gary Kelly describes *The Female Reader* as "hack-work" in *Revolutionary Feminism*, 73.

33. *The Spectator* 10 (12 March 1711).

34. See P. O'Brien, *The Warrington Academy 1757–1786: Its Predecessors and Successors* (Wigan: Owl Books, 1989), 71; Review of *Vindication of the Rights of Woman*, *Monthly Review* 8 (1792), 198–209.

35. See William Enfield, *The Speaker: or, Miscellaneous Pieces, selected from the Best English Writers, and disposed under proper heads, with a view to facilitate the improvement of youth in Reading and Speaking*, a new edition, corrected (London: J. Johnson, 1786); "Dress subservient to useful Purposes" is the title given by Wollstonecraft to an extract from Sarah Trimmer's *The Oeconomy of Charity* (London: J. Johnson, 1787).

36. Letters, 138.

37. See Gerald P. Tyson, *Joseph Johnson: a Liberal Publisher* (Iowa City: University of Iowa Press, 1979).

38. Gregory, *Legacy, Young Lady's Pocket Library*, ed. Jones, 3.

39. Letters, 263.

40. *Paradise Lost*, Book 8, lines 383–4.

41. In chapter 14 of Jane Austen's *Pride and Prejudice* (1813), Mr Collins attempts to read to the Bennet sisters from Fordyce's *Sermons*.

42. James Fordyce, *Sermons to Young Women, in Two Volumes*, 3rd edn., corrected (London: A. Millar and T. Cadell, 1766), 1:99–100.

9

ANNE K. MELLOR

Mary Wollstonecraft's *A Vindication of the Rights of Woman* and the women writers of her day

In *A Vindication of the Rights of Woman*, Wollstonecraft threw down the gauntlet, not only to her male readers, but equally important, to the other women writers of her day, as she called for a "REVOLUTION in female manners." And these women took up Wollstonecraft's challenge. Whether they endorsed her views or contested them, very few women writers of the time ignored them. In this essay, I shall explore the range of responses by women writers to Wollstonecraft's ideas, or, more generally, to the feminist programs she and others espoused, taking the works of Mary Hays, Mary Robinson, Hannah More, Maria Edgeworth, Anna Letitia Barbauld, and Jane Austen as representative.

A Vindication of the Rights of Woman proposed a model of what we would now call "equality" or "liberal" feminism. Grounded on the affirmation of universal human rights endorsed by such Enlightenment thinkers as Voltaire, Rousseau, and John Locke, Wollstonecraft argued that females are in all the most important aspects the same as males, possessing the same souls, the same mental capacities, and thus the same human rights. While the first edition of the *Rights of Woman* attributed a physical superiority to the male, acknowledging his ability to overpower the female of the species with his greater brute strength –

> . . . the female, in general is inferior to the male. The male pursues, the female yields – this is the law of nature; and it does not appear to be suspended or abrogated in favor of woman. This physical superiority cannot be denied – and it is a noble prerogative! (VRW 5:74n4).

– by the end of the second edition, Wollstonecraft has effectively denied the significance and even the necessary existence of male physical superiority. She first reduces the physical difference between males and females, rewriting the above passage thus:

> In the government of the physical world it is observable that the female in point of strength is, *in general*, inferior to the male. This is the law of nature,

141

and does not appear to be suspended or abrogated in favour of women. *A degree of physical superiority* cannot, therefore, be denied – and it is a noble prerogative! (VRW 5:74, my italics).

She then insists that women's virtues – "strength of mind, perseverance and fortitude" – are the "same in kind" if not yet in "degree" (VRW 5:105). She next adamantly denies "the existence of sexual virtues, not excepting modesty" (VRW 5:120), in effect erasing any essentialist difference between males and females. She concludes by suggesting that if females were allowed the same exercise as males, then they would arrive at a "perfection of body" that might well erase any "natural superiority" of the male body (VRW 5:155).

On this philosophical assumption of sexual equality and even potential sameness, Wollstonecraft mounted her campaign for the reform of female education, arguing that girls should be educated in the same subjects and by the same methods as boys. She further advocated a radical revision of British law to enable a new, egalitarian marriage in which women would share equally in the management and possession of all household resources. She demanded that women be paid – and paid equally – for their labor, that they gain the civil and legal right to possess and distribute property, that they be admitted to all the most prestigious professions. And she argued that women (together with all disenfranchised men) should be given the vote: "I really think that women ought to have representatives, instead of being arbitrarily governed without any direct share allowed them in the deliberations of government" (VRW 5:217).

The revolution in female manners demanded by Wollstonecraft would, she insisted, dramatically change both genders. It would produce women who were sincerely modest, chaste, virtuous, Christian; who acted with reason and prudence and generosity. It would produce men who – rather than being trained to become petty household tyrants or slave-masters over their female dependents or "house-slaves" (VRW 5:165) – would treat women with respect and act toward all with benevolence, justice, and sound reason. It would eliminate the "want of chastity in men," a depravity of appetite that in Wollstonecraft's view was responsible for the social production of unmanly "equivocal beings" (VRW 5:208). And it would produce egalitarian marriages based – no longer on mere sexual desire – but on compatibility, mutual affection, and respect. As she concluded,

we shall not see women affectionate till more equality be established in society, till ranks are confounded and women freed, neither shall we see that dignified domestic happiness, the simple grandeur of which cannot be relished by ignorant or vitiated minds; nor will the important task of education ever be properly begun till the person of a woman is no longer preferred to her mind.

(VRW 5:263)

During the heady days of the early 1790s, as the workers and middle classes overthrew the *ancien régime* in France, Wollstonecraft's call for a revolution in female manners was immediately taken up by several of her female compatriots. Her close friend Mary Hays, the daughter of middle-class London Dissenters and the author of a spirited defense of the Unitarian church, *Cursory Remarks on an Enquiry into the Expediency and Propriety of Public or Social Worship* (1791), sprang to the defense of Wollstonecraft's feminist program. Hays's *Letters and Essays, Moral, and Miscellaneous* (1793), a work which Hays submitted directly to Wollstonecraft for her advice and criticism, eloquently attacked the

> mental bondage . . . ; the absurd despotism which has hitherto, with more than gothic barbarity, enslaved the female mind, the enervating and degrading system of manners by which the understandings of women have been chained down to frivolity and trifles, have increased the general tide of effeminacy and corruption. (Letters 3:23)

Hays further endorsed Wollstonecraft's most radical claim, "the idea of there being no sexual character," arguing that the opposite opinion has caused far more dangerous social extremes; moreover, "similarity of mind and principle is the only true basis of harmony" (Letters 3:24). She concluded that "the rights of woman, and the name of Woollstonecraft [sic], will go down to posterity with reverence, when the pointless sarcasms of witlings are forgotten" (Letters 3:29). And in her letter to the Dissenting *Monthly Magazine* for 2 March 1797, published under the running head "Improvements suggested in Female Education," she again invokes Wollstonecraft before concluding:

> Till one moral mental standard is established for every rational agent, every member of a community, and a free scope afforded for the exertion of their faculties and talents, without distinction of rank or sex, *virtue* will be an empty name, and *happiness* elude our most anxious research. (3:195)

Mary Hays based both her novels, *Emma Courtney* (1796) and *The Victim of Prejudice* (1799), on Wollstonecraft's program for social reform. Emma Courtney enthusiastically upholds both Wollstonecraft's and William Godwin's doctrines but brings to them Hays's independent emphasis on the importance of sensibility, of women's capacity for strong emotions and enduring love. Emma falls passionately in love with her mentor Augustus

Harley, a Godwinian philosopher who insists that humans will necessarily perfect themselves through the exercise of reason. Although her offer to give herself to him, even outside of marriage, is coldly rejected by Harley (he is already married), Harley finally vindicates both Emma's sensibility and her desire for a truly companionate relationship by confessing on his death-bed that he has always loved her. In the course of her trials, in which she on one occasion quotes Wollstonecraft's *Rights of Woman*, Emma provides an on-going feminist critique of her society, attacking both the slave trade and the enslavement of women, reflecting "on the inequalities of society, the source of every misery and of every vice, and on the peculiar disadvantages of my sex," and lamenting the "cruel prejudices" that prevented her from being educated "for a profession, for labour" and instead "rendered feeble and delicate by bodily constraint, and fastidious by artificial confinement."[1]

Hays's second novel, *The Victim of Prejudice* (1799), explores the unjust treatment given to women who must pay for a moment of sexual pleasure with a lifetime of ruin, a subject that Wollstonecraft had addressed in the *Rights of Woman* and also, in the minds of many, came in some ways herself to exemplify. Abandoned by her lover, Hays's heroine's mother rapidly sinks into prostitution, is separated from her daughter, and is finally executed as a murderer's accomplice. As she writes to her lost lover, "I perceived myself the victim of injustice, of the prejudice, of society, which, by opposing to my return to virtue almost insuperable barriers, had plunged me into irremediable ruin. I grew sullen, desperate, hardened."[2] Her daughter, the virtuous heroine Mary, is then raped but refuses to marry her traducer. Unable to get honest work since she is now regarded by society as "a fallen woman," Mary is arrested for debt, sent to prison where her health is destroyed, and finally dies, still refusing to marry her (supposedly reformed and repentant) rapist. Mary Hays thus rewrites the narrative of the fallen woman as a story of social prejudice against an unjustly treated and innocent victim, one who preserves her moral integrity and personal independence throughout.

Mary Hays's most radical feminist claims appeared in her *Appeal to the Men of Great Britain in Behalf of Woman*, a tract she wrote before reading Wollstonecraft's *Rights of Woman* but did not publish until 1798. Here Hays is far more critical of men than was Wollstonecraft. She insists throughout on the primary equality of women, arguing that "God created mankind male and female, different indeed in sex for the wisest and best purposes, but equal in rank, because of equal utility."[3] It is men who have defied God, Hays charges, by refusing to educate women, keeping them in "subjection and dependence" (68), in a state Hays memorably defines as "PERPETUAL BABYISM" (97). Prostitution is caused not by female vice but by "the base arts used by profligate men, to seduce innocent and unsuspecting females," and fallen women are thus "more objects of pity than blame" (235–6). And it is men who prefer "folly, vice, impertinence of every kind," who desire women to be solely "their amusement, their dependent; and in plain and unvarnished terms their slaves," because they are terrified that their unearned claims of sexual superiority could be overthrown, terrified "of the frightful certainty of having women declared their equals, and as such their companions and friends" (116).

Hays continued her campaign for liberal feminism even after Wollstonecraft's death, although she was forced by the public denunciation of Wollstonecraft sparked by Godwin's ill-judged publication of his *Memoirs of the Author of the Vindication of the Rights of Woman* in 1798 to speak more circumspectly (her *Appeal* was published anonymously). In 1803 she published her six volume collation of 305 mini-biographies of famous women, *Female Biography; or, Memoirs of Illustrious and Celebrated Women, of all ages and countries* (1803), designed to inspire her female contemporaries to "a worthier emulation" (vi). Here Hays felt compelled by public opinion to omit a biography of Wollstonecraft although she included biographies of such earlier feminists as Mary Astell, Catharine Macaulay, and Madame Roland. Hays's actions here remind us of just how dangerous it had become by 1800 for a woman who hoped to be published and taken seriously to identify openly with Wollstonecraft *as a person*. As Susan Wolfson shows elsewhere in this volume, Wollstonecraft was widely demonized after her death. Nonetheless, many women writers who did not wish to be tarred with the blackened brush of Wollstonecraft's *reputation* still continued to invoke and espouse her ideas. And as the nineteenth century wore on, as Kathryn Gleadle's forthcoming research shows, numerous women writers and thinkers once again openly invoked Wollstonecraft as their noble precursor, both privately in letters and publicly in print.

Reaffirming her commitment both to the education of women and to the importance of the feelings in social intercourse, Hays prefaces the book:

> My pen has been taken up in the cause, and for the benefit, of my own sex. For their improvement, and to their entertainment, my labours have been devoted. Women . . . require pleasure to be mingled with instruction, lively images, the graces of sentiment, and the polish of language. Their understandings are principally accessible through their affections: they delight in minute delineation of character; nor must the truths which impress them be either cold or unadorned.
>
> (*Female Biography*, iv)

Hays here moves beyond her earlier arguments for the equality of the sexes to an even more radical suggestion, that females might potentially be superior to males: "A woman who, to the graces and gentleness of her own sex, adds the knowledge and fortitude of the other, exhibits the most perfect combination of human excellence" (v). In her final work, *Memoirs of Queens Illustrious and Celebrated* (1821), however, Hays returns to Wollstonecraft's equality feminism:

> I maintain . . . that there is, there can be, but *one moral standard of excellence for mankind*, whether male or female, and that the licentious distinctions [between the sexes] made by the domineering party, in the spirit of tyranny, selfishness, and sexuality, are at the foundation of the heaviest evils that have afflicted, degraded, and corrupted society: and I found my arguments upon nature, equity, philosophy, and the Christian religion. (vi)

In the 1790s several women writers endorsed the program of liberal feminism which Wollstonecraft, Catharine Macaulay, and Mary Astell had developed, although none so rigorously or whole-heartedly as did Mary Hays. In *The Female Advocate; or, An Attempt to Recover the Rights of Women from Male Usurpation* (1799), Mary Anne Radcliffe, evoking her personal experiences as a landed Scottish heiress whose ne'er-do-well husband had lost all their money, leaving her destitute and in ill health, bitterly attacked the lack of suitable employment for women. The poet and novelist Mary Robinson, writing as Anne Frances Randall, in her *Thoughts on the Condition of Women, and on the Injustice of Mental Subordination* (1799), attacked the sexual double standard, directly repeating Wollstonecraft's and Hays's argument that male hypocrisy was primarily responsible for female prostitution. At the same time, she celebrated the historical accomplishments, both political and cultural, of contemporary women, citing thirty-nine examples of accomplished female writers, philosophers, historians, translators, and artists, including both Mrs. Woollstonecraft [*sic*] and Miss Hayes [*sic*]. After calling for a university for women, Robinson turned her attention to women's writing as a literary genre. Anticipating Anna Barbauld's later canon-forming claim in her *Essay on the Origin and Progress of Novel-Writing*, the Introduction to the collection of reprints of British novels published by Rivington (1810) and titled *The British Novelists*, Robinson was the first to argue that by 1790 the novel had become a feminine genre:

> The best novels that have been written, since those of Smollett, Richardson and Fielding, have been produced by women: and their pages have not only been embellished with the interesting events of domestic life, portrayed with all the elegance of phraseology, and all the refinement of sentiment, but with forcible and eloquent political, theological, and philosophical reasoning.
>
> (London, 2nd edn., 1799: 95)

At the conservative end of the feminist spectrum in Wollstonecraft's day stood Hannah More, a prolific writer of poems, plays, religious and political tracts and ballads, and fiction. So "Invincibly" opposed to Wollstonecraft was More that she refused even to read the *Rights of Woman*.[4] Often dismissed by scholars and critics as a reactionary thinker dedicated to upholding the status quo, Hannah More developed a feminist program of her own, one based on a theoretical basis different from Wollstonecraft's. But as Mitzi Myers first recognized, More and Wollstonecraft arrived at surprisingly similar conclusions.[5]

Hannah More was the most influential woman living in England in Wollstonecraft's day. Through her writings, political actions, and personal relationships with the Bishop of London and the Evangelical Clapham Sect, she promoted a successful program for social change from within the existing social and political order. She called for a "revolution in manners" or cultural mores, a radical change in the *moral* behavior of the nation as a whole.[6] In contrast to Wollstonecraft's "revolution in female manners," which aimed at transforming the education and behavior of women in particular, Hannah More attempted to change the behavior of all the subjects of the British nation, aristocrats, clergy, the middling classes, workers, *and* women. But insofar as Wollstonecraft's efforts to change radically the social construction of gender in her day entailed a change in the attitudes and daily practices of men as well as women, these two "revolutions in manners" came finally to work toward very similar feminist goals.

As I have argued in my book *Mothers of the Nation*,[7] Hannah More's writings contributed significantly to the prevention of a French-style, violent political revolution in England. They did so by helping to reform, rather than subvert, the existing social order. More's reform efforts were aimed in four directions: at the moral and financial irresponsibility of the aristocracy, at the laxness of the Anglican clergy, at the immorality and economic bad management of the working classes, and most important here, at the flawed education and frivolous behavior of women of all classes. More sought above all to create a new British national identity, one based on a shared value-system grounded on the Christian virtues of rational benevolence, honesty, personal virtue, the fulfillment of social duty, thrift, sobriety, and hard work.

Fundamental to More's project of social revolution was a transformation of the role played by women in the formation of British moral and political culture. Unlike Wollstonecraft, who argued that the two sexes were in all significant aspects the same, Hannah More insisted on the innate difference between the sexes. To women she assigned a greater delicacy of perception and feeling and, above all, a greater moral purity and capacity for virtue.

Men, on the other hand, in More's view, have better judgment, based on their wider experience of the public world; at the same time their manners are coarse, with "rough angles and asperities" ("Introduction" to *Essays on Various Subjects*, 1777; 6: 266). Unlike Wollstonecraft's program of liberal political reform which looked equally to men and to women to institute her new systems of coeducation and egalitarian marriage, if More's "revolution in manners" was to occur, it must be carried out primarily by women.

But first women must be educated to understand their proper function in society. More's *Strictures on the Modern System of Female Education* (1799) laid out her program for the education of "excellent women" (III:200): a systematic development of the innate female capacity for virtue and piety through a judicious reading of the Bible, devotional tracts, and serious literature, extended by rational conversation and manifested in the active exercise of compassion and generosity. The goal of More's educational project for women was no less than a cultural redefinition of *female virtue*. As summed up in that "pattern daughter... [who] will make a pattern wife," Lucilla Stanley (*Coelebs in Search of a Wife*, 1808),[8] female virtue was equated by More with rational intelligence, modesty and chastity, a sincere commitment to spiritual values and the Christian religion, an affectionate devotion to one's family, active service on behalf of one's community, and an insistence on keeping promises. In More's words:

> I call education, not that which smothers a woman with accomplishments, but that which tends to consolidate a firm and regular system of character; that which tends to form a friend, a companion, and a wife. I call education, not that which is made up of the shreds and patches of useless arts, but that which inculcates principles, polishes taste, regulates temper, cultivates reason, subdues the passions, directs the feelings, habituates to reflection, trains to self-denial, and, more especially, that which refers all actions, feelings, sentiments, tastes and passions to the love and fear of God. (*Coelebs*, 13)

More's concept of female virtue – like Wollstonecraft's concept of the rational woman – thus stood in stark contrast to her culture's prevailing definition of the ideal woman as one who possessed physical beauty and numerous accomplishments and whose principal object in life was effectively to entice a man into marriage.

Embedded in More's program for the education of women was a new career for upper and middle-class women, as Dorice Elliot has shown,[9] namely, a sustained and increasingly institutionalized effort to relieve the sufferings of the less fortunate. As Mrs. Stanley defines this career: "*Charity is the calling of a lady; the care of the poor is her profession*" (*Coelebs*: 138; More's italics). While More did not endorse Wollstonecraft's view that women should enter the professions in general (Wollstonecraft had singled out careers in business, medicine, and education as particularly suited to female talents), she did conceptualize for the first time the female professional career of what we would now call the "social worker," the organized and corporate, as opposed to the spontaneous and individualistic, practice of philanthropy. As embodied in Lucilla Stanley, this profession involves spending one day each week collecting "necessaries" for the poor – food, clothing, medicine – and two evenings each week visiting them in their own cottages where she can best determine "their wants and their characters" (*Coelebs* 63).

More advocated that women participate in an even more institutionalized philanthropy, a "regular systematical good" resulting in a "broad stream of bounty . . . flowing through and refreshing whole districts" (*Strictures*, III: 270). She urged her women readers to work aggressively in the organization of voluntary benevolent societies and in the foundation of hospitals, orphanages, Sunday Schools and all-week charity or "ragged" schools for the education and relief of the poor. And her call was heard: literally thousands of voluntary societies sprang up in the opening decades of the nineteenth century to serve the needs of every imaginable group of sufferers. More's Evangelical demand that women demonstrate their commitment to God through a life of active service for the first time gave her upper- and middle-class sisters a mission in life, the personal and financial support of institutionalized charities, from orphanages, workhouses, and hospitals to asylums and prisons. As F. K. Prochaska documented, these philanthropic activities contributed directly to the emancipation and increasing social empowerment of women by teaching them the skills necessary to organize and maintain complex financial institutions.[10]

According to Hannah More, women were particularly suited to the active exercise of charity precisely because of their sexual difference, because women possessed greater sensibility than do men. More defined sensibility as an *active* rather than passive sympathy for the sufferings of others, one that immediately attempts to relieve the misery it perceives. As she invoked it in one of her early poems,

> Sweet Sensibility! thou keen delight!
> Thou hasty moral! sudden sense of right!
> Thou untaught goodness! Virtue's precious seed!
> Thou sweet precursor of the gen'rous deed!
> (*Sensibility: A Poetical Epistle to the Hon. Mrs. Boscawen*,
> 1782, V:336, lines 244–7)

Secondly, women were more versed in what More called "practical piety," the immediate assessment and relief of the day-to-day requirements of the poor, the sick, the dying. Finally, women who had learned how to manage a household properly could more readily extend those skills to the Sunday School, workhouse or hospital.

Implicit both in More's *Strictures on Female Education* and in her novel *Coelebs* is the argument that household management or domestic economy provides the best model for the management of the state or national economy. Here More agrees with Wollstonecraft's similar argument in *Rights of Woman* that the same skills are required to administer the well-run household as to govern the well-run nation. More spelled out this concept of home economics in her *Strictures on Female Education*:

> Economy, such as a woman of fortune is called on to practise, is not merely the petty detail of small daily expenses, the shabby curtailments and stinted parsimony of a little mind operating on little concerns; but it is the exercise of a sound judgment exerted in the comprehensive outline of order, of arrangement, of distribution; *of regulation by which alone well-governed societies, great and small, subsist....* A sound economy is a sound understanding brought into action; it is calculation realized; it is foreseeing consequences, and guarding against them; it is expecting contingencies, and being prepared for them. (III:189–90, my italics)

By assigning to women – and their mentor Eve – the capacity to develop and execute a fiscally responsible plan of household management which satisfies the physical, emotional, and religious needs of all the members of the household (servants as well as family members), More effectually defined women as the best managers of the national estate, as the true patriots. As Kathryn Sutherland has argued, More proposed "a practical politics of domestic reformation, which is national in the ambitious scope of its campaign and personal in its focus on the woman in her family as the source of this larger regeneration."[11] Invoking Milton's Eve as her model of female propriety and "Those thousand *decencies* which daily flow / From all her words and actions," More urged her sisters to "exert themselves with a patriotism at once firm and feminine, for the general good" (*Strictures*, III:14).

It is in the role of mother that More's ideal of the well-educated, fiscally responsible, and morally pure woman finds her fulfillment. But it is crucial to recognize that More's mother is the mother, not just of her own family, but of the nation as a whole. More thus implicitly endorses what I have elsewhere described as Wollstonecraft's "family politics," her argument that the well-managed, co-parented, and egalitarian family provides the best model for the government of the state.[12] As More affirmed in her *Strictures on Female Education*, the great object to which *you*, who are or may be mothers, are more especially called, is the education of your children. If we are responsible for the use of influence in the case of those over whom we have no immediate control, in the case of our children we are responsible for the exercise of acknowledged *power*: a power wide in its extent, indefinite in its effects, and inestimable in its importance. On Y O U depend in no small degree the principles of the whole rising generation.... To Y O U is made over the awfully important trust of infusing the first principles of piety into the tender minds of those who may one day be called to instruct, not families merely, but districts; to influence, not individuals, but senates. Your private exertions may at this moment be contributing to the future happiness, your domestic neglect, to the future ruin, of your country.   (*Strictures*, III:44)

As Mitzi Myers has noted, no one worked harder than More to define a new ideological mission for women: to "educate the young and illiterate, succor the unfortunate, amend the debased popular culture of the lower orders, reorient worldly men of every class, and set the national household in order," thereby elevating women's "nurturing and reformative assignment" into a "national mission."[13] Women can become, in More's view, the Mothers of the Nation.

Emphasizing women's *public* role as mothers of the nation, More necessarily downplayed their more private sexual roles as females. Like Wollstonecraft, More has been criticized by modern feminist critics for insisting on a new ideal of female "passionlessness." As Nancy Cott put it, Hannah More's "work perfected the transformation of woman's image from sexual to moral being," giving women power only at the price of sexual repression. But this is too one-sided a reading of More's campaign. More did not urge women to *deny* their sexual desires, but only to *channel* them into marriage with a morally as well as sexually desirable partner. As Michael Mason has rightly observed, "To Hannah More belongs the distinction of having written at greater length explicitly about sex than any other leading Evangelical" in her novel *Coelebs in Search of a Wife*.[14]

By defining the private household and "private principle" as the source of "public virtue" (*Strictures*, III:44). More implicitly endorsed Edmund Burke's concept in his *Reflections on the Revolution in France* (1790) of the domestic estate as the model for the state of the nation. But rather than assigning to Burke's "canonized forefathers" the ultimate responsibility for the moral improvement and sustenance of the family estate, More like Wollstonecraft explicitly assigned that responsibility to women, to *mothers*. Men may wage battles abroad, but women protect the home front: as she asked rhetorically: "Is it not desirable to be the lawful possessors of a lesser domestic territory, rather than the turbulent usurpers of a wider foreign

empire?" (*Strictures*, III:200). This is why her heroine Lucilla Stanley devotes a great deal of time to *gardening* – to nurturing and controlling the
native land of England, as Eve cultivated the fields of Eden.

In making the private middle-class household the model for the national
household, as had Mary Wollstonecraft before her, Hannah More effectively
erased any meaningful distinction between the private and the broadly defined public sphere. Both More and Wollstonecraft further agreed that it is
women, not men, who are most responsible for carrying out moral reforms
and thus for advancing the progress of civilization as such. As More put it:
"The general state of civilized society depends, more than those are aware
who are not accustomed to scrutinize into the springs of human action, on
the prevailing sentiments and habits of women, and on the nature and degree of the estimation in which they are held" (*Strictures*, III:12). Insisting
on the primary role of women in establishing "true taste, right principle, and
genuine feeling" in the culture of a nation, both More and Wollstonecraft
finally claimed for women the dominant role in what Norbert Elias has since
called the "civilizing process."

Between these two camps of feminist reform, Wollstonecraft's overtly political "revolution in female manners" based on an assertion of sexual equality
and universal human rights and More's more restrictively cultural "revolution
in manners" based on sexual difference and the essential moral superiority of women, other women writers took up more moderate feminist positions. Most notable in their efforts to find a middle ground were the
Dissenters, women whose religion (whether Quaker, Unitarian, or Methodist)
had already granted them a degree of sexual equality based on their capacity for virtue, rationality, and religious leadership.[15] The Quaker philanthropist, Priscilla Bell Wakefield, in her *Reflections on the Present Condition
of the Female Sex; with Suggestions for Its Improvement* (London, 1798),
disagreed with Wollstonecraft's arguments for the equality of women with
men, asserting instead that women should submit to their husbands' superior judgment. And while she singled out Hannah More and Sarah Trimmer
for special praise, she went beyond More to argue that women must be educated in practical vocations so that they could *support themselves*, since the
accidents of fortune often left women of all classes without male economic
support.

The Unitarian Anna Letitia Barbauld, inspired by her education at the
leading Dissenting academy, Warrington Academy, where her father was the
tutor in Classics and Belles Lettres, argued aggressively for the equal rights
of all the subjects of the British nation in 1790 in her fiery denunciation of

the government's refusal to repeal the Corporation and Test Acts which prohibited non-members of the Church of England from holding political office
or attending the established universities, in her political pamphlet *Appeal
to the Opposers of the Repeal of the Corporation and Test Acts*. Barbauld
was the leading female literary critic of her day, arguing forcefully for the
preeminence of contemporary women's writing in the genre of prose fiction.
She also promoted the rational religious education of children in her widely
disseminated *Hymns in Prose for Children* and wrote numerous poems and
tracts attacking the British slave trade, slavery in the British colonies, and the
growing corruption both of the British government and of British commerce
as it extended its empire to India and the Pacific Islands.

Turning her attention to the rights of woman, Barbauld entered into an
extended debate with Wollstonecraft on the proper role of women in society.
Wollstonecraft had attacked Barbauld directly in a footnote to *A Vindication
of the Rights of Woman* (122n5). After endorsing Barbauld's affirmation of
virtue over physical pleasure in her poem "To Mrs. P—, with some drawings
of birds and insects,"

> Pleasure's the portion of the' *inferior* kind;
> But glory, virtue, Heaven for *man* design'd.

(Barbauld is here using "man" in the generic sense, as contrasted to the inferior species of birds and insects), Wollstonecraft then quoted the entire text
of Barbauld's poem "To A Lady, with Some Painted Flowers" (1773), a poem
which she contemptuously dismissed as "ignoble." Wollstonecraft passionately objected to Barbauld's identification of femininity with delicate flowers
"born for pleasure and delight alone" and her conclusion that for women,
"*Your* BEST, *your* SWEETEST *empire* is – to PLEASE" (Wollstonecraft's emphases). Wollstonecraft then commented sardonically, "So the men tell us;
but virtue, says reason, must be acquired by *rough* toils, and useful struggles
with worldly *cares* (123n5).

Barbauld then responded with a poem she chose not to publish, "The
Rights of Woman" (composed 1793, pub. 1825; text given in footnotes[16]).
In this radically destabilized poem, Barbauld first urges "injured Woman,"
quoting Wollstonecraft, to "assert thy right!" (line 1). But for Barbauld, who
endorses Hannah More's belief in innate sexual difference, woman's "rights"
are a "native empire o'er the breast" (line 4), in other words, a greater sensibility, virtuousness or "angel pureness" (line 6). At the same time she mocks
the traditional rhetoric of the battle of the sexes, most famously located perhaps in the image of the "virago Thalestris" in Pope's *Rape of the Lock*,
and instead urges women to resist the conventional notion that they might

be able to attain domination over men through the artillery of their "soft melting tones," "blushes and fears" (lines 11–12), the wiles ("wit and art", line 17) of feminine coquetry. For a female conquest based on the "sacred mysteries" or irrational arts of romantic love only makes "treacherous Man thy subject, not thy friend" (line 20) and leaves women imprisoned in a system of emotional manipulation ("Thou mayst command, but never canst be free," line 20).

Instead Barbauld urges women to use their "angel pureness" to "Awe the licentious, and restrain the rude; / Soften the sullen, clear the cloudy brow" (lines 21–2), in other words, to heighten the moral tone of society and thus advance the civilizing process. She will then become the "courted idol of mankind" (line 25), courted both in the sense that she is sought after or wooed by now-"subdued" man, but also in the sense that she has assumed her rightful place at the center of the now-reigning court of middle-class morality. Once she has raised "subdued" man to her moral level, Barbauld concludes, woman must in turn "subdue" herself, soften her coldness, give up her moral pride, "abandon each ambitious thought" (line 29), any desire for "conquest or rule" over men, and instead submit to "Nature's school" (line 30), a school that teaches that ideally, "separate rights are lost in mutual love" (line 32). Here Barbauld finally foreswears what she sees as Wollstonecraft's overly aggressive demand for the immediate equality or "rights" of woman for a more gradual process of moral development, mutual sexual appreciation, tolerance, and love, a process in which middle-class women recognize and take seriously their ethical responsibilities and emotional capacities to exercise an ethic of care and to prevent conflict and violence at home and abroad (an argument she made at greater length in 1793 in her political pamphlet, *Sins of Government, Sins of the Nation*).[17]

This debate between Wollstonecraft and Barbauld, together with the program advocated by Hannah More, vividly reveals the very real intellectual and psychological tensions that existed between the leading feminists in England in the 1790s. Although each of these three influential female writers advocated the radically improved education of women and increased female control over British social, cultural, and political life, they held distinctly different views as to exactly how women could best exercise that new cultural authority. Wollstonecraft would have women fulfill the social and political roles currently played by men, Barbauld would have women enter the literary realm as didactic writers, educators, and critical judges, while More would have women engage in a life of active service for the welfare of others.

At the end of the century, after the publication of Godwin's loving but ill-judged *Memoirs of the Author of a Vindication of the Rights of Woman* in 1798, it became increasingly difficult for feminist writers openly to endorse even Wollstonecraft's less controversial demands. In the *Memoirs*, Godwin publicly revealed Wollstonecraft's love affair with Gilbert Imlay and his fathering of her illegitimate daughter Fanny, Wollstonecraft's two suicide attempts (in defiance of the Anglican Church's definition of suicide as a sin), and his own sexual liaison with Wollstonecraft long before their marriage. He further asserted, inaccurately, that Wollstonecraft did not call on God on her deathbed. The popular press then widely denounced Wollstonecraft as a whore and an atheist, as well as a dangerous revolutionary. Their attacks were fueled by the chauvinist, anti-French feelings roused by England's declaration of war against France in 1802, and the hysterical British reaction against all French revolutionary ideas and practices during the Napoleonic campaigns.

This wide-spread denunciation of Wollstonecraft's personal life made it increasingly difficult for women writers to invoke Wollstonecraft's writings by name, although many continued to endorse her ideas. Maria Edgeworth took pains to distance herself from Wollstonecraft the person even as she directly advocated Wollstonecraft's "revolution in female manners." In her *Letters for Literary Ladies* (1799), Edgeworth insisted that she was not "a champion for the rights of woman" – which she then narrowly defined as "a vain contention for superiority" by women over men – but was concerned only "to determine what is most for our general advantage."[18] And in her novel *Belinda* (London, 1803), Edgeworth in the seventeenth chapter entitled "Rights of Woman" caricatured her "champion" for women's rights in the figure of Harriet Freke, a cross-dressed, duel-fighting woman who assumes the worst aspects of masculinity – tyranny over the weak (she plays several cruel practical jokes on the black servant Juba), infidelity, and physical violence. The extent to which Edgeworth feels she must go to distance the reader's sympathies from and to punish this early example of what we would today call a macho woman or butch lesbian – Harriet Freke is finally crippled in a "man-trap" – only reveals, as Patricia Juliana Smith has perceptively recognized, Edgeworth's own lesbian panic, her powerful fear that she will be painted with the Wollstonecraft brush, defined as a literary "amazon," and thereby excluded from all "polite society," her reputation as a serious thinker and advocate for the education of women in tatters.[19] At the same time, Edgeworth aggressively promoted her own version of the revolutionary feminist, the new Belinda who will replace Pope's "fairest of mortals" as the envy of her age. Belinda Portman is the embodiment of all that Wollstonecraft called for in women: sound sense, wide reading, prudence, personal modesty, and a loving heart. She makes an egalitarian and companionate marriage with Clarence Harvey (after his own foibles have been exposed) and converts her friend Lady Delacour from a life of aristocratic license and personal anguish to a loving domesticity by reconciling and reuniting her with her estranged husband and daughter.

Like Edgeworth, Jane Austen responded positively to many of Wollstonecraft's feminist arguments without ever mentioning her by name. All of Austen's novels are novels of education, in which her female heroines learn from their reading, their wiser mentors, and their own mistakes to become moral, responsible wives and shrewd judges of human nature. Allusions to and endorsements of ideas promoted in *A Vindication of the Rights of Woman* are scattered throughout Austen's fiction – whether as Elizabeth Bennet's sarcastic condemnation of female "accomplishments" or Wickham's embodiment of Wollstonecraft's critique of standing armies in *Pride and Prejudice*, as the association of the slave trade with the enslavement of British women in *Mansfield Park* (where Fanny Price functions as a house-slave[20]), as the modulated recognition of the competing claims of sense and sensibility which Wollstonecraft had tracked from her *Mary, A Fiction* through *Right of Woman* to *The Wrongs of Woman* in *Sense and Sensibility*, or as the affirmation of Anne Elliot as better qualified to manage the national estate than Wentworth in *Persuasion*. In Anne Elliot, as I have argued in detail in *Mothers of the Nation* (chapter 5), Jane Austen deftly stitches together Wollstonecraft's feminist ideas with those of Hannah More: Anne, Austen's ideal woman, achieves the rational, companionate marriage urged by Wollstonecraft and exemplified in Admiral and Sophia Croft, at the same time that she practices Hannah More's "profession" of caring for the sick, the needy, the poor. Throughout her novels, Jane Austen endorses Wollstonecraft's belief that the best woman is a *rational* woman, a woman of sense as well as sensibility, who seeks a psychologically egalitarian marriage. Within the context of the politicized discourse of the novel in her day, as Claudia Johnson has shown,[21] Jane Austen can be seen as a moderate feminist.

Wollstonecraft's impact on the women writers of her day was incalculably profound. Whether individual writers endorsed Wollstonecraft's specific demands that women enter the professions on a par with men, that they be granted their own "representation" in Parliament, that they be entitled to the legal custody of their own children and to divorce at will, or disagreed with them, very few denied the validity of her key arguments: that women should be rationally educated, that they should be the companions rather than the servants of men, and that they should be responsible, caring mothers and prudent household managers. However reluctant individual female writers may have been to acknowledge directly their indebtedness to *A Vindication of the Rights of Woman*, this ideology which Wollstonecraft so sharply articulated became the dominant belief of the women writers of her day, across the entire feminist spectrum, from the radicals Mary Hays and Mary Robinson through the more moderate Anna Barbauld, Priscilla Wakefield, Maria Edgeworth, and Jane Austen, to the conservative Hannah More.

NOTES

1. Mary Hays, *Memoirs of Emma Courtney*, ed. Marilyn L. Brooks (Peterborough, Canada: Broadview Press, 2000), 88, 65–6. This edition contains the *Monthly Magazine* articles by Hays, as well as a helpful Introduction.
2. Mary Hays, *The Victim of Prejudice* (1799), ed. Eleanor Ty (Peterborough, Canada: Broadview Press, 1998), 66. Also see Eleanor Ty, *Unsex'd Revolutionaries – Five Women Novelists of the 1790s* (Toronto: University of Toronto Press, 1993), chapters. 2–3.
3. Mary Hays, *Appeal to the Men of Great Britain in Behalf of Women* (1798), intro. Gina Luria (New York and London: Garland Publishers, Inc., 1974), 21.
4. See Hannah More's letter to Horace Walpole, 1793, William Roberts, *Memoirs of the Life and Correspondence of Mrs Hannah More*, 4 vols. (London: Seeley and Burnside, 1834), II:371.
5. Mitzi Myers, "Reform or Ruin: 'A Revolution in Female Manners,'" *Studies in Eighteenth-Century Culture*, ed. Harry C. Payne (Madison: University of Wisconsin Press, 1982), 11:199–216. A recent analysis of the intersections as well as the differences in the political discourse of Wollstonecraft and More can be found in Harriet Guest's *Small Change: Women, Learning, Patriotism, 1750–1810* (Chicago: University of Chicago Press, 2000), 271–89.
6. Hannah More, *The Works of Hannah More*, 6 vols. (London: H. Fisher, R. Fisher and P. Jackson, 1834), II:316.
7. See my *Mothers of the Nation – Women's Political Writing in England, 1780–1830* (Bloomington: Indiana University Press, 2000), chapter 1.
8. Hannah More, *Coelebs in Search of a Wife* (London, 1808; repr. Bristol: Thoemmes Press, 1995), 246.
9. Dorice Elliott, "'The Care of the Poor is Her Profession': Hannah More and Women's Philanthropic Work," *Nineteenth-Century Contexts* 19 (1995), 179–204.
10. F. K. Prochaska, *Women and Philanthropy in Nineteenth-Century England* (Oxford: Clarendon Press, 1980), 227 and passim.
11. Kathryn Sutherland, "Hannah More's Counter-Revolutionary Feminism," *Revolution in Writing: British Literary Responses to the French Revolution*, ed. Kelvin Everest (Milton Keynes and Philadelphia: Open University Press, 1991), 27–64, 36.
12. On Wollstonecraft's "family politics," see my *Romanticism and Gender* (New York and London: Routledge Press, 1993), chapter 4.
13. Mitzi Myers, "Hannah More's Tracts for the Times: Social Fiction and Female Ideology," *Fetter'd or Free? British Women Novelists, 1670–1815*, eds. Mary Anne Schofield and Cecilia Macheski (Athens: Ohio University Press, 1986), 264–84, 266.
14. Nancy Cott, *The Bonds of Womanhood: "Women's Sphere" in New England, 1780–1835* (New Haven: Yale University Press, 1977), 226. Michael Mason,

The Making of Victorian Sexual Attitudes (Oxford: Oxford University Press, 1994), 77.

15. Ruth Watts, *Gender, Power and Unitarians in England, 1780–1860* (London and New York: Longman, 1998), Part I.

16. Anna Letitia Barbauld, "The Rights of Woman," *The Poems of Anna Letitia Barbauld*, eds. William McCarthy and Elizabeth Kraft (Athens: University of Georgia Press, 1994), 121–2. The text follows:

> Yes, injured Woman! rise, assert thy right!
> Woman! too long degraded, scorned, opprest;
> O born to rule in partial Law's despite,
> Resume thy native empire o'er the breast!
>
> Go forth arrayed in panoply divine;
> That angel pureness which admits no stain;
> Go, bid proud Man his boasted rule resign,
> And kiss the golden sceptre of thy reign.
>
> Go, gird thyself with grace; collect thy store
> Of bright artillery glancing from afar;
> Soft melting tones thy thundering cannon's roar,
> Blushes and fears thy magazine of war.
>
> Thy rights are empire: urge no meaner claim, –
> Felt, not defined, and if debated, lost;
> Like sacred mysteries, which withheld from fame,
> Shunning discussion, are revered the most.
>
> Try all that wit and art suggest to bend
> Of thy imperial foe the stubborn knee;
> Make treacherous Man thy subject, not thy friend;
> Thou mayst command, but never canst be free.
>
> Awe the licentious, and restrain the rude;
> Soften the sullen, clear the cloudy brow:
> Be, more than princes' gifts, thy favours sued; –
> She hazards all, who will the least allow.
>
> But hope not, courted idol of mankind,
> On this proud eminence secure to stay;
> Subduing and subdued, thou soon shalt find
> Thy coldness soften, and thy pride give way.
>
> Then, then, abandon each ambitious thought,
> Conquest or rule thy heart shall feebly move,
> In Nature's school, by her soft maxims taught,
> That separate rights are lost in mutual love.

17. Different readings of this poem are possible. Many have seen it as a straightforward rejection of Wollstonecraft, penned in anger: see for instance G. J. Barker-Benfield, *The Culture of Sensibility: Sex and Society in Eighteenth-Century England* (Chicago: University of Chicago Press, 1992), 222, 266, and William McCarthy and Elizabeth Kraft, Introduction to *The Poems of Anna Letitia*

Barbauld, xxv. Harriet Guest reads it in a more nuanced way, as an affirmation of women's domestic duty and republican motherhood, in *Small Change*, 226–30.

18. Maria Edgeworth, *Letters for Literary Ladies* (London: Joseph Johnson, 2nd edn., 1799), 89.
19. Patricia Juliana Smith, *Lesbian Panic – Homoeroticism in Modern British Women's Fiction* (New York: Columbia University Press, 1997), 8–11.
20. For this argument, see Moira Ferguson, "*Mansfield Park*: Slavery, Colonialism and Gender," *Oxford Literary Review* 13 (1991), 118–39.
21. Claudia L. Johnson, *Jane Austen – Women, Politics, and the Novel* (Chicago and London: University of Chicago Press, 1988).

10

SUSAN J. WOLFSON

Mary Wollstonecraft and the poets

I. Wollstonecraft reading

A remarkable strategy of Wollstonecraft's cultural criticism, especially on the state of women, is her method of reading society as a text, a "prevailing opinion," so she calls it in the title of chapter v of *A Vindication of the Rights of Woman*.[1] To regard the regulating forms of social existence as "opinion," and not a dictate of divine law or natural order, is to identify a human construction – a set of ideas and practices – that may be subject to critical reading, to revision, to rewriting. Wollstonecraft's method of cultural criticism is at once assisted and logically enabled by her actual literary criticism, applied to such prestigious texts as John Milton's *Paradise Lost* (and its biblical bases), Alexander Pope's epistle *To a Lady, Of the Characters of Women*, Samuel Richardson's epic novel *Clarissa*, J.-J. Rousseau's influential "education" novels, *Emile* and *Julie, ou la Nouvelle Héloïse*, and such works of patriarchal advice as Dr. James Fordyce's *Sermons to Young Women* and Dr. John Gregory's *A Father's Legacy to His Daughters*. Reading the social text and its literary instances, Wollstonecraft sets her sights, and trains ours, on a lexicon (cherished by poets) by which women are flattered into subjection – *innocent, delicate, beautiful, feminine* – to expose a specious syntax of faint praise for "fair defects" of character and a suspect reverence for "angels" and "girls" rather than respect as capable, intelligent adults. She is particularly sharp on how notions of *natural* are summoned to rationalize a social text: worn into "the effect of habit," a social system is "insisted upon as an undoubted indication of nature" (VRW 5:150). "Such is the order of nature," Rousseau intones of man's claims to women's obedience (except in matters of pleasure, where she "naturally" directs him).[2] Taking the form of factual statement about "the order of nature," such assertions conceal a structure of values and power relations, what modern cultural critique would call "ideology."

Women cooperate in and become pernicious texts of ideology themselves, Wollstonecraft suggests, when they accept charming "names" for their degradation: "they act contrary to their real interest on an enlarged scale, when they cherish or affect weakness under the name of delicacy" (VRW 5:116). Linking such names to "the firmly rooted prejudices which sensualists have planted," Wollstonecraft's metaphor is precisely one of culture affecting the name of nature: a seemingly natural character is more accurately the effect of determined planting and cultivation. She carefully sifts the result, asking her readers to read more closely the texts they credit. Fordyce's *Sermons* instructs wives to treat husbands with *"respectful observance* and a more *equal tenderness; studying their humours, overlooking their mistakes, submitting to their opinions,* ... giving *soft* answers to hasty words, complaining as seldom as possible" (her emphasis). "Such a woman ought to be an angel," Wollstonecraft sums the customary praise, then unmasks the dynamic: " – or she is an ass – for I discern not a trace of the human character, neither reason nor passion in this domestic drudge, whose being is absorbed in that of a tyrant's" (VRW 5:165). The innocent angel in the house is unveiled as a tyrant's ignorant, pathetic work-animal.

Wollstonecraft's method of reading throughout *Rights of Woman* is to query the names of "naturalized" habit for women: "why should they be kept in ignorance under the specious name of innocence?" she asks at the opening of her chapter "The Prevailing Opinion" (5:88). At its root, *in-nocent* means blameless (from *nocere*: to harm, *innocuous* is a cognate); the soothing logic is gallant protection, but the material consequence is "ignorance." If Gray, looking back on his boyhood, famously surmised, "where ignorance is bliss, / 'Tis folly to be wise" ("Ode on a Distant Prospect of Eton College," 99–100), Wollstonecraft puts the syllogism under the lens of gender. Gray's college boys, after all, enjoy an education denied to girls in the name of preserving their innocence. Wollstonecraft's equation of innocence and ignorance certainly impressed a poet in her London circle: in *Songs of Innocence and of Experience*, published a couple of years after *Rights of Woman*, Blake assembles a chorus of innocent children who are often fatally ignorant. Wollstonecraft asks her readers to discern the gilded fetters of impotence – intellectual, social, and political – in praises of innocence. When men tell women "to remain, it may be said, innocent[,] they mean in a state of childhood" (VRW 5:130): "in order to preserve their innocence, as ignorance is courteously termed, truth is hidden from them, and they are made to assume an artificial character before their faculties have acquired any strength" (VRW 5:113). With a critical analysis of the artifice of names and terms, Wollstonecraft reads innocence not as a virtue, but as a deficiency, the result of a deliberate method to fashion a specific "character," a kind of text.

Tracing out the architecture of artifice ("ingenious arguments" she calls it at the top of "The Prevailing Opinion"), Wollstonecraft also attends to the cumulative tradition by which it gains reinforcement. A preliminary look at how she addresses the opinion of a chief author, indeed the premier theological poet of English literary tradition, indicates the terrain. Milton matters intensely because of his general prestige in English literary, political, and religious traditions, and more particularly, his esteem in Wollstonecraft's London circle of writers, artists, and political activists, the progressive thinkers to whom she addresses *Rights of Woman*.[3] Her first sustained exercise in literary criticism is focused on his conduct-book modeling of Eve, the archetypal woman on a divinely authorized plan. Eve has "all the 'submissive charms,'" Wollstonecraft remarks (VRW 5:102, citing *PL* 4.498), hitting the adjective that always evokes the disobedience that produced the Fall. Milton delineates her prelapsarian innocence in a keynote syntax of compliance, sexual attractiveness, and subordination to Adam:

> For contemplation he and valor formed,
> For softness she and sweet attractive grace;
> He for God only, she for God in him.
>
> (*PL* 4.297–9)

Aware that this formation has been so credited as to be routinely quoted in conduct tracts such as Fordyce's *Sermons*, Wollstonecraft (re)reads its text back to us: "Thus Milton describes our first frail mother" (VRW 5:88).[4] Satan's temptation cagily appeals to Eve's latent restlessness in her enforced subjection and ignorance. Wollstonecraft in effect joins the devil's party, reforming it as the party of rational faith, with Milton's qualifications (ironically) found wanting:

> when he tells us that women are formed for softness and sweet attractive grace, I cannot comprehend his meaning, unless, in the true Mahometan strain, he meant to deprive us of souls, and insinuate that we were beings only designed by sweet attractive grace, and docile blind obedience, to gratify the senses of man when he can no longer soar on the wing of contemplation.
> How grossly do they insult us who thus advise us only to render ourselves gentle, domestic brutes! (VRW 5:88)

The ground is not ordained; it is a matter of telling and advice, of contingent forming and rendering. Pressing Milton's design of "meaning" into actual social consequence, Wollstonecraft rereads in sweet obedience a blind compliance whose true analogue is (once again) the gentle, domestic brute – "nature" with an insulting vengeance.[5]

To put critical pressure on the poetry formed by and forming the prevailing opinion is a routine procedure of ideological critique today. But as the endurance, even today, of some of the prevailing opinion of Wollstonecraft's day may suggest, her opposition was sufficiently controversial in the 1790s (and decades after) to provoke representations of "Wollstonecraft" by poets determined either to praise or to bury her. Praises were sung by her London circle, but the stronger reflux was an acid wave that crested in the years just after her death, when her husband William Godwin, his judgment clouded by grief and hagiographic devotion, published his *Memoirs of the Author of the Vindication of the Rights of Woman* (1798). Creating a scandal exceeding any produced by Wollstonecraft's own publications, the *Memoirs* embarrassed even fans of *Rights of Woman* while it enabled her critics to link her vindications to a career of "immoral" character and conduct. In 1798, Richard Polwhele cited the *Memoirs* repeatedly in his voluminous footnotes to *The Unsex'd Females*, a satire seemingly devised for the sake of its notes.

Attacks persisted well into the 1970s. Not only was it still possible to stigmatize Wollstonecraft's arguments as sexual deviance, but as the *TLS* review of a new biography demonstrated, the mainstream press could float schoolboy ridicule of her name. Even as he seemed oblivious to his own tempting surname, Richard Cobb declared that "Mary's very surname has about it an unmistakable ring of crankiness, ungainliness, and discomfort, a promise or puritanism and serious intent." David Levine's cartoon of a sour-faced glowerer for *New York Review of Books* (see Poston's edition of *Rights of Woman*, 2nd. ed.: 222) two years before may have been an inspiration, oddly coinciding with Godwin's report of "the preconceived ideas" of a public who expected to meet "a sturdy, raw-boned virago" and instead found "a woman, lovely in her person, and in the best and most engaging sense, feminine in her manners."[6] Just as the anti-Wollstonecraft rants of the late 1790s suppressed for decades the case for the rights of women (modest as the terms were then), the ridiculers of the 1970s were wielding "Wollstonecraft" to impugn what was then called "the women's liberation movement."

This chapter studies the related dynamics of Wollstonecraft's reading of the poets that shaped the text on "woman" in her day, and the reading of "Wollstonecraft" by poets intent to shape the text on her, and implicitly, on the case for the rights of woman.

II. The voices of the poets

Poets' voices, Wollstonecraft knows, are a gordian complication: they are pungent sites of misogyny or agents of dubious praise, all mixed into the poison of prevailing opinion; but they may also instruct in a pleasurable form, and (even in their anti-feminist moods), prove resources for strong, imaginative expression. Wollstonecraft's ways of reading are similarly various: she may call on poets to elevate and fill out her own voice; she may put their words and phrasings in a revisionary syntax; she may read against the grain; she may cite their texts in a general critique of the cultural text. One of her first publications was a poetry-laden anthology, *The Female Reader*, issued under the name "Mr. Cresswick" and graced with a subtitle, *"for the Improvement of Young Women"* (4:53), as if to advertise a conduct manual of sorts. Prefaced by an intent to "imprint some useful lessons on the mind, and cultivate the taste" (4:55), the printing, mostly from the canon of literature and the bible, features more than a few poets: Milton (*Paradise Lost*), William Cowper (*The Task*, "A Fable," "Alexander Selkirk"), Dr. Johnson ("The Natural Beauty"), James Thompson (a paraphrase of a bible passage), Edward Young ("Dying Friends"), Charlotte Smith (some sonnets), Jonathan Swift (some *Stella* poems), Thomas Percy's folk anthology, *Reliques*, Anna Barbauld, Shenstone, Steele, Edward Moore, Merrick, Gay, Elizabeth Carter – as well as ample representation of the poet who by the eighteenth century was regarded as the embodied prestige of English literature itself, William Shakespeare.

Under the aegis of this prestige and the rationale, so states the Preface, of assisting the "desirable attainment" of reading "with propriety" (i.e. "elocution") (FR 4:56), Shakespeare, Wollstonecraft intuited, could sponsor some rather heterodox voices for a young woman.[7] "Mr. Cresswick" contends that his plan is best served by "works addressed to the imagination" rather than "cold arguments and mere declamation" (FR 4:56). So we find Rosalind, Cordelia, Imogen, and Miranda, but also a host of male voices – Orlando (*As You Like It*); Lear, Glocester, Edgar, Edmund, and Kent (*King Lear*); Hubert, Arthur, Executioner, Bastard, and Philip (*King John*); Ferdinand, Ariel, and Prospero (*The Tempest*) – to say nothing of both wicked Macbeths. "A great reader is always quoting the description of another's emotions," Wollstonecraft remarks in her "Hints" for an unrealized sequel to *Rights of Woman* (5:276). She means to praise the originary "imagination" of "strong" writers, but she also aptly describes her life of being "deep read in Shakspeare" (SR: 6:247). Whether in publications or private letters, she summons his language more often than any other poet's to enable, and at time ennoble, her own expression.[8] These summons, moreover, ignore any gender divide: she repeatedly claims emotional and psychological affinity with Shakespeare's tragic men, whose figures of agony speak to her own passions, whose language she seeks, almost magnetically, to elevate her expressions of personal crisis and despair.[9]

Other male poets work this way, too, even one whose "sarcasm" on women (VRW 5:141) tends to spur her polemics. It is Pope who shapes her cautions against feeble learning in *Thoughts on the Education of Daughters* (4:12), and it is his phrase, "grows with his growth, and strengthens with his strength" from *Essay on Man* (2.133–8, about the "principle of death" at work in a "ruling Passion"), that glosses her contempt for the "false notions" of youth (VRM 5:23–4), and their "great effect" on moral development (VRW 5:186), as well as her tracing of the course of melancholy in "the malady of genius" (SR 6:329). Even the opening line of Pope's notorious epistle "To a Lady" gets enlisted for one of her favorite topics: "It has been sarcastically said, by a snarling poet, that most women have no character at all: we shall apply it to their production. – Novels" (a review of 1789 in AR 7:191). So, too, may Milton be applied. In France in 1794, as the ideals of the Revolution were collapsing into the Terror, Wollstonecraft identifies with his sense of himself as "fall'n on evil days" (*PL* 7.25) in the failure of the Puritan Revolution (FR 6:376). In *Rights of Men*, she dismisses the recent sorrows of the French royalty in comparison to the miseries of the poor: "Let those sorrows hide their diminished head before the tremendous mountain of woe that thus defaces our globe!" (VRM 5:58) – echoing, without sympathy, Satan's resentment at how "all the Stars / Hide thir diminisht heads" at the sight of the noonday sun (*PL* 4.32–5).

But like many of her contemporaries (Blake and Godwin especially), Wollstonecraft is drawn to a political and imaginative sympathy with Milton's rebel. With Milton's picture of the "the lovely pair" of Paradise inspiring only her tender condescension, she confesses in a note in *Rights of Woman*, "I have, with conscious dignity, or Satanic pride, turned to hell for sublimer objects" (5:94n).[10] Writing early in 1792, just as she was finishing this work, to William Roscoe, an abolitionist and champion of the French Revolution, about Fuseli's illustrations of *Paradise Lost*, she reports of the artist, "like Milton he seems quite at home in hell – his Devil will be the hero of the poetic series; for, *entre nous*, I rather doubt whether he will produce an Eve to please me in any of the situations, which he has selected, unless it be after the fall" (Letters 206). This reading of prelapsarian paradise as dull and postlapsarian Eve as aesthetic pleasure, and Satanic hell as the more vital intellectual and imaginative terrain would become the temper of the Romantic era. Famously staged by Blake in *The Marriage of Heaven and Hell* (1790), the heroic Satan, in his voice as alienated critic of a tyrannical power, is freshly compelling for Wollstonecraft. Criticizing the ways of a world in which "rank and titles are held of the utmost importance, before which Genius 'must hide its diminished head'" (VRW 5:82), she now echoes Satan's resentment with sympathy.

Despite her nearly reflexive turn from the "paradisiacal pair" of unfallen Eden (VRW 5:94n), even they turn out to have affinities. Writing to her lover

Gilbert Imlay in August 1793, Wollstonecraft evokes Eve's preference for husbandly relation over angelic instruction ("Her Husband the Relater she preferr'd / Before the Angel.../... hee, she knew, would intermix / Grateful digressions, and solve high dispute / With conjugal Caresses, from his Lip / Not words alone pleas'd her" [*PL* 8.52–7]); she will wait with some news until she sees Imlay, because she wants to play Adam to his expectant Eve: "I like to see your eyes praise me; and, Milton insinuates, that, during such recitals, there are interruptions, not ungrateful to the heart, when the honey that drops from the lips is not merely words" (LI 6:370). She summons such recitals again in anticipation of an evening philosophy seminar with Godwin, but sets him more by the book, as Adam to her Eve: "You are to give me a lesson this evening – And, a word in your ear, I shall not be very angry if you sweeten grammatical disquisitions after the Miltonic mode" (15 September 1796; Letters 351).

If Milton's archfiend and even Eve can be reclaimed, what about Shakespeare's misogynists? "You jig and amble, and you lisp, you nick-name God's creatures, and make your wantonness your ignorance," Hamlet sneers at poor exploited Ophelia, dismissing her in his sarcasm to a whore-house: "To a nunnery, go" (3.1.146–51). In *The Sublime and the Beautiful*, Burke gave a picture of female beauty that reversed the terms of Hamlet's contempt for the whole sex: "so far is perfection... from being the cause of beauty," that women, "sensible of this[,]... learn to lisp, to totter in their walk, to counterfeit weakness, even sickness" (Part 3, Section 9). In *Rights of Men*, Wollstonecraft revisits Burke's use of Hamlet in order to underscore the deformation: "they should 'learn to lisp, to totter in their walk, and nick-name God's creatures'" (5:45). And in her Introduction to *Rights of Woman* she borrows Hamlet's litany to satirize in her own voice "the present con-duct of the sex," using third persons: "they dress; they paint, and nickname God's creatures – Surely these weak beings are only fit for a seraglio!" (VRW 5:76) – substituting for Hamlet's rough slang ("nunnery") a scarcely more dignified synonym for "harem." She had further censures of Ophelia, setting up Hamlet for others' espial. Reviewing a book on Shakespeare's characters in 1788, she disputed "the cordial praise" accorded: "Her conduct was mean and unjust; if she acted like a female we pity her weakness, but should not either praise or palliate a fault that no mistaken notion of duty could justify without confounding the distinction between virtue and vice" (AR 7:57).

The emerging affinity with Hamlet is costly purchase not just because it has the advocate of woman's rights underwriting a text of male misogyny but also because it requires Wollstonecraft to split herself rhetorically from her own sex: to make Hamlet's point, she has to rewrite his differentiating *you* as a *they* from which she dissociates herself. That she sensed the problem is suggested by the slightly altered economy of her next voicing of Hamlet, in a complaint about Dr. Gregory's advice to his daughters (in *Legacy*) that they not display their intelligence:

> It is this system of dissimulation, throughout the volume, that I despise. Women are always to *seem* to be this and that – yet virtue might apostrophize them, in the words of Hamlet – Seems! I know not seems! – Have that within that passeth show! (VRW 5:168)

The words of Hamlet are actually, "*I* have that within . . . ," a self-declaring alienation from a corrupt court world, more particularly, a public expression of contempt for his mother's hasty remarriage so soon after his father's sudden death (*Hamlet*, 1.2.76–86). Wollstonecraft converts his syntax into an imperative to all women to have and claim what male instruction would deny them in the promise of social advantage. Women might take on Hamlet's principles and, like Wollstonecraft, disdain the system of female dissimulation. This cross-writing of Shakespeare's misogynists saves him, in effect, for the rights of woman. So, too, when she brings on stage another famous misogynist. Imagining her male readers asking, "But what have women to do in society?" she replies, "surely you would not condemn them all to suckle fools and chronicle small beer!" (VRW 5:218), putting into negative syntax Iago's view of what women are good for. Although she doesn't quote it, she takes the part of Desdemona, who protests his "most lame and impotent conclusion" (*Othello*, 2.1.160–1).

III. Reading poetry, reading the poets

Poets can fill a textbook of misogyny, as the references peppered across *Rights of Woman* to Milton, Cowley, Congreve, Gay, Prior, Swift, Pope, and Shakespeare make clear.[11] But Wollstonecraft did not reduce all poetry to this poison. "I am more and more convinced," she wrote as she was planning a sequel, "that poetry is the first effervescence of the imagination, and the forerunner of civilization;" it "flourishes most in the first rude state of society. The passions speak most eloquently, when they are not shackled by reason" (Hints 5:274, 275). This language seems to relax the reign (and rein) of reason over passion insisted on in *Rights of Woman*. Although Wollstonecraft never completed the sequel, she did publish an essay in *Monthly Magazine* (April 1797) titled "On Poetry, and Our Relish for the Beauties of Nature." Three years in advance of Wordsworth's groundbreaking Preface to *Lyrical Ballads*, which disdained the artificial tastes shaping the popular poetry of the day and urged a return to nature as the soil for a more profound and moral poetry of human feeling, Wollstonecraft had tilled the field. "A taste for rural scenes, in the present state of society, appears to be very often an artificial sentiment, rather inspired by poetry and romances, than a real perception of the beauties of nature," she begins (7:7), using "nature" not as a cover word for suspect artifice, but as the morally positive antithesis. She maps the historical moment of this "real" in the "infancy of society," when poetry was not only "the transcript of immediate sensations" but also the "effusions of a vigorous mind" and "profound thinking" (7:7). This vital intelligence has so decayed in the cultural evolution of poetry that its language has become "unnatural," "disgusting," "servilely copied" from books: "a poet is rather the creature of art, than of nature," she comments (7:8–9), in terms that echo what she has said of women. And like the arts a woman is taught to cultivate, poetic art is more disgusting yet for the way it has to excite "gross minds" with the bait of "forcible representations," lures to "rouse the thoughtless" into "tumultuous emotions" (7:10). It is by force of this art that poetry can erode rational power in both sexes.

At the outset of the decade, Wollstonecraft's tone was more diagnostic than detractive: "Poetry," she proposed in Rights of Men, "naturally addresses the fancy, and the language of passion is with great felicity borrowed from the heightened picture which the imagination draws of sensible objects concentred by impassioned reflection. And, during this 'fine phrensy,' reason has no right to rein-in the imagination" (5:29). She is quoting Shakespeare's Theseus (A Midsummer Night's Dream, 5.1); but whereas he compacts "the poet's eye, in a fine frenzy rolling," with the "seething brains" of lovers and madmen, all exceeding the bounds of what "cool reason ever comprehends," she would exempt the poet. In Rights of Woman she summons Theseus's phrase to insist that in strong poets such as Shakespeare or Milton, indeed in any rational enthusiast, we find no "ravings of imbecility, the sickly effusions of distempered brains; but the exuberance of fancy, that 'in a fine phrenzy' wandering, was not continually reminded of its material shackles" (5:108). Yet the need for distinction suggests the potential dangers and the particular "material" consequences of a too exuberant fancy for women. "On Poetry" closes on a note that chimes right with Rights of Woman: "That the most valuable things are liable to the greatest perversion, is however as trite as true: . . . when sensation, rather than reason, imparts delight," it "frequently makes a libertine" of a man, "leading him to prefer the sensual tumult of love a little refined by sentiment, to the calm pleasures of affectionate friendship, in whose sober satisfactions, reason" holds sway (7:11). Rights of Woman was more blunt: "Novels, music, poetry, and gallantry" (flirtation and coquetry) "all tend to make women the creatures of sensation, and their character is thus formed in mould of folly . . . This overstretched sensibility naturally relaxes the other powers of the mind, and prevents intellect from attaining that sovereignty which it ought to attain to render a rational creature useful to others" (5:130).

Because of its prestige as "art" and refinement, poetry is a subtly dangerous force. And when, as in *Paradise Lost*, it comes with further claims of divine authority and its regent voice of rational faith, it would seem to prevent intellect from critical opposition. It was not possible in Wollstonecraft's day to argue with the Biblical truth without risking charges of heresy, even atheism. But a modern Christian might try, as Wollstonecraft does in *Rights of Woman*, to restrict the question to the Old Testament, reading this book not as revealed truth, but as the poetry of "the first rude state of society" (as she would put it in "On Poetry"). Proposing that "the prevailing opinion, that woman was created for man," arose "from Moses's poetical story" (5:95), she then extends this story to a poetic fiction it clearly inspired: "Milton's pleasing picture" (VRW 5:94n). To link poet Moses to poet Milton is to treat both as story-tellers, subject to literary analysis. The Wollstonecrafted critical tool is gender-neutral "reason," a capacity Milton assigns to men in greater proportion (see *PL* 4.442–3; 8.574, 10.145–56) but which she insists is the general endowment of human being. Reading by "reason," she proposes that "Moses's beautiful, poetic cosmogony," if "literally true," can only be "derogatory to the character of the Supreme Being" (VRW 5:148). This appeal to Supreme Being in terms continuous with human being is a brilliant move: in one stroke, Wollstonecraft invests her social polemic with rational theology and makes a better appeal to divine law than that established in "the prevailing opinion." Poets Moses and Milton do not play as channelers of divine dictation, but as authors of fallible texts that might be treated to critical scrutiny and argued with.

Milton gives Wollstonecraft a way to argue with Scripture, and if he hadn't existed she might have had to invent him for this purpose. That this was a powerful new inspiration for her is suggested by the contrast of her uncritical inclusion in *The Female Reader* of the very passage from *Paradise Lost* (4.598–690) that launches her critique in *Rights of Woman*.[12] *The Female Reader* sets the passage under a rubric of "Dialogues, Conversations, and Fables" with a nonce title: *Conversation Between Adam and Eve on Going to Rest* (4:229, 262). In "The Prevailing Opinion," Wollstonecraft plucks a quintain in Eve's voice (*PL* 4.634–38) for sharp attention, prefaced by a critical pause over that keyword, *innocent*:

> Children, I grant, should be innocent; but when the epithet is applied to men, or women, it is but a civil term for weakness. For if it be allowed that women were destined by Providence to acquire human virtues, and by the exercise of their understandings, that stability of character which is the firmest ground to rest our future hopes upon, they must be permitted to turn to the fountain of

light. . . . Milton, I grant, was of a very different opinion; for he only bends to
the indefeasible right of beauty . . . :

> "To whom thus Eve with *perfect beauty* adorn'd.
> My Author and Disposer, what thou bidst
> *Unargued* I obey; so God ordains;
> God is *thy law, thou mine:* to know no more
> Is Woman's *happiest* knowledge and her *praise.*"

These are exactly the arguments that I have used to children; but I have added,
your reason is now gaining strength, and, till it arrives at some degree of
maturity, you must look up to me for advice – then you ought to *think*, and
only rely on God. (VRW 5:89)

Eve speaks the script of Adam's text, disposed by and obedient to its Author's
intention. To Wollstonecraft, who italicizes the terms of Eve's childishness,
this is an "argument" suitable only for those of immature power. What
does it mean for a man to praise his adult mate as such? Wollstonecraft
unpacks this implication when she addresses the ridicule of women "for repeating 'a set of phrases learnt by rote'" (Swift's sarcasm in the opening line
of "The Furniture of a Woman's Mind"): "nothing could be more natural,"
she retorts, citing "the education they receive, and that their 'highest praise
is to obey, unargued' – the will of man" (VRW 5:187). Reading *Paradise
Lost*, she trumps Milton by presenting herself as a better teacher than his
Adam, one committed to nurturing children of both sexes into the rational capacity by which they may think independently, even argue with their
preceptors.

Wollstonecraft's challenge is evident enough in the way Milton's lines (the
very same) play in a novel by *the* conduct-book manualist of the day. In
Hannah More's *Coelebs in Search of a Wife* (1808), Eve provides a point of
departure for the search, launched by a syntax that means to coopt women
irritated by the pattern:

> I have been sometimes surprised, when in conversation I have been expressing
> my admiration of the character of Eve in her state of innocence, as drawn by
> our immortal poet, to hear objections raised by those, from whom of all critics
> I should have least expected it – the ladies . . .
> [T]hey insist that it is highly derogatory from the dignity of the sex, that the
> poet should affirm, that it is the perfection of the character of a wife,
>
> To study household good,
> And good works in her husband to promote.
>
> . . . [T]he offence taken by the ladies against the uncourtly bard, is chiefly oc-
> casioned by his having presumed to intimate that conjugal obedience
>
> Is woman's highest honour and her praise.

...I would point out to them that the supposed harshness of the observation is quite done away by the recollection, that this scrupled "obedience" is so far from implying degradation, that it is connected with the injunction to the woman "to promote good works" in her husband; an injunction surely inferring a degree of influence that raises her condition, and restores her to all the dignity of equality.[13]

The first inset verse is culled from a later point in the poem, when Adam praises, then chides, Eve's concerns for economy of labor (9.232–4). More's effort to assuage the offense given by the lines in book 4 testifies to the provocation, but misses the point. Coelebs concludes his homage by distinguishing Eve from "a mere domestic drudge," citing Milton's "invariable attention" to her "external elegance" in such lines as "For softness she, and sweet attractive grace" (11–12). More means, clearly, to refute Wollstonecraft's reading of the docile obedient wife as a "domestic drudge" (VRW 5:165), but to have Coelebs read these lines as "combin[ing] intellectual worth and polished manners" (12) is in effect to restate Wollstonecraft's case: to call "intellectual" a being defined by softness and sweet attractiveness is not just patent flattery but contradiction. That More knows Milton has not given the sexes equality, even on the point of "grace," is evident in her decision to have Coelebs address this point:

> If it be objected to the poet's gallantry, that he remarks:
>> Her beauty is excelled by manly grace,
>> And wisdom, which alone is truly fair;
> let it be remembered that the observation proceeds from the lips of Eve herself, and thus adds to her other graces the crowning grace of humility. (12)

This poetry closes Eve's recollection of Adam overcoming her hesitation on their first meeting: "thy gentle hand/Seiz'd mine, I yielded, and from that time see/How beauty is excelled..." (4.488–91). Milton's narrator then congratulates Eve's better seeing and "meek surrender" (492–4). But might the verbs – *seiz'd* and *yielded* – also report coerced lesson-learning and dependent seeing? However one reads the verbs, it is unarguable that what is said to fall "from the lips of Eve herself" is scripted by Milton (even as Coelebs's lesson is scripted by More).

It is exactly on a point of Miltonic contradiction that Wollstonecraft sharpens her critique of Eve's subordination. In a method that we would describe today as a deconstructive reading, and in canny anticipation of a favorite example in late twentieth-century feminist critiques of *Paradise Lost*, Wollstonecraft brings on the text alluded to in her comment that "it would be difficult to render two passages which I now mean to contrast, consistent," pausing for a mildly sarcastic dig that casts Milton as a Miltonic woman, a creature of the senses: "But into similar inconsistencies are great men often led by their senses" (VRW 5:89).[14] In this second passage (*PL* 8.381–92), Milton has Adam complain of his loneliness even among all the creatures in pre-Eve Paradise:

> Yet in the following lines Milton seems to coincide with me; when he makes Adam thus expostulate with his Maker.
>
> > "Hast thou not made me here thy substitute,
> > And these inferior far beneath me set?
> > Among *unequals* what society
> > Can sort, what harmony or true delight?
> > Which must be mutual, in proportion due
> > Giv'n and receiv'd; but in *disparity*
> > The one intense, the other still remiss
> > Cannot well suit with either, but soon prove
> > Tedious alike: of *fellowship* I speak
> > Such as I seek, fit to participate
> > All rational delight – "   (VRW 5:89–90)

Wollstonecraft's italics exonerate Adam against Milton's epic narrator: Adam wants an equal partner, but gets a mate in what Wollstonecraft (with another dig at the "inconsistencies . . . men fall into when they argue without the compass of principles") terms a "line of subordination in the mental powers" (VRW 5:121).[15] The result is a disarray of inequalities: "only 'absolute in loveliness,' the portion of rationality granted to woman, is, indeed very scanty; for, denying her genius and judgment, it is scarcely possible to divine what remains to characterize intellect," she remarks of Adam's first raptures with the Eve his Maker has made for him (VRW 5:121; *PL* 8.547).

A bit into the chapter initiated by this last remark, "Observations on the State of Degradation To Which Woman is Reduced by Various Causes," Wollstonecraft turns more fully to the lines just after "absolute in loveliness," reading in Adam's rapt praises of Eve the grounds of insidious insult:

> Woman . . . thus "in herself complete," by possessing all these *frivolous* accomplishments, so changes the nature of things
>
> > ———"That what she wills to do or say
> > Seems wisest, virtuousest, discreetest, best;
> > All higher knowledge in *her presence* falls
> > Degraded. Wisdom in discourse with her
> > Loses discountenanc'd, and, like Folly, shows;
> > Authority and Reason on her wait." –
>
> And all this is built on her loveliness!
>
> > (VRW 5:128–9; *PL* 8.549–54, her italics)

In a pattern of perfection in which Folly passes as Wisdom and Reason is left hanging, Wollstonecraft traces the fault lines of misogyny. So it comes as no surprise that after the map of Eden undergoes a seismic shift in the Fall, Milton has Adam rant about this same Woman,

> O why did God,
> Creator wise, that peopled highest heaven
> With spirits masculine, create at last
> This novelty on Earth, this fair defect
> Of Nature, and not fill the World at once
> With men as angels without feminine,
> Or find some other way to generate
> Mankind?   (*PL* 10.888–95)

The very deficiency of which he was once enamored is now an indictment of "fair defect."

In 1714 Mary Wray opened her *Ladies Library* in melancholy "musing" on the "general and undistinguished Aspersions" cast by "the most polite Writers of the Age" on the "Composure" of women, including Milton's script for Adam's rant above. Wray entertained the possibility that "the Character of those that speak" might "circumstantiate the thing so as not to make it a Reproach upon Women as such," but she rather doubted it.[16] A credit to her doubt is the way Adam's epithet, "fair defect," was managing to find an uncircumstantiated cultural life of its own. Throughout *Rights of Woman*, Wollstonecraft points to this succinct collation as an oxymoronic logic speaking volumes about the larger economy:

> Inheriting, in a lineal descent from the first fair defect in nature, the sovereignty of beauty, they have, to maintain their power, resigned the natural rights, which the exercise of reason might have procured them, and chosen rather to be short-lived queens than labour to obtain the sober pleasures that arise from equality.   (5:124)

Sounding Adam's postlapsarian oxymoron, Wollstonecraft revisits the commonplace rationale of a "natural" sexual character to propose a broader franchise of "natural rights," rationalized by what Adam originally asked for, "equality." For Eve, there is scarcely a difference between prelapsarian praises and postlapsarian slanders: however "amiable" women may be, as "the fair defects in nature," they "appear to be created not to enjoy the fellowship of man, but ... by playful dalliance to give some dignity to the appetite that draws him to them" (5:136). As she traces the "lineal descent" of this female type, Wollstonecraft emphasizes actions – resignation and choice – that, while compelled, are neither an inevitable nor an immutable order of creation, but a text that might be revised. She begins a chapter titled "The Effect Which an Early Association of Ideas has upon the Character" with this question: "Educated in the enervating style recommended by the writers on whom I have been animadverting; and not having a chance, from their subordinate state in society, to recover their lost ground, is it surprising that women every where appear a defect in nature?" (5:185). It is only "the present modification of society" that requires women to adopt this "style" (5:124); to "submit to be a *fair defect* in creation" a priori is to puzzle the subtlest efforts "to justify the ways of Providence respecting them" (5:114).

With a stress on gender specificity, Wollstonecraft has satirically revised Milton's claiming at the outset of *Paradise Lost* to "assert Eternal Providence,/And justify the ways of God to men" (1.25–6). What of women? With her own philosophy, Wollstonecraft interrogates Adam's rueful oxymoron and its cultural afterlife of faint praise: "As a philosopher, I read with indignation the plausible epithets which men use to soften their insults; and, as a moralist, I ask what is meant by such heterogeneous associations, as fair defects, amiable weaknesses, etc.?" (VRW 5:103). Among these men is Pope, on whose often-quoted phrase "Fine by defect, and delicately weak" ("To a Lady," 44) are Milton's fingerprints. Pope's full sentence is worth review, because it exposes the pernicious binding of fineness and defect that provoked Wollstonecraft:

> Ladies, like variegated Tulips, show,
> 'Tis to their Changes that their charms they owe;
> Their happy Spots the nice admirer take,
> Fine by defect, and delicately weak.   (41–4)

'Tis to viruses that tulips owe their lovely variety, a horticulture of defects that guarantees both charm and constitutional weakness. Wollstonecraft implies this knowledge when she remarks,

> It would be an endless task to trace the variety of meannesses, cares, and sorrows, into which women are plunged by the prevailing opinion, that they were created rather to feel than reason, and that all the power they obtain, must be obtained by their charms and weakness:
> "Fine by defect, and amiably weak!"
> And, made by this amiable weakness entirely dependent, excepting what they gain by illicit sway, on man, not only for protection, but advice, is it surprising that, neglecting the duties that reason alone points out, and shrinking from trials calculated to strengthen their minds, they only exert themselves to give

Mary Wollstonecraft and the poets

their defects a graceful covering, which may serve to heighten their charms in the eye of the voluptuary, though it sink them below the scale of moral excellence? (VRW 5:131)

Her slight misremembering of Pope's phrase aptly registers the social value, of flattery to men (amiability), that sustains a culture of female deficiency.

As Wollstonecraft suggests with other quotations of Pope in *Rights of Woman*, such faint praise is closely allied to damning judgment and uncivil leers. In the same verse paragraph of "To a Lady" in which he sings of fine defects, "Pope has said, in the name of the whole male sex, 'Yet ne'er so sure our passion to create,/As when she touch'd the brink of all we hate'" (VRW 5:95–6). This pithy couplet summary of male sexual desire ("To a Lady," 51–2), Wollstonecraft observes, renders women merely "females," forever "degraded by being made subservient to love or lust" (VRW 5:96).[17] A couplet from one of Dryden's *Fables* drives the point home, a little further along the trajectory of male passion, after the brink has been crossed (VRW 5:189):

> Where love is duty, on the female side,
> On theirs mere sensual gust, and sought with surly pride.[18]

In "Palamon and Arcite," this is the lament of the virgin Emily, pleading to Cynthia, goddess of chastity, to take her as a votress:

> Like Death, thou know'st, I loath the Nuptial state,
> And Man, the Tyrant of our Sex, I hate,
> A lowly Servant, but a lofty Mate.
> Where Love is Duty, on the Female side;
> On theirs meer sensual Gust, and sought with surly Pride.
> (3.227–32)

What makes the system a tyranny of Death from which a retreat from sex itself seems necessary? The culture of "cramping a woman's mind,... in order to keep it fair" leaves Wollstonecraft thinking that women are as damned as Milton's Satan: "would it not be a refinement on cruelty only to open her mind to make the darkness and misery of her fate *visible*?" she asks in the midst of a chapter titled "Animadversions on Some of the Writers Who Have Rendered Women Objects of Pity, Bordering on Contempt" (VRW 5:158). A hopeless world of "No light, but rather darkness visible" is what the hell-flames reveal to Satan, or to any woman who, not realizing her cultural doom, might think of her mind as her salvation (*PL* 1.63).[19]

Wollstonecraft's allusion is a very bitter one, and it is particularly painful to her that along with the "language of men" on "a supposed sexual character,"

175

the "same sentiments" can be voiced by "women of superior sense" such as Barbauld (VRW 5:122), one of the few women in the progressive circles of 1790s London. Back in 1787, as Wollstonecraft was writing *Thoughts on the Education of Daughters: with Reflections on Female Conduct, in the more important Duties of Life*, she was happy to recommend Barbauld's *Hymns in Prose for Children* as a great help from an "ingenious author" in making "the Deity obvious to the senses" (4:10).[20] Even in *Rights of Woman* she could praise Barbauld's good moral sense (5:184), and quote her poetry to make a point about the shallow power men accord to women's beauty:

> They will smile, – yes, they will smile, though told that –
> > "In beauty's empire is no mean,
> > And woman, either slave or queen,
> > Is quickly scorn'd when not ador'd."
> But the adoration comes first, and the scorn is not anticipated.   (5:125)

The poetry is from "Song V" (*Poems* [1773]), in which an "aged Shepherd," hearing the complaint of lovelorn Araminta, advises her with this cold truth. So much for Pope's oft-cited claim that "ev'ry Lady would be Queen for life" ("To a Lady," 218). Under the same hard lesson of "the pernicious tendency of those books, in which the writers insidiously degrade the sex whilst they are prostrate before their personal charms," Wollstonecraft quotes from Dryden's opera, *The State of Innocence: and Fall of Man*:

> —"Curs'd vassalage,
> First idoliz'd till love's hot fire be o'er,
> Then slaves to those who courted us before."
> > (VRW 5:161)

This is Eve's curse (5.1.58–60), the first line of which Wollstonecraft has only partly recalled ("Curs'd vassalage of all my future kind"), truncating a phrase she might have put to work in tracing that male-drawn "lineal descent from the first fair defect in nature" (VRW 5:124).

So when Barbauld takes the male line, Wollstonecraft is sorry, very sorry. She first cites, with emphases, a couplet from Barbauld's "To Mrs. P———, with some Drawings of Birds and Insects" (in *Poems*): "Pleasure's the portion of *th'inferior* kind; / But glory, virtue, Heaven for *man* designed." Barbauld is comparing the endowments of bird-life to those of humankind, here termed "man," with a play upon the Latin root of *virtue* (*vir*: man). "After writing these lines, how could Mrs. Barbauld write the following ignoble comparison?" Wollstonecraft cries (VRW 5:122n). The offence (following Pope on tulips) is "To a Lady, with some painted flowers" (*Poems*), which she quotes in full in a footnote, highlighting with capitals or italics the noxious phrases:

> Flowers to the fair: to you these flowers I bring,
> And strive to greet you with an earlier spring.
> *Flowers* SWEET, *and gay, and* DELICATE LIKE YOU;
> *Emblems of innocence, and beauty too.*
> With flowers the Graces bind their yellow hair,
> And flowery wreaths consenting lovers wear.
> *Flowers, the sole luxury which nature knew,*
> In Eden's pure and guiltless garden grew.
> *To loftier forms are rougher tasks assign'd;*
> *The sheltering oak, resists the stormy wind,*
> *The tougher yew repels invading foes,*
> *And the tall pine for future navies grows;*
> *But this soft family, to cares unknown,*
> *Were born for pleasure and delight* ALONE.
> Gay without toil, and lovely without art,
> *They spring to* CHEER *the sense, and* GLAD *the heart.*
> Nor blush, my fair, to own you copy these;
> *Your* BEST, your SWEETEST *empire* is – to PLEASE.

"So the men tell us," Wollstonecraft dryly remarks (bracketing the praises as "the language of men") and at grievous cost to women: "but virtue, says reason, must be acquired by *rough* toils, and useful struggles with worldly *cares*" (VRW 5:122–3). Degendering male-rooted "virtue" in the open franchise of reason, Wollstonecraft refutes Barbauld's comparison of the "Lady" to sweet, weak, delicate, passive, pleasure-devoted flowers; the trope "nips reason in the bud," she warns, exfoliating Barbauld's dominant metaphor (5:125).

IV. The poets read Wollstonecraft

"There is no bond of union among literary women," Barbauld curtly replied when popular novelist Maria Edgeworth proposed in 1804 that they coedit a periodical featuring this community. Barbauld cited, among other things, "different sentiments." About ten years earlier she had answered Wollstonecraft's critique of her poetry in *Rights of Woman* with a poem of friendly amendment, "The Rights of Woman."[21] Its first six stanzas resound Wollstonecraft's disdain of female pride in their specious power in the game of love, their realm of "rule in partial law's despite." So situated, "injured Woman" – "too long degraded, scorned opprest" – can "rise" and "assert [her] right" by ruling heartlessly over men's hearts. Satirizing a conduct instructor, Barbauld exhorts, "Go, bid proud man his boasted rule resign, / And kiss the gold sceptre of thy reign" (7–8); "Make treacherous Man thy subject, not thy friend" (19). Her summary caution is of a piece with the lines Wollstonecraft quoted from "Song V": "But hope not, courted idol of mankind, / On this proud eminence secure to stay" (25–6). Yet instead of projecting a fall into abjection and scorn, Barbauld proposes a remedy that nowhere appears in Wollstonecraft's view of the relations of the sexes, except as passionless friendship. Urging the coquette to abandon the power-plays of courtship, Barbauld summons nature not as Wollstonecraft does, the specious rationale for social oppression, but as the truest mentor of the heart, "In Nature's school, by her soft maxims taught, / That separate rights are lost in mutual love" (31–2).

Barbauld offers this solace in partial Law's despite, but she envisions no reform of the law itself. If Wollstonecraft, too, is silent on such remedy (scarcely thought of in the 1790s), unlike Barbauld she still had a systemic instead of a personal cure in mind. This was a paired reform in state education and what she was willing to advertise in her conclusion to *Rights of Woman* as "a REVOLUTION in female manners" (5:265). And it was this rhetoric, fresh on the heels of the French Revolution, that Reverend Richard Polwhele, high Church and Tory, shuddered at and broadcast in *The Unsex'd Females* (1798) – a satire loudly praised in anti-Jacobin (reactionary) quarters for its disciplinary zeal:[22]

> Survey with me, what ne'er our fathers saw,
> A female band despising NATURE's law,
> As "proud defiance" flashes from their arms,
> And vengeance smothers all their softer charms.
>   *I* shudder at the new unpictur'd scene,
> Where unsex'd woman vaunts the imperious mien.
>   (11–16)

We can do the Wollstonecraft-work on "NATURE's law" (an ideology, and thus not "natural" at all), but what can Polwhele mean by "unsex'd"? His scene throngs with sexual wild-women, all hopped up on French ideas and French licentiousness.[23] Polwhele means that a public protest and a disdain of "softer charms" render women unfeminine, "unsexed."

Yet the oversexed female is a peculiar vehicle for publicizing this scandal, given Wollstonecraft's own exhortations, in the passages of *Rights of Woman* Polwhele must have missed (if he read it at all), of modesty and chastity (sexual self-control in marriage) as necessary to rational behavior. What we see by the contradictory lines of Polwhele's cartoon of "Wollstonecraft" is the emerging cultural transformation of Rationalist Wollstonecraft into Radical Wollstonecraft, her liberal causes reducible to libertine promiscuity:

> See Wollstonecraft, whom no decorum checks,
> Arise, the intrepid champion of her sex;
> O'er humbled man assert the sovereign claim,
> And slight the timid blush of virgin fame.
> "Go, go (she cries) ye tribes of melting maids,
> "Go, screen your softness in sequester'd shades."
>
> (63–8)

As Polwhele does seem aware, Wollstonecraft had challenged women to refuse not only the cant of "Nature's law" but also the flattery of a revered canon of poets, which he sums as "the rapt Bard":

> "Tho' the rapt Bard, your empire fond to own,
> "Fall prostrate and adore your living throne,
> "The living throne his hands presum'd to rear,
> "Its seat a simper, and its base a tear;
> "Soon shall the sex disdain the illusive sway,
> "And wield the sceptre in yon blaze of day;
> "Ere long, each little artifice discard,
> "No more by weakness winning fond regard;
> "Nor eyes, that sparkle from their blushes, roll,
> "Nor catch the languors of the sick'ning soul,
> "Nor the quick flutter, nor the coy reserve,
> "But nobly boast the firm gymnastic nerve;
> "Nor more affect with Delicacy's fan
> "To hide the emotion from congenial man;
> "To the bold heights where glory beams, aspire,
> "Blend mental energy with Passion's fire,
> "Surpass their rivals in the powers of mind
> "And vindicate *the Rights of womankind.*"
>
> (73–90)

Except for the sarcasm and the hysteric conclusion that such women can want only to "surpass" men (always viewed as "rivals" in the exercise of mental "power") so as to "wield the sceptre" themselves, Polwhele, as much as More's Coelebs, all but vindicates Wollstonecraft. He means to present his dire reports – "artifice discard," "no more of weakness," "gymnastic" pride, disdain of "Delicacy," and "mental energy" – as shocking negations of what defines and honors "the sex"; but his obsessive sputtering of these Wollstonecrafted points paradoxically confirms their force.

His next verse paragraph as much as concedes this force with a mock-epic catalog of all the women (he sounds the alarm) who have "caught the strain" (91–106) – among them, poets Mary Robinson, Charlotte Smith, Helen Maria Williams, Ann Yearsley, and Barbauld. The venom commands not only several footnotes sneering at Wollstonecraft's arguments and the scandals of Godwin's *Memoir* – her infatuations with Fuseli and Imlay, her suicide attempts and her refusal of established religion (pp. 25–30) – but also several more verses ridiculing her failure, in the sway the "licentious love" (156), to live by her code of reason. Polwhele even gloats over her death in childbirth ("the destiny of women"), discerning a "visible" "Hand of Providence" to punish her challenge (pp. 28–30).

Polwhele dedicated his bile to T. J. Mathias, whose Preface to the Fourth Dialogue of *The Pursuits of Literature* (1797) gave him his title, the inspiration featured on the title page: "Our unsex'd female writers now instruct, or confuse, us and themselves, in the labyrinth of politics, or turn us wild with Gallic frenzy" – the ideas and mores stirred by the regicidal French Revolution. To complement the compliment, Mathias included a set of equally venomous anti-Wollstonecraft stanzas in a satire he published the next year, as replete as Polwhele's with such lengthy notes on Godwin's *Memoirs* as to suggest that his verse was mere pretextual scaffolding:

> Fierce passion's slave, she veer'd with every gust,
> Love, Rights, and Wrongs, Philosophy, and Lust.[24]

The Anti-Jacobin Review piled on in 1801 with *The Vision of Liberty*.[25] After a dolorous tour of the decapitated corpses of the French royal family, its poet-dreamer enters "The house of liberty" (stanza VIII) to behold monstrous images of Voltaire, Paine, and various Jacobin criminals:

> Then saw I mounted on a braying ass,
> William and Mary, sooth, a couple jolly;
> Who married, note ye how it came to pass,
> Although each held that marriage was but folly? –
> And she of curses would discharge a volley
> If the ass stumbled, leaping pales or ditches:
> Her husband, sans-culottes, was melancholy,
> For Mary verily would wear the breeches –
> God help poor silly men from such usurping b——s.
>
> Whilom this dame the Rights of Women writ,
> That is the title to her book she places,
> Exhorting bashful womankind to quit
> All foolish modesty, and coy grimaces;
> And name their backsides as it were their faces;

Such licence loose-tongued liberty adores,
Which adds to female speech exceeding graces;
Lucky the maid that on her volume pores,
A scripture, archly fram'd, for propagating w——s.

William hath penn'd a waggon-load of stuff,
And Mary's life at last he needs must write,
Thinking her whoredoms were not known enough,
Till fairly printed off in black and white. –
With wondrous glee and pride, this simple wight
Her brothel feats of wantonnness sets down,
Being her spouse, he tells, with huge delight,
How oft she cuckolded the silly clown,
And lent, O lively piece! herself to half the town!

(stanzas XV–XVII)

The visionary prods readers to recall that the *Anti-Jacobin*'s debut issue (July 1798) indexed "Prostitution" apparently for the sake of the cross reference, "*See* Mary Wollstonecraft" (*Anti-Jacobin*, 859).

American poet Adrienne Rich took this libel to heart in her stanza on Wollstonecraft in *Snapshots of a Daughter-in-Law* (1963), published almost a decade before a reinvigorated twentieth-century feminism became an Anglo-American movement. Her italicized, poeticized epigraph is a modest proposal from Wollstonecraft's *Thoughts on the Education of Daughters*.[26]

"*To have in this uncertain world some stay*
which cannot be undermined, is
of the utmost consequence."
Thus wrote
a woman, partly brave and partly good,
who fought with what she partly understood.
Few men about her would or could do more,
hence she was labeled harpy, shrew and whore.

(Section 7)

Rich is only partly right, however, for there were a few good men in Wollstonecraft's own day who also contested the label, even as they were aware of its adhesiveness.

William Roscoe's satirical ballad on Edmund Burke was one of the first to do so, praising the bold rebuttal of his *Reflections on the Revolution in France* in her *Vindication of the Rights of Men* – a tribute for which Wollstonecraft thanked Roscoe as she was finishing her next *Vindication* (Letters 206). As Roscoe knew, the revelation that *Rights of Man* was a woman's writing roiled the initial reviews,[27] and he celebrates this extraordinary female performance:

An[d] lo! an Amazon stept out,
    One WOLSTONECRAFT her name,
Resolv'd to stop his [Burke's] mad career,
    Whatever chance became.

An oaken sapling in her hand,
    Full on the foe she fell,
Nor could his coat of rusty steel
    Her vig'rous strokes repel.

When strange to see, her conq'ring staff,
    Returning leaves o'erspread,
Of which a verdant wreath was wove,
    And bound around her head.[28]

In Roscoe's baroque image, the oaken sapling as weapon and metaphoric pen generates the material for Wollstonecraft's honors: it sprouts the leaves (with a pun on pages) that supply the headwreath that signifies a poet laureate.

To similar gender-bending praise in the wake of *Rights of Woman* another member of the Wollstonecraft's London circle, George Dyer, was inspired. His "Ode on Liberty" (1792) hails "Liberty" for having chosen "to warm/ With more than manly fire the female breast," fueling "Wollstonecraft to break the charm, / Where beauty lies in durance vile opprest" (stanza VIII).[29] To this praise Dyer appends a lengthy explanatory note:

> Author of the *Rights of Woman*. I have observed, that the most sensible females, when they turn their attention to political subjects, are more uniformly on the side of liberty than the other sex. This may be accounted for without adopting the sentiments or the language of gallantry. The truth is, that the modes of education and the customs of society are degrading to the female character; and the tyranny of custom is sometimes worse than the tyranny of government. When a sensible woman rises above the tyranny of custom, she feels a generous indignation; which, when turned against the exclusive claims of the other sex, is favourable to female pretensions; when turned against the tyranny of government, it is commonly favourable to the rights of both sexes. Most governments are partial, and more injurious to women than to men.

Where Rich will reiterate "partly" to mean both "incompletely" and "with a bias," Dyer locates all fault in a system of injurious "partial" privileges. Dyer puts Wollstonecraft in impressive female company, including Williams, Barbauld, Smith, and Macaulay. Robert Southey found her unique, praising her in some elegiac verses of 1797 as one "Who among women left no equal mind / When from this world she passed; and I could weep, / To think that *She* is to the grave gone down!" While she was alive, Southey wrote "To Mary Wolstoncraft" (1795), one of the two dedicatory sonnets to *The Triumph of*

Woman. He attempted to restore some of the traditional poets' praises of woman:[30]

> The lily cheek, the "purple light of love,"
> The liquid lustre of the melting eye, –
> Mary! of these the poet sung, for these
> Did Woman triumph: turn not thou away
> Contemptuous from the theme. No Maid of Arc
> Had, in those ages, for her country's cause
> Wielded the sword of freedom; no Roland
> Had borne the palm of female fortitude;
> No Cordé, with self-sacrificing zeal,
> Had glorified again the Avenger's name,
> As erst when Cæsar perished...   (lines 1–11)

Despite the heroic analogues (the revolutionary martyrs Joan of Arc, Madame Roland, Charlotte Corday), that phrase in quotation is just the sort to provoke Wollstonecraft to animadversion: "O'er her warm cheek and rising bosom move / The bloom of young desire and purple light of love," wrote Gray in *The Progress of Poetry* (40–1). Southey adored Wollstonecraft, but he was uncomfortable with her disdain of conventional poetic praises, and wished her to moderate her contempt with some forgiveness for the pace of progress.

Another poet in the Johnson circle saw in the treatment of Wollstonecraft, especially after the outrage ignited by Godwin's *Memoirs*, a mirror of his own felt persecution for heterodoxy. In "Mary" (1802–3, but not published until 1866), Blake celebrates an unembarrassed, radiant beauty (lines 9–12) with a bountiful hand (lines 23) – an allusion to the work of her pen:

> Some said she was proud some calld her a whore
> And some when she passed by shut to the door.
>   (lines 16–17)

Blake's calumniated "Mary" is a martyr to her ideals:[31]

> She went out in Morning in plain neat attire
> And came home in Evening bespatterd with mire.
>   (lines 35–36)

> With Faces of Scorn & with Eyes of disdain
> Like foul Fiends inhabiting Marys mild Brain
> She remembers no Face like the Human Divine
> All Faces have Envy sweet Mary but thine
> And thine is a Face of sweet Love in Despair

And thine is a Face of mild sorrow & care
And thine is a Face of wild terror & fear
That shall never be quiet till laid on its bier.
                    (lines 41–8)

For most of the nineteenth century, British culture put Wollstonecraft on its own bier, burying her critical challenges in the scandal of her name. Yet among some radical poets she remained a living light. In the Dedication of *Laon and Cythna* (1817) to Mary Wollstonecraft Godwin, Percy Shelley eulogizes her mother both as a lost light and a continuing inspiration:

> ... One then left this earth
> Whose life was like a setting planet mild,
> Which clothed thee in the radiance undefiled
> Of its departing glory; still her fame
> Shines on thee, through the tempests dark and wild
> Which shake these latter days ...
>   (Dedication 102–7)

In the metaphor of shining light glistens Wollstonecraft's devotion to rational enlightenment. "A pretty woman, as an object of desire, is generally allowed to be so by men of all descriptions," she sighed in *Rights of Woman*, "whilst a fine woman, who inspires more sublime emotions by displaying intellectual beauty, may be overlooked or observed with indifference, by those men who find their happiness in the gratification of their appetites" (5:116). Her lament clearly caught Shelley's attention, and he redeemed it for one of the most passionate statements of his philosophy, published the same year he wrote the dedicatory lines above, "Hymn to Intellectual Beauty."

Shelley's poem is a redemptive operation, but in *The Wrongs of Woman, or Maria*, the political fable Wollstonecraft left unfinished at her death, poetry retains the deeply ambiguous role enacted by her own disciplines and pleasures. It is woven into the system of wrongs, but it may also provoke a sense of rights. Incarcerated by a treacherous husband, Maria hears another inmate, reported to be "a lovely maniac," singing "the pathetic ballad of old Robin Gray with the most heart-melting falls and pauses." This popular poem by Anne Lindsay (first published in 1770s) is "pathetic" for its tale of how severe economic hardship forced the singer into marriage with kind old Rob and the consequent loss of her beloved Jamie. Taken to the maniac's chamber, Maria expects to embrace a sympathetic double in the "lovely warbler," and is appalled by "a torrent of unconnected exclamations and questions ... interrupted by fits of laughter, so horrid, that Maria shut the door" (1.95). She then learns that the maniac was made so by a darker Robin Gray, a brutally jealous, rich old husband. Maria closes the door, but *Maria* keeps it open, to show the social, political, and psychological entailments of aesthetic pleasure. The enchanting poetry is a text of error and its revealed context a text of illumination. A little earlier that same day, Maria had received a packet of books from another inmate (his identity a mystery):

> Dryden's Fables, Milton's Paradise Lost, with several modern productions, composed the collection. It was a mine of treasure. Some marginal notes, in Dryden's Fables, caught her attention: they were written with force and taste. (1.93)

It's a Wollstonecraft poetry shelf, perhaps even a Wollstonecraft scene of instruction, of thinking in the margins of poetry. Although this scene has other latencies, including the dubious character of the bibliophile, it survives as a local reference to Wollstonecraft's way of reading the poets. To the extent that cultural criticism today is involved with reading the social text and its books of poetry, Wollstonecraft alerts us to the complicated attractions. Reading the poets may solicit a fall into error, but it may also become an education in error. The reader who writes in the margins of poetry is no passive, uncritical recipient of opinion, but an active producer, unmaking, remaking, making opinion anew – in the root sense of "making," another poet.

NOTES

1. Milton's *Paradise Lost* is abbreviated *PL*. Quotations from well-known poets are given without a specific edition.
2. See the passage she quotes, 4:159. *Emile* abounds with assertions of "natural" female character (see, for instance, 5:94 and the passages focusing her extended "animadversion" on *Emile* in VRW chapter v:1 [5:147–60]). "The worthy Dr. Gregory fell into a similar error" in "his celebrated Legacy to his Daughters": "cultivate a fondness for dress, because a fondness for dress, he asserts, is natural to them," Wollstonecraft reports, treating the asserted order of nature as just a man's text, poorly argued: "I am unable to comprehend what either he or Rousseau mean, when they frequently use this indefinite term" (5:97). Throughout, she reinforces the point that "natural" is a usage, not a fact: a girl is brought up in a way that guarantees that she is "rendered dependent – dependence is called natural" (5:110) and man is designated "their *natural* protector" (5:131).
3. For a reading of Wollstonecraft as so intimidated by Milton that she could manage her resistance only in the indirect attacks of allusions and italics, see Mary Poovey, *The Proper Lady and the Woman Writer: Ideology as Style in the Works of Mary Wollstonecraft, Mary Shelley, and Jane Austen* (Chicago: University of Chicago Press, 1984), 72–3. As shall be apparent, I see far more direction than indirection in Wollstonecraft's staging of her reading; even her allusions and italics seem quite pointed.

4. Cited in 5:88n. A progressive thinker such as William Hazlitt, writing to the radical newspaper *The Examiner*, could assert "That line in Milton is very striking – 'He for God only, she for God in him.' Such is the order of nature and providence... Women are what they were meant to be" – a state he has described as one of "no ideas, except personal ones," driven by "their senses, their vanity, or their interest" ("The Round Table" 12 February 1815, 108).

5. Wollstonecraft is anticipated by Pope's contemporary Richard Bentley, who was prompted to save Milton from himself with a correction in his edition of *Paradise Lost:* "A shameful error to have pass'd through all the Editions. The Author gave it, *He for God only, She for God* AND *Him*" (*Milton's "Paradise Lost"* [London: Tonson & c, 1732], 117n). Bentley's substitution at least allows Eve her own line of relation to God.

6. Cobb, review of Claire Tomalin, *The Life and Death of Mary Wollstonecraft*, *TLS*, 6 September 1974, 941–4; Godwin, *Memoirs*, 1st edn., eds. Pamela Clemit and Gina Luria Wakler (Ontario: Broadview Press, 2001), 76.

7. See my essay, "Shakespeare and the Romantic Girl Reader," *Nineteenth-Century Contexts* 21 (1999), 191–234.

8. For interweavings of Shakespeare's terms, phrases, and wording into her own or her heroines' language, see *Mary* (1:31, 63), *Rights of Men* (5:9 and 60), *Rights of Woman* (5:108, 180, 214, 221), *Hints* (274), *Short Residence* (6:322, 324, 337),*Wrongs of Woman* (1:85, 167, 176). The index to *Works* provides further guidance; see also Lorne Macdonald's superb index to the Broadview edition of the two *Vindications*.

9. For pungent incorporations of Hamlet's voices of distraction, misery, anger, or sarcasm, see *Historical and Moral View of the French Revolution* (6:58), *Short Residence* (6:332, 336), *Letters to Imlay* (6:377, 403, 416) and Maria in *Wrongs of Woman* (1:90); for Lear's anger, see LI 6:421, and for Macbeth 's anxiety, M 1:49 and LI 6.378. For the presence of *Hamlet* in*Wrongs of Woman*, see Claudia L. Johnson, *Equivocal Beings: Politics, Gender and Sentimentality in the 1790s, Wollstonecraft, Radcliffe, Burney, Austen* (Chicago: University of Chicago Press, 1995), 62.

10. Glossing a comment on the status of women as amusements inspiring tenderness but little "respect," this note begins, "Similar feelings has Milton's pleasing picture of paradisiacal happiness ever raised in my mind." "Whenever [I] read Milton's description of paradise," she wrote to her sister two years before, "the happiness, which he so poetically describes fills me with benevolent satisfaction – yet, I cannot help viewing... the first pair – as if they were my inferiors – inferiors because they could find happiness in a world like this" (Letters, 195).

11. See, in addition to the texts I discuss in this essay, 5:104, 138, 145, 187, and 192.

12. *The Female Reader*, observes Tilottama Rajan, assigns women to the domestic sphere without commenting on "social psychology as something historically produced. Its instructional form assumes the anterior presence of universal truths, without raising the question of their representation" (*The Supplement of Reading* [Ithaca: Cornell University Press, 1990], 171).

13. *Coelebs in Search of a Wife* (London: James Blackwood, 1809), 9–10. In the table of contents, chapter 1 is titled "Milton on Eve – Opinions of the Ladies not correct."

14. In *Feminist Milton* (Ithaca: Cornell University Press, 1987), Joseph Wittreich proposes that Milton has "calculated" such "contradictions" to thwart a regard of him as a unified voice of orthodoxy or an equation of his views with those of his dramatic speakers, such as Adam or even the epic narrator. Arguing that Wollstonecraft produces Milton as "an advocate for women, not their adversary" (41–2), Wittreich misses not only her critical tone but also the fact that she has included him in, indeed made him the epitome of, the insulting view that women were formed for softness and sweet attractive grace (VRW 5:88). Against his report, Wollstonecraft's note (VRW 5:94) which he cites as praise of Milton, expresses restlessness with "Milton's pleasing picture of paradisiacal happiness."

15. That Wollstonecraft has quoted Adam's argument for the virtues of equality in *Rights of Men* (5:39) suggests that she is alert to Milton's self-contradiction on the issue of gender arrangements. For the shapes and consequences of this contradiction, see Ronald Levao, "'Among Unequals What Society': *Paradise Lost* and the Forms of Intimacy," *Modern Language Quarterly* 61.1 (2000), 79–108; especially 96 and n26.

16. *The Ladies Library. Written by a Lady*, 3 vols. (London: Steele, 1714), 1:2–4. Wittreich cites Wray as an example of Milton's availability for a "defense" of women (54), but Wray says otherwise: to the possibility that Adam's rant is his and not Milton's view, she replies, "if the Author had right Sentiments of Woman in general, he might more emphatically aggravate an ill Character, by Comparison of an ill to an innocent and vertuous one, than by general Calumnies without Exception" (4).

17. For other references in *Rights of Woman* to the misogyny in Pope's epistle, see 5:96, 141, 187, 241, 260. In a weird misremembering of the most luridly misogynist scene in *Paradise Lost* (2.746–814) – a misprison that Poovey sees reflecting Wollstonecraft's fear that female desire may justify misogyny (*Proper Lady*, 76) – she writes in her conclusion, "What are the cold, or feverish caresses of appetite, but sin embracing death, compared with the modest overflowings of a pure heart and an exalted imagination?" (VRW 5:264; "Modest" means "rationally governed"). In Milton's allegory, Death (the issue of Satan's rape of his daughter Sin) rapes his mother, who gives birth to the hellhounds that eternally torture her by gnawing at her womb. This is Milton's first image of birth-giving in the poem, and it is one whose terms of description draw in unfallen Eve.

18. This couplet appears on the title page of William Thompson and Anna Wheeler's *Appeal of One Half the Human Race, Women, Against the Pretensions of the Other Half, Men, To Retain Them in Political, and Thence in Civil And Domestic Slavery* (1825), the most important appeal after Wollstonecraft's, published in a decade when her name and cause were still a scandal.

19. See also her reference to this Satanic purview in *Mary*, chapter 19, as Mary describes her hopelessness (1:49), and in *Rights of Men*, describing Catholicism in the advent of the Protestant Reformation: "this faint dawn of liberty only made the subsiding darkness more visible" (5:12).

20. See also the praise lavished on Barbauld later in *Thoughts* (4:57) and some of her reviews for the *Analytical Review* (7:35, 72, 417). In *The Female Reader* (1789) Wollstonecraft includes several of her prose pieces as well as three of the 1773 *Poems: The Mouse's Petition, A Character, An Address to the Deity*, and *On a Lady's Writing* – this last a trio of neoclassical couplets in which writing

pertains not just to her script but also to the cultural "writing," or inscription, of female conduct ("Her even lines her steady temper show" is the first line). I quote from the "new edition" (London: Joseph Johnson, 1792).

21. This poem was written soon after Wollstonecraft's tract appeared (1795 or so) but not published until *The Works of Anna Lætitia Barbauld, with a Memoir*, ed. Lucy Aikin, 2 vols. (London: Longman, 1825) 1:195–7. Barbauld's comment to Edgeworth is reported by Anna Letitia Le Breton, *Memoir of Mrs. Barbauld* (London: George Bell, 1874), 86–7.

22. *The Unsex'd Females: A Poem* (London: Cadell and Davies, 1798).

23. Claudia L. Johnson suggests that the problem is that they seem oversexed, ungovernable; see her trenchant discussion, *Equivocal Beings*, 9.

24. *The Shade of Alexander Pope on the Banks of the Thames, A Satirical Poem, With Notes*, by the Author of *The Pursuits of Literature* (London: T. Becket, 1799), 47–8. The nearly full-page footnotes run 44–53.

25. Signed "C. K.," *Anti-Jacobin Review and Magazine, or, Monthly Political and Literary Censor* 9 (April-August, 1801), 515–20; I quote from 518. Clemit and Walker identity C. K. as C. Kirkpatrick Sharpe (192).

26. This is the last sentence in the section titled "Artificial Manners" (4.15). *Snapshots* appears in a volume of the same title (New York: Harper & Row, 1963), reissued 1967 and 1970.

27. The *Analytical Review* hooted, "how deeply must it wound the feelings of a *chivalrous knight*, who owes the fealty of 'proud submission and dignified obedience' to the fair sex, to perceive that two of the boldest of his adversaries are women!" (8 [1790], 416); the other was Catherine Macaulay, whose *Observations on Burke* was reviewed immediately after. *Critical Review*, having assumed a male author until the second signed edition, vindicated its blunt response with an appeal to chivalry: "a lady should have been addressed with more respect," it apologized in a note appended to the title line, but insisted that when a she-author "assumes the disguise of a man, she must not be surprised that she is not treated with the civility and respect that she would have received in her own person" (70 [1790], 694). The *English Review* did treat this masculine performance with civility and respect: "The language may be thought by some too bold and pointed for a female pen; but when women undertake to write on masculine subjects, and reason as Miss Wollstonecraft does, we wish their language to be free from all female *prettinesses*, and to express with energy and perspicuity, the ideas they mean to convey" (17 [1791], 61). *Gentleman's Magazine* saw the point, too, and could manage its discomfort only in the genre of farce, leading its review with a mock broadcast of a scandal: "The *rights of men* asserted by a fair lady! The age of chivalry cannot be over, or the sexes have changed their ground . . . Mrs. Wolstencraft enters the lists armed *cap-à-pie*" (61/1 [1791], 151).

28. "The Life, Death and Wonderful Atchievements of Edmund Burke: a new ballad" (1791), *William Roscoe of Liverpool*, ed. George Chandler (London: B. T. Batsford, 1953).

29. *Ode VII. On Liberty*, in G. Dyer, *Poems* (London: J. Johnson, 1792).

30. For Southey's verses, see *Memoirs* (ed. Durant), xxx–xxxi.

31. *Mary* gave Emily Sunstein her title for *A Different Face: the Life of Mary Wollstonecraft* (New York: Harper & Row, 1975): "O why was I born with a different Face" (21).

11

CLAUDIA L. JOHNSON

Mary Wollstonecraft's novels

Beyond the sphere of Wollstonecraft studies, *Mary, A Fiction* (1788) and *The Wrongs of Woman, or Maria* (1798) typically receive scant attention. As if her novels had little intrinsic interest, most histories of the novel do not mention Wollstonecraft's contributions to the genre, and until relatively recently Wollstonecraft scholars in a way have seemed to concur, largely ignoring the first and reading the last either as an extension of her biography or as a fictionalization of *A Vindication of the Rights of Woman*. At first glance, some skepticism about Wollstonecraft's contributions to the English novel seems only too reasonable. Although she became a woman of letters – "moralist" would probably have been the eighteenth-century term for her – Wollstonecraft's career did not develop around a single genre. All of her works are of a piece in their very diversity, blending overlapping discourses of education, political commentary, travel literature, autobiography, moral philosophy, and fiction by turns, and while this makes for challenging and often bracing reading, it is also probably a little dizzying to audiences whose generic expectations are more straightforward, who expect novels to execute a well-managed plot or to unfold incrementally developing character. Moreover, like most women writers of the time, Wollstonecraft had little in the way of formal education and is not a remarkably deft writer, lacking the ease and fluency of novelists like Ann Radcliffe, Charlotte Smith, the dramatic flair of Elizabeth Inchbald, let alone the comprehensive mastery of narration, dialogue, and pacing of someone like Jane Austen. She mostly wrote topically and in haste, rarely polishing what she had done, and she did not even finish such major works as *Rights of Woman*, *Historical and Moral View of the French Revolution*, and, of course, *Wrongs of Woman*. When we add to this the fact that Wollstonecraft's articles for the *Analytical Review* and her arguments in *Vindication of the Rights of Woman* frequently decry the trashiness of novels, especially by women, and the fact that her own novel *Mary* characterizes them more or less as soft porn – "delightful substitutes for bodily dissipation"(M 1:8) – the case against a separate treatment of her work as a novelist seems sound.

But during the eighteenth century – and well beyond – novelists routinely decry their craft; indeed it is almost a matter of convention to do so (Jane Austen makes a serious and extended joke about this "ungenerous and impolitic custom" in the fifth chapter of *Northanger Abbey*), and accordingly we should not be put off. The fact is that novels are the very bookends of Wollstonecraft's life as a writer, both pre- and post-dating her attempts at direct political intervention. She turns to the novel when she attempts to inaugurate her career in 1787, the year *Mary* was written,[1] and to the novel again, after the disappointment of her political hopes in 1796, when she started *Wrongs of Woman*, dying a year later from complications resulting from childbirth before it was completed. The novel's accessibility to authors lacking a classical education, its relatively wide public, and its formal suppleness made it a natural choice for an aspiring writer interested in treating the subjects of virtue, desire, education, genius, sociability, sensibility, and justice.

Although Godwin believed that *Mary, A Fiction* was enough "to establish the eminence of her genius" with "persons of true taste and sensibility",[2] late in her life Wollstonecraft seems to have felt less than proud of it. "As for my Mary," she wrote her sister Everina in 1797, "I consider it as a crude production, and do not very willingly put it in the way of people whose good opinion, as a writer, I wish for; but you may have it to make up the sum of laughter" (Letters, 385). But the same "crudeness" that embarrassed the older Wollstonecraft evidently struck the younger author – who also wanted people's good opinion *as a writer* – as a sort of proof of its merits as a ruggedly original work that bravely dared to depart from common practice. *Mary, A Fiction* is indeed a bold and suggestive novel that addresses the fundamental relationship of gender to the novel as a genre. In the Advertisement Wollstonecraft proposes to do something that had never been done before in novels, and her claim is stunning both in its simplicity and its ambition: to represent "the mind of a woman who has thinking powers" (M 1:8). Wollstonecraft's audacity deserves some attention. She differentiates her (let's face it) decidedly fledgling accomplishment in *Mary* not from that of forgettable and forgotten novels of her time, novels she would almost routinely deride in *The Analytical Review*, as Mitzi Myers shows here. Instead, she is saying that her achievement is better than what then were and still are the eighteenth century's best most compelling novels, Jean-Jacques Rousseau's *Emile* and Samuel Richardson's *Clarissa* and *Sir Charles Grandison*. The implication hardly needs spelling out: despite the memorable heroines of these novels and their enormous appeal to women and men alike, these novels somehow feature women who do not have "thinking powers" of their own, but rather (presumably) only feeling powers, sensibilities that bind them closely to approval and disapproval of their communities and thus circumscribe them as independent moral agents.

Mary, A Fiction is a daring and difficult novel, and I suspect many readers share my sense that it is often hard to figure out exactly what on earth the narrator and heroine are talking about. Why is this so? In 1787 Wollstonecraft herself stated that *Mary* "is a tale, to illustrate an opinion of mine, that a genius will educate itself." Disdaining false modesty, she bluntly continued: "I have drawn from Nature" (Letters, p. 162). In this autobiographical novel, then, Wollstonecraft undertakes to show how an unusual and gifted woman learns to think and act for herself – through the solitary contemplation of the works of God in nature, through reading works of religious philosophy and later even medicine, through travel and through sociable intercourse with her two particular "friends" – and in the process she becomes one of "the chosen few" who "wish to speak for themselves, and not to be an echo" (M 1:5). The sometime high-blown, portentous quality of the prose shows us an author wishing to say what has never been said and so achieve a true grandeur. The epigraph printed on the title page of the novel — "*L'exercise des plus sublime vertus éleve et nourrit le génie*" [The exercise of her various virtues gave vigor to her genius[3]] – comes from Rousseau's *Lettres de deux amants* (1761) and many have seen Rousseau's novel about a hero's education into personal as well as civic maturity, *Emile*, as the fictional prototype for *Mary*. But while Wollstonecraft's debts to Rousseau are many, Wollstonecraft's Advertisement disputes it. Here – and for the rest of her career – she is painfully aware that Rousseau himself would recoil from a woman like her heroine Mary, a woman who is indifferent to the cultivation of feminine charms and personal attractions, particularly as these are to be deployed in eliciting, taming, and socializing the erotic sentiments of men; a woman who is clearly idiosyncratic, intense, and autonomous rather than obliging, soft and softening, or domesticated; a woman who spends her time indulging in vatic utterances about complex subjects such as God, duty, sublimity, sensibility, and the afterlife. To be sure, Rousseau would not only disapprove of such a woman; he would also in all probability run away from her as fast as he could.

One important prototype for *Mary* was Samuel Johnson's *Rasselas* (1759), a formative influence generally overlooked by scholars who read Wollstonecraft exclusively as a Jacobin writer and in the process confine her literary horizons solely to the period of the 1790s.[4] Wollstonecraft met Samuel Johnson in 1784, the year he died, and she demonstrably had his quasi-oriental tale on her mind during this period, for she engaged and reworked it in her fragment "The Cave of Fancy," begun and abandoned in 1787: "Ye who expect constancy where every thing is changing, and peace in the midst of tumult, attend to the voice of experience, and mark in time the footsteps of disappointment" (CF 1:191). Likewise beginning with an admonitory "Ye who listen with credulity to the whispers of fancy, and persue with eagerness the phantoms of hope," *Rasselas* features a group of male and female protagonists impelled by their desire for happiness to escape from the prison of their coddled community in the Happy Valley, and together to survey and discuss the modes of life best able to promote durable happiness – the life of philosophy, of pleasure, of retirement, of marriage, of celibacy, of religious devotion, etc. – only to terminate in "A Conclusion in which nothing is concluded," human desire being fundamentally incommensurate with the possibilities for satisfaction. Describing her novel as an "artless tale, without episodes," Wollstonecraft similarly takes her heroine from her sheltered life into the wide world without much attention to conventional plotting, along the way endowing her with grave Rasselasian reflections galore (e.g., "only an infinite being could fill the human soul, and that when other objects were followed as a means of happiness, the delusion led to misery, the consequence of disappointment" [M 1:16]. Yet in neither Johnson's tale nor Wollstonecraft's is this abstruse but conventional-sounding moral used as a club to beat down the desire for happiness and teach stoic resignation instead. Written within a Lockean tradition of liberal psychology which stresses how we are actuated by the desire for happiness, *Rasselas* licenses the restlessness of desire that sends its thoughtful protagonists roaming beyond the confines of what has been proscribed for them, even as it acknowledges that happiness is not available here below, and the gender neutrality of this account of human motivation appealed to Wollstonecraft. Eschewing the marriage plot, *Rasselas* represents women and men similarly impelled by the desire for happiness and as equally capable of reflection upon it. Mary taps into *Rasselas*, then, to support the philosophic voice of its narrator and heroine, and to authorize the dignity Wollstonecraft solicits for her thwarted *thinking* heroine.

In de-orientalizing *Rasselas*, and transforming it into a work with greater claims to realism, Wollstonecraft is attempting something highly experimental, and this shows in the unusualness of her subtitle: a *fiction*. "Novel," "romance," "tale," or "history" would be likelier generic terms than "fiction" to designate prose narrative of this length. But Wollstonecraft refuses them, because their conventions implicate women in desires she resists. But as we shall see, the promise of gender neutrality Wollstonecraft gets from *Rasselas* is not fully sustainable. Throughout this text, the heroine appears superior in part because the objects of her desires are not fully intelligible and namable, and not readily conformable to the plots that typically describe women and literally inscribe them into narrative. Disentangling the relation of gender and genre is thus one of the central objectives of *Mary, A Fiction*. No sooner does the "fiction" open than it launches into a stinging attack on Mary's novel-reading mother Eliza, an attack which foregrounds the problem of desire for women in particular. As Mary Poovey has put it in a critique that bears as much on *Wrongs of Woman, or Maria* as it does on *Mary*, Wollstonecraft sets out to challenge the delusoriness of "romantic expectations" that trivialize women and invite them to desire the wrong things, only herself to be seduced by versions of those expectations which her own writing reproduces.[5] *Mary, A Fiction* does indeed begin with an effort of dissociation that it cannot keep up indefinitely, but the "romantic expectations" the novel eventually indulges aren't exactly identical to those it initially assails, but have been somewhat recast and transformed.

Eliza is Wollstonecraft's typical romantic heroine familiar to any reader of the period's sentimental fiction: fatuous, insipid, and unthinking. Along with her unreflective acceptance of the ways of the world, Eliza's asthenia is marked out for particular abuse. What with her "sickly die-away languor," it is no wonder her earthy husband prefers the "ruddy glow" of his female tenants to his wife's pallor, "which even rouge could not enliven" (M 1:7). Like her mind, her voice is "but the shadow of a sound" and her body so delicate "that she became a mere nothing" (M 1:7). While Eliza may think of herself as sensitive and elevated, her sentiments have actually debased and denaturalized her desires – which we see in her inappropriate attachment to her lapdog, her indifference to maternal responsibilities, and above all in her fondness for novels such as *The Platonic Marriage* (1787) and *Eliza Warwick* (1777), which in idealizing romance, lead her peevishly to blame her admittedly coarse husband because he does "not love her, sit by her side, squeeze her hand, and look unutterable things" (M 1:9) the way heroes do in novels.

Mary, A Fiction, we are to understand by implication, will not be the kind of novel that caters to the thwarted sexual desires of female readers such as the heroine's mother, Eliza. At first glance, however, Wollstonecraft does not appear to make good on this claim. Like her mother, Mary too searches "for an object to love" (M 1:11) in a heartless world that affords her little affective sustenance; she too is forced to marry a man to whom she is indifferent, and she too has a yearning for an illicit love. And the "die-away languor" that is supposed to be contemptible when it characterizes the mother somehow appears "interesting" and attractive when it characterizes other characters whom Mary adores. And finally, like her mother, Mary attempts to satisfy frustrated desire through fantasy – "tales of woe" (M 1:11) in Mary's case, and through sentimental novels in Eliza's. And yet, despite these close similarities to her mother, Mary finds herself in the grip of desire which, far from being the wearisomely hackneyed stuff of popular fiction, is unable to speak its name at all. Mary first turns to Ann "to experience the pleasure of being beloved" (M 1:13). This is no ordinary friendship, we gather. In their relationship Mary is coded as masculine (agentive, sublime) while Ann is stereotypically feminine in the "die-away" delicacy she shares with Eliza. True, Mary is disappointed to discover that Ann does not reciprocate the fullness and intensity of her passion: Ann feels only "gratitude" in return. But this disappointment does not quell Mary's love. She still "loved Ann better than any one in the world" and dreams: "To have this friend constantly with her . . . would it not be superlative bliss?" (M 1:20).

The eighteenth century of course did have a term for women's passionate attachment to each other. The boy to whom Mary is yoked in marriage uses it when he refers to it as "romantic friendship" (M 1:25). This licit category grants passionate attachments between women some visibility, to be sure, but at the same time nervously divests them of significance. Young Charles's reliance upon it demonstrates his vulgarity. He tolerates Mary's "romantic friendship" because he cannot imagine that could possibly rival Mary's sentiments towards himself. For her own part, Mary does not describe her relation to Ann as a "romantic friendship," and part of the real interest of the novel derives from the fact that the prose seems to dissolve under the stress of having to describe this relation at all. The narrator frequently and explicitly denies that Mary's love for Ann is the sort of passion a woman might feel for a man. But denial often implies the presence of something to be denied, and sometimes the very gaps in Wollstonecraft's prose seem to open up and afford space to the unspeakable, and as such have an uncanny brilliance all their own. For example, when Ann's mother urges Mary to care for her daughter, Mary's father intrudes to carry her home to marry a boy-groom in order to solve a property dispute and to please her dying mother in one swoop. As Mary emerges from the state of shock in which this sudden news throws her,

> a thousand [thoughts] darted into her mind, – her dying mother, – her friend's miserable situation, – and an extreme horror at taking – at being forced to take, such a hasty step; but she did not feel the disgust, the reluctance, which arises from a prior attachment.
>
> She loved Ann better than any one in the world – to snatch her from the very jaws of destruction – she would have encountered a lion. (M 1:20)

Notice that in this relatively early effort of free indirect discourse, Mary does not register that her love for Ann, imperfect and not even fully reciprocated though it is, has something to do with her aversion to marriage: the dashes elide this connection as well as advertise it as something repressed, unrealized. Her love for Ann can not be understood as a "prior attachment" because only men are signified by that phrase. After Mary willy-nilly gets written into a marriage plot, pronouncing "the awful [marriage] vow without thinking of it" (M 1:20), Ann is not merely tolerated but actively sought as a companion by Mary's father precisely because she has no official status as a significant attachment.

As *Mary, A Fiction* continues, the impossibility of articulating Mary's attachment becomes more conspicuous. The friendship of Ann and Mary is repeatedly distinguished from the sexual – "I mentioned before," the narrator writes, "that Mary had never had any particular attachment, to give rise to the disgust [for her husband] that daily gained ground" (M 1:25). Mary herself concedes that her devotion to Ann needs to be accounted for, so she asks that her husband permit her to travel to Portugal with Ann on the grounds that she takes a "maternal" interest in her health (M 1:25). Yet as if, on the one hand, these disclaimers had never been made, and because, on the other, they have, the unaccountability slips out in unguarded moments. In one of the few truly dramatic passages in the novel, Mary, distraught about Ann's imminent death, rushes to her traveling companions for help:

> The ladies... began to administer some common-place comfort, as, that it was our duty to submit to the will of Heaven, and the like trite consolations, which Mary did not answer; but waving her hand, with an air of impatience, she exclaimed, "I cannot live without her! – I have no other friend; if I lose her, what a desart will the world be to me." "No other friend," re-echoed they, "have you not a husband?"
> Mary shrunk back, and was alternately pale and red. A delicate sense of propriety prevented her from replying; and recalled her bewildered reason.
>
> (M 1:32)

The precise cause of the embarrassment that makes Mary blanch and blush by turns is hard to fathom: is it the impropriety of her indifference to her husband, or is it the impropriety of her desperate attachment to her dying friend? The silly ladies dismayed by Mary's grief are linked to her silly husband through their allegiance to the "common-place" (the worst insult in Wollstonecraft's lexicon), for it was he who indulged in dismissive and "commonplace remarks on [Mary's] romantic friendship" (M 1:20) to begin with.

As Ann wanes into death, Henry waxes into Mary's affections, and this tale of forbidden and unnarratable passionate friendship becomes a tale of forbidden but narratable adulterous love. Yet Mary's desire for Henry also resists articulation in conventional terms. First of all, despite the fact that Henry's certifiably masculine and expansive mind expands Mary's smaller one, his manners and sensitivity are feminine, and (as is the case with Ann) have the effect of immasculating Mary by comparison,: his "voice" is "musical" and his expression "elegant" (M 1:28); his disposition "gentle, and easily to be intreated" (M 1:33). Styling himself a "die-away swain" (M 1:41), he has all the earmarks of the decaying sentimental heroine "disappointed" (M 1:41) in love that litter the pages of eighteenth-century novels – heroines such as Maria's own mother, Eliza (whose "die-away" languor the narrator scorns, however [M 1:7]), and, of course, Ann. Like Ann, he has given his heart to a lover "not worthy of my regard" (M 1:40), only to become so crushed that he is "dead to the world," now awaiting his "dissolution" (M 1:40). Like Ann again, he offers Mary "friendship" (M 1:41) which is something more than a friendship, lives with his mother, and becomes intimate with Mary through the license permitted by the sick-bed.

If Henry's gender-ambiguity complicates the nature of Mary's desire for him, so too do the terms in which he describes and she responds to it, which are hardly straightforward. Looking at Mary, Henry asks "in the most in-sinuating accents,"

> . . . if he might hope for her friendship? If she would rely on him as if he was her father; and that the tenderest father could not more anxiously interest himself in the fate of a darling child, than he did in her's. (M 1:41)

The narrator very subtly but unmistakably makes it clear that Henry is at-tempting to seduce Mary: "He had exerted himself to turn her thoughts into a new channel, and had succeeded" (M 1:41). He succeeds in part because for Mary "friendship" is an ecstatically if obscurely charged word. The nar-rator steps in to observe that Mary did not "know that love and friendship are very distinct" (M 1:42); indeed, for Mary, though evidently not for Henry it appears, love and friendship are not distinct at all. The desire Mary finds herself feeling for Henry is striking and powerful precisely because it blurs so many distinctions at once:

> she thought of him till she began to chide herself for defrauding the dead, and, determining to grieve for Ann, she dwelt on Henry's misfortunes and ill health . . . she thought with rapture that there was one person in the world who had an affection for her, and that person she admired – had a friendship for.
> He had called her his dear girl . . . My child! His child, what an association of ideas! If I had a father, such a father! – She could not dwell on the thoughts, the wishes which obtruded themselves. Her mind was unhinged, and passion unperceived filled her whole soul. (M 1:41–2)

What makes Wollstonecraft's prose throughout *Mary* so difficult is that her subjects seem so unbounded, so beyond the pale of the ordinary that they are buried in multiple references that are as haunting and nebulous to the character as they are to the reader. Who precisely is the "dead" person Mary fears she is defrauding, for instance? On one hand it is the beloved Ann, whom Mary guiltily feels she is betraying when she responds so powerfully to Henry's erotic allure. But just as Mary herself had earlier described her own interest in Ann as "maternal" (M 1:25), Henry (ingenuously or disingenuously) describes his sentiment for Mary as paternal – and as a result the "dead" person Mary fears she is defrauding also refers to Mary's own miserable father. And finally, of course, since Mary also expresses a rapturous relation to her heavenly "Father" (M 1:26) and "Almighty Friend" (M 1:27), God Himself gets mixed up in the nexus of overlapping and not fully distinguishable desires Mary experiences here. The point is not that Mary is confused, or that she is deceiving herself or being deceived. She comes to us as a rare woman with thinking powers after all, and this means that she is impelled by yearnings that are extraordinary, expansive, tinged with the sublime and therefore not fully speakable or intelligible. Indeed, as in other classics of sentimental fiction such as Laurence Sterne's *Sentimental Journey* (1768) and Henry Mackenzie's *Man of Feeling* (1771), here sensitive characters again and again forebear to speak, and it is assumed that the most authentic and deeply felt sentiments shrink from the publicity of speech or print, and are therefore to be sought in the dashes or asterisks or silences. Only common – and therefore unworthy – things can be said starkly, and only shallow worldings chatter.

After Ann's death, as she decides whether to return to the husband she loathes or take up with the man she loves, Mary contemplates being inscribed onto conventional, if illicit or tormented, plots: "One moment she was a heroine, half-determined to bear whatever fate should inflict; the next, her mind would recoil–and tenderness possessed her whole soul" (M 1:64). One minute, in other words, Mary is a character in a novel that has already been written, a "Clarissa, a Lady G– , or a Sophie," an exemplary woman whose body has been disciplined in the sentimental tradition, and the next she is a woman who possesses a "mind" with "thinking powers" and who dares to think for herself and choose uncommon, transgressive desire. But Mary resists the pull of all plots. Her ministrations to a poor, sick, and ungrateful woman follow the trajectory of the friendship narrative, and when we see Mary recoil from drunken prostitutes – "the manner of those who attacked the sailors, made her shrink into herself, and exclaim, are these my fellow creatures" (M 1:48) – she is thinking about the grossness of the primal scene toward which the romantic narrative with Henry leads her. Eventually, *Mary* seems to become a romantic novel rather than a successful experimental fiction, for Mary sinks into hyper-femininity at the end after all. One letter from Henry makes her a lovesick girl: just as Ann had been monomaniacal in the recollection of the man she loved – playing the "tunes her lover admired, and handl[ing] the pencil he taught her to hold" (M 1:18) – Mary too turns obsessive: "To beguile the tedious time, Henry's favorite tunes were sung; the books they read together turned over; and the short epistle read at least a hundred times" (M 1:62).

Thus by novel's end, the singular, uncommon Mary appears to become absorbed into utterly commonplace narrative about blasted romantic love as experienced by sensitive souls; she seems, in other words, to become divested of her thinking powers. But the very same conventions that seem to coopt her also save her. Sentimental heroines typically die for their love, but Wollstonecraft delivers this commonplace of sentimental narrative with a twist. After Henry's death, Mary honors his wish that she fulfill her "destined course" as Charles's wife. But her body revolts: Mary faints when her husband approaches, and whenever he mentions "anything like love, she would instantly feel a sickness, a faintness in her heart, and wish, involuntarily, that the earth would open and swallow her" (M 1:72). Mary is a wife at last, but ordinary domesticity is entirely forestalled. In becoming the heroine of a love story, Mary gets a "die-away" body, but her death becomes an exit from an intolerable narrative. *Mary, A Fiction*, its heroine, and its plot finally give way to the categories of gender and genre without really giving into them. For like the conclusion of *Rasselas*, which looks forward to eternity as the only venue for durable happiness, *Mary* concludes by looking forward to another, better world where a woman's desire is not trammeled by the compulsory love plot, a world "*where there is neither marrying*, nor giving in marriage" (M 1:73, emphasis Wollstonecraft's). In a gesture both visionary and proto-radical, the last words of Wollstonecraft's first novel yearn for the annihilation of the marriage plot, where that plot is understood both as a sort of conspiracy that seduces and traps women, and as a literary structure that can mis-describe and mis-shape their desires in the novels women read.

While the preface to *Mary, A Fiction* introduces Mary as a "mind" with "thinking powers" and who therefore requires a different kind of literary work, in the preface to *The Wrongs of Woman, or, Maria* Wollstonecraft seems to have no problem in referring to her text as a "novel," and she links it to the female body while refusing to consider this as a pathology or defect: this novel originates in the specificity of womanhood, and it is *not* an "abortion of distempered fancy" or the ravings of a "wounded heart" (WWM 1:83). We first encounter Maria as a female body – abused in its uniquely female sentiments (Maria is "tortured by maternal apprehension" for the child wrested from her), and hindered in its uniquely female physical functions (Maria's breasts are "bursting with the nutriment for which this cherished child might now be pining in vain" [WWM 85]). The change in genre – from experimental "fiction" to novel pure and simple – corresponds to a change of heart and mind about gender, and to understand this change we need to consider the intervening polemical writings. Predating Wollstonecraft's political coming-to-consciousness; *Mary* is a hermetic novel in part because it has no politics, no wish to or grounds for generalizing her extraordinary heroine's experience, no access to solutions in the public sphere that might apply to women as a whole. Given the aversion to debilitated sentimental femininity evinced in *Mary*, it is easy to see why the liberal feminism of *Rights of Woman* seemed promising and necessary. There, she would insist, virtue had no sex. But the subject of liberalism is always implicitly masculine, even when it touts its neutrality. For Wollstonecraft too at this stage, women should be encouraged to be manly – sturdy, rational, independent, and self-responsible. In the ideal republic, men and women would not be frivolous or purely private (as they are in *Mary*) but civic minded and purposive; they would be active citizens and busy parents. But however hopeful, the *Rights of Woman* was always fighting something of a lost cause, addressed not to reactionaries after all, but to political allies who, even before the Revolution degenerated into Terror, had already disappointed her by clinging to demeaning notions of sexual difference. When we consider the failure of the French Revolution as well as the crushing derelictions of her fellow radical and lover Gilbert Imlay, who abandoned her and their child, we can imagine in what frame of mind Wollstonecraft reconsidered the question of femaleness and its relation to virtue. If *Mary, A Fiction* treats the female body and its desires as the problem to be overcome, and if the *Rights of Woman* assumes that it can be subsumed under masculinity, *The Wrongs of Woman; or, Maria* begins to wonder whether the female body can be treated as a solution.

The plot of *Wrongs of Woman* retrospectively narrates Maria's struggles with a typical unreclaimed male, in the person of her monstrous yet also banal husband, George Venables, and also prospectively narrates Maria's fragile and incomplete disenchantment with republican masculinity, in the person of Darnford. In the process, the plot also adumbrates hopes specific to women and their fellowship. This fellowship is important. While Mary came to us as a passionately if tragically sociable creature, one who lives for love, she is paradoxically isolated as well, for uncommonness is the absolute condition of her genius. One of the central rhetorical gestures of that novel, therefore, is invidious distinction, or contrast: time after time the narrator intervenes with defensive asides, telling us how her novel is different from and better than common sentimental novels, how Mary is different from, and better than, the common sort. The structure of *The Wrongs of Woman*, on the other hand, is incorporative and inclusive. Not only does it everywhere absorb and transform texts by Dryden, Rowe, Rousseau, Shakespeare, Johnson, Burney, Godwin, to name only a few – indeed its opening gestures is an extended, one-upping allusion to Radcliffean gothic – but its characteristic gesture is comparison. Here, we have not a heroine who is different, but one who is (alas) like all the other women we meet, "caught in a trap, and caged for life" (WWM 1:138).

Bringing the conventions of gothic fiction to bear on present-day England, *The Wrongs of Woman* opens with disorienting power *in medias res*. Maria has been immured in a decaying mansion which is at once a prison and a madhouse. As a prison, this mansion literalizes the condition of women across the kingdom: "Was not the world a vast prison, and women born slaves?" (WWM 1:88). Maria herself avers, "Marriage had bastilled me for life...fettered by the partial laws of society, this fair globe was to me an universal blank" (WWM 1:146), and women have the same experience all the way the down the social ladder. At the first house where Maria seeks refuge from her husband, she discovers a haggard landlady who timorously avers, "when a woman was once married, she must bear every thing" (WWM 1:158), for her own drunken husband "would beat her if she chanced to offend him, though she had a child at the breast" (WWM 1:158). Maria's second landlady bores and irks Maria with a story that follows the same outline, also foreshadowing Maria's later experience before the court of law: having had no choice but to suffer the depredations of a husband who, under the protection of the law, pawns her clothes for whores and drink, she observes, "women always have the worst of it, when law is to decide" (WWM 1:165). Although these tales expose myths about domesticity, the case of Jemima is even worse. Having been raped and debauched of character and reputation since childhood, she is excluded from domestic service, and can only subsist through prostitution.

These episodes of *The Wrongs of Woman, or, Maria*, which construct a web of carceral imagery, flesh out the intention Wollstonecraft formulated in the letter Godwin made into the Preface of the novel: "to show the wrongs of different classes of women, equally oppressive, though, from the difference of education, necessarily various" (WWM 1:84). But Maria's prison is also an insane asylum, and as such calls our attention to the complex issue of madness and delusion in the novel. Maria, after all, is a prisoner to her marriage but is also in a larger sense a prisoner to the delusoriness of love that chained her to Venables in marriage to begin with, a love that enchains her to

---

Darnford as well. This enthralling delusion is conveyed through the pervasive allusions to *Hamlet*. Like Hamlet, Maria meditates upon the rottenness of the kingdom as she looks out her window upon a "desolate garden" gone to seed, at "a huge pile of buildings" fallen "to decay" and "left in heaps in the disordered court" (WWM 1:86). Recasting Hamlet's famously misogynist "Frailty, thy name is woman," Maria soliloquizes, "Woman, fragile flower! why were you suffered to adorn a world exposed to the inroad of such stormy elements?" (WWM 1:95), and the fragility she refers to is not women's susceptibility to carnal appetite, but their lack of the material, legal, and personal resources necessary to withstand brutality: the Ophelia she contemplates is a fellow inmate–"a lovely maniac," yet another womanly "warbler" singing in her cage – driven out of her mind by the brutish and "rich old man" to whom she was forcibly married "against her inclination" (WWM 1:95). And finally, like Hamlet Maria seems doomed to painful lucidity that makes her look like the crazy one in the corrupted and corrupting world she lives in. To the stern judge presiding not only over Maria's case at the end of the novel – someone who represents and enforces the rules of established power, as distinct from genuine social justice – a woman's refusal of her husband's conjugal rights on the grounds that her erotic feelings are equally legitimate smacks of insurrectionary "French principles," of "new-fangled notions" inimical to the "good old rules of conduct," and at the same time that refusal marks her as someone who is *not* "of sane mind" (WWM 1:181) and therefore not entitled to the autonomy she claims as her right.

The "narrative" (WWM 1:145) which Maria writes for her daughter's edification is calculated to prove just the opposite: to show that Maria was insane when she fell *in* love with her husband, not when she fell *out* of love with him. Maria describes her initial attraction to George Venables as a projection onto him of the virile qualities she herself possesses in greater abundance. He effectively "buys" Maria, when he contributes a guinea (the currency not coincidentally minted with the gold mined from Africa and linked to the slave trade) to Maria's charitable projects on behalf of an old woman, she believes him the soul of excellence: "I fancied myself in love–in love with the disinterestedness, fortitude, generosity, dignity, and humanity, with which I had invested the hero I dubbed" (WWM 1:127). Wollstonecraft's hostile reader at *The Anti-Jacobin Review and Magazine* maintained that since Maria had erroneously "fancied him a miracle of goodness" in the first place, she should be reproaching her own silliness rather than carrying on about the "wrongs of woman."[6] And there is troubling evidence that Wollstonecraft's own friends, like the stern judge, did not "get" the political point of Maria's delusions. In a letter of 1797 to George Dyson, Wollstonecraft acknowledges the rawness of her sketch, but expresses dismay at Dyson's opinion that Maria's domestic unhappiness is not moving, and Wollstonecraft attributes this insensitivity to the fact that he is a male:

> "I have been reading your remarks and I find them a little discouraging.... I was perfectly aware that some of the incidents ought to be transpossed [sic] and heightened by more harmonious shading; and I wished to avail myself of yours and Mr G's criticism before I began to adjust my events into a story ... yet I am vexed and surprised at your not thinking the situation of Maria sufficiently important, and can only account for this want of – shall I say it? delicacy of feeling by recollecting that you are a man" (Letters: 391–2).

It is unfortunate but quite telling, given his tendency to cast his wife as a woman of feeling, that Godwin, who used much of the rest of this letter as a Preface to his edition of *The Wrongs of Woman, or, Maria*, published after Wollstonecraft's death, actually omitted the contextualizing section quoted here. Wollstonecraft apologizes for Maria's "sensibility" not because she is committed to fine feeling, but because even a well-disposed male reader failed "to be disgusted with him [Venables]!!!" and thus failed to understand why Maria gets upset. Such failure undermines the premise of the entire novel, that women as a class of persons are systematically "wronged." Wollstonecraft's entire point in protesting Maria's situation as a political rather than merely personal wrong is that her delusion is hardly self-induced. In sentimental culture, no one considers it suspect to find the "beauty of a young girl ... much more interesting than the distress of an old one" (WWM 1:130). Maria, of course, eventually sees that she was deluded to consider "that heart as devoted to virtue, which had only obeyed a virtuous impulse" (WWM 1:131) inspired by her erotic presence: he behaved well only because he wanted to get the girl.

Maria's critique of what the world regards sane or insane about love continues as she defends the reasonableness of her revulsion from her husband. Refuting popular moralizers such as Dr. Gregory, author of the popular conduct book *A Father's Legacy to His Daughter* (1774), as well as heterodox and controversial figures like Rousseau, she rejects the maxim that women should cultivate a "coldness of constitution," and yield to the "ardour" of their husbands only occasionally and out of duty: both would concur with the judge at Maria's trial: "What virtuous woman thought of her feelings? – It was her duty to love and obey the man chosen by her parents and relations" (WWM 1:131). Countering the position that sensible women anaesthetize their feelings, Wollstonecraft asserts women's legitimacy as affective and erotic subjects. Mary's revulsion from her husband in *Mary* emanates from a disgust so visceral as to appear pathological; but in *Wrongs* Maria's revulsion seems an altogether rational, enlightened response to a man whose libertine habits she had been too benighted to recognize at first, and whose "tainted breath, pimpled face, and blood-shot eyes" (WWM 1:145) now appear as they in fact are: disgusting.

In a complex structural decision on Wollstonecraft's part, the memoirs Maria writes for her daughter are withheld from the reader until chapters seven through ten, when Darnford reads them. By encountering the memoirs so late, by reading them just as the Darnford–Maria relationship develops, we are placed in a position to recognize how Maria's love for him recapitulates the error she made with Venables, although here it is not the "happy credulity of youth" (WWM 1:131) that carries her forward but the urgency of sexual desire itself. In *Rights of Woman*, "voluptuousness" is a pejorative, particularly when denoting the culpable sensuality of male vice. But in *Wrongs of Woman* Wollstonecraft accepts Maria's "voluptuousness" and claims that "it inspired the idea of strength of mind, rather than of body" (WWM 1:104), as if the manifestly (female) sexed substantiality of Maria's body could heighten rather than detract from her dignity. Here, when the "air swept across her face with a voluptuous freshness that thrilled to her heart" (WWM 1:95) after Maria has been reading Rousseau's sentimental novel, *La Nouvelle Héloïse*, in her cell, we side with the body and the instincts that seek to expand beyond the constraints that fetter them. And these instincts are decidedly heteroerotic. Mary finds a man as etiolated as Ann, but Maria fantasizes masculine virtues embodied in an almost hypervirile man. Darnford's doughty insistence – "I *will* have an answer" (WWM 1:98) – contrasts to Henry's intense reserve, just as the force potency of his presence – "His steady step, and the whole air of his person, bursting as it were from a cloud" (WWM 1:96)" – contrasts with Henry's retiring, die-away languor.

There is considerable disagreement among scholars and critics about the degree to which Wollstonecraft is consciously critiquing the Maria/Darnford relationship, some contending that the novel itself is unwittingly seduced by romance yet again, and others maintaining that it opens out a new space for critical distance.[7] To a large extent, one's interpretation depends on the kind and degree of narrative control one is willing to extend to Wollstonecraft as a novelist. To me, Wollstonecraft's irony seems clear. When the narrator asks, "what chance had Maria of *escaping*" (WWM 1:104, emphasis added), we are being told that this love is yet another form of incarceration from which *escape* is as necessary as it is unlikely. What deludes Maria this time into casting her lover as "a statue in which she might enshrine" all "the qualities of a hero's mind" (WWM 1:105)? The menace turns out to be republican ideology itself, something that was supposed to lead the entire world out of its prison of darkness. Maria reads Darnford's composition about "the present state of society and government, with a comparative view of the politics of Europe in America" (WWM 1:93), and she is convinced that because his politics are progressive, his love will be different. Yet, while a man like Venables practices active deceit, Darnford's narrative really says it all: it is a self-mystifying tale of intrepid, republican manhood, part self-pity ("I never knew the sweets of domestic affection" [WWM 1:100]) and part braggadocio ("with my usual impetuosity, [I] sold my commission, and travelled..." [WWM 1:101]). But the fact that Maria shares his political views makes her fatally deaf to Darnford's ludicrously obnoxious account of himself. Maria was ignorant of Venable's "habits of libertinism" (WWM 1:127), but Darnford makes it a point to brag about them: "And woman, lovely woman!" he boasts, " – they charm every where" (WWM 1:101). Worse, he brandishes his fancy for prostitutes: "the women of the town (again I must beg pardon for my habitual frankness) appeared to me like angels" [WWM 1:102]. But republican discourse having clothed what might formerly be damned as "libertine" grossness in the new garb fashioned of frankness, Maria sees his selfishness as admirable inservility, sees his impulsiveness as manly resoluteness and sees his gallantry as liberality, and as a result the ardent Maria is completely taken in, her judgment clouded. Obviously a rendering of Wollstonecraft's experience with Imlay, the Darnford/Maria episodes finally judge male culture to be so corrupt as to make reciprocity between the sexes impossible. Indeed, even before the concluding hints inform us that Darnford deserts Maria, the narrator unequivocally damns him: "A fondness of the sex often gives an appearance of humanity to the behaviour of men, who have small pretensions to the reality; and they seem to love others, when they are only pursuing their own gratification" (WWM 1:176).

The most disturbing proof that Maria's love for Darnford is a form of derangement is her apathy upon learning that she is free to leave her prison: "[L]iberty has lost its sweets." Maria imagines that in Darnford "she had found a being of celestial mould" (WWM 1:173) and feels too happy with her madhouse to leave. Significantly, it is Jemima rather than a lover who takes Maria out of her bedlam, and brings her back from death in the final provisional fragment. Maria's attachment to Jemima is new in the history of the novel, and in representing a turn towards solidarity and affective community even with the most despised and unlovely of women, it suggests an alternative to the disastrousness of heterosocial relations.[8] Here again Wollstonecraft's manipulation of pacing and sequence is brilliant, repaying close attention. Just when we think we are going to get an idealized, even corny, love scene between Maria and Darnford, Jemima barges in, clearly unwanted, interrupting the panting lovers, and she commences a very long and brutal story that could chill anybody's ardor. The conclusion of Jemima's narrative binds her to Maria and pointedly leaves Darnford out. When Jemima accounts for her hard-heartedness by retorting, "Who ever risked any thing for me? – Who ever acknowledged me to be a fellow creature?" (WWM 1:119), Maria answers by taking her hand, and on the basis of this connection, Jemima proves the deliverer Maria insanely hoped Darnford would be.

This novel uses the common narrative device of inset tales which correct and broaden the heroine's and the reader's vision and which reflect on each other in illuminating ways. In narrating his tale, Darnford, for example, blunders when bragging/confessing, "I was taught to love by a creature I am ashamed to mention; and the other women with whom I afterwards became intimate, were of a class of which you can have no knowledge" (WWM 1:100–1). Had Darnford paid attention to Maria's memoirs, which we know he has read, he would have learned as we have that he is quite wrong on this score, of course: Maria does know this "class" of "creature" – first as the "wantons of the lowest class" whose "vulgar, indecent mirth" roused the "sluggish spirits" (WWM 1:139) of her husband. Moreover, undercutting Darnford (who adores "women of the town" [WWM 1:102]) as well as Venables, Jemima's story gives us a truer view about being, precisely, such a "creature." Challenging tales about prostitutes as Maria, Venables, and Darnford have told them, Jemima's experience exposes the truths concealed by ideologically loaded assumptions about and practices of female propriety and respectability,[9] showing that prostitutes neither enjoy their work, nor pine for their heartless seducers, but are, like wives, an exploited class, despising the men on whom they are dependent. Similarly, when Maria herself heaps scorn upon "the savage female," the "hag" (WWM 1:121) who takes over when Jemima temporarily leaves the asylum, we can see – even if Maria yet cannot – that this woman may simply be another Jemima, who has not yet been reached by human affection, and that Maria's harsh epithets withhold them from emancipatory fellowship.[10]

As mothers and as daughters, Maria and Jemima share a blighted story, and their bond is based in a kindred warmth which they associate with motherhood. Representing romantic love as warped beyond the possibility of correction, *Wrongs of Woman* locates the "humanizing affections" in maternal nurturance instead.[11] Permeated with images of nursing, the novel feminizes the imagery of natural blossoming Tom Paine used to characterize revolution as a natural and life-affirming process, the giving way of the wintery and withering old regime to the warmth and vitality of the new. In Wollstonecraft's novel, this sort of revolution is in turn linked to the redemptive emergence of the mother – daughter relation: "The spring was melting into summer, and you, my little companion, began to smile – that smile made hope bud out afresh, assuring me the world was not a desert" (WWM 1:167). But it is not subjected and generic men, then, but hounded women with infant daughters at their nursing breasts who are the "tender blossoms" which ought to burst from their cells into the fullness of life. The radical Darnford is accessible to authentic moral feeling only to the extent that he mimics the maternal, as when "he respectfully pressed [Maria] to his bosom" (WWM 1:172). Conversely, "'the killing frost'" (WWM 1:167, another allusion to Shakespeare) is not repressiveness with which privileged men of the old regime repress other men in general, but the very particular brutality with which patriarchal culture in post-revolutionary England severs women from each other: the frost that blasts Maria's daughter, kidnapped from her mother by a father determined to get his hands on the property to which she is heir, has also already injured Maria (whose mother favored sons) as well as Jemima, whose "humanity had rather been benumbed than killed, by the keen frost she had to brave at her entrance into life" (WWM 1:120), in turn cutting her off from fellow feeling by making her unwilling in turn to "succour an unfortunate" like Maria (WWM 1:88).

Jemima and Maria repair their injuries in their relations to one another and in their joint relation to Maria's daughter. Maria first dreams about Darnford partly because she wants her daughter to have "a father whom her mother could respect and love" (WWM 1:97). But as this fantasy of domesticity vanishes, Maria turns to Jemima not to take the father's place but rather to double in the mother's: "I will teach her to consider you as a second mother" (WWM 1:120). Allured by this promise, Jemima persuades Maria to leave the madhouse/prison with her because of the primary affective duty they owe each other. "[O]n you it depends to reconcile me to the human race" (WWM 1:174), she admonishes, as if the offer of co-mothering were a marriage vow binding even when they believe "their" daughter is dead. The household they set up is, as Gary Kelly has so aptly put it, "prefigurative" of a feminist solidarity it would take later generations to realize fully.[12] It does not conceal the difficulty of class difference or entirely reinscribe gender as class: although Maria promises Jemima a position equal to her own – she is to be a "second mother" rather than a nurse or mammy – Jemima insists on the wages that insure her independence even as she would appear to collaborate as a co-mother. In the last fragment, when Maria is in agony, Jemima reappears with the lost daughter, whom she has tutored to say the magic word, "mamma!" (WWM 1:203). The word gives Maria something to live for beyond the romantic plot which has been inscribed for her. That child is treasured not because she is the progeny of a fickle but still-beloved male like Darnford, but, on the contrary, despite its relationship to the loathsome Venables. The daughter's word "mamma" gives Jemima, her "second mother," something to live for too, an arena for kindred affection not determined by biological kinship.

This is not a story which *The Wrongs of Woman* fully tells. The novel is in fragments. The dissolution of Maria's relation with Darnford is hardly depicted at all, and her eventual independence does not appear to be voluntary. Clearly, Maria's despondency is hardly overcome. Still, as Janet Todd has aptly put it, Maria's history is thus marked by two movements, "one circular and repetitive, and the other linear and developmental. The circular binds her to male relationships . . . the linear tends towards freedom and maturity."[13] To the extent that freedom is achieved at all in this fractured and unfinished work, it is in the cooperative and mutually respecting partnership Jemima and Maria seem to verge on achieving.

Wollstonecraft's novels may not be masterpieces in the old-fashioned, traditional sense. They are brave attempts, not polished performances. But as such they evince qualities that typify Wollstonecraft's best work. They are startlingly innovative in their methods and their subjects, sometimes clumsy and sometimes breathtakingly brilliant, and in close dialogue with the forms of fiction they are attempting to supersede. Both novels are written either about or for those "who will dare to advance before the improvement of the age" (WWM 1:83), to exceptional minds in other words, who are not confined by ideology, but who can peer just above or ahead of it, and who because they are relatively unblinkered, will pass over the novels' imperfection and comprehend both their despair of the present and their hope in the future.

NOTES

1. Wollstonecraft's first publication was actually *Thoughts on the Education of Daughters* (1787), educational tracts being, like novels, good sellers. This relatively modest and conventional work does not attempt the boldness to which Wollstonecraft aspires in *Mary, A Fiction*.

2. *Memoirs of the Author of "The Rights of Woman,"* ed Richard Holmes (Harmondsworth: Penguin Books, 1986), 223–4. This edition appears with Wollstonecraft's *A Short Residence*. Godwin goes on: "The story is nothing. He that looks into the book only for incident, will probably lay it down with disgust. But the feelings are of the truest and most exquisite class; every circumstance is adorned with that species of imagination, which enlists itself under the banners of delicacy and sentiment." (*Memoirs*, 223–4). Godwin here recalls Johnson's remarks on *Clarissa*.

3. This is the very approximate translation Wollstonecraft herself offers in Chapter 13 of *Mary*.

4. For a corrective discussion, see James Basker "Radical Affinities: Mary Wollstonecraft and Samuel Johnson," *Tradition in Transition: Women Writers, Marginal Texts, and the Eighteenth-Century Canon*, eds. Alvaro Ribeiro and James G. Basker (Oxford: Clarendon Press, 1996), 51–5.

5. Mary Poovey, *The Proper Lady and the Woman Writer: Ideology as Style in the Works of Mary Wollstonecraft, Mary Shelley, and Jane Austen* (Chicago: University of Chicago Press, 1984), 98.

6. See *Anti-Jacobin Review and Magazine* (1798), 92–93, 92.

7. For an impressive reading of *The Wrongs of Woman* as recapitulating romantic error, see Poovey, *The Proper Lady and the Woman Writer*. Gary Kelly takes the a more emancipatory view in *Revolutionary Feminism: the Mind and Career of Mary Wollstonecraft* (New York: St. Martin's Press, 1992).

8. See Anne K. Mellor, "Righting the Wrongs of Woman: Mary Wollstonecraft's *Maria*," *Nineteenth-Century Contexts* 19 (1996), 413–24.

9. Jemima's story also corrects Wollstonecraft's own highly sentimentalized representation of "ruined" women in *Rights of Woman*, where she imagines them worthy of respect only insofar as they carry a torch for their first seducer.

10. Employing a deconstructive rather than historicist approach, Tilottama Rajan similarly argues that the inset tales together with the rest of the novel constitute an assemblage of texts calling for readings which invite and make possible large and accommodating perspectives. See *The Supplement of Reading: Figures of Understanding in Romantic Theory and Practice* (Ithaca: Cornell University Press, 1990).

11. In path-breaking essays, Cora Kaplan maintained that Jemima is a working-class heroine compromised by the middle-class romantic sentimentality of Maria and Wollstonecraft alike. See "Pandora's Box: Subjectivity, Class and Sexuality in Socialist-Feminist Criticism," *Making a Difference: Feminist Literary Criticism*, eds. Gayle Greene and Coppelia Kahn (London and New York: Methuen, 1985), 146–76. I am most indebted to this essay, as to Kaplan's other discussion of Wollstonecraft in "Wild nights: pleasure/sexuality/feminism," *The Ideology of Conduct: Essays in Literature and the History of Sexuality*, eds. Nancy Armstrong and Leonard Tennenhouse (London: Methuen, 1987), 160–84. For a discussion of masculine appropriations of maternity of the sort I see Wollstonecraft trying to resist in *Wrongs of Woman*, see Ruth Perry's fine "Colonizing the Breast: Sexuality and Maternity in Eighteenth-Century England," *Journal of the History of Sexuality*, 2 (1991), 204–34.

12. Gary Kelly, *English Fiction of the Romantic Period* (London; New York: Longman, 1989) 4.

13. Todd, *Women's Friendship in Literature* (New York: Columbia University Press, 1980), 211–12.

12

MARY A. FAVRET

Letters Written During a Short Residence in Sweden, Norway and Denmark: traveling with Mary Wollstonecraft

> I perceive, but too forcibly, that happiness, literally speaking, dwells not here.
> And that we wander to and fro in a vale of darkness as well as tears.
>
> (VRM 5:76)

From the title of the last book published before her death, *Letters Written During a Short Residence in Sweden, Norway and Denmark* (1796), we can guess that for Mary Wollstonecraft the word "residence" reflects little stability or rest. A short residence in three countries? Over the course of one summer? Upheaval writes itself into the title, and becomes the motor of this peculiar but lovely book. Here Wollstonecraft takes the restlessness and dislocation that marked her own life, as well as the society she observed in northern Europe, and tries to shape them into a style, an argument, and a political stance. "The art of travelling," she remarks elsewhere, "is only a branch of the art of thinking."[1] In the *Short Residence* the thinking subject herself cannot be distinguished from constant movement. Her travelogue thus tells us more about the mind of the traveler-subject, charting her path through a "heterogeneous modernity," than about the three countries she visits.[2] During her *Short Residence*, the narrator adopts several modes of travel but never settles: her account of boat trips, carriage rides, ferry passages, walks, and, most significantly, flights of fancy, purposefully has no end. As the *Short Residence* unfolds, however, the mobility of the subject, which had initially presented itself as both liberating and creative, modulates into something compromised, inescapable. In her *Vindication of the Rights of Men* (1790), Wollstonecraft first signaled this thought: "I perceive, but too forcibly, that happiness, literally speaking, dwells not here. And that we wander to and fro in a vale of darkness as well as tears" (VRM 5:76). As if confirming this passage six years later, the final letter of the travelogue understands travel as the misery of wandering – and thinking:

> Adieu! My spirit of observation seems to be fled – and I have been wandering around this dirty place, literally speaking, to kill time; though the thoughts, I

would fain fly from, lie too close to my heart to be easily shook off, or even beguiled, by any employment, except that of preparing my journey to London.

(SR 6:345)

Certain things fly away, others refuse to budge, and the one thing her traveling cannot free her from is the need to keep moving. Her desire to escape ("I would fain fly"), a recurring motif, is finally mocked by the more pedestrian employment of packing. In the course of these twenty-five letters of erratic length, while sorting through modes of physical as well as mental travel, Wollstonecraft tests – and loses – her faith in the freedom of movement.

Revising travel

From her earliest writings, Wollstonecraft exhibits a sense of herself as a person on the move. "I have had a number of drawbacks," she writes to her sister in 1789, "but still I cry avaunt despair – and *I push forward*." (28 February 1789; her italics). As she continues to write, she promotes forward motion as the basis for intellectual achievement:

> A present impulse pushes us forward, and when we discover that the game did not deserve the chace [sic] we find that we are gone over much ground, and not only gained many new ideas, but a habit of thinking. The exercise of our faculties is the great end, though not the goal we had in view when we started with such eagerness.　(VRM 5:29)

The analogy of physical movement to mental exercise, or even physical exercise to the movement of thought (in *A Vindication of the Rights of Woman*, she fuses these into "the locomotive faculty of body and mind") reappears later as a central structuring device for her *Short Residence*, body and mind legitimating each other by covering ground (VRW 5:141). "Exercise" will remain a valued word for Wollstonecraft throughout her career, connoting as it does deliberate and vigorous activity as opposed to "indolence," which she only mentions with contempt. But even as it asserts itself against the immobility of "indolence" or "idleness," "exercise" shakes off the possibility of another sort of motion – what Wollstonecraft calls elsewhere "waywardness" or "aimlessness" or, as we have seen, "wandering to and fro." The *Short Residence* exposes most dramatically the confrontation between Wollstonecraft's desire to view movement as progressive, purposeful exertion (even when the purpose seems lost, or vain) and the threat that movement may have no clear end. Thus, even as her travels cast themselves against the dangers of inertia, they call up the specter of pointless locomotion.

For Wollstonecraft, an individual moves (or not) with philosophical, political, and moral freight. Like other ambitious writers of the middle class, she subscribed to a theory of class mobility that rewarded hard work and determination. It was common for radicals of the middle class to picture the aristocracy as especially languid, lethargic figures, ensconced on their sofas and sated with pleasure. Comprehending both political hierarchy and social convention, the status quo was static for reformers like Wollstonecraft. Members of the lower classes too, if not hailed for their relentless labor, could be labeled, as Wollstonecraft demonstrates in *Short Residence*, "clods" who were going nowhere. In contrast, these writers identified themselves with a middle-class ethos of movement, distilled in such favorite terms as enlargement, expansion, advancement, progress, or, in less aggressive moments, dilation and diffusion. Though often applied to intellectual and moral terrain, these words all connote some movement through space. They were understood as the end products of two other privileged terms in the 1790s reformer's lexicon: exertion and industry, without which individuals as well as society would remain inert. The desire to move forward and outward was thus inextricably linked, for writers in Wollstonecraft's milieu, with work and economic status as well as political reform. Motion as metaphor brought with it high stakes, as can be glimpsed in this quotation from the reformer Jeremy Bentham:

> Indigence is the centre to which inertia alone, that force which acts without relaxation, makes the lot of every mortal gravitate. Not to be drawn into the abyss, it is necessary to mount up by continual effort, and we see by our side the most diligent and the most virtuous slipping by one false step, and sometimes thrown headlong by inevitable reverses.[3]

Bentham imagines life as a perilous mountain-climbing expedition, where, unless the climbers move continuously and unerringly, they will fall into the abyss of poverty, a form of inertia at the other end of the spectrum from the static rich. Constant exertion is the only solution to the nearly physical force of economic inertia, "which acts without relaxation." For Wollstonecraft, composing her travel letters, danger presents itself less as poverty than as having no place to go, no end to her exertions.[4] Thus, while the *Short Residence* charts a progressive path, endorsing the liberty that attends energetic movement, it also charts a counter-path through the dark side of mobility.[5]

For a clearer picture of the forces involved in the issue of mobility, we might recall that Mary Wollstonecraft spent her life moving. Born in Spitalfields, on the edge of London, her family relocated when she was two to the countryside, and shuttled between it and the city. At six, she moved with her family to a farm at Barking, where her father planned to shed his urban roots and settle down as a gentleman farmer. When this venture failed, the

Wollstonecrafts moved again, this time to Yorkshire, in the north; further difficulties prompted further uprooting: back to London, then to Laugharne, in Wales, then back to London. At the age of eighteen, Mary Wollstonecraft had lived in seven different residences. As one biographer explains, "Her father's remedy for failure was to move on"; movement as necessity – or solution – became a fixture of the writer's life.[6]

So began a series of journeys for the young woman, most of them dictated by the need for money and the desire to escape a difficult home life. Traveling as a paid lady's companion, she visited England's fashionable resorts; then came a brief stop in Newington Green, to establish a school for girls; when the school failed, she jumped to Ireland, where she lived for a year as a governess; in 1787 she arrived in London to forward her career as a writer. She also traveled for love: to Portugal in 1785 to comfort her dying friend, Fanny Blood. Later, having made a name for herself as a radical writer with *The Vindication of the Rights of Men* (1790) and *A Vindication of the Rights of Woman* (1792), Wollstonecraft uprooted herself again, this time to Paris in 1792, to witness and write about the enormous upheaval of the French Revolution. Her residence in Paris lasted six months; from there she moved to the suburb of Neuilly, for safety, and several months later, pregnant with her first child, on to Le Havre, where Fanny was born. From Le Havre she traveled back to London to join up with Fanny's father, the American Gilbert Imlay, who had, Wollstonecraft learned with pain, himself moved on to another woman. In London in 1795, Wollstonecraft planned one final trip: a suicide attempt. But Imlay intervened and, once her health appeared restored, sent his ex-lover off to yet another residence – in Scandinavia. This was a voyage of escape, money and love: Imlay wanted Wollstonecraft to serve as his agent in pleading for reparation for a lost ship in which he had invested; he, and perhaps Wollstonecraft herself, also hoped the trip would pull her from the fatal depression into which his infidelity had cast her.[7] In any case, travel, rather than a long rest at home (but where was home?), seemed the solution to several problems. From this voyage came Wollstonecraft's most moving piece of writing, *Letters Written During a Short Residence in Sweden, Norway and Denmark* (1796), her meditation on the value of movement.

We find in Wollstonecraft's biography of "short residences" a condensed history of an age in upheaval, registered by bodies continuously displaced. Though the late eighteenth century is recognized as the dawn of modern travel, it must also be remembered as a time of massive social and demographic dislocation. The desperate removals of a family on the run from debtors, or a young person finding and losing employment, or, in fact, an abandoned woman and her illegitimate child, rarely earn the label "travel."

These are movements dictated by economics, deprivation, shame, and grief; we typically consider them as profoundly constrained and over-determined trajectories, rather than the freely chosen and pleasurable excursions enjoyed, as Wollstonecraft writes, by "those favourites of fortune who travel for pleasure."[8] But if we keep in mind James Clifford's proposal that the term "travel" might encompass a wide range of individual and mass itineraries, *and* that these itineraries, perhaps more than notions of settlement or dwelling, underwrite the experience of modern culture, we can add another wrinkle to Wollstonecraft's investigation into movement and the thinking subject: not simply whether or not movement is carried out with determination, but who or what makes that determination, gives movement its end.

There were at least two ways of categorizing movement at the end of the eighteenth century in Great Britain, the Continent, and their imperial domains, and both feed into Wollstonecraft's relationship to travel. One might be called constrained movement, determined jointly by economics and politics. It included the mass emigration of rural people to the metropolis in response to the Enclosure Acts; the mobilization of men for warfare across the globe; the political exile of aristocrats and clerics, as well as rebels and republicans; the forced transport of slaves; and the deportation of British men and women to distant colonies. The other logic might be called open or free movement, imagined in terms of its goals rather than its determinants: social progress, or what Wollstonecraft sometimes liked to call "civilization" was one version; individual education, cultural or technological refinement were others. Travel, of course, was the privilege of fortune's favorites, and epitomized the freedom of movement that was thought to characterize both advanced societies and high rank. Travel was supposed to be undertaken and written about by individuals, not the wayward masses. Yet Wollstonecraft typically yokes these two sorts of movement in a way that demonstrates her own ambivalent status. Her emphasis on exercise and determination in her travels (travel writing is useful, she tells us, "if the traveler always has a particular pursuit in his head") quietly hints at the *travail*, the work or suffering that lies beneath the word travel, even as it constructs an image of self-possession or independence.[9]

To translate the first logic of movement into the second, to give openness and value to forced dislocation, is the work of an enormous amount of literature at the turn of the eighteenth century. In first-person slave narratives, in gothic novels with their abducted heroines, in poetic encounters with vagrants, soldiers, beggars, and forsaken women, or in the haunting figures of Ancient Mariners, Wandering Jews, and Vampires, we find testament to the broader cultural need to give meaningful form to types of rootlessness that do not meet the elevated status of leisurely "travel." In these works, as in *Short Residence* a deep ambivalence develops around the middle-class, progressive valuation of movement. Wollstonecraft's travel writing, even as it tests ways to translate constraint into freedom, translates in the opposite direction as well, demonstrating in a variety of ways the dangers of imagining we are moving by ourselves, freely.

In the *Short Residence* the letter writer appears to us as someone seeking to move from oppression to freedom: the opening two pages describe her "confinement" aboard a ship and her longing to be liberated. When no rescue boat, no "liberator" appears on the horizon, the narrator casts off her passive role and takes charge, convincing the captain of her boat to send her ashore (SR 6:243–4). Throughout the book the narrator will experiment with different means of exerting herself physically and mentally to escape an oppressive stasis. She will rewrite her prescribed itinerary – a business trip – into an account of her own freely determined movements, her travels. If at times reluctant captains, tedious convention or bad weather slows her down, she will find other means to continue her movement. At first, flights of fancy seem to offer the best escape from a too-restrictive world; but with each successive fanciful excursion, the narrator finds herself edging closer and closer to aimlessness and to losing her self-determination altogether. Freedom of movement, these flights seem to suggest, may not be the solution the letter writer seeks.

Flights of Fancy

From the opening pages of *Short Residence* we are engaged with an energetic narrator, a singular woman who cannot stand confinement, yearns to be walking "abroad," advertises her intrepid climbs over rocks and hills, and, to highlight the value of her exertions, contrasts them with the "idleness" of the local Swedes. Whether despotism "cramps the industry" of the population around her, or whether living "so near the brute creation" keeps them "rooted in the clods they so indolently cultivate," it is clear that the traveler's restless rootlessness signals her superiority over all she surveys (SR 6:243, 245). When she moves, she moves by herself. "Men with common minds seldom break through general rules," she blithely asserts at the outset. "Prudence is ever the resort of weakness; and they rarely go as far as they may in any undertaking who are determined not to go beyond it on any account" (SR 6:244). The narrator will "go far" by "going beyond"; her accomplishments will be offered as feats of physical as well as intellectual strength, but they will also be measured by the ceaselessness of her movement. As she adopts more and more rarified forms of movement, however, the narrator twists her writing into a critique of her own belief in the freedom offered by "going beyond." We begin to understand the traveler's flights less as examples of freedom and more as efforts to escape, and therefore testaments to the constraints under which she operates.

The climax of the first letter calls attention to the essential mobility of the traveler. The narrator retires to bed, though "I would gladly have rambled about much longer" outside. While all around her "nature [is] at rest," her imagination refuses to settle. This agitation opens into the first of the book's remarkable reveries:

> – What, I exclaimed, is this active principle which keeps me still awake? – Why fly my thoughts abroad when every thing around me appears to be at home?.... Some recollections attached to the idea of home, mingled with reflections respecting the state of society I had been contemplating that evening, made a tear drop on the rosy cheek I had just kissed [her daughter's]; and emotions that trembled on the brink of extasy and agony gave a poignancy to my sensations, which made me feel more alive than usual.
>
> What are these imperious sympathies?... I have considered myself as a particle broken off from the grand mass of mankind; – I was alone, till some involuntary sympathetic emotion, like the attraction of adhesion, made me feel that I was still part of a mighty whole, from which I could not sever myself – not, perhaps, for the reflection has been carried very far, by snapping the thread of an existence which loses its charms in proportion as the cruel experience of life stops or poisons the current of the heart. (SR 6:248–9)

A crucial feature of these thoughts flying abroad is their ability, as we would say, to "free associate": to jump from one topic to another at will. The dashes, so characteristic of Wollstonecraft's prose in this work, and especially of her reveries, highlight the leaps her mind is making. The narrator wavers irresolute between the image of herself as an untethered, independent individual "broken off from the grand mass of mankind" and herself as "part of the mighty whole," bound by "imperious sympathies." Yet the point even of this wavering is to assert the power of her mind to carry her reflections "very far," even if that movement envisions "snapping the thread of . . . existence" in order, paradoxically, to keep the current of the heart flowing. Here, at the outset of her travels, Wollstonecraft wants to insist that this "active principle," the mobility of her soul, will travel beyond the bounds of mortality itself.

As Julie Ellison has observed, the work of fancy, so central to the literature of sensibility in the eighteenth century, and active in these reveries, depends upon and validates the perceived power of motion itself. Fancy, Ellison writes, represents subjectivity that is at once ungrounded – liberated from or deprived of territory – and mobile, committed to ambitious itineraries through international space and historical time.[10]

Flights of fancy thus accomplish exactly the sort of conversion Wollstonecraft seems to be aiming at: turning dislocation and deprivation into ambition and freedom. As allegory and extension of the idea of upward mobility, flights of fancy allow this traveler to "walk in the footstep" of queens, kings and nobles or drop "down from the clouds in a strange land" like a deity (SR 6:329, 330, and 269). Furthermore, while fancy can project the fancier through time and space, it can also pitch her, as Wollstonecraft hopes, outside convention and routine. For the narrator, already moving through foreign territories, fanciful reveries send her into an realm without boundaries or binding attachments. "I have frequently strayed, sovereign of the waste," she tells us, while fancy, "taking its flight with fairy wing to the misty mountains that bounded the prospect, . . . tript over new lawns, more beautiful even than the [ones] . . . before me" (SR 6:279–80). Beyond the bounds of this world, fancy promises to turn her "straying" into something more, better and her own.

And yet, despite the freedom such transcendent travel seems to offer and the energy to which it attests, any claim to truly independent motion falters in these reveries. In the second letter, for instance, where hospitality evokes the writer's scorn as a sign of "indolence," a "pleasure where the mind gets no exercise," and where "tiresome civility" serves as a "continual constraint on all your actions," she flees an endless dinner party to venture into the woods. Here as elsewhere we see Wollstonecraft identifying the domestic sphere with inertia and pointless routine. Her walk outdoors is her chance to determine freely where and how she will move. But rather than describe where she actually goes and what she sees, the narrator waxes fanciful.

> [L]et me, kind strangers, escape sometimes into your fir groves, wander on the margin of your beautiful lakes, or climb your rocks to view still others in endless perspective; which, piled by more than giant's hand scale the heavens to intercept its rays, or to receive the parting tinge of lingering day – day that, scarcely softened into twilight, allows the freshening breeze to wake, and the moon to burst forth in all her glory to glide with solemn elegance through the azure expanse. (SR 6:252)

Again we see the freely associative syntax which emerges in the writing whenever the letter writer "stray[s] abroad" (SR 6:252). But as her thoughts move, so do the source and agent of motion. At first the apostrophe seems to give her hosts the authority to determine whether or not she can "escape," "wander," "climb." Then we enter a fantastic, anthropomorphic realm where the walker disappears, but rocks "scale the heavens" with Miltonic echoes, day "lingers," breezes "wake," and, in the grand finale, the feminine moon "bursts forth" and "glides" through an expansive sky.[11] Agency or authority proves to be as slippery as movement itself in this passage: something "more than giant's hand" has placed the rocks so they might "scale"; a waning day "allows" the breeze to awaken and the moon to begin her majestic procession. This is "the witching time of night," we are told, and indeed, some extra-human magic, or fancy itself, sets the surrounding world in motion.

Wollstonecraft again pushes the principle of movement beyond mortal and physical borders, but in doing so she pushes it beyond her very self.

> Spirits of peace walk abroad to calm the agitated breast. Eternity is in these moments; worldly cares melt away into the airy stuff that dreams are made of; and reveries, mild and enchanting. . . . carry the hapless wight into futurity[.]
>
> (SR 6:252)

Where has the narrator gone? Is she one of those spirits of peace "walk[ing] abroad" (language she often uses to characterize her own activity)? Is she the hapless wight being carried off into futurity? The principle of movement, even as it opens itself as widely as one can imagine, reveals itself as a principle of displacement.

Subsequent reveries offer similar confusions about agency and the source or even path of motion. In Letter v, the moon again focuses this confusion:

> I should not have wondered at [Edward Young's] becoming enamoured of the moon. But it is not the queen of the night alone who reigns here in all her splendour, though the sun, loitering just below the horizon, decks her with a golden tinge from his car, illuminating the cliffs that hide him; the heavens also, of a clear, softened blue, throw her forward. . . .   (SR 6:267)

Who reigns here? The moon, the behind-the-scenes sun, the circumambient heavens, or the writer who orchestrates this series of deflections?[12] It appears the solitary walker, for all her intrepidity, cannot or does not want to venture into this vast region alone, on her own authority. Her own nocturnal wanderings are displaced onto the moon, and the moon is merely "thrown forward," not venturing by her own will. These reveries, moreover, the sign of her mind's free and creative mobility, disclose other luminaries – Milton, Shakespeare, Young – who, like the hiding sun, undermine the writer's sovereignty while illuminating her path.

Most of the book's reveries occur during or just after her walking, and most of them have the same direct aim – to futurity or eternity or immortality, as if the purpose of bodily exercise were to fling the letter writer outside her body. Yet two paradoxes present themselves in these exercises. First, if these

movements, walking and reverie, share a determined end, that end is endlessness. Thus on one occasion the narrator may finish her reverie with a powerful gesture of transcendence: "I stretched out my hand to eternity, bounding
over the dark speck of life to come" (SR 6:311; see also 279); but on another
occasion she confesses her dread of being lost in that endlessness: "I cannot
bear to think of being no more – of losing myself.... nay it seems impossible
to me ... that this active, restless spirit, equally alive to joy and sorrow, should
only be organized dust – ready to fly abroad the moment the spring snaps"
(SR 6:281). The most liberating strategy of movement, then, the one that
will free her from the cares and constraints of this world, cannot guarantee
that she will not end up lost, diffused into the atmosphere. The second paradox involves the source or authority for movement. Though it is clear that
she can choose to walk alone outside, and does so in the face of convention
(the Swedish women, she relates, "were astonished that I should [walk], for
pleasure" [SR 6:282]), the narrator's flights of fancy often deflect their impetus onto external, magical but also conventional, sources. The reverie which
concludes Letter x makes this paradox explicit, asserting her "strong imagination" even as it collapses into the arms of "phantoms of bliss! Ideal forms
of excellence!" (SR 6:294). Increasingly, the narrator cannot rely on herself
to provide the forward momentum she desires. Spirits, nature, Shakespeare
(especially *The Tempest*) all step in as surrogate motors for transport:

> I must fly from thought and find refuge from sorrow in a strong imagination –
> the only solace for a feeling heart. Phantoms of bliss! Ideal forms of excellence!
> Again inclose me in your magic circle.   (SR 6:294)

> [T]here was an enchanting wildness [in the sound of a horn echoing in the
> caves] in the dying way of reverberation, that quickly transported me to Shake-
> speare's magic island. Spirits unseen seemed to walk abroad, and flit from cliff
> to cliff.   (SR 6:297)

> [T]he impetuous dashing of the rebounding torrent... produced an equal ac-
> tivity in mind: my thoughts darted from earth to heaven, and I asked myself
> why I was chained to life and its misery?... [M]y soul rose, with renewed dig-
> nity, above its cares – grasping at immortality – it seemed as impossible to stop
> the current of my thoughts, as of the always varying, still the same, torrent
> before me –   (SR 6:311)

Even in this last passage, where the mind and soul take an active role ("my
thoughts darted," " my soul rose"), the narrator nevertheless surrenders to
the activity of the torrent, helpless to stop herself. Her mental exertions fold
into passivity.

One explanation for the narrator's deliquescence in the face of absolute
freedom could be gender: the woman traveler dare not claim authority to

carry herself into these areas. On one occasion, the narrator "pierces the fleecy clouds" of mortality only to "bow before the awful throne of my Creator" (SR 6:280), acknowledging that the territory she has entered belongs to a sovereign Lord. Elsewhere she disguises her "straying" as the operation of forces beyond her: spirits or scenery or special effects "move" her and it is "impossible to stop." Legitimate male poets thus provide cover for a woman writer venturing out of her body, into sublimity. On the other hand, the writer has already called attention to herself as someone who refuses the limitations of gender, who will "go beyond" rules. Rather than covering up, she frequently calls attention to the fact that she is "straying," both in her walks and in her writing. Her constant apologies to her reader for these digressive reveries indicate that she claims responsibility for her movements, however vagrant they appear: "But whither am I wandering?" she writes after one (SR 6:269); "But I have rambled away again" (SR 6:289); "But I have flown from Norway" (SR 6:307); "But to go further a-field" (SR 6:341); and, in an apology that indicates what the reveries resist: "But to return to the straight road of observation..." (SR 6:326). To wander from the straight road may indicate a sort of freedom, but, as the reveries themselves demonstrate, it may also signal an inability to locate oneself. One can read the series of flights of fancy in *Short Residence* as an exposé of the belief in transcendent movement, a discovery that such movement always reveals itself to be subject to something else, to be, in fact, not freedom but displacement, a removal of the self. A crucial turn in the book occurs in Letter XII, where the writer confesses that the movement of fancy incapacitates her: "I cannot write composedly – I am every instant sinking into reveries – my heart flutters, I know not why. Fool! It is time thou wert at rest" (SR 6:299; see also 333). As this realization plays itself out in the course of *Short Residence*, the traveler abandons her flights and concentrates more on the worldly movements that keep her restless – especially economics and war.

Systems of motion

In the middle of *Short Residence* the narrator turns to interpret her travels no longer in the light of fancy, but in the context of pressing political and economic movements. Letter XII opens happily, as the narrator once again leaves her "confinement" on a boat to reach shore: "It seemed to me a sort of emancipation," she writes, and "elysian scenes" welcome her back to land. Her emancipation, however, quickly qualifies itself: there is no one to greet her in this place; she dreads "the solitariness of her apartment," she longs "to close her eyes on a world where I was destined to wander alone." Her freedom of movement reveals itself as a purely negative freedom:

"I walked, till I was wearied out, to purchase rest – or rather forgetfulness" (SR 6:298). No wonder she is provoked to cry out to herself, "Fool! It is time thou wert at rest!" (SR 6:299). The letter ends with two images – a "wild-goose chase" [sic] and migratory birds – indicative of her reevaluation of her previous flights (SR 6:299).

The sense of defeat so palpable in Letter XII converts itself into harsh critique in Letter XIII, as the writer's individual misery gives way to a larger sense of oppression. The shift announces itself immediately in Letter XIII, where, in the commercial city of Moss, the narrator retracts her earlier, admiring assessment of Norway's institutions and elaborates her disaffection.[13] Three figures emerge to focus this no longer personal disappointment: the peasant drafted into war, the enslaved criminal (in Norway some crimes were punished by sending the offender into years of slave labor), and the political prisoner. For Wollstonecraft each case represents a "tyrannical" constraint on movement. Military service "trammels" Norwegian men; most shocking to the writer is the fact that, by pre-selecting which men will go to the navy, which to the infantry, the state forbids a man "to follow his inclination, should it lead him to go to sea" (SR 6:301). It seems to come to her as a revelation that the military might get in the way of one's travel preferences. Later, in Christiana, as she walks to relieve an "oppressed heart," her steps lead her to the site of more material oppression. "Chance directed my steps to the fortress, and the sight of the slaves, working with chains on their legs, only served to embitter me more against the regulations of society" (SR 6:305). "[A] degree of energy in some of their countenances" draws forth her sympathy and respect, and she contrasts the ornamented merchants and officers she has met in society with these chained laborers, confessing her suspicion that "the former produced the latter" (SR 6:306). During her walk around the fortress, the narrator also tries to catch a glimpse of a man "confined six years for having induced the farmers to revolt," presumably against high taxes. Thanks to political machinations and legal loopholes, the man's sentence remains indeterminate; he may never go free. The narrator's fascination with him is apparent: "He must have possessed some eloquence, or have had the truth on his side, for farmers rose up by hundreds to support him" (SR 6:305).

Amidst her anger at the power of state institutions to delimit human movement, the traveler's eye in this letter fixes on such "risings up." Prior to her account of the farmers' insurgence, she reports that "a few months ago, the people of Christiana rose" to protest the gouging price and scarcity of grain:

They threw stones at Mr. Anker [a local grain merchant] . . . as he rode out of town to escape from their fury; they assembled about his house. And the people demanded afterwards, with so much impetuosity, the liberty of those who were taken up in consequence of the tumult, that the Grand Bailiff thought it prudent to release them.   (SR 6:304)

These two popular uprisings, one over grain, the other over taxes, recall the initial stirrings of the French and American revolutions. They also transfer the question of movement from the individual to the collective. The pairing of a success story with a stark failure registers again Wollstonecraft's ambivalence: how viable is self-determined forward – or upward – movement? And who is the determining self? Here law, in the form of the Grand Bailiff, bows to the will of the people and releases its prisoners; there its faceless machinery squelches a popular "rising up" by locking up one man for life. Throughout this political see-sawing, it is clear that the narrator is working to make some exchange between her own situation and that of the people. Before her walk to the fortress, she pictures this exchange almost allegorically:

> the fire of fancy [in me], which had been kept alive in the country, was almost extinguished [in Christiana] by reflections on the ills that harass such a large portion of mankind. – I felt like a bird fluttering on the ground unable to mount; yet unwilling to crawl tranquily [sic] like a reptile, whilst still conscious it had wings.   (SR 6:305)

Sandwiched between the two stories of people who "rose up" against political and economic oppression, the image of the narrator's momentary paralysis between earth and sky points the question of how she will continue to move.

Her answer, in part, is to merge her own predicament with that of the people, and to find in the systems that determine their movement (or confinement) the source of her own restlessness. Letter XIII thus unleashes her strongest critique yet of commerce, "the noble science of bargain making," "the tricks of trade" which dictate not only the movement of goods and money, but of the traveler as well, for, as frequent hints have informed us, she is traveling on business. Disparaging comments about the evils of speculators and the "narrowness" of merchants dot the first half of *Short Residence*, but here the attack escalates. Commerce is a "pursuit" or exercise that "wears out the most sacred principles of humanity and rectitude"; speculation is "a species of gambling, I might have said fraud, in which address generally gains the prize." Subsequent letters add to her charges against the ubiquitous movements of trade, culminating in a five-page tirade near the end of her journey. Her report from Hamburg analyzes in detail the "secret *manoeuvres* of trade," which disguise themselves as productive growth but effectively move in empty rotation, the "ups and downs of fortune's wheel" (SR 6:340).

Wollstonecraft exposes the promises of mobile capitalism as, in fact, vain motion or alternatively, constraint. Hamburg, she tells us, shuts its gates early every night, "lest strangers, who have come to traffic [there], should prefer living,... and spend[ing] their money out of the walls of the Hamburgers' world" (SR 6:340). The greed which motivates capitalism threatens to shut down the world, and thereby "embrute" humanity.

This stifling of the world, it turns out, has been stifling the letter writer as well. The critique of commerce veers away from dispassionate observation to a more pointed and personal complaint, and in doing so, demonstrates how the very correspondence before us has been written under the thumb of commerce. Now it begins to wrench itself free. The "you" whom the letter writer has been trying to engage, even placate, can now be acknowledged as an "embruting" speculator. As she recounts the frauds practiced by merchants during wartime to receive compensation for damaged or nonexistent goods, the traveler's criticism suddenly points to her correspondent: "This censure is not confined to the Danes! Adieu!" (SR 6:304). And later, near the close of the letters: "But you will say I am growing too bitter, perhaps too personal. Ah! Shall I whisper to you – that you – yourself, are strangely altered, since you have entered deeply into commerce – more than you are aware of – never allowing yourself to reflect and keeping your mind, or rather passions, in a continual state of agitation –" (SR 6:340–1). Her earlier celebrations of ceaseless industry devolve into a condemnation of the "continual state of agitation" produced by a commercial world. In the motion produced by commerce – "the ups and downs of fortune's wheel," the "continual state of agitation" – it is hard not to find analogues, if not explanations, for the letter writer's own emotional turbulence; her own feelings have gone up and down throughout the course of letters. Displaying her most intimate, personal tone in this passage, the narrator accentuates the shifting of the site of movement away from the self to this impersonal and depersonalizing system: this "you" could be anybody, could be the economic system itself. At the same time, it registers how an impersonal system weighs upon our most intimate selves.

Complicit with the "whirlpool" of commerce are the movements of war; indeed the swindles practiced by speculators depend on a war economy. The letter writer has her eyes open to the injustices of the war economy from the moment she arrives in Scandinavia: she registers that it prompts unjust taxation, induces merchants in neutral countries to sell abroad; and obstructs the free flow of goods, money, and jobs. Yet war claims its own role as a dominant force shaping her travels. Warfare, as it distributes populations and civilizations, makes its appearance in almost every letter: in slight mentions of a Norwegian pilot who fought in the American War of Independence, or of a ruined fort overlooking a river; in large-scale meditations on the sacrifice of young lives; or in the actual threat of violence that sends her fellow travelers scurrying home at the end of the book. When the narrator sees a flock of tents outside the walls of Copenhagen, she cycles through various interpretations of something that looks like travel: she "suppose[s] that the rage for encampments had reached this city," that is, that people were engaged in recreational camping. She soon learns that these are refugees from the recent fire that had raged through the capital (SR 6:319). But the contemporary imagery of war – of besieged cities, refugees and military encampments – also obviously emanates from this scene, which ends with the narrator's thoughts taking her "in search of houseless heads" (SR 6:320).

Yet just as her early letters applaud industry while dismissing speculators, so too do they lament the "effects of war" while admiring military heroes (SR 6:254). In some instances, the courage of military heroes shadows her flights of fancy, adding plausibility to Ellison's notion that fancy mimics the movement of conquerors. Before moving to the "queen of the night" passage, Letter v offers an elegy for Sweden's Charles XII, "an ambitious military man" of the beginning of the eighteenth century, who, Carol Poston's notes inform us, "assembled one of the most effective armies in history."[14] The narrator classes Charles XII with Alexander the Great, both men's "force of mind" and "individual exertions" having contributed to the "general improvement," "acquirements, even the virtues" of humanity (SR 6:267). Emphasis falls on these military men as movers and shakers, who "went beyond" general rules and pulled posterity along with them.

Her appeal to Charles XII and Alexander harkens back to a remarkable reverie about human evolution earlier in Letter v, where the narrator actually places warfare at the heart of human progress. Arguing that the "first dwellings of man" must have been in the north, she imagines a primitive migration toward a divine sun "so seldom seen":

> Man must therefore have been placed in the north, to tempt him to run after the sun, in order that the different parts of the world might be peopled. Nor do I wonder that hordes of barbarians always poured out of these regions to seek for milder climes, when nothing like cultivation attached them to the soil; especially when we take into view that the adventuring spirit, common to man, is naturally stronger and more general during the infancy of society. The conduct of the followers of Mahomet, and the crusaders, will definitely corroborate my assertion.   (SR 6:263–4)

The passage envisions the dislocations and violence or war as an almost pre-ordained geographical and historical progress, the innocent movements of "infancy." An adventuring spirit characterizes the warrior, along with a quasi-religious desire to move; they characterize the writer in her early reveries as well.

Just as they pull away from their admiration of industry and activity, so too the letters eventually shed their heroic and nostalgic image of war as progressive movement. They begin to focus more carefully on the contemporary war disrupting Europe and its colonies, they also focus more on the bodies mobilized by warfare. From Norwegian men conscripted to the army or navy, to soldiers exercising in their barracks in Copenhagen, the narrator carries us, at the end of her journey, to the castle of Sleswig, where she views "with pity and horror, these beings training to be sold to slaughter, or be slaughtered" (SR 6:336). A new sort of reverie about military movement overtakes her as she walks:

> I crossed the draw-bridge, and entered to see this shell of a court in miniature, mounting ponderous stairs, it would be a solecism to say a flight, up which a regiment might have marched, shouldering their firelocks, to exercise in vast galleries, where all the generations of the princes of Hesse-Cassel might have been mustered rank and file, though not the phantoms of all the wretched they had bartered to support their state, unless these airy substances could shrink and expand, like Milton's devils, to suit the occasion. (SR 6:336)

The passage reads almost as a direct refutation of previous "flights," where phantoms and spirits are transformed into slaughtered soldiers and their diabolic emanations, military princes turn out to be barterers and butchers, and history becomes an infinite regress of "exercises" leading to violence and death.

While the "tricks of trade" replace the supernatural magic of her roving fancy, and recast emotion as empty agitations ("But to commerce every thing must give way," she writes, " . . . 'double–double, toil and trouble'"), the architectonics of warfare determine the movement of the body itself, even to death (SR 6:343). Almost no form of motion practiced by the narrator in these letters remains free from the grip of these two systems. The "going beyond" trumpeted at the outset converts to the thought that men under capitalism are "machines" who "allow themselves to break with impunity over bounds" (SR 6:342). Thus, in these last pages she falls away from the very ethos of travel: "I do not feel inclined to ramble any further this year; I am weary of changing the scene, and quitting people and places the moment they begin to interest me." But even as she hopes to quit quitting, she knows she is trapped in ceaseless movement: " – This also is vanity!" she moans, and she sets out to walk the dirty streets of Dover "as if to kill time" (SR 6:345). There is no homecoming, no finale to her travels. The final pages of *Short Residence* take the platitude, "life is a journey" and transform it into an impassioned cry against oppression and injustice, seen now as forms and engines of motion.

Coda

Throughout *Short Residence* the letter writer cycles back to the question that organizes her first reverie: is she a solitary traveler, "a particle broken off from the great mass of mankind," or "a part of the mighty whole, from which I could not sever myself?" (SR 6:249). In some sense, the path of these letters is the path between these two poles, a continual travel out of the self and back again, as if travel for Wollstonecraft required the repeated disso-lution of the self, and travel writing the recognition of that process. Clearly this process can be written in a variety of ways, through fanciful reveries or political critique or the rhetorical leaps made between them. But it is hard to ignore, as one reads this travelogue, that it can also be written as the route taken by emotion. Readers since its publication have tended to notice first how *moving Short Residence* is, and the work proved to be Wollstonecraft's greatest critical and financial success. In a typical assessment, the *Monthly Review* reports that the expressions of this "writer's heart" will "never fail to touch the reader . . . [R]eaders will seldom see reason to censure her feel-ings and never be inclined to withhold their sympathy." "Perhaps a book of travels that so irresistibly seizes upon the heart of its reader never, in any other instance, found its way to the press," wrote William Godwin, in a exaggerated but not unrepresentative response to *Short Residence*.[15] Wollstonecraft demonstrates that movement and emotion are inextricable. She understands the ambivalent position of her narrator, wavering between self and mass, as essentially moving precisely because it describes the position of emotion itself.

In the Advertisement that precedes the letters, Wollstonecraft points to her use of the first person as a convenient fiction: "I found I could not avoid being continually the first person – 'the little hero of every tale.'" And she justifies her choice, adding that "[a] person has a right . . . to talk of himself, when he can win our attention by acquiring our affection" (SR 6:241). The self portrayed in the letters is a ruse whereby the writer wins our sympathies so as to grab our attention. Without that self, presumably, our attentions would wander. Yet that self is itself marvelously mobile: it wanders because of the need to evoke emotion from a large public.

Wollstonecraft has constructed her narrative so as to suggest that emotion, too, travels, that it derives not from some fixed dwelling in a single individual, but rather from its inability – or disinclination – to locate itself. As with any migrant, if emotion doesn't move, it doesn't work. This is not simply to say that the emotion of the letter writer fluctuates in the course of the narrative, even in the course of one passage, from despair to elation, from confidence to grinding doubt, though this is true. It is to suspect that emotion here is deliberately ungrounded, dislocated, covering the ground between any self the writing offers and a mass of potential readers.[16] The grief that threatens to overwhelm the narrator, like the moments of ecstasy, arrives out of thin air: it is given few specifics, no origin. Precisely because she refuses to explain these feelings, Wollstonecraft achieves an unusual sense of intimacy with her reader, as the letters repeat, "you know.... you know.... you know." And the reader knows, or thinks she knows, not because she has any privileged information about the writing self, the MARY— who signs the letters (most contemporary readers would have been ignorant of the details of Wollstonecraft's life), but because Wollstonecraft has given us an array of stock characters to channel emotion. The narrator is alternately the intrepid adventurer, the anxious mother, the dispassionate observer, the too-sensitive dreamer, the wronged woman, the contemplative philosopher, the pugnacious radical; she picks up and drops each role as need be. She moves her readers in voices she assumes are familiar: Shakespeare, Milton, Dryden, and Christian scripture. When, in her penultimate letter, she unleashes her most wrenching outburst – "Why should I weep for myself? – 'Take, O world! Thy much indebted tear!'" – she borrows the utterance from Edward Young's *Night Thoughts*, one of the most popular poems of the century. At the same time, she acknowledges that emotion belongs outside and beyond any single "I." What moves the reader, in other words, is the mobility of emotion, the way that it travels away from any fixed location and disperses itself into cultural references, convention, the world.

NOTES

1. Review of William Hamilton, *Letters Concerning the Northern Coast of the Country of Antrim* (1790) (AR 7:277).
2. I borrow this phrase and the larger thought of this sentence, from James Clifford, *Routes: Travel and Translation in the Late Twentieth Century* (Cambridge and London: Harvard University Press, 1997), 3:

   Dwelling was understood to be the local ground of collective life, travel as a supplement.... But what would happen, I began to ask, if travel were untethered, seen as a complex and pervasive spectrum of human experiences? Practices of displacement might emerge as *constitutive* of cultural meanings rather than as their simple transfer or extension.... As I began to consider diverse forms of "travel," the term became a figure for routes through a heterogeneous modernity.

3. From Bentham, *Theory of Legislation*; quoted in Gary Harrison, *Wordsworth's Vagrant Muse: Poetry, Poverty and the Poor* (Detroit: Wayne State University Press, 1994), 195–6.

4. Still, it is worth remembering that Wollstonecraft wrote this book for economic independence. See Letters, 328–9.

5. See Harrison, *Wordsworth's Vagrant Muse*, chapter 4, especially 115–16: "Given the value of industry for the middle classes, it should surprise us little that when cultural production fell primarily into their hands, industriousness was . . . depicted as . . . a projection of middle-class interest in economic security and social mobility."

6. Claire Tomalin, *The Life and Death of Mary Wollstonecraft*, rev. edn. (Harmondsworth: Penguin Books, 1992), 18.

7. The best account of the circumstances of this trip is Per Nyström, "Mary Wollstonecraft's Scandinavian Journey," *Acts of the Royal Society of Arts and Letters of Gothenburg, Humaniora* 17 (1980).

8. From her review of William Gilpin, *Three Essays: On Picturesque Beauty; On Picturesque Travel; and On Sketching Landscape* (1792), (AR 7:456).

9. For more on the status of the traveler, see James Buzard, *The Beaten Path: European Tourism, Literature, and the Ways to "Culture" 1800–1918* (Oxford: Clarendon Press, 1993). Wollstonecraft often inverts the terms and hierarchies that cluster around travel. Her travel reviews, for instance, rewrite the aristocratic, leisured traveler as aimless slave to the smallest change in circumstance (e.g. AR 7:276). See also her comments in the *Short Residence* about keeping a travel journal as a means of determining the purpose of travel and fighting off "idleness" (SR 6:256).

10. Julie Ellison, *Cato's Tear and the Making of Anglo-American Emotion* (Chicago; University of Chicago Press, 1999), 100. Fancy also provides what Ellison calls a "purportedly victimless kind of imagination," a feature that runs alongside the confusion of agency in Wollstonecraft's flights of fancy.

11. Wollstonecraft echoes *Paradise Lost*, 4.354–5: "and in th'ascending Scale / Of Heav'n the Stars that usher evening rose."

12. Later the narrator will echo both these passages on the moon when, "straying" near a ruined fort, "sovereign of the waste," she finds her "very soul diffused into the scene, – and seeming to become all senses, glided," and "melted in the freshening breeze" (SR 6:280).

13. See Letter VII for her more positive appreciation of Norway's institutions.

14. See Poston's edition of Wollstonecraft's *Letters Written During a Short Residence in Sweden, Norway and Denmark*, ed. with intro. Carol Poston (Lincoln and London: University of Nebraska Press, 1976), 49n.

15. *Monthly Review* 20 (1796), 251 and William Godwin, *Memoirs of Mary Wollstonecraft*, ed. W. Clarke Durant (1798); rpt. (London; Constable & Co., Ltd., 1927), 84–5.

16. For an excellent study of the mobility of emotion in the thinking of this period, see Adela Pinch, *Strange Fits of Passion: Epistemologies of Emotion fom Hume to Austen* (Stanford; Stanford University Press, 1997).

13

ANDREW ELFENBEIN

Mary Wollstonecraft and the sexuality of genius

For a reader coming to the life and work of Mary Wollstonecraft for the first time, one of the most compelling aspects of her career is its power to unsettle the homosexual/heterosexual split that the twentieth century made so rigid. This unsettling occurs partly because Wollstonecraft, like all eighteenth-century writers, had no words like "homosexual" or "heterosexual" in her vocabulary. Sexuality had no language of its own in the eighteenth century. Instead, writers understood sexual roles through the vocabulary of gender: certain modes of sexual behavior were the supposed prerogatives of masculinity; others, of femininity.[1]

What is so interesting about the eighteenth century is that neither "masculinity" nor "femininity" was a fixed category. When eighteenth-century writers argued about virtually anything (education, aesthetics, law, natural philosophy, religion, politics), they usually did so in loudly gendered terms. However, gender definitions were not necessarily the same in each discourse; they were as likely to differ as to complement one another. Consequently, eighteenth-century writers like Wollstonecraft could set different definitions against each other, using those from one discourse to criticize those in another. For example, in *A Vindication of the Rights of Woman*, Wollstonecraft creatively adapts gender definitions from the political discourse of civic humanism to counter the stereotypes of female conduct books, as when she prefers to judge women by what had traditionally been seen as the "manly" quality of virtue rather than by the angel-like traits idealized by conduct-book writers. Criticizing James Fordyce's comparison of women to angels, she notes that for him women "are only like angels when they are young and beautiful; consequently, it is their persons, not their virtues, that procure them this homage" (5:164).[2] Since all gender definitions suggested differing possibilities for relations between and among the sexes, a simple homo/hetero binary rarely does justice to eighteenth-century writing.

For Wollstonecraft, the topic that encouraged the most experimentation with sex and gender roles was that of genius. Genius as a category received an enormous amount of attention from eighteenth-century writers in general and from Wollstonecraft in particular. Nevertheless, at first glance, it may seem an odd topic for an essay about sexuality. Many readers have learned to think that if an author is truly a genius, his or her work will transcend the particulars of sexual behavior. I want to argue instead that genius, as understood by eighteenth-century writers, helps to explain the most salient characteristics of Wollstonecraft's thoughts about sexuality: her deep mistrust for conventional forms of erotic relationships and her profound doubt about lasting love in a world that victimizes women who have any sensitivity whatsoever. In much of her writing, Wollstonecraft's project was less to be homosexual or heterosexual, feminine or masculine, than to understand the consequences of linking the category of genius to the category of woman. The results, however, were some of the most daring and unconventional treatments of sexuality in all eighteenth-century literature.

The biographical tradition about Wollstonecraft has largely masked such daring. While writers admit that she experimented with gendered behavior and sexual relationships, a counter narrative usually runs through their work to suggest that she really was not as startling as she seemed and that, when all is said and done, she only wanted a good marriage. This counter narrative makes its case by reading her life in terms of a movement from youthful proto-lesbianism, perceived as vaguely distasteful, to adult heterosexuality, perceived as healthy or at least sympathetic. It also treats her eventual marriage to William Godwin as the real goal of her life, thereby ignoring the expansive, unconventional, and sometimes rocky modes of heterosexuality that Wollstonecraft experimented with in her relations with Henry Fuseli, Gilbert Imlay, and Godwin himself. This tidying-up of Wollstonecraft's sexuality dates back to the first biography of her, Godwin's *Memoirs of Mary Wollstonecraft*, which is worth examining in some detail because of its immense later influence.

Godwin's discussion of *A Vindication of the Rights of Woman* initiates the biographical tradition of both acknowledging Wollstonecraft's daring and mistrusting it. While he claims to like her "very bold and original production," he immediately backtracks: "There are also, it must be confessed, occasional passages of a stern and rugged feature."[3] His clause "it must be confessed" flows from him all too easily. In his eyes, *A Vindication of the Rights of Woman* is an embarrassment because of its supposed lack of feminine grace: Wollstonecraft's authorial character has a "rigid, and somewhat amazonian temper." The result: "Many of the sentiments [in *A Vindication of the Rights of Woman*] are undoubtedly of a rather masculine description" (*Memoirs*, 231). Evidently, masculinity in a woman necessarily leads to violence: Wollstonecraft "repels the opinions of Rousseau, Dr Gregory, and

Dr James Fordyce" and she "explodes the system of gallantry" that oppresses women (231).

For eighteenth-century writers, female masculinity of the kind that Godwin described could point in two directions: asexuality and lesbianism. Although they are quite different modes of sexual behavior, they could quickly blur into each other because both set women against the presumed norm of bourgeois heterosexuality. If relations between the sexes presupposed the belief in their mutual sexual desirability, the possibility of a woman who either was not interested in sex or was not interested in men was threatening because she forced relations between men and women to assume an entirely new footing. Godwin's discomfort reveals how deeply sexuality was supposed to determine the female character. If Wollstonecraft's masculinity "explodes the system of gallantry," then it was not clear how a man might behave toward such a woman.

Not only was Wollstonecraft masculine; according to Godwin, her early love interests were homoerotic. Specifically, as a young woman, she fell in love with Fanny Blood, "for whom," Godwin writes, "she contracted a friendship so fervent, as for years to have constituted the ruling passion of her mind" (*Memoirs*, 210). For the most part, Godwin is neutral or even admiring in his treatment of Wollstonecraft's love for Blood; when he interjects notes of disapproval of Blood's character, they usually come from Wollstonecraft's own comments. Only one small revision to the *Memoirs* suggests some concern on Godwin's part that her relation with Blood might foreground her troubling masculinity. He omitted in the second edition a sentence describing their first meeting: "The situation in which Mary was introduced to [Blood], bore a resemblance to the first interview of Werter with Charlotte" (*Memoirs*, 210). Given Werter's fame as a paragon of all-consuming love, the comparison may have made too obvious a link for Godwin between Wollstonecraft's masculinity and her love for Blood.

In the larger course of his narrative, Godwin neutralizes Wollstonecraft's masculinity by showing that it vanished after Blood's death in childbirth. Instead of turning to other women, Wollstonecraft fell in love with a series of men: Fuseli, Imlay, Godwin. According to Godwin, the affair with Imlay was so powerful that it eradicated her masculinity altogether:

> Her whole character seemed to change with a change of fortune . . . She was playful, full of confidence, kindness and sympathy. Her eyes assumed new lustre, and her cheeks new colour and smoothness. Her voice became chearful; her temper overflowing with universal kindness; and that smile of bewitching tenderness from day to day illuminated her countenance.　　(*Memoirs*, 242)

Loving Imlay, according to Godwin, makes Wollstonecraft a real woman: the Amazon suddenly becomes the model heterosexual partner. He describes her so vividly that one might think he had seen this transformation himself. Actually, this supposed change occurred when she was in Paris, when we have no reason to believe that he had any contact with her. But Godwin's lack of first-hand knowledge does not stop him from lavishing attention on this fantasy. His description is all the more remarkable given the affair's miserable outcome: we might have expected him to be more reserved when describing a relationship that turned out terribly for Wollstonecraft. Instead, he halts his narrative to devote an entire paragraph to the marvelously beneficial effects of loving a man on the female character. In Godwin's fairy tale, the love of a handsome man (Gilbert Imlay) turns the ugly duckling (stern, rugged, harshly masculine Wollstonecraft) into a beautiful swan (confident, bewitching, beautifully feminine Wollstonecraft).

Godwin thus fits Wollstonecraft into one of the master plots of female development in Anglo-American literature: the movement from same- to opposite-gender attachments as a metaphor for the movement from youth to maturity. This master plot was hardly new to the late eighteenth century: it can be found in William Shakespeare's *A Midsummer Night's Dream* and appears in a sexually explicit version in John Cleland's pornographic *Memoirs of a Woman of Pleasure*. It undercuts the mystique of opposite-gender attraction as an unspeakable, forbidden love by admitting that women might desire other women, but only when they are young and immature. Real life supposedly begins once they leave other women and turn to men.[4] In Wollstonecraft's case, according to Godwin, she came to value heterosexual attachment as an ultimate good: "She set a great value on a mutual affection between persons of an opposite sex. She regarded it as the principal solace of human life" (*Memoirs*, 235). He strategically forgets Wollstonecraft's relationship to Blood in order to make her a prime spokesperson for love between men and women.

In a few cases, Godwin's contemporaries ignored his treatment of Wollstonecraft and represented figures based on her as more or less openly desiring other women. The most notorious is the character of Harriot Freke in Maria Edgeworth's novel *Belinda*, although Freke should be understood as a representation less of Wollstonecraft than of the sexually uncontrolled woman that she was supposed to embody. Freke dresses in men's clothes, aggressively pursues other women, and cries, "*Vive la liberté* ... I'm a champion for the Rights of Women."[5] Nevertheless, for the most part, Wollstonecraft's biographers have not made her into Harriot Freke. On the contrary, they have largely accepted Godwin's account of her, complete with its mistrust of the supposedly masculine traits in her character.

An example of the durability of Godwin's account is the extraordinary afterlife of his derogatory adjective "amazonian" as a shorthand for the twinning of asexuality and lesbianism in Wollstonecraft's character. Claire Tomalin chose "The Amazon" as the chapter title for the section in her biography dealing with *A Vindication of the Rights of Woman*.[6] Emily Sunstein's biography contrasts two portraits of Wollstonecraft: in the first, commissioned by William Roscoe, she is an "intellectual Amazon," while in the second, by John Opie, she is "a woman of more graceful *tenue* and a deeper, subtler look, with soft cheeks and an almost tender mouth." Sunstein's desexualizing adjective "intellectual" prepares for Wollstonecraft's later emergence into conventional feminine sexuality: "She felt she had been too rigid, frugal, and self-denying, and in a fashion she had never before permitted herself, transformed her appearance, enhanced her femininity."[7]

Richard Holmes in his biographical essay on Wollstonecraft in *Footsteps* also contrasts the Roscoe and Opie portraits to make their sexual associations more explicit. According to him, the first shows her in "her Amazonian phase," while the second "shows her as a thoroughly romantic *femme de trente*." He adds, with sigh of relief, that the differences between them "belie any suggestion of mannish coldness or lesbian hauteur."[8] His phrases are classic examples of the doubling of lesbianism ("mannish," "lesbian") and asexuality ("coldness," "hauteur") in the treatment of women who do not fit conventional sexual categories. Like Godwin, he is relieved to absolve Wollstonecraft from both charges by noting that she eventually abandoned her crypto-lesbianism for a "romantic" (i.e., heterosexual) character. Even less openly homophobic critics of Wollstonecraft still read her life in terms of the erotic sequence first mapped out by Godwin: Fanny Blood, Henry Fuseli, Gilbert Imlay, William Godwin. They thereby retain his master plot (Wollstonecraft's movement from homoerotic to heteroerotic relationships) by suggesting that affairs with men ultimately dominated her life.

Some of this master plot's durability arises from a historical accident: more of Wollstonecraft's letters to men have survived than her letters to women. For example, while many painful letters to Imlay exist, albeit in heavily edited form, not until quite recently has it become known that Wollstonecraft actually corresponded with Catharine Macaulay, whom she singles out in *A Vindication of the Rights of Woman* as her most admired female author.[9] Biographers can easily analyze her relationships with men because they took place partly through writing, especially those with Imlay and Godwin (her letters to Fuseli were destroyed). Yet if we look not only at Wollstonecraft's correspondents but also at her day-to-day life, it is clear that she spent most of her time with women: her sisters, Eliza and Everina; her daughter Fanny; her maids, especially Marguerite, who accompanied her to Scandinavia;

and the intellectual women of Paris and London, such as Mary Hays, Ruth Barlow, Madeleine Schweizer, Ann Cristall, Amelia Alderson (later Opie), Sarah Siddons, Maria Reveley, and others. Whereas biographers give her affairs with men lots of space, these ties to women fade into the background because less written evidence survives about them. Admittedly, these women were family members, employees, or social acquaintances, not lovers, and I am not suggesting that Wollstonecraft had affairs with them, or even liked many of them. My point, rather, is that by following the accidents of the written record and paying so much attention to Wollstonecraft's affairs with men and so little to her relations with women, her biographers have hyper-heterosexualized her.

Even in the treatment of Wollstonecraft's heterosexual relations, biographers use the fact that she eventually married Godwin to imply that, throughout her life, she was really just waiting to settle down in an ordinary marriage. Her experimental, daring relation to heterosexuality is dismissed sneeringly as sheer naivete. For example, her desire to live with Fuseli as a spiritual rather than as a sexual partner has not been treated kindly. Tomalin is typical in calling it an "absurd and innocent request."[10] Yet, given the brilliance with which Wollstonecraft dissected the brutal effects of the sex/gender system on women in her *A Vindication of the Rights of Woman*, her search for a different kind of relationship with Fuseli could be seen not as absurd but as a risky, innovative attempt to live out her own principles. Similarly, her resistance to marriage and her insistence that she and Godwin live in separate houses even after their marriage reveal an effort to separate heterosexuality from its stifling associations with bourgeois domesticity that deserves more respect than it often has gotten from Wollstonecraft's critics.

To take account of the full range of experimentation in Wollstonecraft's relation to sexuality, I want to return the discussion to an eighteenth-century context. I will argue that the eighteenth-century language of genius and its consequences for sexual roles provided Wollstonecraft with an alternative to the increasingly restrictive roles being foisted on women by novels, conduct books, medical tracts, and religious sermons. Throughout her authorial career, Wollstonecraft used the role of genius as a means of reinventing possibilities for the woman writer and her sexuality.

Today, "genius" as a label has been applied so often and so loosely that it is virtually meaningless. In literary criticism, it has faintly conservative associations as a means of preserving standards of quasi-divine achievement. In the eighteenth century, however, genius was far more exciting. Its attraction was simple: it could shatter the traditional hierarchies of artistic achievement because anybody could potentially be a genius, not just the upper-class, university-educated men who ruled the literary establishment.

Shakespeare was the prime example of a man with (supposedly) little education and humble lineage who, by virtue of his genius, had become a great writer. Eighteenth-century audiences were fascinated by examples of "natural" genius: authors like Robert Burns and Ann Yearsley who seemed to have miraculously overcome their supposed lack of education to become distinguished poets. For writers who came from classes or groups that traditionally had no place in the English literary market, genius was a wedge into a hitherto closed system. Not surprisingly, many members of the radical circles in which Wollstonecraft moved in the 1790s were deeply invested in the category of genius. Wollstonecraft's friend, the poet Mary Robinson, composed an elaborate ode celebrating its power; William Godwin devoted the first several issues of *The Enquirer* to an inquiry about its roots; and William Blake repeatedly hailed it as the only source of great poetry.

Wollstonecraft herself first became interested in genius during her time as a governess in Ireland. While there, she read "Blairs lectures on genius taste &c &c [Hugh Blair's *Lectures on Rhetoric and Belles Lettres*]," in which Blair defines genius as a capacity that "imports something inventive or creative; which does not rest in mere sensibility to beauty where it is perceived, but which can, moreover, produce new beauties, and exhibit them in such a manner as strongly to impress the minds of others."[11] Suddenly, "genius," a term that does not appear in Wollstonecraft's earlier letters, crops up frequently in her writing. It gave her a weapon of self-assertion when, as a governess, she was feeling the effects of a hierarchical class system most painfully. In her early fragment "The Cave of Fancy," she wrote proudly: "The genius that sprouts from a dunghil [sic] soon shakes off the heterogeneous mass" (CF 1:196). In her letters, she tried to prove that she was shaking off the mediocre heterogeneity around her. For example, she found that her employer, Lady Kingsborough, had an understanding that "could never have been made to rise above mediocrity." She added, "I am very well persuaded that to make any great advance in morality genius is necessary–a peculiar kind of genius which is not to be described, and cannot be conceived by those who do not possess it."[12] Although she did not quite identify herself as having such genius, her criticism of Lady Kingsborough was possible only if she had what her employer lacked.

Even as Wollstonecraft borrows the idea of genius from Blair, she also revises it. Blair, like most other eighteenth-century writers, argues that genius differs from taste because genius involves production, whereas taste involves consumption. The genius produces new works of art, new scientific discoveries, great speeches, and so forth.[13] For Wollstonecraft, however, genius loses its productivity. In her essay "On Poetry," she defines genius against Blair as "only another word for exquisite sensibility" (OP 7:9). There is a gendered edge to Wollstonecraft's downplaying of genius's productions: if geniuses are expected always to be creating, then few women would ever be able to demonstrate genius. Even women like Wollstonecraft, who were professional authors, would not have had much opportunity to show their "exquisite sensibility" in a way that anyone would take seriously. While Wollstonecraft was hardly unproductive, relatively little of her work, such as her reviews or translations, offered an outlet for the kind of genius that she described in "On Poetry." A woman needing to write for a living had to write what would make money rather than what would demonstrate the originality supposedly characteristic of genius.

But if woman's genius was not productive, what good was it? Men could point to concrete results of their genius in their works. A woman, however, might possess exquisite sensibility, but she would have a difficult time in demonstrating it or, more seriously, making it useful. The fear haunts Wollstonecraft's work that genius in a woman is a waste of time. It distinguishes a woman in potentially dangerous and unhelpful ways by making her discontent with ordinary femininity, but leaving her powerless to realize her distinctiveness. The result for the female genius is the danger of perpetual solitude, given the difficulty of finding any outlet for her abilities.

Nevertheless, Wollstonecraft found positive aspects in appropriating genius for women that counterbalanced its potential deficiencies. Most obviously, genius was potentially free from restrictive gender associations.[14] As Christine Battersby has demonstrated, although eighteenth-century writers assumed that geniuses were men, they tended to describe them as feminized ones: "Before the eighteenth century there had been a direct link between the word 'genius' and male fertility; now 'genius' was presented as both an expression of, and a threat to, maleness. Genius was seen to feminise the male body and mind."[15] For example, in *An Essay on Original Genius*, William Duff describes the poetic genius as metaphorically female: "A glowing ardor of Imagination is indeed . . . the very soul of Poetry. It is the principal source of INSPIRATION; and the Poet who is possessed of it, like the *Delphian* Priestess, is animated with a kind of DIVINE FURY."[16] Drawing on a long tradition associating femininity with loss of self-possession and control, he compares the genius to the inspired priestess at Delphi. Duff's genius inherits a mode of femininity that the proper bourgeois femininity of the eighteenth century strove to erase: femininity as monstrous, uncontrolled, undisciplined, and excessive. At the same time, as Battersby notes, genius was still supposed to belong to biological males, even though they might have feminized traits.

Proof of geniuses' gender deviance, for eighteenth-century theorists, was that they were supposedly unsuited for marriage. Duff refused to believe that geniuses could be tied down by any conventions: "Every species of original Genius delights to range at liberty... This noble talent knows no law, and acknowledges none in the uncultivated ages of the world, excepting its own spontaneous impulse, which it obeys without control."[17] While he does not mention marriage specifically, the absence is itself telling: genius has no need for domesticity. Isaac D'Israeli's *Manners and Genius of the Literary Character* made explicit what was implicit in Duff: "I remark that many of the conspicuous blemishes of some of our great compositions may reasonably be attributed to the domestic infelicities of their authors."[18] Marriage, by imposing trivial cares and anxieties on the genius, led to "blemishes" on what otherwise would have been even more perfect works.

The freedom of genius from conventional class hierarchies, gender categories, and marriageability meant that the category offered Wollstonecraft a rare space for experimentation with sexual roles. The result was her extraordinary novel *Mary, A Fiction*, the first attempt by anyone to represent a female genius. Wollstonecraft was quite plain that the heroine of her novel was meant to be a genius. In her letter to the Reverend Henry Dyson Gabell, she explains that she wrote it to illustrate "that a genius will educate itself."[19] She borrowed this thesis from Rousseau and indicated her further indebtedness to his treatment of genius with her novel's epigraph by him, "L'exercice des plus sublimes vertus élève et nourrit le génie" [The exercise of the most sublime virtues elevates and nourishes genius]" (M 1:3). Throughout the novel she makes clear that her heroine Mary is meant to embody this genius: "Her joys, her ecstasies, arose from genius" (M 1:16); "Genius animated her expressive countenance" (M 1:33); "The exercise of her various virtues gave vigor to her genius" (M 1:35); "Her genius, and cultivation of mind, roused his curiosity" (M 1:60).

As her Advertisement to the novel emphasizes, Wollstonecraft is quite aware of how daring she was in representing a female genius: "In delineating the Heroine of this Fiction, the Author attempts to develop a character different from those generally portrayed . . . In a fiction, such a being may be allowed to exist; whose grandeur is derived from the operations of its own faculties, not subjugated to opinion; but drawn by the individual from the original source" (M 1:5). Mary, in other words, possesses originality, the most distinctive trait of genius. Wollstonecraft registers this originality partly by distinguishing Mary from the female character as "generally portrayed." Wollstonecraft satirizes such a conventional female character in her treatment of Mary's mother: "Her voice was but the shadow of a sound, and she had, to complete her delicacy, so relaxed her nerves, that she became a mere nothing" (M 1:7). Mary, the female genius, is the opposite: her original voice is loudly heard, and she acts with an energy and decisiveness that prevent anyone from dismissing her as a nothing.

Consequently, just as the male genius of the eighteenth-century theorists is feminized, so Wollstonecraft's female genius is masculinized. In letting Mary take on the gender-questioning status of genius, Wollstonecraft revises the long misogynistic tradition of female masculinity.[20] In eighteenth-century satire, female masculinity was a convenient and seemingly inexhaustible satirical target in the person of the virago, who was usually characterized by excessive and violent behavior, somewhat like Wollstonecraft-as-Amazon in Godwin's *Memoirs*. In some cases, as in Samuel Richardson's Mrs. Sinclair in *Clarissa* or Henry Fielding's representation of Mary Hamilton in *The Female Husband*, such women were associated with desire for other women, but female masculinity never automatically signaled same-gender desire. It could also suggest asexuality (lack of interest in any sexual activity) or, in some cases, hyper-sexuality (a frenetic desire for partners of any stamp). Throughout the century, male satirists endlessly abused female masculinity and female same-gender desire in tones ranging from the amused to the outraged. In *Mary*, Wollstonecraft uses female genius to turn this long tradition on its head.

Specifically, Wollstonecraft reinvents female masculinity as a positive trait. In the novel, Mary's positive masculinity is established by contrasting her energy and decisiveness with the passivity and sickliness of her love objects, Ann and Henry, who are both invalids. For example, when Henry tries to convince her that she might one day be reconciled with her husband, she responds with a force and certainty not found in traditional eighteenth-century heroines: "My opinions on some subjects are not wavering; my pursuit through life has ever been the same: in solitude were my sentiments formed; they are indelible, and nothing can efface them but death–No, death itself cannot efface them, or my soul must be created afresh, and not improved" (M 1:46). At this moment, Mary's masculinity resides not in dressing like a man or in violently assaulting men but in having strong, original opinions to which she adheres in the face of conventional wisdom.[21]

Since one of Mary's original opinions is that she has no obligation to endure the masquerade of a loveless marriage, the novel supports eighteenth-century theorists like Duff and D'Israeli in treating marriage as completely inadequate to genius. Mary is trapped by her parents into an arranged marriage and soon finds it to be "a dreadful misfortune" and a "heavy yoke" (M 1:22). Wollstonecraft is not simply making a point about the oppressiveness of marriage. She is entering into the familiar eighteenth-century insistence that marriage enchains genius. As many critics have noted, the real focus of Mary's passion is not her conventionally loveless relation to her husband but her unconventional love for her friend Ann: "Her friendship for Ann occupied her heart, and resembled a passion" (M 1:25). Wollstonecraft's message is plain: the passion of geniuses exceeds the boundaries imposed by common practice, and a female genius is more interested in loving another woman than in settling down to a bourgeois marriage.

Although some critics have tried to lessen Wollstonecraft's daring by arguing that a female–female attachment was not remarkable in the eighteenth century, Wollstonecraft's novel suggests otherwise.[22] Faced with Ann's declining health, Mary despairs to a group of "fashionable ladies": "I have no other friend; if I lose her, what a desart will the world be to me." When they drily respond, "Have you not a husband?" Mary "shrunk back, and was alternately pale and red. A delicate sense of propriety prevented her replying; and recalled her bewildered reason" (M 1:32). The ladies' question brings Mary up short by confronting her with the social unacceptability of her feelings for Ann. In the face of their assumption that care for a husband takes precedence over care for another woman, Mary remains silent, pointedly refusing to affirm their standards of feminine feeling and behavior.

As Claudia Johnson has demonstrated, Mary's love for Henry, which develops after the death of Ann, does not reject her love for another woman but continues it.[23] The narrative explicitly aligns her feelings for Henry with her feelings for Ann, as when Mary tells Henry: "Talk not of comfort... it will be in heaven with thee and Ann" (M 1:67). Both loves are illicit because neither Henry nor Ann is Mary's husband. In accordance with the traditional eighteenth-century characterization of genius, marriage is the last place in which a genius will be able to find true partnership. Even when Mary is involved in a heterosexual relationship, it still struggles against the restrictions of bourgeois convention. For the female genius, sexuality is inherently transgressive because the mores of society are completely inadequate to her desires. The gender of the object of desire may be less important than the impossibility of containing that desire within acceptable social forms.

After *Mary*, when Wollstonecraft turned to political writings, her approach to genius and its encouragement of unconventional sexual roles changed dramatically. Genius was less useful to her in these writings because she needed to describe ordinary men and women so that she could make broadly applicable political arguments. Often, she downplayed the language of genius because, as she recognized, a belief in it could have dangerous political consequences in the wrong hands. For example, in her *Historical and Moral View of the French Revolution*, she admits that "there is a superiority of natural genius among men" and that "in countries the most free there will always be distinctions proceeding from superiority of judgement." Yet she goes on to argue that even though only a few have such natural genius, the state nevertheless must educate everyone because "the advantages of civilization cannot be felt, unless it pervades the whole mass" (HMV 6:220). She counters the position that education belongs only to those with genius because, in her eyes, everyone is "susceptible of common improvement" (HMV 6:220). To concentrate on genius would depoliticize her work or make it antidemocratic because she would be seeming to argue for qualities possessed only by a few. Even as she wishes to identify herself as belonging to that few, she is concerned that such a privileging of genius would leave the ordinary person without education or rights.

In *A Vindication of the Rights of Woman*, Wollstonecraft similarly concentrates on the average mind rather than the exceptional one and therefore, for the most part, avoids the vocabulary of genius: "I have confined my observations to such as universally act upon the morals and manners of the whole sex" (VRW 5:145). Yet she cannot let genius go altogether. For example, when she is about to discuss the importance of educating even ordinary minds, she pauses for a short rhapsody:

> The understanding, it is true, may keep us from going out of drawing when we group our thoughts, or transcribe from the imagination the warm sketches of fancy; but the animal spirits, the individual character, give the colouring. Over this subtile electric fluid, how little power do we possess, and over it how little power can reason obtain! These fine intractable spirits appear to be the essence of genius, and beaming in its eagle eye, produce in the most eminent degree the happy energy of associating thoughts that surprise, delight, and instruct. These are the glowing minds that concentrate pictures for their fellow-creatures; forcing them to view with interest the objects reflected from the impassioned imagination, which they passed over in nature.
>
> (VRW 5:185–6)

Although Wollstonecraft attributes these traits to "the man of genius" (VRW 5:186), her use of the first-person pronoun in this passage suggests she believes that they apply to her as well. Throughout her description of "the essence of genius," she is careful to follow the eighteenth-century convention whereby genius unsettles obviously gendered language. She skillfully sets off feminized characteristics like the "warm sketches of fancy" with masculinized descriptions like "intractable spirits" so that no one gender has a monopoly on genius's traits. She also uses biological and scientific phrases like "animal spirits" and "subtile electric fluid" to avoid locating genius obviously in one gender. As she describes it, genius has the privilege of avoiding all conventions of categorization.

The sexual implications of Wollstonecraft's identification with genius in *A Vindication of the Rights of Woman* surface only at the margins of her argument. For example, in a footnote, she lists female geniuses whom she admires because they received a "masculine education": "Sappho, Eloisa,

Mrs Macaulay, the Empress of Russia, Madame d'Eon, etc." (VRW 5:146). The list is quite a remarkable one in terms of sexuality: it begins with a woman famous for loving other women and ends with a male-to-female transvestite. Except for Mrs. Macaulay, the sexuality of all these women is characterized by the same association with illicit, extra-marital love that characterized Wollstonecraft's heroine Mary. The footnote is a little flash of the sexual daring that Wollstonecraft's understanding of genius licenses, but it is one that she hides throughout most of *A Vindication of the Rights of Woman*.[24]

Wollstonecraft recognizes that the identification with genius will not help her argument, which has to be about ordinary women and ordinary love. Much as she admires the genius's gender-bending status and sexual freedom, she insists on clearly marked gender roles for men and women in *A Vindication of the Rights of Woman* because she hopes that doing so will prevent the wrong kinds of gender-crossing and sexuality that supposedly come from moral corruption. In her eyes, society has been ruined by the growth of tyrannical women, who represent the very mode of female masculinity that she was revising in *Mary*, and effeminately sensual men, who "attend the levees of equivocal beings, to sigh for more than female languor" (VRW 5:208). She pushes her rejection of genius so far that *A Vindication of the Rights of Woman* rejects sexual desire. For Wollstonecraft, rational friendship should replace love: "Friendship is a serious affection; the most sublime of all affections, because it is founded on principle, and cemented by time. The very reverse may be said of love" (VRW 5:142).[25] In moving from the private arena of *Mary* to the public one of *A Vindication of the Rights of Woman*, Wollstonecraft discovers that genius shares too much with forms of sexuality that she needs to stigmatize to be useful to her.

After this politicized rejection of genius, however, Wollstonecraft returned to the category and its possibilities for sexual experimentation in her great unfinished novel *The Wrongs of Woman*. In it, she politicizes genius in a way that she had not done either in *Mary* or in *A Vindication of the Rights of Woman* by using it to characterize women's relationship to sex. As in *Mary*, she is indebted to the eighteenth-century theorists of genius, but, also as in *Mary*, she takes their ideas in entirely new directions. Among politically progressive writers, it was a commonplace that genius depended on liberty. In his *Lectures on Rhetoric*, Hugh Blair paraphrases Longinus to argue that oratory flourishes only in a free state: "Liberty, he remarks, is the nurse of true genius; it animates the spirit, and invigorates the hopes of men; excites honourable emulation, and a desire of excelling in every art." He adds that "all other qualifications . . . you may find among those who are deprived of liberty; but never did a slave become an orator; he can only be a pompous flatterer."[26] In *The Wrongs of Woman*, Wollstonecraft adapts Blair to make his politicization of liberty matter to female sexual experience.

To do so, she alters her understanding of genius from something belonging only to an exceptional individual to a capacity available to all who can exercise their minds at liberty. Whereas Mary was always a genius, Maria experiences an influx of genius only when she briefly frees herself from an oppressive situation. In general, Maria is "a woman of sensibility, with an improving mind" (WWM 1:83), but not an exceptional genius, and she lacks the masculine traits that characterized Mary. Her oppression instead is meant to be typical of all middle-class women; the novel's message depends on the possibility of generalizing from Maria's experience to larger political claims. This typicality might seem to demand avoiding genius as a category, much as Wollstonecraft did in *A Vindication of the Rights of Woman*. Instead, Wollstonecraft connects genius to liberation from constrained heterosexual relations.

In a climactic scene, Maria vows to leave her husband after discovering that he is planning to sell her body. In front of him, she removes her ring and swears to leave his house forever. We might imagine that a woman in such a situation would worry about her future: a place to live, means of support, concern about her reputation. While Maria eventually has to face those worries, her first reaction is quite different. Rather than troubling about details, she rhapsodizes:

> "Was it possible? Was I, indeed, free?"... How I had panted for liberty – liberty, that I would have purchased at any price, but that of my own esteem! I rose, and shook myself; opened the window, and methought the air never smelled so sweet. The face of heaven grew fairer as I viewed it, and clouds seemed to flit away obedient to my wishes, to give my soul room to expand. I was all soul, and (wild as it may appear) felt as if I could have dissolved in the soft balmy gale that kissed my cheek, or have glided below the horizon on the glowing, descending beams. A seraphic satisfaction animated, without agitating my spirits; and my imagination collected, in visions sublimely terrible, or soothingly beautiful, an immense variety of the endless images, which nature affords, and fancy combines, of the grand and fair.   (WWM 1:152–3)

It would be easy to dismiss this passage as one more sentimental effusion so common in late eighteenth-century texts, but doing so would miss the point. This passage is not a stock bit of sentiment but a demonstration that aesthetic capacities depend on political ones. While subject to "ignoble thraldom" (WWM 1:156) in the form of her tyrannical husband, Maria's imaginative abilities wither. As soon as she frees herself, she feels less that she has taken the moral high ground than that she has soared to imaginative heights. Rather than being a genius, like Mary, Maria experiences a moment of "true sensibility, the sensibility which is the auxiliary of virtue, and the soul of genius" (WWM 1:163).

The passage is memorable because it is virtually the only moment of real happiness that Maria experiences. It is also, metaphorically, the best sex she has in the whole novel. Evidently, the "soul of genius" is a highly erotic one. Having just rejected the empty sexuality to which her husband would have sold her, she experiences the figurative sexuality of genius, which is far more complete. Feeling her soul expand, she longs to dissolve in the gale that kisses her cheek, glide on descending beams, and enjoy "seraphic satisfaction." It is especially notable, given Wollstonecraft's mistrust of passion in *A Vindication of the Rights of Woman*, that Maria emphasizes that her spirits are not agitated. While in *A Vindication of the Rights of Woman*, Wollstonecraft could recommend only a passionless friendship between men and women, the "soul of genius" in *The Wrongs of Woman* experiences passion that carries none of the dangers of heterosexual romance. Instead, a "calm delight" is "diffused" through Maria's heart, a far cry from the bitterness and suffering produced by her husband or the tumult caused by Darnford. No man can offer the erotic satisfaction that Wollstonecraft suggests that nature can give to a woman inspired by genius.

In this scene, Wollstonecraft translates the politics of genius into the concrete situation of women's relationship to sex. Sex with men in *The Wrongs of Woman* is uniformly a disaster because it is fundamentally unfree and therefore chokes a woman's capacity for genius. Much of the pathos of the passage describing Maria's vision is that she will never again experience the erotic transport she here describes. She is soon locked in a madhouse by her husband, where she becomes a prey to desperation and melancholy, and consequently turns to the untrustworthy Darnford. When describing Maria's affair with Darnford, Wollstonecraft is careful to emphasize that "true sensibility" is not at work but a deluded, fevered imagination: "The heart is often shut by romance against social pleasure; and, fostering a sickly sensibility, grows callous to the soft touches of humanity" (WWM 1:177). The fragility of Maria's possession of genius allows Wollstonecraft to demonstrate the fundamental lack of freedom that conditions normative sexual relations in her society.

It is also a reminder that men, and even other people, are hardly necessary to provide women with satisfactory erotic experience. A woman of genius may find, as Maria does, that her own liberated imagination provides more satisfaction than does the seeming romantic hero Darnford. Wollstonecraft revises the asexuality sometimes associated with masculine women into this erotically fulfilling fantasy of a transfigurative relationship to nature. The tragedy of the novel is that women are not allowed to enjoy this liberated imagination for long because the forces conspiring to imprison them are so powerful. But in this one passage, Wollstonecraft glimpses a utopian sexual possibility, an eroticism that is genuine but not implicated in the impossible tangles of human relations. Genius has its own sexuality that refuses to fit into ready patterns of social acceptability.

The challenge of bringing together "woman" and "genius" thus leads Wollstonecraft to reject the privileging of bourgeois marriage as the only acceptable mode of sexuality. In *Mary*, she suggests that a female genius is as likely to favor a female object of desire as a male one; in *Wrongs of Woman*, she suggests that women can experience genius only when they have escaped the bondage of men, and that doing so provides more erotic satisfaction than physical sex. More subtly, in her *A Vindication of the Rights of Woman*, she suggests that she herself aspires to the gender-questioning authority of genius and the sexual freedom that accompanies it, even as she recognizes the need to ground her argument in firm gender distinctions and sexual roles. Although there is no discourse of sexuality to which Wollstonecraft responds, the discourse of genius leads her to treatments of sexuality quite unlike those of any other eighteenth-century writer.

For later women writers, Wollstonecraft made it possible to take seriously a woman who claimed the authority of genius. With this claim came new experimental possibilities, especially in relation to female sexuality. As the bourgeois couple became ever more normative in the nineteenth century, the character of the female genius became virtually the only site through which women writers could seriously question the assumed inevitability of marriage. This questioning had a cost: female geniuses rarely lived happily ever after, or, if they did, they usually had to give up some of the qualities that made them seem like geniuses. Yet, as Wollstonecraft had also shown, a woman writer was not obliged to strive for happy endings. She would have agreed with another writer who claimed genius for himself, Oscar Wilde, that such endings were terribly unfair, especially for women whose abilities gave them the right to expect something more than conventional domestic happiness.

NOTES

1. For useful backgrounds to eighteenth-century sexuality, see Terry Castle, *The Apparitional Lesbian: Female Homosexuality and Modern Culture* (New York: Columbia University Press, 1993); Emma Donoghue, *Passions Between Women: British Lesbian Culture, 1668–1801* (London: Scarlet Press, 1993); Anthony Fletcher, *Gender, Sex, and Subordination in England, 1500–1800* (New Haven: Yale University Press, 1995); Michael McKeon, "Historicizing Patriarchy: the

Emergence of Gender Difference in England, 1660–1760," *Eighteenth-Century Studies* 28 (1995), 295–322; Lisa L. Moore, *Dangerous Intimacies: Toward a Sapphic History of the British Novel* (Durham: Duke University Press, 1997), 1–21; Randolph Trumbach, *Sex and the Gender Revolution* (Chicago: University of Chicago Press, 1998).

2. For this analysis, see Claudia L. Johnson, *Equivocal Beings: Politics, Gender, and Sentimentality in the 1790s, Wollstonecraft, Radcliffe, Burney, Austen* (Chicago: University of Chicago Press, 1995), 23–46.

3. Godwin, *Memoirs of the Author of The Rights of Woman* (published together with Mary Wollstonecraft, *A Short Residence in Sweden, Norway and Denmark*), ed. Richard Holmes (Harmondsworth, Middlesex: Penguin, 1987), 231.

4. See Valerie Traub, "The (In)significance of 'Lesbian' Desire in Early Modern England," *Erotic Politics: Desire on the Renaissance Stage*, ed. Susan Zimmerman (New York: Routledge, 1992), 150–69; Elizabeth Susan Wahl, *Invisible Relations: Representations of Female Intimacy in the Age of Enlightenment* (Stanford: Stanford University Press, 1999).

5. Maria Edgeworth, *Belinda*, ed. Kathryn Kirkpatrick (Oxford: Oxford University Press, 1994), 229. For discussion, see Moore, *Dangerous Intimacies*, 75–108.

6. Claire Tomalin, *The Life and Death of Mary Wollstonecraft*, rev. edn. (Harmondsworth, Middlesex: Penguin, 1992), 121–30.

7. Emily Sunstein, *A Different Face: the Life of Mary Wollstonecraft* (New York: Harper and Row, 1975), 203–4.

8. Richard Holmes, *Footsteps: Adventures of a Romantic Biographer* (Harmondsworth, Middlesex: Penguin, 1985), 92–3.

9. Bridget Hill, "The Links between Mary Wollstonecraft and Catherine Macaulay: New Evidence," *Women's History Review* 4 (1995), 177–92.

10. Tomalin, *Life and Death of Mary Wollstonecraft*, 151–2.

11. Wollstonecraft, letter to Everina Wollstonecraft, 12 February 1787, in Letters, 138; Hugh Blair, *Lectures on Rhetoric and Belles Lettres* (Philadelphia: James Kay, 1844), 3 vols. (facsimile edition; New York: Garland, 1970), 1:52.

12. Wollstonecraft, letter to Everina Wollstonecraft, 3 March 1787, Letters, 140.

13. See Blair, *Lectures*, 1:52–3.

14. The argument in the next two paragraphs is indebted to my discussion of genius in *Romantic Genius: the Prehistory of a Homosexual Role* (New York: Columbia University Press, 1999), chapter 1.

15. Christine Battersby, *Gender and Genius: Towards a Feminist Aesthetics* (Bloomington: Indiana University Press, 1989), 86.

16. William Duff, *An Essay on Original Genius*, ed. John L. Mahoney (facsimile edition; Gainesville: Scholars' Facsimiles, 1964), 171.

17. Ibid., 283.

18. Isaac D'Israeli, *An Essay on the Manners and Genius of the Literary Character* (facsimile edition; New York: Garland, 1970), 58.

19. Wollstonecraft, letter to Rev. Henry Dyson Gabell, 13 September 1787, Letters, 162.

20. On eighteenth-century female masculinity, see Judith Halberstam, *Female Masculinity* (Durham: Duke University Press, 1998), chapter 2.

21. For more on Mary's masculinity and her relationships with Ann and Henry, see Johnson, *Equivocal Beings*, 48–58, and Ashley Tauchert, "Escaping Discussion:

Liminality and the Female-Embodied Couple in Mary Wollstonecraft's *Mary, A Fiction*," *Romanticism on the Net* 18 (May 2000), June 10 2000 <http://users.ox.ac.uk/~scato385/18tauchert.html>.

22. See in particular Gary Kelly, who notes, "Such homosocial intensity was and is not uncommon, was licensed to a degree by social convention at that time, and was indeed encouraged in the culture of Sensibility" ("[Female] Philosophy in the Bedroom: Mary Wollstonecraft and Female Sexuality," *Women's Writing* 4 [1997], 143–53; 148).

23. Johnson, *Equivocal Beings*, 56–7.

24. See Tauchert, "Escaping Discussion."

25. On heterosexual desire in Wollstonecraft, see Cora Kaplan, "Pandora's Box: Subjectivity, Class, and Sexuality in Socialist-Feminist Criticism," *British Feminist Thought: a Reader*, ed. Terry Lovell (Oxford: Blackwell, 1990), 345–66.

26. Blair, *Lectures*, 2:180.

14

CORA KAPLAN

Mary Wollstonecraft's reception and legacies

Virginia Woolf, in 1929, described Mary Wollstonecraft's remarkable "form of immortality" through the memorable conceit that "she is alive and active, she argues and experiments, we hear her voice and trace her influence even now among the living."[1] A strong sense of unfinished business hovers about Wollstonecraft's legacy – the effects of a life cut short and a political agenda not yet met, but also of something less straightforward, emanating from the combined – but disjunctive – force of her life and work as well as yoked with the seductive fiction that revolution and romance have some natural and dangerously volatile affinity. For "even now," at the beginning of the twenty-first century, Woolf's perception of an embodied, social and affective presence – "alive . . . among the living" – captures what has proved most enduring but also most troubling about Wollstonecraft's reception, the aura of unreconciled emotion that hovers around her shifting reputation. Wollstonecraft remains an ambiguous symbol both of feminism and of femininity, her significance disputed most strongly by the diverse western feminisms of the last quarter of the twentieth century which have made her and her feminist peers living and legible in her own time and in theirs. Their disagreements have been productive as well as divisive; it is to the credit of Wollstonecraft's interpreters that she remains a restive presence, who cannot be easily framed or honorably laid to rest as the distinguished foremother of modern feminism.

In *A Vindication of the Rights of Woman*, Wollstonecraft argued that women's "virtue is built on mutable prejudices" (VRW 5:171), that fluctuation of opinion which constructs women's understanding of what "virtue" is. "Mutable prejudice" felicitously characterizes the historical mobility of Wollstonecraft's own reception and influence. Her mutable legacies – better thought of perhaps in the plural – have proved a rich but unstable mix of traceable influences and uncanny resemblances. In this essay I pursue some selected strands of those legacies as they have emerged in twentieth-century feminism and in the related commentary of its male fellow travelers, sketching a cognitive map through which we might begin to trace her movements and effects in the more recent history of feminism and modernity.

Curiously, for an author–activist adept in many genres – a career to which many feminists have aspired – up until the last quarter-century Wollstonecraft's life has been read much more closely than her writing, which has sometimes seemed a mere pretext for telling and retelling her personal story. Yet now that her work too has at last received the attention it deserves there is a sense in which she seems to offer the present too much – both an emotional and sexual history whose notoriety has inhibited access to the writing, and a body of work at once so discursively emphatic and elusive that it upsets the tidy categorizations and standard narratives of social, political, and cultural history. Wollstonecraft's standing today is at once higher and less settled than at any time since her reincarnation in the early 1970s as the origin and avatar of western feminism. Late twentieth-century feminism adopted Wollstonecraft as an icon for its success in placing women's rights and sexual difference at the center of social and political debates, and in so doing, making the genealogy of feminist ideas in modernity of interest to a wider public. In the 1970s and 80s when feminist optimism was high, it was hoped that creating a new public forum for issues of gender and sexuality would lead to their speedy and progressive resolution, an outcome that appears less and less likely. Wollstonecraft's legacies do not preside, in any sense at all, over a postfeminist utopia; rather it is the stubborn persistence into the new millennium of those nagging questions about gender, sexuality, and modernity first raised in the late eighteenth century by Wollstonecraft and her contemporaries that has led to the centrality of gender in the current rethinking by historians, literary scholars, political scientists, and philosophers of the mixed origins of modernity.

As a result, women's writing and thought is now taken much more seriously as an object of study by scholars of this period. Wollstonecraft herself is now regularly discussed in relation to a much wider field of women writers and intellectuals than was true a generation ago, yet she has kept her preeminence among them – a fact that would have gratified the woman who so strongly desired to be "first" in friendship, love, and reputation. Wollstonecraft scholarship has played a leading role in a shift, which as Harriet Guest has recently noted, has moved on from "the study of the experience or writings of women as a separate category of literary or historical analysis, and toward the complex involvement of women and of gender difference in all areas of eighteenth-century life and thought."[2] Mary Wollstonecraft herself has slowly but surely become an indispensable figure for thinking through this crucial shaping moment of modernity: the tensions within and between her ideas and her life are seen as indicative of the contradictions thrown up, not just for women but for whole societies, by the entwined but often conflicting impulses of progressive politics in its various forms and the expanding market economy. The problems she posed about the future of gender in modern societies appear both actively in her work, and passively through the interpretations made by subsequent generations of what Woolf called her "experiments in living."

Of all the questions Wollstonecraft asked, and of which she often appears to be the exemplary text, none remain so insistent or so agonistic as those that ask how or whether we should gender and moralize emotion. Increasingly human affect has come to be seen as the key to understanding a whole host of questions about eighteenth-century culture, and by implication, our own. The vocabulary of that eighteenth-century debate – sensibility, sentimentality, and sympathy – are still in such common usage today that we are often too quick to translate the eighteenth-century debates into our own meanings and values. Yet although their context and meaning have altered, there are striking continuities. Sentimentality in particular continues to function, rather as it did in the last decades of the eighteenth century, as a kind of moral and aesthetic watershed, the supposed dividing line between true and false feelings as they are expressed by individuals and by groups, and as they are represented in works of art. (Claudia Johnson has noted, for example, the "ritual acts of disavowal" which have prefaced critical work on the "sentimental fiction of the 1790s", as if critics must acknowledge the aesthetic inferiority of such affect-drenched prose for their analyses to be taken seriously.[3]) The reactionaries and rebels of the eighteenth-century world that Wollstonecraft inhabited were engaged in lengthy, nuanced discussions about the character, causes, and consequence of human affect. Rousseau pinned his hopes of a free and just society on its supposed asymmetry in men and women; the young Edmund Burke hung his influential aesthetic theories on just such a lop-sided psychology, while Adam Smith made the affinity between self-love and sympathy the basis of both the social bond and the rivalrous commerce that he thought would ensure the wealth and coexistence of nations. These old arguments continue to mutate and resonate, so much so that while not every revaluation of Wollstonecraft's work and reputation in the twentieth century makes the question of emotion central, we can in retrospect see that most biographical and critical comments do address her shifting perspective on gendered feeling.

This essay will focus on Wollstonecraft's mixed reception and complex influence in the late twentieth century but her treatment in the early twentieth century provides a necessary and revealing starting point. Woolf's celebration of Wollstonecraft, for example, is one decisive sign of the positive turn in her reception by feminists. Wollstonecraft had provided a lifeline as well as a foil for nineteenth-century feminism, which sometimes chose to promote its legitimacy through a vociferous disavowal of her scandalous life. When her rehabilitation began, in the later part of that century, it was painfully slow. Rediscovery by twentieth-century feminists whose agendas placed sexual and emotional freedom among the most important rights of woman radically shifted the terms in which she would be received. It is not surprising to see that Wollstonecraft is a heroine for such disparate sexual radicals as Virginia Woolf and Emma Goldman,[4] appropriated by them for the very different iconoclasms of Bloomsbury and international anarchism, but it is striking that for each of them Wollstonecraft's life is the more enduring and interesting text.[5]

Goldman's imagination was most taken with Wollstonecraft's tragic passion for Imlay, rather than the "sweet and tender camaraderie" of her liaison with Godwin, whom she credits with being "the first representative of Anarchist Communism."[6] She puts the priority of biography at its most extreme: "Had Mary Wollstonecraft not written a line, her life would have furnished food for thought" (Goldman, "Tragic Life," 256). Woolf, too is gripped by Mary's unhappy love affair with Imlay, and she cannot resist interpreting its dynamic, rather even-handedly too, with sympathy for both parties, but her identification is, predictably, with Wollstonecraft's companionate and intellectually egalitarian alliance: Wollstonecraft's relation with Godwin was her "most fruitful experiment" (Woolf, "Four Figures," 163). Neither Goldman nor Woolf in their short essays dwell on the specifics of Wollstonecraft's feminism as expressed in her writing. For them, what had become standard, if by no means fully realized, demands for educational and legal parity seemed to need no further glossing or scrutiny – "their originality has become our commonplace" says Woolf ("Four Figures," 158) – and each felt quite free to reinvent Wollstonecraft as their contemporary. Goldman's Mary is a universalist, a vanguard figure very much in Goldman's own image, fighting as she did, as much for the affective and sexual "freedom for the whole human race" as for its civil and economic rights; Mary/Emma is the pathfinder and pioneer, whose life "proves that economic and social rights for women alone are not enough . . . to fill any deep life, man or woman."(Goldman, "Tragic Life," 251) The moving rhetoric of romantic radicalism slips too easily into the hackneyed language of sensation fiction. In an unconscious parody of Wollstonecraft's own intermittent resort to an overripe language of sensibility, Goldman endows Mary with a "burning, yearning soul," a spirit which "reached out to great heights" and which also "drained the cup of tragedy." (250–1) For Goldman, Wollstonecraft's life represented the extreme difficulty, perhaps the ultimate impossibility, of combining high passion and political and intellectual work, of living successfully at the edge of feeling. Goldman's idealization of Mary's near fatal passion for Imlay rather than for the more politically sympathetic Godwin, reflects her own mixed experience of liaisons within the anarchist movement, and her limited success in persuading leading male figures in the movement as a whole that the cause of sexual freedom should be high on their agenda. In an oblique rebuke to their skepticism she exalts such passion as an extreme example of libertarian thinking, giving a kind of nobility to *not* surviving "the tempest" of "infatuation" and unrequited love. Almost glorying in Mary's defeat in "the struggle between her intellect and her passion," Goldman interprets her relationship with Imlay as a high moment of reckless but sublime excess that her life with Godwin could not repair or replace (256). Choosing a therapeutic figure, at once maternal and asexual, Goldman imagines the liaison with Godwin as "a cold hand upon a burning forehead" (256). A further and more final cooling follows. Wollstonecraft's death becomes, for Goldman, fortuitous and exemplary, as well as a fate that waits for romantics of any period or gender, since "he who has ever tasted the madness of life can never again adjust himself to an even tenor" (256).

Writing some years later, Woolf implicitly associates Mary with the profound changes wrought by World War I, so that her essay begins with the general comment that "Great wars are strangely intermittent in their effects," leaving the lives and attitudes of some individuals untouched, but utterly transforming others ("Four Figures," 156). In Wollstonecraft's case the "Revolution . . . was not merely an event that had happened outside her; it was an active agent in her own blood," a catalyst, Woolf thought, for an already rebellious spirit. In Mary, a lifelong revolt, "against tyranny, against law, against convention" joins personal and political revolt, and finds an "eloquent and daring" expression in her two Vindications (158). It is particularly interesting how "war" and "revolution" as motors of progress and experiment become elided in Woolf's account. The social and political revolution that England did *not* have in the 1790s, and the First World War whose upheaval effected social change but whose overt politics were hardly progressive, are cleverly merged in Woolf's essay, just as her evocation of the sexually egalitarian coteries of the London intelligentsia in the time of the French Revolution seem like costume versions of their early-twentieth-century incarnations. That "party of ill-dressed, excited young men" with "middle-class names" and a woman "with very bright eyes and a very eager tongue" called simply by her surname "as if it did not matter whether she were married or unmarried, as if she were a young man like themselves" which met in Somers Town "over the tea-cups," Woolf's vignette of dissenting circles in North London in the 1790s, calls up the social and intellectual milieu of Gordon Square, in the Bloomsbury of her own time, its middle-class young men and women also deep in those scandalous conversations and experiments which they hoped would demolish the last vestiges of the late Victorian and Edwardian conventions of their parents. (156–7) Wollstonecraft's implied androgyny – "as if she were a young man" – even evokes Woolf's gender-bending protagonist Orlando in her 1928 novel of the same name. As Woolf reimagines Wollstonecraft, it is the "contradictions" in her life and work that fascinate rather than her ideologically driven agenda, however daring, for Mary, says Woolf, was "no pedant, no cold-blooded theorist."(159) Woolf's essay pinpoints those key moments when theory and practice conflict: the pity Mary unexpectedly felt on seeing the Louis XVI that she had reviled in her work on his way to the National Assembly, her incompatible desires both for free love and emotional security. The moment of Louis's downfall, when Wollstonecraft "saw the most cherished of her convictions put into practice – and her eyes filled with tears" is for Woolf the exemplary instance in which the true complexity of life and the limits of utopian politics are revealed: the point at which the rationality of political belief is undercut by an experience that produces an upsurge of feeling (159). This, perhaps, is Woolf's most interesting insight, but also the one which, as we will see, would become most contested, as Wollstonecraft's tears are reinterpreted as mere sentimentality.

Wollstonecraft's urgent plea to her own and future generations of women in *A Vindication of the Rights of Woman*, her repeated insistence that women must train and exercise their "understanding," is only one strand in her legacy for twentieth-century feminism, and perhaps, taken alone, misleading. More accurate is her opinion that "the most perfect education...is such an exercise of the understanding as is best calculated to strengthen the body and form the heart" (VRW 5:90). The emphasis she placed on education, independence, and rationality was, even at the beginning of the twentieth century, already incorporated into a broadly based agenda for women's emancipation. Much more equivocal – then as now – was the role of "the heart," or affect – the whole spectrum of the emotions from maternal devotion to sexual desire in the reform and liberation of woman. What makes Wollstonecraft often seem so eerily modern to different generations of women are the recurring contexts of radical political agitation and reaction in which the sexual division of the emotions which distinguish femininity from masculinity has been debated. Goldman and Woolf used Wollstonecraft to validate the importance of women's affective life rather than women's equal civil status. Goldman, the activist, thought that romantic excess – "the madness of life" – was both opposed to and unsustainable within the political agendas of what we tend to think of as that most passionate of radical traditions, anarchism. Woolf brings the perspective of the novelist into her analysis, reading the expression of emotion as the beginning of real enlightenment, at the point where one intuitively acknowledges both the complexity and the limits of utopian thinking.

This reinstatement of Mary Wollstonecraft's sexual and emotional "experiments" as the most liberating and progressive elements of her thinking spoke to a concern expressed by many women thinkers, especially women novelists, between the world wars. Getting the vote had opened the door to civil and economic equality, but while sexual mores were changing, emotional and sexual autonomy was still tantalizingly out of reach. By the 1960s and 70s, the years when Wollstonecraft studies started to take off, it was becoming clear that the road to women's economic, social, and political, emancipation was also steeper than had been anticipated and would not be quickly solved merely by access to the polling booth. Resisting a call to return to their proper place in the home, more women were entering the workforce, and more were in white collar and professional occupations, which were nevertheless still male strongholds. The immediate postwar period, in both Britain and the United States, was marked by the resurgence of social, political, and sexual conservatism that frequently follows the more liberal and liberated regimes of wartime, a conservatism that championed the expansion of women's education, at least in the United States, but also targeted, in the popular press and in social policy, women's failure to find marriage and reproduction an adequate career as perverse and even pathological. This oddly contradictory stance, promoting university education for women, but preferring that its benefits equip them to be civic wives and mothers rather than independent professionals, has its parallels in Wollstonecraft's own temperate approach to such issues in *Rights of Woman*. In this climate of social conservatism, with the Cold War looming but before the surging tide of postwar feminism, Wollstonecraft emerges as an inspiring heroine for postwar liberals of both sexes, her life and career evoking a kind of revolutionary golden age, newly labeled as the age of democratic revolutions to distinguish them from later, tainted socialist revolution. Mary's enthusiasm for, as well as her critique of, the French Revolution could now be positioned as a more emotionally appealing alternative to what liberal Americans and Britons increasingly saw as the repressive, frigid post-revolutionary societies of the Soviet bloc. Reacting against, but also influenced by, this increasingly conservative national mood, a new and major biography of Wollstonecraft came out of the American midwest, written by an academic based at the University of Omaha and published by the University of Kansas Press in 1951.

Ralph Wardle's *Mary Wollstonecraft: a Critical Biography* treats her writing seriously, and its final pages emphasize, rightly, the discontinuous history of feminist thought, but it ends by contradicting the evidence he provides on her mixed reception in the nineteenth century and minimizing the direct effect of Wollstonecraft's writing on the generations that succeeded her, by arguing that although she was a pioneer, her work had "little traceable influence on the course of female emancipation."[7] *A Vindication of the Rights of Woman*, Wardle thought, was an "original, if not an influential, book" but it was "Mary's personality that has kept her memory alive. Surely dozens of readers have thrilled to her history or been fired by her example for every one who has read his way through *Rights of Woman*" (341). And Wardle, who had himself objected that earlier champions had made her unrecognizably into a "saintly lady" (339) sums her up, equally incredibly, in the soft-focus language of idealistic postwar Hollywood heroines, who, "once she had rid herself of the brashness displayed in the years of her first successes" became, "above all, a woman of personal charm . . . not the placid charm which rises from beauty and graciousness alone; it was the positive, energetic charm of a courageous woman eager to serve humanity" (341). The woman was never "mean" or "dull," but *Rights of Woman*, Wardle implies, is still a daunting, difficult read – while the life has the appeal of popular film or genre fiction, but with an improving political message. Yet his biography does highlight Mary's intellectual and political trajectory. Rather like Woolf, Wardle celebrates Wollstonecraft's fusion of political, social, and emotional rebellion; like Woolf it is the persona that he in part invents rather than the texts before him that stirs his imagination.

Wardle's interest in Wollstonecraft during the socially and politically conservative 1950s did not strike a collective chord for almost another generation, until the "second wave" of the women's movement adopted Wollstonecraft as foremother and sometime heroine. As one critic has remarked, Wollstonecraft has been, if anything, "over-biographied" and never more so than in the 1970s when six studies of her life appeared in just six years – by Margaret George (1970), Edna Nixon (1971), Eleanor Flexner (1972), Emily Sunstein (1975), Claire Tomalin (1974), and Margaret Tims (1976) – so many indeed, that we might cynically see some of them as responding at least as much to a publishing opportunity as to a cause. Feminism sought and found an audience of women readers, but publishers eagerly built on the rarely flattering and often sensational public image of the women's movement, to buy and commission more books by and about women in general, targeting not only an appetitive younger feminist readership, but cleverly catering for women who were anxious about the turn which postwar feminism was taking. But six biographies in as many years speak to more than commercial opportunism. Mary's life suddenly becomes an incendiary precedent for what postwar feminism sometimes implied it was inventing anew. Her story revised the more airbrushed accounts of feminism's history revealing its deep roots in a wider political context. But something remains disturbingly hidden in this sudden excess of biography, as if Wollstonecraft's life must be repeated again and again, more like a symptom that conceals a fear, a symptom that must be expressed but not named, than an heroic and tragic story whose time for retelling had come.

While Wollstonecraft's life was being introduced to a new generation of women readers the paradox that she was often seen to represent – the passionate life in apposition to the radical and rationalist agenda – was being summarized in the best-known slogan of the Women's Movement. "The personal is political" became the gnomic catchphrase of feminism in the seventies, not, as is sometimes said, a license for unrestrained individualism or the self-indulgence of confession, but as a challenge to political discourses that were unwilling to debate the traditional divisions of labor in the home, violence against women, or the contested issues of sexuality and reproductive rights. The slogan itself spawned vigorous but also productive disagreement about what constituted a politically progressive "personal" agenda. Feminists who were at heart social conservatives shunned the sexual libertarianism of artistic and cultural avant gardes, disliked the sixties for its dangerous mix of sex, drugs, radical politics, and rock and roll, and worried that postwar feminisms were incorporating aspects of the politics of pleasure into its cultural sensibility rather than just critiquing its misogyny. But even among women who really welcomed the more emotionally and sexually expressive culture of the seventies, there were residual anxieties about the place of sexuality and emotion on the feminist agenda. Of the major strands of competing white feminisms of the seventies – liberal, radical, and socialist – both liberal feminism, with its emphasis on equality within existing capitalist democracies, and socialist feminism, with its more far-reaching analysis of the relationship between women's oppression and free-market economics were dedicated, if in slightly different ways, to rationality as the basis for the parity between men and women. Initially at least, the equal capacity to reason was associated with feminism's ethical claims for full civic subjectivity for women – rationality provided the imprimatur both for women's equal footing in the existing liberal humanism of Western democracies and for their equal participation in socialist alternatives. The largely unexamined, commonsense assumption of this argument is that reason and feeling are compartmentalized aspects of mental life, that they exist in direct proportion to each other, and that a necessary balance between them is destabilized when emotion overcomes reason. Following this train of thought, too great an emphasis on sexual freedoms, including homosexuality as well as permissive heterosexuality, might act as a diversion from the main priorities and alienate just those women – and men – that they wished to persuade.

Wollstonecraft's life, read in this context, seemed somehow to illustrate this half-recognized conundrum that continued to fascinate biographers and their readers, but it could simultaneously appall. This latter response is conspicuous in the most conservative of the Wollstonecraft biographies of this period. By 1973, in the American Penguin edition of Eleanor Flexner's *Mary Wollstonecraft*, publisher and author seem at once to be exploiting Wollstonecraft's life and distancing themselves from its supposed transgressive elements, now seen to be taken further forward by what the popular press and academic social conservatives, each identified as the "extremism" of modern feminism. Flexner, author of the groundbreaking *Century of Struggle: the Woman's Rights Movement in the United States* (1959) is quoted in the front-of-book blurb as a self-described "moderate" who "vehemently favors equal rights, equal opportunity, and equal pay for women."[8] This dry list of political and economic aims, tactically lubricated only by the adjective "vehemently," inserted to show that the biographer too had her political passions, very deliberately excluded an endorsement of forms of sexual radicalism. Flexner's conclusion emphasizes Mary's advocacy of "rational thought" for men and women, and her call to conventional forms of duty – "the duty of being human, of being women – as mothers and wives as well as citizens. Mary Wollstonecraft's own life, except for the few occasions when she strayed to the verge of aberration, exemplified that belief. It is surely not irrelevant today" (Flexner, *Biography*, 266). Mary's "aberrations" are not restricted to her emotional excesses but also to her egotism – Mary's treatment of her sisters and her adopted daughter Ann as well as her desperate attachment to Imlay are, says Flexner, hard to "explain" or "understand." Flexner's "psychological" portrait has it both ways, reproducing the scandal in loving detail, but moralizing Wollstonecraft's life so that her "aberrations" can retrospectively serve both as negative examples and minor hiccups in an otherwise exemplary career. In this way she can be rewritten as an appropriate origin for a sanitized, and fairly conventional, liberal feminism. Flexner is as severe on the writing as on the life, finding *A Vindication of the Rights of Woman* alarmingly full of digressions, and interpreting what she calls Wollstonecraft's inability "to follow a consistent train of thought" a sign of Mary's lack of education. Her pedantic judgment reads like a school report: "She is incapable either of the coherent organization of ideas or of avoiding repetition" (Flexner, *Biography*, 164). Nor did Mary's novels rescue her: "she had no talent whatever for writing fiction" (249). This monitory tone infantilizes Wollstonecraft, replacing the high-minded if less-than-readable stylist of Wardle's biography, with that of an undisciplined and wayward teenager, full of grandiose plans and chaotic desires: melodramatically emotional, man-chasing, mean to her relatives, failing her lessons – in short exhibiting all those symptoms of adolescent femininity that never fail to irritate – and frighten – adults. There is an issue about class and gentility embedded in this portrait also; Mary's lack of formal education does not, for Flexner, make her a successful autodidact, but more like a disadvantaged twentieth-century daughter, too poor to be sent to college where strict training would smooth the rough edges, fill in the intellectual gaps, and teach her an acceptable prose style. Her life and work are offered to the impressionable reader as a cautionary tale with an oblique health warning against the undisciplined rhetoric and emotion equally visible in her actions and her prose: the causal connection between the two never quite stated but always implied. There is a calculated echo here, for any reader of the second *Vindication* of Wollstonecraft herself, who voiced the common view among reforming women – both radicals and conservatives – that women were peculiarly vulnerable to the corrupting influence of badly written sensational fiction whose "stale tales and meretricious scenes" (cliche and inauthenticity combined) could inflame the imagination, leading readers into "actual vice" (VRW 5:256). In Flexner's own imagination, the "aberrant" side of Mary, which includes her incoherent writings, becomes just such a "meretricious" but dangerously active text.

We cannot fully understand the nervous moralizing with which Flexner, the self-designated feminist moderate, approached the subject to which she was also so attracted without exploring further the context in which it was being composed. For in spite of the undercurrent of anxiety about the way in which emotion and sexuality were being highlighted in some parts of the women's movement, it was clear that the time for such issues had come, and at some level they define the difference between the "first wave" of feminism that brought about the franchise in the late nineteenth and early twentieth century, and the second wave. For Flexner and those who shared her views, the supposed aberrations of Mary's life were being writ large in the fiery polemic – and the highly colored publicity that it attracted – of the more radical tendencies within the women's movement in the late sixties and early seventies. Feminism, it must have seemed to them, had been reborn as a politicized juvenile delinquent pursuing a scandalous celebrity, reveling both in public attention and a kind of anti-intellectual populism – at once hyperfeminine and full of "masculine" aggression. At the same time, prominent and headline-grabbing elements of feminism were launching powerful critiques of the patriarchal state and of the androcentric social arrangements fostered by liberal capitalist democracies; radical feminists in particular were highlighting abortion and sexual choice as leading issues around which to campaign. Basic demands such as equal pay, education, and equal rights before the law became indelibly associated in the public mind with the more divisive issues of reproductive rights, sexual freedom, and, most contested of all, lesbianism. A standard strategy of anti-feminist rhetoric was to imply that female autonomy would inevitably lead to heterosexual promiscuity at best and lesbianism at worst, "choices" which were seen as undermining marriage, the family, and the state, a position that is still with us today. While the debates within Anglophone feminism – about sexuality, about race, about class, about theory and practice – reached their apogee between the mid-seventies and mid-eighties, divisions within the Women's Movement were already taking shape in the period when Flexner was reconstructing Wollstonecraft's life and work to serve both as an origin and a warning for late-twentieth-century feminism.

It is both moving and distressing to see feminism revisit, albeit in a post-Freudian context, those questions about the gendered division of feeling and thinking that had so fascinated and troubled men and women from the middle of the eighteenth century to its close. We must ask why they have been so important in feminist thinking, so significant in shaping gender, subjectivity, and sexuality, both at that early period when capitalism and the modern nation state are taking their recognizably modern form and again when the categories of the self and of economic and political structures seem under such radical revision?

The how and why of that return can be illuminated through a brief reprise of the criticism and historiography surrounding Wollstonecraft, from the mid-seventies, when the impulse to write and rewrite her biography gives way to a more serious and detailed project aimed at analyzing Wollstonecraft's writing in terms of eighteenth-century society and its debates – to offer historical readings which would provide a scholarly view of the lineage of modern feminism and make Wollstonecraft more significant for the eighteenth century, but perhaps less easily or happily appropriated to our own. Predictably the initial thrust of this work highlighted Wollstonecraft's ideas on education, treating her not as a lone woman speaker but as one voice among many across the political spectrum of the late eighteenth-century advocating the moral reform of bourgeois society through the reform of middle-class women's education.

By no means all critics of this period see Wollstonecraft's views as particularly daring – and where they do make this claim the "life" is almost always drawn in to supplement the works. Where she is mentioned as a part of a coterie of radical writers, the supposed poor quality of her fiction demotes her; Marilyn Butler, for example who would later become a leading editor of Wollstonecraft's work, mentions Wollstonecraft only briefly in her brilliant revisionist study *Romantics, Rebels and Reactionaries: English Literature and its Background 1760–1830* (1981). While it was still the convention to see the radical and reactionary women as representing quite different cultural and political trajectories, in an influential essay from 1982 Mitzi Meyers argues that on many issues concerning domesticity, and the reform of wives and mothers, the views of the political radical, Mary Wollstonecraft and the conservative Hannah More were closely allied.[9] A year after Meyers highlighted what she believed to be the central preoccupation of *A Vindication of the Rights of Woman*, feminist historian Barbara Taylor, in *Eve and the New Jerusalem*, identified Wollstonecraft as a "feminist democrat" whose "project took her right to the limit of the bourgeois-democratic outlook and occasionally a little way past it."[10] For Taylor, Wollstonecraft and her associates in the 1790s, like Rousseau before them, "envisioned" a "new age as a time of perfect harmony between the aspirations of the individual and the collective needs of humanity as a whole," rather than as an irreconcilable contradiction (5–6). Both that radical impulse, Wollstonecraft's appetite for major changes not minor reforms, and the "whirlpool of excitement and controversy which lasted for decades" created by *Rights of Woman* made Wollstonecraft and her work a precursor of the Owenite Socialist women of later decades (Taylor, *Eve*, 1). Members of Wollstonecraft's circle, including of course William Godwin, belonged to a long tradition of "utopian visionaries," whose interest in gender egalitarianism often extended, as in Godwin's *Political Justice*, to the abandonment of marriage in favor of free liaisons "based on mutual desire and affection" (Taylor, *Eve*, 8). The sexual heterodoxy of the Owenites as well as their utopian feminism, could be traced back, Taylor argued persuasively, to Wollstonecraft and her peers.

1983 was a bumper year for widely different representations of Wollstonecraft and her legacy. My own contribution to the debate, an essay entitled "Wild Nights: Pleasure/Sexuality/Feminism" argued that however Wollstonecraft's views altered in later years, *Rights of Woman* could in no way be construed as a text promoting sexual radicalism, but rather mounted a "negative and prescriptive assault on female sexuality"; Wollstonecraft, I suggested, figured "feeling" itself, as "almost counter-revolutionary."[11] *Rights of Woman*, if not Wollstonecraft's other writing, headed a long tradition of feminist moralization of sexuality that stretched from Wollstonecraft to the prescriptive and polemical writing of the feminist poet and critic Adrienne Rich.[12] There was something about radical and revolutionary moments, I suggested, that simultaneously inspired open-ended explorations of "experiments in living" and its converse, the policing of desire and sexuality. A year later, in 1984, Mary Poovey's study, *The Proper Lady and the Woman Writer*, drawing on a much wider range of Wollstonecraft's work, but also focusing on *Rights of Woman*, read Wollstonecraft's denial of female sexuality in that text as "a *defense* against what she feared: desire doomed to repeated frustration. Contrary to her assertions, Wollstonecraft's deepest fear centers not on the voraciousness of male sexual desire but on what she fears is its brevity."[13] Exploring the ideologies of gender and sexuality in both *Vindications, Letters Written During a Short Residence in Norway, Denmark and Sweden* and *The Wrongs of Woman, or Maria*, Poovey argues that the distinctions that Wollstonecraft was attempting to make between forms of sensibility and sentiment, do not add up to the full scale critique of "sentiment," because sentiment provided the structure that supported an individualism Wollstonecraft could not jettison. "Wollstonecraft's refusal to abandon the ideal of 'true sensibility,' even after she had recognized that the romantic expectations endemic to such sensibility were agents of the very institutions she was trying to criticize, reflects her persistent yearning for some connections between spiritual values and real, everyday experience" (*Proper Lady*, 108). "Perhaps," Poovey continues "the two most fundamental problems with sentimentalism's solution to this longing lay in its celebration of immaterial, romantic rewards and in its emphasis on individual feeling" which, substitute for or sublimate "more 'real' – because more socially effective goals" (109).

Looking back on these assessments almost a generation later, it is revealing to see how profoundly at odds Taylor, Poovey, and I were on questions of affect and imagination and the place they held in Wollstonecraft's life and work. Both Taylor and Poovey, for example, highlighted the centrality of the imagination for Wollstonecraft and her time, but for Taylor this placed Wollstonecraft at the head of a neglected tradition of utopian socialist feminism, while for Poovey its overemphasis left Wollstonecraft stranded in the world of individualized, bourgeois desire. All three of us were writing within a socialist-feminist paradigm, but on questions of fantasy and desire, of the imaginative anticipation both of a future society or future personal relationships we "heard" Wollstonecraft saying very different things in relation to a set of questions that modern feminism continued to frame as discrete alternatives. Was the erotic and affective imagination, gendered or universal, a blessing or a curse for women? Was it indispensable to radical consciousness, irrefutably a part of human psychic life, or was it something that could and should be jettisoned or retrained? If gendered identity was largely a matter of social construction, as most of the feminists I have been citing believed, then could a brave new world reconstruct its unconscious as well as its conscious wishes? These ambitious questions were being asked by all varieties of feminism with a special kind of urgency in the early to mid-1980s.

In the nineteen eighties, contention about Wollstonecraft's legacy came to be implicated in a cluster of related debates within feminism, on the reading of popular romance, on pornography and on lesbian sado-masochism that focused on the politics of the sensual and sentimental imagination, debates known in the history of modern feminism as "the sex wars." Wollstonecraft's almost material presence inhabits the return, in the early 80s of the debate about the corrupting effect of romantic and sensational fiction on women readers, an issue extensively addressed by Wollstonecraft as well as by more conservative or conventional figures, such as More and Austen. There is a direct parallel between the anxieties generated by the expansion of female literacy and the sentimental fiction written for and by women in the 1780s and 90s and the democratization of reading in the post World War II period, when the fear is that unrestrained access to print culture and Hollywood cinema, rather than family, church, and education will socialize young women into transgressive femininity. While eighteenth-century commentators on the spread of literacy often used the just-literate servant girl as the reader who would be most easily corrupted by sensational tales, writers from Wollstonecraft to Austen worried more about what women of their own class were reading. In the twentieth century there is a distinct elitist bias to the debates about mass culture and its female audience. Women often "stand in" in cultural analysis from the left and right sides of the political spectrum for all peculiarly vulnerable and impressionable readers and viewers. Although they are undoubtedly related, there is crucial difference between this general anxiety and the specifically feminist struggle for the hearts and minds of women both within and beyond the educated middle classes who formed its primary constituency. Feminism worried that fast-food romantic and sentimental narrative was the not so secret addiction of women of all classes, blunting their intellectual appetites and absorbing their psychic energy, its emotional seductions leading women down the garden path to the wrong kind of utopian thinking. The debate at first naively assumed that women readers naturally and exclusively identified with the heroines of romance – an odd view, if one thinks about it, for the largely literary trained academics in the debate to hold. Ann Snitow led the attack with an essay provocatively titled "Mass-market Romance: Pornography for Women is Different"; her argument frames the case against such reading in terms of its reproduction of women's subordination, and their psychic abjection. *Loving With a Vengeance: Mass Produced Fantasies for Women* (1984), Tania Modleski's interpretation of romance reading, as providing a way for women to imagine revenge and autonomy, gives the individualism that romantic and sentimental narratives encourage a more sympathetic feminist spin, while Janice Radway's fascinating sociological exploration of a group of mass-market romance readers, *Reading the Romance*, is more ambivalent about the individualism that the private act of reading and fantasizing engenders, but she is sure that it cannot be the route to mobilization for any kind of collective resistance to the public forms of patriarchal power.[14] The narrative and rhetorical structures of romance reading and the fantasizing it induces, are, in these accounts the affective routes through which female subjectivity is shaped or distorted. The debate itself was underpinned by an under-argued and sometimes only half-articulated assumption that the psychic economies of affect have fixed limits as well as strict forms of distribution – too much sexual fantasy, not enough rationality, ergo not enough political activism.

The link between sentimental and erotic fantasy and political transformation (or the lack of such a link) gave even these very scholarly exchanges on romance reading a certain polemical tone in the early 1980s. Not so the debates on heterosexual pornography and lesbian erotica which escaped the pages of academic books and journals, spilling over into angry public confrontations and eventually, in the case of pornography, into contested legislative moves. These "sex wars" within feminism were at their most intense in the early to mid 1980s, in a period which, while still characterized by optimism about feminism's capacity to change laws, manners, and morals, was threatened by the general move towards more conservative social attitudes and policy in Britain and America with the elections of Republican and Conservative governments. Calls for, and passionate resistance to, the moralizing and gendering of imagination and fantasy were therefore raised in the waning moments of what was sometimes called, with more rhetorical optimism than absolute accuracy, "a revolutionary moment." We should see both responses as part of that "revolutionary" consciousness, exemplifying equal if opposed visions of the kinds of social subjects and social relations that might emerge from a period of fundamental and rapid change. Feminism argued vigorously on both sides of the question: condemning popular romance as a harmful drug which keeps women in abjection; defending it as a site of fantasy which allows women to identify across gender and imagine themselves otherwise; targeting pornography for men as the theory of which rape is the practice; defending the whole spectrum of representations of sexuality on the grounds that censorship can only rebound on women's right to expression; damning anything that smacks of the perverse in lesbian sexuality and its representations as the willful reenactment of the violence of the heterosexual imagination; praising it as exemplary of consensual, liberating, experimental acts. The sex wars within feminism did not just generate heat and light: they put the assumptions of each side under close intellectual scrutiny. By the mid-90s the arguments on both sides of these questions had become more nuanced and complex. If still unresolved, they were no longer such urgent or contested issues on feminism's agenda, in part because the optimistic dreams of social transformation that had fueled them seemed ever less achievable.

The debate about psychic life and gender within feminism was symptomatic of a shift in the way affect in general, and in its particular instances, were being theorized and historicized from the late 80s, a shift which would have a profound impact on Wollstonecraft scholarship from that period forward. Psychoanalytic feminism had strongly queried the model of human consciousness which divided the rational and the feeling self; so too, although from slightly different premises, did other strands of theory – poststructuralism, deconstruction, postmodernism. An interest in the "history of the affections" was also reemerging in the work of male and female historians and critics, more skeptical about psychoanalysis but whose socialist inflected humanism saw complementarity not impasse between individual affection and revolutionary passion.[15] This was particularly true for male commentators, friendly to feminism, and sympathetic to Romanticism's privileging of affect, who come to the topic with less personal and political investment in the way the gendering of affect had historically subordinated women.

What would become emotion's more positive role in Wollstonecraft's fin-de-siècle incarnation is adumbrated in Richard Holmes 1987 Penguin Classics edition of Wollstonecraft's *Letters Written During a Short Residence in Sweden, Norway and Denmark*[16] and Godwin's *Memoirs of the Author of the Rights of Woman*, the first Wollstonecraft's most popular publication in her own lifetime, the second the book which undid her influence and reputation for almost a century. In bringing these, the most affective texts of the couple together, Holmes attempts a retroactive rapprochement between Godwin's revelations with Wollstonecraft's legacy, embracing them both as new forms of "confessional" literature, enacting a "revolution in literary genres," transforming both travel literature and biography (Holmes, Introduction, 16). Calling them "forgotten classics of English eighteenth-century non-fiction" Holmes judges these "short, factual, readable and, in different ways, intensely passionate" works as "the best books that either wrote" (9). Through them Wollstonecraft and Godwin together become founding figures of literary and political Romanticism. *A Short Residence* in particular had, Holmes believes, a direct influence on the romanticism of his own biographical subjects, Coleridge and Shelley. Holmes reminds us that to Wollstonecraft and Godwin's radical contemporaries, as well as to "the larger body of liberal opinion, and to many of the younger writers of the day" their liaison was "a kind of culmination: a consecration of that New Sensibility in which the rational hopes of the Enlightenment were catalyzed by that element of imagination and personal rebellion which we now know as Romanticism....They were seen as transitional figures, pointing towards a freer life and a more just society, and the new 'empire of feeling'" (15). Positioning them thus, Holmes incorporates and indeed echoes Woolf's admiration for Wollstonecraft's "experiments in living"; without glossing over the "intense disruption" of "hope and feeling," the "pain, discontent and frustrated happiness" in both texts he avoids the kind of moralizing that we have seen so easily attached itself to Wollstonecraft's life and work (16). Against feminism's rebuke to Godwin for aligning Wollstonecraft with the intuitive rather than the rational, Holmes, the neo-Romanticist, mounts a spirited and detailed defense of the *Memoir*'s appreciation of Wollstonecraft's intellectual achievements, which he believes, celebrates "Imagination" not simply as the gendered complement of rationality but the *sine qua non* of the creative faculty. Obliquely countering censures of Wollstonecraft's writing for style or content, Holmes puts a strong case for that literary innovation – Wollstonecraft's and Godwin's – which successfully marries fact and affect. But if Wollstonecraft/Godwin as reread by Holmes become an eighteenth-century avant-garde double-act, at least in literary terms, Holmes's focus on the Imlay–Wollstonecraft–Godwin triangle locks Wollstonecraft back into the heteronormativity from which postwar feminism had partly liberated her. And by aligning himself unapologetically with the Romanticism he believes they represent, Holmes reproduces rather than resists the old gendered binary between reason and feeling which still remain, in his essay, symbolized respectively by Godwin and Wollstonecraft. While Holmes defends Godwin against charges of sexism in his characterization of Wollstonecraft's talents, his own choice of adverbs betrays his identification with a gendered division of style: Holmes admires the "wildness and richness of emotional rhetoric" in *A Short Residence* which is matched by the "frankness and understatement" of Godwin's *Memoirs* (16).

Holmes's essay is the harbinger of a positive turn in Wollstonecraft's reception which would become more marked in the decade to follow. Looking back one can see that the energy with which some feminists *dis*identified with Wollstonecraft in the 1980s was symptomatic of the unreconciled elements that affected most Western feminisms – their origins and sensibilities so normatively assessed as a product of bourgeois and liberal ideologies but their aims so often linked to radical communitarian and sometime revolutionary dreams. World events in 1989 were to destabilize that fragile equilibrium between identities and aims further, and to have a profound effect on Wollstonecraft studies. The fall of the Berlin wall between East and West Germany and the crumbling of communist and socialist regimes across Eastern and Central Europe signaled the triumph of democracy and capitalism, revealing the history and significance of Western revolutions and the role of their founding figures in a new light. To Western observers the power of public feeling against corrupt and repressive regimes, the engine behind the bloodless transformation of Europe and the former Soviet Union, was perceived as miraculous and uplifting, giving new ethical value to the association of "sensibility" and revolution, even as it quenched, finally, hopes for a return to socialism in the West. The after-shocks of 1989, which have included the resurgence of violent nationalisms and the brutal effects of unregulated capitalism have been more sobering. And for historians of all persuasions, as for the general public, the past, present, and future of social and political radicalism, including feminism in all its manifestations, has required fresh scrutiny, perhaps especially in terms of the politics of affect. In the last part of this essay I want to look at the implications of this new perspective on Wollstonecraft's reception and legacy.

Virginia Sapiro's *A Vindication of Political Virtue: the Political Theory of Mary Wollstonecraft* published in 1992, the two hundredth anniversary of *A Vindication of the Rights of Woman*, makes the post 1989 context of her reappraisal explicit in her introduction, as she writes of tuning in to "the latest news from Eastern Europe" while reading about the fall of the Bourbon's in Wollstonecraft's *An Historical and Moral View of the French Revolution*. In her mind, she says, the tyrannical Bourbons and Romania's brutal communist leaders, Nikolai and Elena Ceausescu "fell at the same moment...so that it would have been strange had the political questions these events raised not become entangled."[17] Sapiro highlights an issue that she never quite pursues. But the implications of the altered political landscape are drawn out, if only obliquely, in other work on Wollstonecraft in the 1990s and following.

Gary Kelly's *Revolutionary Feminism: the Mind and Career of Mary Wollstonecraft*, also published in 1992, is the first of these.[18] Building upon and integrating the new social and cultural analysis of the previous two decades, especially the work of feminist scholars, *Revolutionary Feminism* is a dramatically revisionist study, refuting or jettisoning many of the debates and divisions that were its ground. Kelly's Wollstonecraft becomes the figure through whom a series of political and philosophical oppositions which in past decades fueled the struggle over Wollstonecraft's legacy, are seemingly reconciled including the disjunction between reason and feeling which Kelly brings together persuasively under the inclusive category of "mind." Kelly argues that "Sensibility" in its role as a formal category of the period "appealed particularly to those who were socially marginalized" and this possibility, he suggests "gave Sensibility a revolutionary potential" (*Revolutionary Feminism*, 41), as did Wollstonecraft's rejection of the "gendering of subjectivity." Yet these initiatives were all too soon undermined, he argues, by a ruthless masculine hegemony that appeared in the early years of the nineteenth century.

There is however an analytic and political price to be paid for Kelly's desire to downplay, even submerge, the conflicts and contradictions between affective desires and political aspirations of which Wollstonecraft herself was so conscious, and which drove her own thinking forward. Even more puzzling is his move to cordon off Wollstonecraft's lasting contribution from the realm of the political, claiming her permanent influence on the "cultural revolution that founded the modern state in Britain" (1). He explains that while "the 'Revolutionary' feminists of the 1790s advocated the rights and claims of women within an intense debate over a sudden and violent revolution" it was the "less sudden" revolution in which "gender difference was a major issue, deeply implicated in other major revolutionary issues and in the struggle to define and lead the classes by and for whom the cultural revolution was being carried out" (2). Kelly's "cultural revolution" at first looks like a hold-all phenomenon in which progressive and conservative aims are not only entwined but almost undifferentiated, merged in the relentless process of modernization that is eventually realized in the dominant middle-class ideology of State and Nation, the triumph of liberal capitalism, exemplified in the late twentieth century by selfish and elite competition, "where feminisms contend for leadership among themselves largely within the dominant professional culture" and "most women, like other subordinated groups" are left to their own devices to improvise resistance in "the bricolage of everyday life" (228). This bleak judgment, sounding the death knell of any progressive politics that reaches out to the poor beyond middle-class aspiration, is a familiar response of some radical scholars to the triumph of liberal capitalism that 1989 was seen to represent. It erupts almost without warning at the end of a study that overtly offers a nuanced understanding and celebration of Wollstonecraft, at odds with the downbeat tone of these final pages, which describe a limited and short-lived emancipatory project generating a legacy hardly worthy of mourning or recovery. In this conclusion Wollstonecraft seems suddenly to become a condensed and displaced figure for a more generalized despair at the defeat and/or retrospective irrelevance of any utopian agendas that stand outside the competitive demand of market societies, making her modern influence seem an ignoble footnote to a long-lost cause.

Pessimism however, is only one response to the seismic shift in Western political culture, and a more mixed response dominates eighteenth-century scholarship over the last decade in which work has been further enriched by the contributions of lesbian, gay, and queer as well as feminist critics and historians. Wollstonecraft studies has contributed to and profited from the increasing centrality of gender and sexuality to history and criticism, especially as it has encouraged writers to address the question of affect, subjectivity, and politics through a deeper and less tendentious exploration of what G. J. Barker-Benfield has termed the "culture of sensibility" of the late eighteenth century. A spate of work from the mid-80s through the early 90s give the debates over the rights and wrongs of affective thinking greater scope as a discourse through which the great changes in the societies that bordered the Atlantic were interpreted, critiqued, and legitimated.[19] The rise and fall in the reputation of that imagined figure, the man and woman of feeling, and the fictional, philosophical and polemical texts in which they were both created and dissected, has been shown as indissolubly bound at once to the definition of civic virtue and aesthetic value and the gendered identities that commodity culture required. In these analyses scholars overcome the twentieth century's intellectuals' almost phobic response to "sentiment" and the sentimental, seeing the gendered rhetoric of both sentiment and sensibility as driving the language of politics, articulating the deep structure of economic as well as social change, as a language of self and other appropriated simultaneously and in turn by both radicals and conservatives.

This perspective has resulted in fascinating work on Wollstonecraft and her contemporaries. I want to conclude by looking at just two examples of how Wollstonecraft is rewritten within this evolving paradigm. Claudia L. Johnson, exploring the writing and careers of Wollstonecraft in tandem with her contemporaries, Ann Radcliffe and Fanny Burney, writers whose careers she argues "are organized around the nexus of politics, affectivity, and gender" relishes and rehabilitates the fiction of the last decades of the eighteenth century so ritually relegated for its "over the top" emotional rhetoric, hearing in its sentimental excesses a deadly serious debate about the politics of feeling (*Equivocal Beings*, 15). So Johnson, looking at Wollstonecraft's theorization of sentiment and sensibility across the two *Vindications* and in both her novels, *Mary, A Fiction* and the unfinished *Wrongs of Woman* suggests that Wollstonecraft's polemic against the sentimental in men and women, especially her stinging critique of sentimental masculinity, runs alongside a fantasy of same-sex attachment that cannot be fully imagined in a period where the gendered divisions of sentiment are represented as a reformed heterosexuality which has become the keystone of conservative and radical politics. Nevertheless, Johnson argues that the peculiarly restrictive logic of these categories produces some unforeseen, ironically capricious effects. It leads Wollstonecraft to her scornfully homophobic characterization of Burke as an "equivocal being" – his corrupt sentiment becoming a dangerously polymorphous subjectivity. This critique, as Johnson suggests, is extended and elaborated in her fiction in the negative portraits of feminized and sentimental males. But the strictures which governed the moralization of gender and sentiment meant that all cross-gendered identifications became suspect, forcing Wollstonecraft to imagine her own eccentric femininity in the same hybrid and ambiguous terms.

My second example, Harriet Guest's *Small Change: Women, Learning Patriotism, 1750–1810*, also asks how masculinity and femininity were imagined within the period's rhetoric of feeling, focusing on those emotions seen as necessary to the making of modern market economies. Her exploration of how educated British women came to imagine themselves as political subjects in a culture increasingly visualized through the lens of commerce takes up an issue which Wollstonecraft and her contemporaries thought of great importance. The last section of her study on the 1790s reads Wollstonecraft, Hannah More, and Mary Hays in apposition. Guest suggests that these writers reacted to the impossible demands commercial culture makes on femininity by recourse to the language of professionalization, which they use to reclaim respectability for the notion of virtuous femininity (287). The public world in which this virtue is to be practiced is also, however, depicted by them as saturated in affect. When Wollstonecraft suggests "The world cannot be seen by an unmoved spectator, we must mix in the throng, and feel as men feel" (VRW 5:170) she voices something that will strike a chord with feminism down the centuries, its last phrase echoed almost word for word in Jane Eyre's cry from the rooftops, and in every text thereafter that takes the extra-domestic (which must also necessarily be, in part, the tainted world of commerce) as the sphere that women must enter to imagine themselves active and "free." The contradiction embedded in this view is made explicit as Guest turns to that "touchstone" question in Wollstonecraft studies, Wollstonecraft's attack on sensibility in early works and her recourse to it in the brief period from *Short Residence* to the end of her life. Reading this shift in terms of the counter-revolutionary mood and collapsed "revolutionary"' possibilities of the late 90s, Guest suggests that in this political climate it is increasingly difficult to distinguish a virtuous sensibility that women might hold as separate from the commercial world with its morally muddied affect. The libidinized emotions necessary to commodity culture, the seductive language of the successful merchants whose materialism Wollstonecraft decries in the *Short Residence*, are simulacra therefore of the restless and forceful desire which evokes what Wollstonecraft eloquently calls the "imperious sympathies," those draw humans willy-nilly out of isolation into social life, and which may fuel ambitions of all kinds.[20] The problem, Guest concludes, is that "the domestic and intimate world of sensibility is folded into that other sphere, those other elements of modern society, not just by the presence in that world too of men who rule. It is also folded in, I suggest, because for women to think of themselves as modern subjects necessarily involves a refusal of the exclusion, the division, fundamental to modernity: it involves thinking of themselves as modern because their desires are structured and articulated as those of commercial agents and political citizens" (*Small Change*, 312).

Johnson's and Guest's Wollstonecrafts no less, for example, than Woolf's and Goldman's, are hostage to the hopes and fears of their own moment. From our present political perspective at the opening of the twenty-first century we seem to have a special sympathetic resonance with the dilemmas faced by Wollstonecraft and her radical contemporaries in the conservative modernity of the late 1790s. Mary Wollstonecraft and her peers seem not a ghostly but a living presence in an ongoing struggle to wrest a more fluid language of gender, sexuality, and subjectivity from the grip of a still determining hetero-normative discourse. We seem uncannily to echo them when we ask whether it is possible to dream of and work for a just society by harnessing the affective rhetoric we must of necessity share with the languages of the global market. Feminism at the opening of the new millennium is accordingly less likely to chide Wollstonecraft for not having an uncompromised critique of her world, but this greater tolerance is also a function of the times – and may pass. The less moralized, more nuanced Mary Wollstonecrafts who have been slowly emerging from the scholarship of the last decade are figures whose complex relationship to the discourses of feeling of her day and ours offers us new perspectives on the historical limits and possibilities of the political imagination, but they no more than their earlier incarnations stand outside the moods and concerns of their construction, a reminder that the analytic impulse itself always has, perhaps must have, a blind spot or two. Wollstonecraft, the iconic representative of modern feminism's multiple narratives, has at times in the last quarter century suffered a harsh and judgmental scrutiny, infantilizing her as if she were the wayward child of an over-exacting feminism rather than its revered and chosen ancestor. This suspicious turn of the genealogical impulse, one which disinherits itself of the inheritance it also claims, is typical just now of the uncertain status accorded to the founding figures of any grand historical or political narrative, for those narratives often seem in their present scarcity and vulnerability, at once utterly fallible and peculiarly precious.

Wollstonecraft's personal history as a radical story still holds an abiding fascination for us, as the success of Janet Todd's impressive recent biography that unashamedly calls itself *A Revolutionary Life* attests.[21] I have tried to argue throughout this essay that Wollstonecraft's particular treatment by her critics and biographers must be read in counterpoint to the shifting terms

of feminist debates about the sexual and affective imagination, debates that
were of critical importance to Wollstonecraft's work and world and centrally
implicated in its wider politics – and ours. As for Mary Wollstonecraft, as
novelists used to say, we are unlikely to have heard the last of her. Her
virtues, like those of women themselves, will continue to be revised through
the "mutable prejudices" of the future. Her story in its broadest definition, as
legacy and reception together, seems more complicated and unfinished than
ever, offering just now the kind of open-ended anti-moral narrative that, if
we think about it, is as sentimental in its own way as the more conventional
ones that we have cast aside. Luckily for her admirers and detractors alike,
Wollstonecraft is too volatile and too evasive a figure to become even a fixed
point of unstable reference, and will go on to act as a constant provocation
to her interlocutors.

NOTES

1. Virginia Woolf, "Four Figures", *The Common Reader*, 2nd Series, ed. Andrew
   McNeillie (London: Hogarth Press, 1986), 163. The individual essay on Mary
   Wollstonecraft collected in 1932 with three others under the title "Four Figures"
   was first published in the *Nation and Athenaeum*, 5 October 1929 and reprinted
   in the *New York Herald Tribune*, 20 October 1929.
2. Harriet Guest, *Small Change: Women, Learning, Patriotism, 1750–1810* (Chicago:
   University of Chicago Press, 2000), 2.
3. Claudia L. Johnson, *Equivocal Beings: Politics, Gender, and Sentimentality in
   the 1790s, Wollstonecraft, Radcliffe, Burney, Austen* (Chicago: University of
   Chicago Press, 1995), 1.
4. Emma Goldman (1869–1940) was an eloquent speaker as well as an anarchist
   activist imprisoned for her radical activity and deported from the United States
   in 1919.
5. Neillie notes that Woolf's reading for the essay was largely biographical, including Godwin's *Memoirs* and C. Kegan Paul's *William Godwin and his Friends
   and Contemporaries* (London, 1876).
6. Emma Goldman, "Mary Wollstonecraft: Her Tragic Life and Her Passionate
   Struggle for Freedom" Mary Wollstonecraft, *A Vindication of the Rights of
   Woman*, ed. Carol H. Poston, 2nd edn. (New York: W.W. Norton & Co.,
   1988), 256.
7. Ralph M. Wardle, *Mary Wollstonecraft: a Critical Biography* (Lincoln: University
   of Nebraska Press. 1967), 341.
8. Eleanor Flexner, *Mary Wollstonecraft: a Biography* (Baltimore: Penguin Books,
   1973), frontispiece.
9. Mitzi Myers, "Reform or Ruin: 'A Revolution in Female Manners,'" *Studies in
   Eighteenth-Century Culture* 11 (1982), 199–216.
10. Barbara Taylor, *Eve and the New Jerusalem: Socialism and Feminism in the
    Nineteenth Century* (London: Virago, 1983), 6.
11. *Sea Changes: Culture and Feminism* (London: Verso, 1986), 35.

12. *Signs; Journal of Women in Culture and Society*, 5/4, 631–60.

13. Mary Poovey, *The Proper Lady and the Woman Writer: Ideology as Style in the Works of Mary Wollstonecraft, Mary Shelley, and Jane Austen* (Chicago: University of Chicago Press, 1984), 74.

14. Ann Snitow, "Mass Market Romance: Pornography for Women is Different," in *Powers of Desire: The Politics of Sexuality*, ed. Ann Snitow, Christine Stansell, and Sharon Thompson (New York: Monthly Review Press, 1983); Tania Modleski, *Loving With a Vengeance: Mass-produced Fantasies for Women* (Hamden: York: Archon Books 1984); Janice Radway, *Reading the Romance: Women, Patriarchy and Popular Literature* (London: Verso, 1987).

15. At least one strand of this tradition in social history should be traced back to the work of E. P. Thompson, especially *The Making of the English Working Class* (London: Victor Golancz, 1963).

16. Richard Holmes, Introduction, Mary Wollstonecraft and William Godwin, *A Short Residence in Sweden and Memoirs of the Author of The Rights of Woman* (London: Penguin Books, 1987). Note that Holmes uses the short title, *A Short Residence in Sweden, Norway and Denmark*.

17. Virginia Sapiro, *A Vindication of Political Virtue: the Political Theory of Mary Wollstonecraft* (Chicago: University of Chicago Press, 1992), xvi.

18. Gary Kelly, *Revolutionary Feminism: the Mind and Career of Mary Wollstonecraft* (London: Macmillan, 1992).

19. See, for example Janet Todd, *Sensibility: an Introduction* (London: Methuen, 1986); John Mullan, *Sentiment and Sociability: the Language of Feeling in the Eighteenth Century* (Oxford: Clarendon Press, 1988); G. J. Barker-Benfield, *The Culture of Sensibility: Sex and Society in Eighteenth-Century Britain* (Chicago: University of Chicago Press, 1992); Jessie Van Sant, *Eighteenth-Century Sensibility and the Novel: the Senses in Social Context* (Cambridge: Cambridge University Press, 1993).

20. See this citation from *Letters* in the context of Guest's analysis, *Small Change*, 309–10.

21. Janet Todd, *Mary Wollstonecraft: a Revolutionary Life* (London: Weidenfeld and Nicholson, 2000).

SELECT BIBLIOGRAPHY

The following are among the most important and widely cited works about Wollstonecraft and her period. For a comprehensive listing of books and articles about Wollstonecraft from her own time through 1975, see Janet Todd's *Mary Wollstonecraft: an Annotated Bibliography* (New York: Garland Publishing, 1976).

Biographical Studies

Flexner, Eleanor. *Mary Wollstonecraft*. New York: Coward, McCann & Geoghegan, 1972.

George, Margaret. *One Woman's "Situation": a Study of Mary Wollstonecraft*. Urbana, Chicago and London: University of Illinois Press, 1970.

Godwin, William. *Memoirs of the Author of a Vindication of the Rights of Woman*, London, 1798. Also the supplemented edition by W. Clark Durant. London: Constable; New York: Greenberg, 1927.

Hays, Mary. "Memoirs of Mary Wollstonecraft." *Annual Necrology*, 1797-8. (London: 1800), 411-60.

James, H. R. *Mary Wollstonecraft, a Sketch*. London: Oxford University Press, 1932.

Nixon, Edna. *Mary Wollstonecraft: Her Life and Times*. London: Dent, 1971.

Paul, C. Kegan. *William Godwin, his Friends and Contemporaries*. London, 1876.

Pennell, Elizabeth Robins. *Mary Wollstonecraft Godwin*. London, 1885.

Sunstein, Emily. *A Different Face: the Life of Mary Wollstonecraft*. Boston and Toronto: Little, Brown and Co, 1975.

Taylor, G. R. Stirling. *Mary Wollstonecraft: a Study in Economics and Romance*. London: Secker, 1911.

Todd, Janet. *Mary Wollstonecraft: a Revolutionary Life*. London: Weidenfeld and Nicholson, 2000.

Tomalin, Claire, *The Life and Death of Mary Wollstonecraft*. London: Weidenfeld and Nicholson 1974. Rev. edn. Harmondsworth: Penguin, 1992.

Wardle, Ralph M., *Mary Wollstonecraft: a Critical Biography*. Lawrence: University of Kansas Press, 1951.

Selected editions of letters and works

A Vindication of the Rights of Woman. Ed. Carol H. Poston. 2nd edn. New York: W. W. Norton & Company, 1988.

A Short Residence in Sweden, Norway and Denmark and William Godwin, Memoirs of the Author of "The Rights of Woman." Ed. Richard Holmes. London: Penguin, 1987.

The Collected Letters of Mary Wollstonecraft. Ed. Ralph M. Wardle. Ithaca: Cornell University Press, 1979.

The Letters of Mary Wollstonecraft. Ed. Janet Todd. Forthcoming Penguin Press 2002.

The Vindications. Eds. D. L. Macdonald & Kathleen Scherf. Peterborough, Ontario: Broadview Press, 1997.

The Works of Mary Wollstonecraft, 7 vols. Eds. Marilyn Butler and Janet Todd. London: Pickering & Chatto; New York: New York University Press, 1989.

Books and articles about Wollstonecraft and her age

Barker-Benfield, G. J. "Mary Wollstonecraft: Eighteenth-Century Commonwealth-woman." *Journal of the History of Ideas* 50 (1989): 95–115.

The Culture of Sensibility: Sex and Society in Eighteenth-Century Britain. Chicago: University of Chicago Press, 1992.

Basker, James. "Radical Affinities: Mary Wollstonecraft and Samuel Johnson." *Tradition in Transition: Women Writers, Marginal Texts, and the Eighteenth-Century Canon.* Eds. Alvaro Ribeiro and James G. Basker. Oxford: Clarendon Press, 1996: 51–5.

Butler, Marilyn. *Romantics, Rebels and Reactionaries: English Literature and its Background 1760–1830.* Oxford, New York: Oxford University Press, 1981.

Butler, Marilyn, ed. *Burke Paine, Godwin, and the Revolution Controversy.* Cambridge: Cambridge University Press, 1984.

Conger, Syndy. "The Sentimental Logic of Wollstonecraft's Prose." *Prose Studies* 10/2 (September 1987): 143–58.

Mary Wollstonecraft and the Language of Sensibility. London: Associated University Presses, 1994.

Davidoff, Leonore, and Hall, Catherine. *Family Fortunes: Men and Women of the English Middle Class, 1780–1850.* London: Hutchinson, 1987.

Deane, Seamus. *The French Revolution and Enlightenment in England, 1789–1832.* Cambridge: Harvard University Press, 1988.

Everest, Kelvin, ed. *Revolution in Writing: British Literary Responses to the French Revolution.* Milton Keynes and Philadelphia: Open University Press, 1991.

Favret, Mary. *Romantic Correspondence: Women, Politics, and the Fiction of Letters.* Cambridge: Cambridge University Press, 1993.

Ferguson, Frances. "Wollstonecraft Our Contemporary." *Gender and Theory: Dialogues in Feminist Criticism.* Ed. Linda Kauffman. Oxford: Blackwell, 1989: 51–62.

Furniss, Tom. "Gender in Revolution: Edmund Burke and Mary Wollstonecraft." *Revolution in Writing: British Literary Responses to the French Revolution.* Ed. Kelvin Everest. Milton Keynes and Philadelphia, Open University Press, 1991.

Edmund Burke's Aesthetic Ideology: Language, Gender and Political Economy in Revolution. Cambridge: Cambridge University Press, 1993.

Goldman, Emma. "Mary Wollstonecraft: Her Tragic Life and Her Passionate Struggle for Freedom." *Feminist Studies* 7 (1981): 114–21.

Gubar, Susan. "Feminist Misogyny: Mary Wollstonecraft and the Paradox of 'It takes one to Know One.'" *Feminist Studies* 20:3 (1994): 453–73.

Guest, Harriet. "The Dream of a Common Language: Hannah More and Mary Wollstonecraft." *Textual-Practice* 9:2 (Summer 1995): 303–23.

"Eighteenth-century Femininity: 'A Supposed Sexual Character.'" *Women and Literature in Britain 1700–1800*. Ed. Vivien Jones. Cambridge: Cambridge University Press, 2000: 46–68.

Small Change: Women, Learning, Patriotism, 1750–1810. Chicago: University of Chicago Press, 2000.

Guralnick, Elissa. "Radical Politics in Mary Wollstonecraft's *A Vindication of the Rights of Woman*." *Studies in Burke and Hist Time* 18 (1977): 155–66.

"Rhetorical Strategy in Mary Wollstonecraft's *A Vindication of the Rights of Woman*." *Humanities Association Review* 30 (1979): 174–85.

Hill, Bridget. *The Republican Virago: the Life and Times of Catharine Macaulay*. Oxford: Clarendon Press, 1992.

"The Links between Mary Wollstonecraft and Catharine Macaulay: New Evidence." *Women's History Review* 4 (1995): 177–92.

Jacobus, Mary. "The Difference of View." *Women Writing and Writing about Women*. Ed. Mary Jacobus. New York: Barnes and Noble, 1979: 1–21.

"In Love with a Cold Climate: Traveling with Wollstonecraft." *First Things: the Maternal Imaginary in Literature, Art, and Psychoanalysis*. New York and London: Routledge, 1995: 63–82.

Janes, R. M. "On the Reception of Mary Wollstonecraft's *A Vindication of the Rights of Woman*." *Journal of the History of Ideas* 39 (1978): 293–302.

Johnson, Claudia L. *Equivocal Beings: Politics, Gender, and Sentimentality in the 1790s, Wollstonecraft, Radcliffe, Burney, Austen*. Chicago: University of Chicago Press, 1995.

Jones, Chris, *Radical Sensibility*. London: Routledge, 1993.

Jones, Robert. *Gender and the Formation of Taste in Eighteenth-Century Britain: the Analysis of Beauty*. Cambridge: Cambridge University Press, 1998.

Jones, Vivien. "Women Writing Revolution: Narratives of History and Sexuality in Wollstonecraft and Williams." *Beyond Romanticism: New Approaches to Texts and Contexts, 1780–1832*. Eds. Stephen Copley and John Whale. London and New York: Routledge, 1992: 178–99.

"The Seductions of Conduct: Pleasure and Conduct Literature." *Pleasure in the Eighteenth Century*. Eds. Roy Porter and Marie Mulvey Roberts. London and Basingstoke: Macmillan, 1996: 108–32.

"The Death of Mary Wollstonecraft." *British Journal for Eighteenth-Century Studies*. 20:2 (Autumn 1997): 187–205.

Jump, Harriet Devine, "No Equal Mind: Mary Wollstonecraft and the Young Romantics." *Charles Lamb Bulletin*, New Series, 79 (July 1992): 225–38.

Mary Wollstonecraft: Writer. New York: Harvester Wheatsheaf, 1994.

Kaplan, Cora. "Wild nights: pleasure/sexuality/feminism." *The Ideology of Conduct: Essays in Literature and the History of Sexuality*. Eds. Nancy Armstrong and Leonard Tennenhouse. London: Methuen, 1987: 160–84.

"Pandora's Box: Subjectivity, Class, and Sexuality in Socialist-Feminist Criticism."
  British Feminist Thought: a Reader. Ed. Terry Lovell. Oxford: Blackwell, 1990:
  345–66.
Kay, Carol. "Canon, Ideology, and Gender: Mary Wollstonecraft's Critique of Adam
  Smith," *New Political Science* 15 (Summer 1986): 63–76.
Kelly, Gary. "Mary Wollstonecraft as Vir Bonus." *English Studies in Canada* 5 (1979):
  275–91.
"Expressive Style and 'The Female Mind': Mary Wollstonecraft's *Vindication of the
  Rights of Woman*." *Studies on Voltaire and the Eighteenth Century: Transac-
  tions of the Fifth International Congress on the Enlightenment* 4 (1980): 1942–9.
English Fiction of the Romantic Period. London, New York: Longman, 1989.
Revolutionary Feminism: the Mind and Career of Mary Wollstonecraft. London:
  Macmillan; New York: St. Martin's Press, 1992.
Women, Writing and Revolution, 1790–1827. Oxford: Clarendon Press, 1993.
"[Female] Philosophy in the Bedroom: Mary Wollstonecraft and Female Sexuality."
  Women's Writing 4 (1997): 139–54.
Klein, Lawrence. "Gender, Conversation and the Public Sphere in early Eighteenth-
  Century England." *Textuality and Sexuality: Reading Theories and Practices*.
  Eds. Judith Still and Michael Worton. Manchester: Manchester University Press,
  1993.
Landes, Joan B. *Women and the Public Sphere in the Age of the French Revolution*.
  Ithaca: Cornell University Press, 1988.
"Mary Does, Alice Doesn't: the Paradox of Female Reason in and for Feminist
  Theory." *Mary Wollstonecraft and 200 Years of Feminism*. Ed. Eileen Janes
  Yeo. New York: Rivers Oram Press, 1997: 50–60.
Langbauer, Laurie. *Women and Romance: the Consolations of Gender in the English
  Novel*. Ithaca: Cornell University Press, 1990.
Lloyd, Genevieve. *The Man of Reason: "Male" and "Female" in Western Philosophy*.
  Minneapolis: University of Minnesota Press, 1984.
Mellor, Anne K. *Romanticism and Gender*. New York and London: Routledge Press,
  1993.
"Righting the Wrongs of Woman: Mary Wollstonecraft's *Maria*." *Nineteenth-
  Century Contexts* 19 (1996): 413–24.
Mothers of the Nation: Women's Political Writing in England, 1780–1830. Bloom-
  ington: Indiana University Press, 2000.
Maurer, Lisa Shawn. "The Female (As) Reader: Sex, Sensibility, and the Maternal in
  Wollstonecraft's Fictions." *Essays in Literature* 19 (1992): 36–54.
Moore, Jane. *Mary Wollstonecraft*. Plymouth: Northcote House, 1999.
Myers, Mitzi. "Politics from the Outside: Mary Wollstonecraft's First Vindication."
  Studies in Eighteenth-Century Culture 6 (1977): 113–32.
"Wollstonecraft's Letters Written … in Sweden: Towards Romantic Autobiogra-
  phy." *Studies in Eighteenth-Century Culture* 8 (1979): 165–85.
"Impeccable Governesses, Rational Dames, and Moral Mothers: Mary
  Wollstonecraft and the Female Tradition in Georgian Children's Books."
  Children's Literature, eds. Margaret Higonnet and Barbara Rosen (New Haven
  and London: Yale University Press, 1986), XIV.31–59.
"'A Taste for Truth and Realities': Early Advice to Mothers on Books for Girls."
  Children's Literature Association Quarterly 12/3 (Fall 1987): 118–24.

"Pedagogy as Self-Expression in Mary Wollstonecraft: Exorcising the Past, Finding a Voice." *The Private Self: Theory and Practice of Women's Autobiographical Writings.* Ed. Shari Benstock. Chapel Hill: University of North Carolina Press, 1988: 192–210.

"Sensibility and the 'Walk of Reason': Mary Wollstonecraft's Literary Reviews as Cultural Critique." *Sensibility in Transformation: Creative Resistance to Sentiment from the Augustans to the Romantics.* Ed. Syndy Conger McMillen. Rutherford: Fairleigh Dickinson University Press, 1990: 120–44.

Nyström, Per. "Mary Wollstonecraft's Scandinavian Journey." *Acts of the Royal Society of Arts and Letters of Gothenburg, Humaniora* 17 (1980).

Paulson, Ronald, *Representations of Revolution.* Yale University Press, New Haven and London, 1983.

Pocock, J. G. A. *Virtue, Commerce, and History.* Cambridge: Cambridge University Press, 1985.

Poovey, Mary. *The Proper Lady and the Woman Writer: Ideology as Style in the Works of Mary Wollstonecraft, Mary Shelley, and Jane Austen.* Chicago: University of Chicago Press, 1984.

Poston, Carol H., and Todd, Janet M. "Some Textual Variations in the First Two Editions of *A Vindication of the Rights of Woman.*" *Mary Wollstonecraft Journal* 2:2 (May 1974): 27–9.

Rajan, Tillotama. "Wollstonecraft and Godwin: Reading the Secrets of the Political Novel." *Studies in Romanticism* 27 (1988): 221–51.

The Supplement of Reading: Figures of Understanding in Romantic Theory and Practice Ithaca: Cornell University Press, 1990.

Rendall, Jane. *The Origins of Modern Feminism: Women in Britain, France and the United States, 1780–1860.* London: Macmillan, 1985.

Reiss, Timothy. "Revolution in Bounds: Wollstonecraft, Women, and Reason." *Gender and Theory: Dialogues in Feminist Criticism.* Ed. Linda Kaufman. Oxford: Blackwell, 1989.

Richardson, Alan. *Literature, Education, and Romanticism: Reading as Social Practice, 1780–1832.* Cambridge: Cambridge University Press, 1994.

Robbins, Caroline, *The Eighteenth-Century Commonwealthman.* Cambridge: Harvard University Press, 1959.

Roper, Derek. "Mary Wollstonecraft's Reviews." *Notes and Queries* n.s. 5 (January 1958): 37–8.

Reviewing before the "Edinburgh," 1788–1802. London: Methuen, 1978.

Sapiro, Virginia. *A Vindication of Political Virtue: the Political Theory of Mary Wollstonecraft.* Chicago: University of Chicago Press, 1992.

Shevelow, Kathryn. *Women and Print Culture: the Construction of Femininity in the Early Periodical.* London: Routledge, 1989.

Stewart, Sally. "Mary Wollstonecraft's Contributions to the *Analytical Review,*" *Essays in Literature* 11:2 (Fall 1984): 187–99.

Taylor, Barbara. *Eve and the New Jerusalem: Socialism and Feminism in the Nineteenth Century.* London: Virago, 1983.

Mary Wollstonecraft and the Radical Imagination. Cambridge: Cambridge University Press, 2002.

Tauchert, Ashley. "Maternity, Castration and Mary Wollstonecraft's *Historical and Moral View of the French Revolution.*" *Women's Writing* 4:2 (1997): 173–99.

"The Union of the Sexes: Female Embodiment and Same Sex Desire in Mary Wollstonecraft's *Vindication of the Rights of Woman*." QWERTY 9 (October, 1999): 281–9.

"Escaping Discussion: Liminality and the Female-Embodied Couple in Mary Wollstonecraft's *Mary, A Fiction*." *Romanticism on the Net* 18 (May 2000), 10 June 2000 <http://www.users.ox.ac.uk/~scato385/18tauchert.html>.

Thiebaux, Marcelle. "Mary Wollstonecraft in Federalist America." *The Evidence of the Imagination*. Eds. Donald Rieman, Michael C. Jaye, and Betty T. Bennet. New York: New York University Press, 1978: 195–235.

Todd, Janet. "The Language of Sex in *A Vindication of the Rights of Woman*." *Mary Wollstonecraft Newsletter* 1 (1973): 10–17.

"The Polwhelan Tradition and Richard Cobb." *Studies in Burke and His Time* 16 (1975): 271–7.

"The Biographies of Mary Wollstonecraft." *Signs* 1 (1976): 721–34.

Women's Friendship in Literature. New York: Columbia University Press, 1980.

Sensibility: an Introduction. London: Methuen, 1986.

The Sign of Angelica: Women, Writing, and Fiction, 1660–1800. New York: Columbia University Press, 1989.

"Mary Wollstonecraft and the Rights of Death." *Gender, Art and Death*. Cambridge: Polity Press, 1993: 102–19.

Ty, Eleanor. *Unsex'd Revolutionaries – Five Women Novelists of the 1790s*. Toronto: University of Toronto Press, 1993.

Tyson, Gerald P. *Joseph Johnson: a Liberal Publisher*. Iowa City: University of Iowa Press, 1979.

Wang, Orrin N. C. "The Other Reasons: Female Alterity and Enlightenment Discourse in Mary Wollstonecraft's *A Vindication of the Rights of Woman*." *Yale Journal of Criticism* 5:1 (1991): 129–49.

Wardle, Ralph M. "Mary Wollstonecraft, *Analytical Reviewer*." PMLA 62:4 (December 1947): 1000–9.

Woolf, Virginia. "Mary Wollstonecraft." *The Nation and Athenaeum* 46 (5 October 1929): 13–15. Rpt. "Four Figures." *The Common Reader*, 2nd Series. London: Hograth Press, 1932: 140–72.

INDEX

Addison, Joseph
  Spectator, The, 128, 131, 133
advice literature, 129–40
  See also Education
Aiken, John, 29, 43
Alembert, Jean Le Rond d', 65
Almeria Belmore, 87
American Revolution, 42, 47, 63, 221–2
  passim
  Analytical Review, 4, 8, 18, 24, 43, 51,
    62, 82–98
  See also titles of MW's works
ancien régime, 52, 54–7, 61–2, 70–5 *passim*,
  143
Anti-Jacobin Review, 1, 180, 181, 201
Arden, Jane, 13, 15, 16
Armstrong, Nancy, 121
asexuality *See* sex and sexuality
associationist psychology, 24, 25, 27
Astell, Mary, 104, 145, 146
Augustine of Hippo, St., 103, 115
Austen, Jane, 8, 83, 86, 92, 141, 156–7,
  189, 260
  Mansfield Park, 156
  Northanger Abbey, 19, 190
  Pride and Prejudice, 156
  Sense and Sensibility, 156

Bage, Robert
  Man As He Is, 93
Baillie, Joanna, 27
Barbauld, Anna Letitia, 25, 43, 45, 131–2,
  141, 146, 152–4, 157, 164, 176–7,
  180, 182
  *Appeal to the Opposers of the Repeal of
    the Corporation and Test Acts*, 153
  "Essay on the Origin and Progress of
    Novel Writing", 146
  Hymns in Prose for Children, 153, 176
  Lessons for Children, 38

  Poems, 176
  "The Rights of Woman", 153–4, 177–8
  Sins of Government, 154
Barker-Benfield, G. J., 266
Barlow, Ruth, 232
Battersby, Christine, 235
benevolence, 45–6, 48, 53, 57, 148–9
Bentham, Jeremy, 211
Bishop, Elizabeth Wollstonecraft (MW's
    sister), 8, 9, 14, 15, 22, 232
  marriage to Meredith Bishop, 17
Blair, Hugh, 8, 9, 234–5, 240–1
  Letters on Rhetoric, 8
Blake, William, 2, 28, 132, 234
  Marriage of Heaven and Hell, The, 165
  "Mary", 183–4
  Songs of Innocence and Experience, 44,
    161
Blood, Fanny, 13, 14, 16, 17, 212,
  230–2
Blood, George, 9, 13, 14, 18
bluestockings, 10
Brissot de Warville, J.-P., 43
  Travels to America, 53
Brown, John, 104
Burgh, Hannah, 125
Burgh, James, 42, 125
  Thoughts on Education, 126, 133
Burke, Edmund, 3, 45–8 *passim*, 50, 51, 55,
    57, 60, 61, 64, 111, 115, 128, 135,
    137, 248
  Reflections on the Revolution in France,
    19, 44, 55, 60, 62, 74, 122,
    151, 181
Burney, Frances, 8, 86, 200, 266
Burney, Sarah Harriet
  Clarentine, 86
Burns, Robert, 234
Butler, Marilyn, 257
Byron, George Gordon, sixth baron, 8, 19

Carter, Elizabeth, 10, 164
Cartwright, Major, 47
Ceaucescu, Nikolai and Elena, 264
Chapone, Hester, 121, 130, 132, 134
  Letters on the Improvement of the Mind,
    121
Chesterfield, Philip Dormer Stanhope, fourth
    earl of
  Letters to His Son, 136
Christie, Thomas, 43, 49, 55, 65
Church of England, 42, 59, 100, 155
citizenship, 48–51
  See also Public sphere
Cleland, John, 231
Clifford, James
Cobb, Richard, 163
Cobbett, William, 57
coeducation See education
Constitution, English, 47, 51, 61
Cott, Nancy, 151
Coleridge, Samuel Taylor, 45, 46, 50, 52,
    57, 262
commerce, 51, 53, 54, 57, 78, 102, 123,
    128, 221
conduct books, 106, 119–40 passim, 162,
    170
  See also education
Congreve, William, 167
Corday, Charlotte, 183
Cowley, Abraham, 167
Cowper, William, 132, 133, 164
  The Task, 164
Cristall, Ann, 233

Day, Thomas, 29
  Sandford and Merton, 29, 30, 32
deviance, 1, 55, 163, 178–9, 228–43; and
    MW, 234–43
Diderot, Denis, 62
Dissenters, 25, 42–4, 47, 59, 107, 108, 110,
    111, 114, 123, 125–7, 131, 132, 135,
    143, 152
Dissenting academies, 28, 36, 42, 43,
    131, 152
domesticity, 25, 26, 35, 121–3, 126, 128,
    147–8, 150
  domestic bonds, 34, 45, 46, 57
  domestic education, 34
  domestic sphere as national sphere,
    147–52
Dryden, John, 200
  Fables, 175, 185
  State of Innocence, 176

Duff, William, 235–7 passim
Dyer, George, 50, 182
  "Ode on Liberty", 182
Dyson, George

Edgeworth, Maria, 83, 92, 141, 155, 157,
    177, 231
  and Richard, 27, 29, 34
    Parent's Assistant, The, 38
    Practical Education, 27
  Belinda, 155–6
  Edward and Harriet, 89
  Letters for Literary Ladies, 155
education, 4, 24–41, 49, 119–40, 142, 148
  and duty, 120–1
  and gender, 31
  and National Schools, 34–6, 63
  MW's role in, 82–98
  political nature of, 75
  reason and, 26, 31, 39
effeminacy, 43–4, 51–2, 54–5, 61, 74
  See also gender
Elfenbein, Andrew, 5
Elias, Norbert, 152
Eliza Warwick, 193
Elliot, Dorice, 148
Ellison, Julie, 215, 223
Enfield, William, 28, 43
  The Speaker, 28, 131–2
English Reaction, 8, 32, 39, 68, 155, 178
English Review, The, 129
Enlightenment, Age of, 22, 47, 53, 99, 107,
    108, 119, 132, 133, 136, 141, 262
enthusiasm, 59, 60, 62, 73, 78, 102, 114, 168
equality, 32–6 passim, 53, 71, 75, 76, 141–6
    passim, 152, 154, 171, 173
Evangelicals, 105, 147, 149
Eve, 109, 123, 126, 136, 150, 152, 162, 166,
    169–72 passim, 176
exertion, 210 ff.

Fair Hibernian, The, 87
fancy, 214–7
femininity, 228–30 passim, 235–43
  See also gender, modesty, propriety
feminism, 22, 31, 39, 41
  and advice literature, 119–40
  and education, 24–41
  and MW's legacy, 246–69
  and MW's literary reviews, 82–98
  and modernity, 247
  and women's rights, 24, 62, 63, 122, 134,
    155, 247

as ideological critique of literature, 160–88
of MW, compared to her female
    contemporaries, 141–59
political traditions of, 42–58
religious basis of MW's, 99–118
twentieth-century histories of, 246–69
Fénelon, François
    Instructions to a Governess, 129
Fenn, Eleanor
    Cobwebs to Catch Flies, 38
Ferguson, Adam, 51
Fielding, Henry, 237
Flexner, Eleanor, 253, 255
Fordyce, James, 106, 137, 161, 228
    Sermons to Young Women, 122, 136,
        137, 162
Franklin, Benjamin, 42
French Revolution, 2, 4, 8, 19, 32, 46, 47,
        52, 54, 56, 59–80, 104, 135, 199,
        221, 250–2
    and Bastille, 32, 38, 56, 59, 71, 73, 132
    and *Declaration of the Rights of Men and
        of Citizens*, 48, 55, 62
    and French national character, 54–5, 70–1,
        73–5, 77, 78
    and Girondins, 65, 66
    and Jacobins, 24, 63, 65–7, 73, 180, 191
    and March on Versailles, 55, 60, 61, 72
    and National Assembly, 55, 62, 72–5
    and terror, 2, 19, 53, 55, 64, 67, 68, 199
Furniss, Tom, 4
Fuseli, Henry, 12, 13, 19, 64, 132, 165, 180,
        229, 230, 232, 233

Gabell, Henry, 9, 10, 18, 236
Gay, John, 164, 167
gender
    and civil humanism, 48–52, 228
    and education
    and poetry, 160–88
    and religion, 99–116
    critiqued in MW's *Reviews*, 82–94
    See also effeminacy, femininity, masculinity
Genlis, Mme de (Stephanie-Felicité)
    Tales of the Castle, 132
genius, 5, 22, 90–1, 190–1, 199
    and liberty, 240–1
    and MW, 57, 234–43
    and radical circles, 233–4
    and sex/gender deviance, 228–43
    as above ideology, 207
George, Margaret, 253
Gleadle, Kathryn, 145

Glorious Revolution, 42, 47, 59
Godwin, William, 2, 7, 11–3, 19–22 *passim*,
        26, 37, 43, 45, 46, 50, 52, 56, 84, 100,
        101, 143, 165, 166, 190, 200, 202,
        225, 232–4 *passim*, 250, 262
    Memoirs, 2, 3, 12, 13, 101, 102, 145,
        154–5, 163, 183, 229–31, 237, 262
Goethe, Johann Wolfgang von, 19
    Sorrows of Young Werther, 19, 20, 102
Golden Age, 44, 47, 57
Goldman, Emma, 249–51, 268
Gouges, Olympe de, 62
Gray, Thomas
    "Ode on a Distant Prospect", 161
    "The Progress of Poetry", 183
Gregory, John, 33, 106, 123, 133, 135,
        137–8
    and Scottish Enlightenment, 133, 135
    *Comparative View of the State and
        Faculties of the Mind*, 132, 133
    Father's Legacy, A, 119, 122, 133, 136,
        160, 167, 202
Guest, Harriet, 247, 267–8

Hardy, Thomas, 68
Harrington, James, 43
Hays, Mary, 8, 10, 15, 22, 25, 101, 114, 141,
        142–6, 157, 233, 267
    Appeal to the Men of Great Britain, 144
    Cursory Remarks on an Enquiry,
        143
    Emma Courtney, 143
    Female Biography, 144, 145
    Letters and Essays, 143
    *Memoirs of Queens Illustrious and
        Celebrated*, 146
    Victim of Prejudice, 143, 144
Heloise, 20
heteronormativity
    and genius, 228–45
    and MW's reception history, 246 ff.
    and narrative, 192–207
    and religion, 112–16
    See also sex and sexuality
heterosexuality, 112, 134–7, 228–43
    See also sex and sexuality
Holcroft, Thomas, 132
Hollis, John, 43
Holmes, Richard, 232, 262–3
homosexuality, 1, 55, 178–9, 228–43
    See also sex and sexuality
Hume, David, 44
Hutcheson, Francis, 44, 45

Imlay, Gilbert, 2, 10–3 passim, 15, 19–21, 67, 68, 77, 166, 180, 229, 230–2, 249–50
Inchbald, Elizabeth
 Simple Story, A, 88, 189
independence, 33, 37, 43, 45, 49, 50, 57, 125, 126, 128, 135, 138
Islam
 women in, 103, 162, 223
Israeli, Isaac D', 236, 237

Jefferson, Thomas, 42
Joan of Arc, 183
Johnson, Claudia L., 156, 238, 248, 266–8 passim
Johnson, Joseph, 9, 11, 12, 15, 18, 25, 26, 28, 43, 59, 64, 82–4, 130–2, 183
Johnson, Samuel, 3, 90, 164, 191, 200
 Rasselas, 191–2, 198
Jones, Chris, 4
Jones, Vivien, 4
Jump, Harriet, 26

Kaplan, Cora, 2, 113
Kay, Carol, 3
Kelly, Gary, 206, 264–5
Kingsborough, Lord and Lady, 18, 28, 29, 234
Knowles, E. H., 12
Knowles, John, 12, 13

Lady's Magazine, The, 129, 130
Lavater, Thomas
 Aphorisms on Man, 132
lesbianism, 155, 229, 232, 236–8, 257, 261, 265
 See also sex and Sexuality
Levine, David, 163
liberty, 42, 44, 47, 49, 50, 52, 59–61 passim, 66, 73, 75, 76, 108, 109, 126, 132, 135, 137, 180, 182, 211, 221
Lindsay, Anne, 184
Lloyd, Genevieve, 83
Locke, John, 24, 29, 34, 46–9 passim, 108, 127, 141, 192
 and education, 26–7, 31, 38, 131
 Second Treatise of Government, 60
 Some Thoughts Concerning Education, 24, 26, 125
Longinus, 240–1

Louis XVI (King of France), 64, 65, 251
 court of, 70
 execution of, 66
 luxury, 51–4, 61, 71, 123, 134

Macaulay, Catharine, 11, 25, 39, 42, 43, 45, 47, 55, 145, 146, 182, 232, 240
 Letters on Education, 25, 32
MacKenzie, Henry
 Man of Feeling, 197
Marguerite (MW's maid), 232
Marie Antoinette (Queen of France), 49, 61, 62, 67
 as actress, 70
marriage, 120, 124, 126, 134, 235–9, 241–3
Mason, Michael, 151
masculinity, 51, 228, 229, 235, 237
 See also gender
Mathias, T. J.
 Pursuits of Literature, 180
Merrick, James, 164
Mellor, Ann, 5
Mill, John Stuart, 2
Millar, John, 51
Milton, John, 4, 19, 109, 115, 126, 130, 135, 136, 150, 165, 167, 168, 217
 Paradise Lost, 109, 123, 160, 162, 164, 169, 170 ff., 185
misogyny, 103, 128, 163, 166, 167, 173
modesty, 33, 35, 36, 39, 116, 131, 142, 148, 155, 178, 181
Modleski, Tania, 260
Montague, Lady Mary Wortley, 10
Monthly Magazine, 167
Monthly Review, 225
Moore, Edward, 164
 Fables for the Fair Sex, 127
More, Hannah, 25, 37, 104, 105, 121, 123, 141, 147–52, 153, 156, 157, 260, 267
 Coelebs in Search of a Wife, 148, 150–1, 170–1, 179
 Essays on Various Subjects, 148
 "Sensibility", 149
 Strictures on Female Education, 37, 148, 150–2 passim
Moses, 169
motherhood, 35, 37–8
 and education, 25, 26, 38, 84, 151
 as duty, 120, 123 ff., 134, 150
 as normative basis of solidarity, 198 ff.
Myers, Mitzi, 4, 147, 151, 190, 258

nature, 160 ff.
Newington Green, 17, 25, 26, 42, 59, 107, 120, 125, 212
Nixon, Edna, 253
nonconformity See Dissenters
Norman, Elizabeth
  Child of Woe, The, 86

Opie, Amelia Alderson, 7, 15, 232
Opie, John, 232
Orleans, Duke d' (Philippe Égalité), 55
Ovid
  Heroides, 20
Owen, Robert, 57, 258

Paine, Thomas, 42, 43, 46, 47, 55, 65, 180, 205
  Age of Reason, The, 47
  Common Sense, 47
  Rights of Man, The, 51
Paul, St., 104
Pennell, Elizabeth Robins, 2, 12
Pennington, Sarah, 124, 126, 130
  Unfortunate Mother's Advice to Her Absent Daughters, An, 124
Percy, Thomas, 164
periodicals, 128, 129, 131, 133
philanthropy See benevolence
Pinkerton, Miss, 21
Plato, 115
Platonic Marriage, 193
politeness, 44, 54-5
  and literature of advice, 128 ff.
Polwhele, Richard, 1, 163, 178-80
Poovey, Mary, 113, 121, 258-9
Pope, Alexander, 4, 85, 128, 132, 155, 165, 167, 175
  "Epistle to a Lady", 127, 165, 174, 176
  Essay on Man, 165
  Rape of the Lock, 153
Price, Richard, 3, 25, 43-5 passim, 50, 53, 59, 60, 107, 108, 125
  Discourse on the Love of Our Country, 59
  Observations on the Nature of Civil Liberty, 47
  Review of the Principal Questions and Difficulties of Morals, A, 109, 111
Priestley, Joseph, 43, 47, 107, 131
Prior, Matthew, 167
Prochaska, F. K., 149

progress, 45, 48, 51, 52, 56, 57, 69, 75-6, 78-9
property, 49, 50, 51, 61, 142
propriety, 119-40
public sphere
  and education, 32-9
  and politeness, 128 ff.
  republicanism and, 42-58
  women writers and, 141-59

Radcliffe, Ann, 200, 266
  Italian, The, 93, 189
Radcliffe, Mary Anne, 121
  Female Advocate, The, 146
radicals, 15, 25, 30, 31, 35, 43-5, 47, 54, 59-79 passim, 102, 107, 108, 122, 123, 125, 126, 128, 132, 156, 179, 184, 211, 212, 226, 234
Radway, Janice, 260
Randall, Anne Frances
  See Robinson, Mary
reading, 82-98, 119-40, 160-88
reason, 7, 12, 21, 25-38 passim, 62, 69, 71-6 passim, 82-94 passim, 100, 101, 107-16 passim, 123-38 passim, 147, 148, 152, 153, 156, 167-79 passim, 184, 263
religion, 4, 10, 48, 99-116, 124-7
  and equality of women, 103 ff.
  See also Dissenters
Republicanism, 42-50, 61, 66, 203 ff.
  and friendship, 46, 51
Revely, Maria, 233
Rich, Adrienne, 181, 182
  Snapshots of a Daughter-in-Law, 181, 258
Richardson, Alan, 4, 122
Richardson, Samuel, 73, 86, 237
  Clarissa, 166, 190
  Sir Charles Grandison, 190
rights
  and liberal feminism, 141-6
  and religion, 99-118
  discourses of, 42-58, 59-81
Robespierre, Maximilien, 43
Robinson, Mary, 10, 141, 157, 180, 234
  Hubert de Sevrac, 93
  Thoughts on the Condition of Women (Randall, Anne Frances), 146
Roland, Mme (Marie-Jeanne), 43, 56, 67, 145, 183
romantic friendship, 194-5
Romantic poets, 5, 57, 91

Roper, Derek, 88
Roscoe, William, 11, 15, 64, 165, 181–2, 232
Rousseau, Emile, 19, 28, 29, 33, 34, 36, 105, 115, 116, 135, 160, 190
La Nouvelle Héloïse, 115, 116, 160, 191, 203
Rousseau, Jean-Jacques, 3, 28, 29, 44, 48, 51, 63, 84, 102, 109, 135, 141, 160, 200, 236, 248
Rowan, Archibald Hamilton, 15
Rowe, Nicholas, 200

Sapiro, Virginia, 264
Savile, George (Marquis of Halifax)
Lady's New Year's Gift, The, 124, 127, 136
Schweizer, Madeline, 233
scriptures
used in arguments regarding gender, 169 ff., 226
used in education, 28
self-help, 24–41 *passim*, 50, 51, 119–40 *passim*
See also independence
sensibility, 44–6, 48–9, 61, 62, 69, 102, 105, 132, 133, 143, 149–50, 168, 241, 248 ff.
and MW's reputation, 246–70
and religion, 102
MW's attitude toward, 82–98
sentimentality
in novels, 82–94, 189–208
Sévigné, Marie de Rabutin-Chantal, 19, 20
sex and sexuality, 1, 5, 20, 36, 39, 65, 112–6, 119–20, 135 ff., 151, 228, 229, 233
and MW's reputation, 247 ff.
and narrative, 189–207
"sex wars", 259 ff.
Seymour Castle, 85
Shaftesbury, Anthony Ashley Cooper, seventh earl of, 44
Shakespeare, William, 4, 28, 130, 131, 164, 167, 200, 206, 217, 231
As You Like It, 164
Hamlet, 166–7, 201
King Lear, 164
Midsummer Night's Dream, A, 168
Othello, 167
Tempest, The, 164, 218
Shelley, Mary Wollstonecraft (MW's daughter), 12, 184
Shelley, Percy Bysshe, 57, 184, 262
"Laon and Cyntha", 187
"Hymn to Intellectual Beauty", 184

Shelley, Sir Percy Florence, 12
Shenstone, William, 164
Siddons, Sarah, 233
Smith, Adam
on sensibility, 44, 53
slavery, 54
as analogy central to MW's work, 45, 126, 132, 137, 142
Smith, Charlotte, 84, 87, 89, 164, 180, 182, 189
Emmeline, 89
Smith, Patricia Juliana, 155
Snitow, Ann, 260
sociability, 44, 49, 51, 52, 53, 83–94
Southey, Robert, 13, 182
Steele, Richard, 164
Spectator, The, 128
Sterne, Lawrence, 86
Sentimental Journey, A, 197
strength, 33, 34, 141–2
Sunstein, Emily, 232, 253
Sutherland, Kathryn, 121, 122, 150
Swift, Jonathan, 164, 167, 170

Talbot, Catherine, 10
Talleyrand-Perigord, Charles Maurice de, 49
Taylor, Barbara, 4, 258, 259
Test Acts, 108, 153
Thelwall, John, 68
Thomson, James, 164
Tims, Margaret, 253
Todd, Janet, 3, 268
Tomalin, Clair, 59, 64–7 *passim*, 232, 233, 253
Tooke, John Horne, 43, 68
travel, 209–227
as freedom, 210 ff.
MW's ambivalence about, 209–29
treason trials, 68
Trimmer, Sarah, 27, 50, 132
Turner, James, 115

Unitarians, 50, 107–8, 125, 143, 152
See also Dissenters
utopianism, 36, 43, 57, 100, 102, 243, 252, 258–60 *passim*, 265

virtue, 14, 25, 27, 30, 32–6, 43–52 *passim*, 61, 62, 66, 71, 72, 93, 99, 100, 105, 106, 109–16 *passim*, 119, 125–34 *passim*, 137, 138, 142–53 *passim*, 161, 166, 167, 176, 179

Voltaire, François Marie Arouet de, 65, 141, 180

Wakefield, Priscilla, 121, 157
  Reflections on the Present Condition of the Female Sex, 152
Walpole, Horace, 1, 9, 19
Wardle, Ralph, 2, 3, 11, 83
Waterhouse, Joshua, 13
Wedgewood, Josiah, 22
Whigs, 42, 47, 60, 61
White, James
  Earl Strongbow, 93
Wilkes, Wetenhall, 121
Williams, David
  Lectures on Education, 29
Williams, Helen Maria, 43, 53, 56, 64, 65, 66, 87, 180, 182
  Julia, 87, 92
  Letters Written in France, 62
Wolfson, Susan, 4, 145
Wollstonecraft, Charles (MW's brother), 15
Wollstonecraft, Edward (MW's brother), 16
Wollstonecraft, Edward John (MW's father), 15
Wollstonecraft, Elizabeth Dickson (MW's mother), 17
Wollstonecraft, Everina (MW's sister), 13–5 *passim*, 17, 18, 67, 114, 190, 232
Wollstonecraft, Fanny (MW's daughter), 19, 26, 37, 38, 212
Wollstonecraft, Mary
  and Blair, 234–5
  and Fanny Blood, 16–17, 230, 232
  and "rational passion", 12, 48–9, 55
  and relation to Godwin, 12 ff., 249 ff., 229 ff., 262
  and relation to Imlay, 10, 11, 19, 199, 204, 211, 249, 255, 263
  and relation to male poets, 160–88
  and relation to women writers, 5, 86 ff., 141–59, 228–43
  and religion, 4, 99–118
  and sensibility, 82–98
  and travel to Scandinavia, 9–11, 19, 209–26 *passim*
  as novelist, 189–207
  attempt to reconcile reason and passion, 7, 12, 21, 83 ff.
  biographical traditions, 1–2, 162–3, 229–30, 246–70
  demonization of, 1, 39, 154, 155, 163, 177–81

  determination to become writer, 9 ff.
  development as a feminist, 82–94
  dislocation, MW's early experiences, of, 211–14
  emotional conflicts, 7–23
  life of, in *Letters*, 9–23
  life of, in *Short Residences*, 209–27
  literary style of, 7, 8, 10, 91–3, 190 ff., 197
  and development of voice, 82
  and synthesis of reason and passion, 82–94
  optimism of, 69 ff.
  reception of, 246–69
  reputation of, 246–69
  suicide attempts of, 12, 19, 55, 180, 212
  works of
    Analytical Review, 4, 8, 18, 29, 32, 53, 62, 82 ff., 130, 189, 190; attribution of, 82–3
    "Cave of Fancy", 114, 115, 192, 234
    Female Reader, 28, 33, 119, 120, 128, 129–34, 136, 164, 169
    "Hints", 37, 84, 91
    Historical and Moral View of the French Revolution, 4, 8, 52, 53, 54, 67, 68, 69–77; sovereignty of people in, 65, 71, 72, 74, 75; violence in, 76–7, 238–9
    Lessons, 24, 37, 38, 39
    "Letter on the Present Character of the French Nation", 66
    Letters, 7–23
    Letters on the Management of Infants, 20, 24, 37, 38
    Letters Written during a Short Residence in Sweden, Norway, and Denmark (= *Short Residence*), 2, 4, 20, 53, 77–9, 100, 209–27, 259, 262–3, 267
    Mary 2, 24, 53, 84, 105–8 *passim*, 115, 120, 125, 156, 189–98, 236–8, 240, 243
    "On Poetry, and Our Relish for the Beauties of Nature" ("On Artificial Taste"), 84, 91, 167, 234–5
    Original Stories, 24, 28–32, 36, 38, 39, 53, 106, 120
    Posthumous Works, 12, 37
    Thoughts on the Education of Daughters, 24, 26–8, 33, 36, 100, 119, 120–30, 135, 136, 176, 181
    Vindication of the Rights of Men, A, 4, 8, 11, 12, 26, 32, 44, 45, 48, 49, 52, 55, 60, 108, 111, 128, 135, 165, 166

Vindication of the Rights of Woman, A,
  1, 4, 8, 11, 12, 18, 26, 32, 37, 44, 49,
  54, 57, 62, 63, 70, 84, 85, 87, 89, 90,
  99, 106–8, 110–11, 114–15, 119,
  122–3; and female education, 1–3, 32,
  34–6, 39, 83, 89, 133–9; and MW's
  intellectual development, 135 ff.,
  141–57, 160, 203, 228–9, 232–3,
  239–43, 248; religious basis of,
  99–118
Works of Mary Wollstonecraft (eds.
  Butler and Todd), 2, 4
Wrongs of Woman, or Maria, 2, 21, 24,
  28, 30, 87, 92–3, 156, 184–5,
  198–201, 240–3
Young Grandison, 37

women's movement
  and reception of MW, 246–70
Woolf, Virginia, 248, 249, 250–1,
  268
Wordsworth, William, 28, 57, 68,
  167
  on domestic feeling, 45
  Preface to Lyrical Ballads, 167
  Prelude, 28
Wray, Mary, 173

Yearsley, Ann, 180, 234
Young, Edward, 164, 217
  *Complaint,The, or Night Thoughts
    on Life, Death and Immortality*,
    226